EMERGING PERSPECTIVES ON MANAGING ORGANIZATIONAL JUSTICE

Edited by
Stephen W. Gilliland, Dirk D. Steiner,
and
Daniel P. Skarlicki

INFORMATION AGE
PUBLISHING

80 Mason Street
Greenwich, Connecticut 06830

Library of Congress Cataloging-in-Publication Data

Emerging perspectives on managing organizational justice / edited by
Dirk D. Steiner, Daniel P. Skarlicki, and Stephen W. Gilliland.
   p. cm. – (Research in social issues in management ; v. 2)
Includes bibliographical references.
  ISBN 1-931576-36-X (pbk.) – ISBN 1-931576-37-8 (Cloth)
  1. Organizational justice. I. Steiner, Dirk (Dirk Douglas) II.
Skarlicki, Daniel. III. Gilliland, Stephen. IV. Series.
  HD6971.3 .E45 2002
  658.3'14–dc21
                                                2002008912

Copyright © 2002 Information Age Publishing Inc.

All rights reserved. No part of this publication may be reproduced, stored in a retrieval system, or transmitted, in any form or by any means, electronic, mechanical, photocopying, microfilming, recording or otherwise, without written permission from the publisher.

Printed in the United States of America

CONTENTS

Preface
Dirk D. Steiner, Daniel P. Skarlicki, and Stephen W. Gilliland,   vii

Part I.   Interdisciplinary Perspectives on Organizational Justice

1. Economic and Noneconomic Mechanisms in Interpersonal Work Relationships: Toward an Integration of Agency and Procedural Justice Theories
   M. Audrey Korsgaard and Harry J. Sapienza   3

2. The Religious Underpinnings of Social Justice Conceptions
   Dianna L. Stone and Eugene F. Stone-Romero   35

3. Patients and Physicians as Stakeholders: Justice in the Medical Context
   Carol T. Kulik and Robert L. Holbrook, Jr.   77

4. A Social Information Processing View of Organizational Justice
   Barry M. Goldman and Sherry M. B. Thatcher   103

Part II.   Expanding the Domain of Unfairness

5. A Third-Party Observer's Reactions to Employee Mistreatment: Motivational and Cognitive Processes in Deservingness Assessments
   John H. Ellard and Daniel P. Skarlicki   133

6. Employee Stress, Injustice and the Dual-Position of the Boss
   Riel Vermunt   159

7. Distribution of Tasks: A View from the Social Psychology of Justice
   Gerold Mikula   177

8. "Hot Flashes, Open Wounds": Injustice and the Tyranny of Its Emotions
   Robert J. Bies and Thomas M. Tripp   203

Part III.   Commentary

9. Some Reflections on the Morality of Organizational Justice
   Russell Cropanzano and Deborah E. Rupp   225

10. Information on Contributing Authors   279

PREFACE

Dirk D. Steiner, Daniel P. Skarlicki, and Stephen W. Gilliland

As in Volume 1 of *Research in Social Issues in Management*, the theme of this second volume is new perspectives on organizational justice. Whereas Volume 1 was entitled *Theoretical and Cultural Perspectives on Organizational Justice*, the current volume takes justice beyond the organizational context. That is, it recognizes that what happens in organizations both influences aspects of our lives that take place outside of the workplace and is influenced by things that go on outside of organizations. As in Volume 1, many of the chapters in this volume were produced as a result of the first International Round Table on Innovations in Organizational Justice which took place in Nice in June of 1999. Authors enriched and modified their work as a result of these exchanges, and additional contributors were solicited to complete this volume.

The volume is composed of three parts. The first part is concerned generally with expanding our understanding of perceptions of what is fair by including interdisciplinary perspectives in our conceptualizations of organizational justice. The second part attends to outcomes of justice that go beyond the traditional organizational variables of performance and satisfaction with decisions. Finally, the chapter by Russell Cropanzano and Deborah Rupp composes the third part of the volume. These authors contribute an integrative view of justice perspectives that goes well beyond a summation of the preceding chapters.

Part One begins with a chapter by Audrey Korsgaard and Harry Sapienza who provide an integration of agency and procedural justice theories. Agency theory is an economic theory of organizational relationships that focuses on relationships between principals (e.g., owners or employers) and agents (e.g., managers or employees). As a microeconomic theory, the focus of agency theory is on costs and economic returns, rather than on social relations. On the other hand, procedural justice theories have addressed fairness in decision-making procedures associated with social relationships. Korsgaard and Sapienza argue that accounting for both perspectives is important in understanding the fairness of interpersonal relations, particularly when the economic stakes are high. They apply this integrated perspective to the context of entrepreneur-venture capitalist relations.

The second chapter, a contribution by Dianna Stone and Eugene Stone-Romero, represents an under-examined area of study in work on organizational justice, that is, the role of religious beliefs. Because this is such a vast topic, their chapter focuses on perspectives different religions may have on distributive justice only. Their analysis shows a number of striking similarities and interesting differences in how different religions suggest that resources be allocated. They limit their examination of these questions to the religious beliefs of Judaism, Christianity, Confucianism, and Buddhism, which generally represent either the major world religions or the basis for them. Some parallels with Islam are also developed in these pages.

In the third chapter, Carol Kulik and Robert Holbrook extend justice theories into the realm of doctor-patient relationships. The authors propose that one of the most important problems in the physician-patient relationship is the failure of patients to follow through on physicians' recommended treatments. Kulik and Holbrook use patient adherence to treatment regimens as one example of a common organizational dilemma—how can authorities achieve compliance with their directives? They present a model that explores how characteristics of a patient-physician encounter influence patient reactions and physician outcomes. They use fairness judgments as a central, mediating variable to understand how patients interpret their physician's behavior, decide whether to follow through on the physician's recommended treatment, and ultimately manage the uncertainty inherent in the medical context.

Concluding Part One is a contribution by Barry Goldman and Sherry Thatcher that examines the potential contribution of social information processing (SIP) research to organizational justice theories. Despite the assumption that fairness perceptions lie in the eyes of the beholder, relatively little justice research to date has investigated the impact of social influences on organizational justice. Goldman and Thatcher explain the mechanisms by which social information can affect justice judgments and individuals' responses to (un)fairness in terms of attitudes and behaviors. The authors develop a model that specifies the particular linkages and incorporates the implications of SIP as applied to fairness theory (Folger & Cropanzano, 2001) and fairness heuristic theory (Lind, 2001). Goldman and Thatcher develop a research agenda relating to theoretical, substantive, and methodological issues.

The starting point for Part Two, the treatment of non-work reactions to organizational justice, is the chapter by John Ellard and Daniel Skarlicki who focus on fairness perceptions of third-party observers—individuals who may not be directly affected by employee mistreatment, but who make fairness judgements nonetheless. Observers can include investors, customers, and potential employees as well as arbitrators and judges. In particular, the authors propose that an understanding of deservingness perceptions can be useful for predicting third-party observers' fairness judgements and their reactions to employee mistreatment. Deservingness reflects observers' sense that the employee is more or less deserving of his or her fate by virtue of the employee's actions or who the employee is, which in turn affects fairness judgments. Implications of a deservingness analysis of observer reactions for both theory and practice are considered.

In the following chapter, Riel Vermunt utilizes Injustice-Stress Theory (IST) to explain why an exceedingly large percentage of Dutch employees enter into the country's disablement program. Many of these employees report having problems with their bosses; in particular their supervisors' unjust behavior. Vermunt describes the dual position of the boss as an important factor for why bosses maintain their unjust behavior. In brief, he proposes that the boss is confronted with two forms of fairness, one form has to do with allocating resources to subordinates (proactive justice; Greenberg. 1996), and the other is reactive justice and has to do with the evaluation of allocation behavior by the boss' superior. Vermunt argues that because of the dual position of the boss, appearing fair towards his/her subordinates may be preferred to actually being fair, given the potential for negative consequences in terms of subordinates' behavior. Vermunt offers some suggestions for improvement.

Gerold Mikula, in Chapter 7, addresses justice issues associated with the distribution of tasks. Traditionally, organizational justice research has addressed the fairness of rewards and punishments, as well as the procedures associated with these outcomes. Mikula argues that the distribution of tasks, such as work tasks, may invoke a different set of distributive rules than has been studied in distributive justice research. He argues that the nature of the tasks being distributed and the nature of the social system both influence the types of distributive rules that become salient. Results are reported from preliminary empirical studies that demonstrate how it may be possible to study the distributive justice issues associated with task distributions.

The concluding chapter of Part Two, by Bob Bies and Tom Tripp, deals with emotions as a generally neglected consequence of organizational injustice. In their analysis, these authors first focus on unfair treatment because such experiences incite the strongest reactions by employees. They then show that such injustices initiate a process by which employees attempt to understand them, and that this usually begins by assigning blame. They then draw on their research and that of other authors to analyze the different characteristics of emotions that arise as a consequence of unfair treatment. The interplay of cognition and emotion is also examined, and new perspectives for research should give rise to a better understanding of the consequences of more rational or more emotional responses by employees faced with injustice.

Part 3, a commentary on the chapters in this volume, is an interesting contribution to the organizational justice literature in its own right. Russell Cropanzano and Deborah Rupp have succeeded in couching the various individual contributions of this volume in a much broader perspective which provides a complete examination of the morality of organizational justice. Indeed, they show, with a number of relevant illustrations from a variety of researchers, that in order to understand justice motives, it is necessary to integrate three perspectives: the instrumental approach which insists on rather self-serving motives for some decisions; the interpersonal approach which emphasizes our relations with others and social identity; and the deontological perspective which shows that sometimes we are simply motivated by what is right or moral in making decisions. Because the third approach is often ignored and is relatively less-researched than the other two, Cropanzano and Rupp show its relevance for the contributions in this volume where the role of morals was not explicit.

In conclusion, there is a lot of new material in this volume which illustrates both the progress that has been made in organizational justice research and valuable new directions for research. We hope that you will find these contributions as inspiring as we did and that they contribute to bringing attention to the fact that justice at work goes well beyond the organization.

REFERENCES

Folger, R., & Cropanzano, R. (2001). Fairness theory: Justice as accountability. In J. Greenberg & R. Cropanzano (Eds.), *Advances in organizational justice* (pp. 1-55). Stanford, CA: Stanford University Press.

Greenberg, J. (1996). *The quest for justice on the job.* Thousand Oaks, CA: Sage.

Lind, E. A. (2001). Fairness heuristic theory: Justice judgments as pivotal cognitions in organizational relations. In J. Greenberg & R. Cropanzano (Eds.), *Advances in organizational justice* (pp. 56-88). Stanford, CA: Stanford University Press.

PART I

INTERDISCIPLINARY PERSPECTIVES ON ORGANIZATIONAL JUSTICE

CHAPTER I

ECONOMIC AND NONECONOMIC MECHANISMS IN INTERPERSONAL WORK RELATIONSHIPS:

Toward an Integration of Agency and Procedural Justice Theories

M. Audrey Korsgaard and Harry J. Sapienza

ABSTRACT

Procedural justice provides a powerful framework for understanding how the fairness of decision-making procedures affects the relationships individuals have with each other and with institutions or organizations. In the context of work organizations, procedural justice has been particularly useful in explaining employees' commitment to the organization and trust in its agents. However, in applying procedural justice to work organizations, limited attention has been given to the unique aspects of the organizational context, specifically, the economic dimension of relationships in organizations and the vulnerability of the organization. In contrast, economic theories of organizational relations, such as agency theory, focus on the economic dimension of inter- and intra-organizational relationships but are relatively mute on the role of social bonds in such relationships. We argue that accounting for both perspectives is important to understanding interpersonal relations in work organizations, particularly those relationships where the economic stakes are very high, such as the relationship between entrepreneurs and venture capital investors. We discuss implications for research on procedural justice. We then apply this integrated perspective to the high-stakes context of entrepreneur-venture capitalist relations.

Research on procedural justice has demonstrated that the fairness of procedures and treatment are important sources of employee attitudes and behavior (Greenberg & Cropanzano, 1997). Findings in this area also suggest that fairness influences the quality of the relationship between the employer and employee as well as employees' feelings about being a member of the organization. In particular, fair treatment and procedures have a positive impact on employees' trust in management (Konovsky & Pugh, 1994; Korsgaard, Schweiger, & Sapienza, 1995) and commitment to the organization (Folger & Konovsky, 1989; Konovsky & Cropanzano, 1991; Korsgaard et al., 1995; Schaubroeck, May, & Brown, 1994). These findings are consistent with recent developments in procedural justice theory that emphasize assessments of the decision maker's intent and trustworthiness (Folger & Cropanzano, 2001; Lind, 2001) and that portray identity concerns (Tyler & Balder, 2000) as central mechanisms underlying procedural and interactional justice effects. These recent formulations represent a dramatic departure from early notions of rational self-interest as the primary psychological mechanism underlying procedural justice effects (Lind & Tyler, 1988).

Our understanding of the nature and effects of procedural justice in organizations has its roots in social psychological theory on procedural justice (Lind & Tyler, 1988; Thibaut & Walker, 1975), where procedural justice concepts were applied to a variety of social settings, such as interactions between citizens and police and defendants' experiences with legal systems (Greenberg & Cropanzano, 1997). However, applications of this framework to work organizations may have given inadequate consideration to the uniqueness of the work context. Clearly, at the center of the organizational context is an economic exchange relationship *between* employee and employer. Yet procedural justice theories and research focus on the vulnerability of employees to employers' decisions, a focus that has ignored the economic rationale behind decisions and the active role the employee plays. Consequently, although much has been learned about employees' reactions to decisions, the current literature provides little insight into why managers or employers might behave unjustly, what actions might reduce these tendencies, or how employees' behavior affects the decision process (Folger, 1993; Folger, & Skarlicki, 2001; Korsgaard, Roberson, & Rymph, 1998).

In developing procedural justice theory as a means of explicating individuals' reactions to decision processes, theorists have tended to highlight factors beyond self-interest and rationality. Self-interest and rationality have by no means been ignored in justice research. For example, research on equity theory and distributive justice clearly illustrate the importance of material outcomes to employees' attitudes and motivation (Brockner & Wiesenfeld, 1996); such results suggest that employees evaluate and react to transactions with their employer in a somewhat self-interested and calculative way. Similarly, some theory and research on procedural justice suggest that self-interest or "instrumental" mechanisms underlie—at least in part—the effects of procedural justice (Lind & Tyler, 1988). Nonetheless, theorists interested in the unique effect of procedural justice and in the joint effects of procedural and distributive justice (Brockner & Wiesenfeld, 1996) have tended to focus attention on the psychological significance of decision-making processes. Theory for these effects emphasize the role of less deliberative processes, such as heuristic processing (Lind, 2001) and counterfactual thinking (Folger & Cropanzano, 2001), and motivations that are less self-focused, such as social identity (Tyler & Blader, 2000) and terminal values (Folger, 1998).

In contrast, rational self-interest is a strong, explicit assumption in microeconomic theories. One branch of microeconomics, new institutional economics, which focuses on the arrangement of economic exchanges or transactions (Nilakant & Rao, 1994), is particularly relevant to understanding the employer-employee relationship. One of the dominant theories in this field is agency theory, which examines how the relationship between a principal (owner/employer) and agent (manager/employee) is structured so as to maximize the return for the principal and minimize the costs of delegating authority. Agency theory has been criticized for exaggerating the role of self-interest to the exclusion of other-oriented motives and behavior (Perrow, 1986). Furthermore, some critics have argued agency theory neglects the role of social relations in economic exchanges (Nilakant & Rao, 1994); that is, it assumes that only the outcomes of transactions have value and that there is no value or significance to the exchange process or relationship. Despite these criticisms, agency theory appears useful for explaining a variety of behaviors exhibited by both the employer and the employee (Eisenhardt, 1989).

Agency theory addresses how to ensure that exchanges between the principal and agent are conducted properly, or, in the language of organizational justice, that the outcomes of exchanges are fair. Given this focus, agency theory has obvious connections to distributive justice in that both emphasize the exchange outcomes and rational self-interest. However, agency theory differs from distributive justice in that agency theory focuses on how to structure the exchange relationship so as to ensure or compel agent compliance. That is, the central concern of agency theory focuses on the procedures used to govern exchanges. Many of the issues examined in agency theory research therefore have overlap with and implications for the phenomena studied in procedural justice research. Thus, although agency theory has much in common with distributive justice, the emphasis on the role of governance procedures in fair exchanges suggest that agency theory may have more in common with procedural justice research.

In this chapter, we examine these theoretical perspectives, identifying ways in which each complements and potentially enhances the explanatory power of the other. While the two perspectives address overlapping phenomena, the focus of each theory differs, and perhaps more significantly, the emphasis given to various underlying cognitive and motivational mechanisms differs substantially. These differences point to how these perspectives might address deficiencies in each other. Specifically, the emphasis of procedural justice on cognitive processes and social relations can help address the limitations of agency theory's strong assumption of unconstrained self-interest. Similarly, agency theory's insight into the perspective and vulnerability of the principal addresses the limitations of the employee-centered emphasis of procedural justice research. The purpose of this paper is to integrate justice and agency theory into a more comprehensive, explanatory framework for the employee-employer relationship. In the following pages, we briefly review these theoretical perspectives, discuss their commonalties and differences, and present a tentative integrated framework. We then discuss a research agenda that flows from this model and apply this framework to the case of investor-entrepreneur relationships.

THEORETICAL BACKGROUND

Procedural Justice

Procedural justice concerns the fairness of procedures used to make decisions. The concept of procedural justice can be distinguished from the concept of distributive justice, which concerns evaluations of decision outcomes. A variety of procedural factors contribute to the perception of procedural justice. Perhaps the most widely documented factor is the opportunity for voice in the procedure (Thibaut & Walker, 1975). Additionally, building on the work of Leventhal (1980), several procedural criteria contributing to perceptions of fairness have been investigated in organizational settings, including: judgment based on evidence, correctability or refutability of the decision, and consistent application of procedures (Folger, Konovsky, & Cropanzano, 1992; Kim & Mauborgne, 1991, 1993). Researchers have drawn the distinction between determinants of procedural justice that pertain to formal procedures and those that pertain to the decision maker's conduct, the latter being referred to as interactional justice (Tyler & Bies, 1990). The two main facets of interactional justice are interpersonal sensitivity (the extent to which individuals are treated with respect and dignity) and informational justice (the extent to which individuals are given adequate and timely information regarding the decision procedure and outcome); both procedural and interactional factors give rise to judgments of procedural justice, although the relevance or importance of particular factors may vary somewhat depending on the decision context (Greenberg, 1993; Greenberg & Cropanzano, 1997).

Research on the consequences of procedural justice reveals two main findings. First, procedural justice can have a unique and unqualified effect on attitudes and behaviors (Lind, 2001). People are more willing to accept a decision when they perceive decision procedures as just (Korsgaard et al., 1995; Schaubroeck et al., 1994). Moreover, individuals are more likely to cooperate with a decision (Kim & Mauborgne, 1993) and with the organization (Konovksy & Pugh, 1994; Moorman, 1991) if they perceive the procedures to be just. Similarly, when procedures are unjust, individuals are likely to engage in antisocial or retaliatory behavior (Greenberg, 1990; Skarlicki & Folger, 1997). Second, procedural justice interacts with distributive justice to affect attitudes and behavior such that the impact of procedural justice is stronger when distributive justice is lower (Brockner & Wiesenfeld, 1996). This finding seems to suggest that perceptions of procedures may influence the sense-making process that is triggered when unfavorable or negative outcomes occur (Folger & Cropanzano, 2001).

Numerous theoretical explanations for the effects of procedural justice have been offered. The earliest explanation was material self-interest: individuals value fair procedures because they ensure that their material interests will be protected, at least in the long run (Lind & Tyler, 1988). That is, even if the immediate outcome of a decision is unfair, fair procedures ensure that over time individuals will receive what they are due. This explanation is consistent with the assumption of rational, economic self-interest, albeit not as rigorously applied as it is in equity theory or in agency theory. Rather, this explanation of procedural justice effects suggests a willingness to suspend self-interest in the short term if the procedures signal long-term returns. Indeed, recent theoretical work on the judgment processes underlying fairness perceptions suggests individuals rely on a less deliberative process than on a careful weighing of inputs to outcomes.

Theoretical explanations pointing to a less calculative process suggests that judgments are based on assessments of decision makers' intent or character (Folger & Cropanzano, 2001; Lind, 2001; Mikula, 1998). For example, the relational model (Tyler & Lind, 1992; Tyler & Blader, 2000) identifies three beliefs that are shaped by procedural justice: standing, neutrality, and trust; the latter two specifically concern assessments of intent and character. Neutrality refers to the extent to which individuals feel the decision maker treats them equally. Trust refers to the belief that the decision maker intends to be fair, ethical, and benevolent. While neutrality and trust have implications for the protection of self-interest in that one would expect a neutral, trustworthy decision maker to make distributively just decisions, Lind (2001) argues that these judgments do not appear to influence behavior through a strictly rational or calculated judgment process. Recent empirical and theoretical work on fairness heuristic theory (Lind, 2001; Lind, Kulik, Ambrose, & de Vera-Park, 1993) suggests that individuals are unlikely to carefully weigh the personal costs and benefits of a given decision outcome but rather apply the heuristic of procedural fairness to determine the trustworthiness of a decision maker. Only when individuals sense that procedural justice has been violated do they become more deliberative in their assessments of exchanges.

Additionally, theory suggests that motives may involve some bases other than self-interest or self-focus. Both the heuristic model of procedural justice (Lind, 2001) and the relational model (Tyler & Blader, 2000; Tyler & Lind, 1992) propose that individuals value fair procedures because such procedures affirm their standing in relationships with authorities and with groups. Such affirmations are *inherently* valued because individuals' identities are based at least in part on their membership in groups. This explanation is based on the concept of social identity, which concerns how individuals come to identify and form bonds with various groups and organizations (Deaux, 1996). This perspective suggests that people have a fundamental need to form relationships with others such that they base their self-identities on their membership in various groups. Therefore, it is highly important for individuals to maintain good standing in the groups to which they belong, for if their standing in a group is threatened, their identity is threatened.

Some have speculated that the group identity explanation of procedural justice effects simply reflects self-interests of a social-emotional nature rather than a material nature (Cropanzano & Ambrose, 2001). However, social identity theory suggests that processes underlying social identification are quite different from those underlying more self-interested thought and action. Specifically, social identity theory specifies that identification involves a process of depersonalization in which the basis of perception and action shifts from the self to the group (Hogg & Terry, 2000; Turner & Oronato, 1999). Further, theory suggests that, in addition to self-esteem, identity effects are motivated by uncertainty reduction (Hogg & Terry, 2000), an epistemic motivation to make meaning of the world, which is not directly related to self-concerns. Thus, identity concerns underlying procedural justice may not be self-focused and in fact may have little to do with self-concerns.

Agency Theory

In contrast to procedural justice, rational self-interest looms large in agency theory. Agency theory is part of a broader class of microeconomic theories that include property rights theory and transaction cost theory (Nilakant & Rao, 1994). These theories are concerned with the efficient arrangement of economic exchanges. Agency theory (Eisenhardt, 1989; Jensen & Meckling, 1976; Pratt & Zeckhauser, 1991) is particularly relevant because it is readily applicable to dyadic relationships across various levels of the organizational hierarchy. Agency theory concerns an exchange wherein a principal delegates the performance of a task to an agent in exchange for compensation. Agency theory focuses on how principals attempt to structure the relationship to protect their interests against the self-interests of the agent. In work settings, agency theory has often been applied to explain the relationships between outside owners of the firm (as principals) and top managers (as agents). However, the CEO and managers can be viewed as both principals and agents because they serve in the role of agents relative to the owners of the company and as principals relative to the role of their subordinates (Scarpello & Jones, 1996).

Agency theory makes several assumptions regarding individuals' propensities and the effects of the exchange context (Eisenhardt, 1989; Jensen & Meckling, 1976). First, both the principal and the agent are assumed to be motivated to maximize their own individual utilities. Further, the theory assumes bounded rationality and, in particular, that incomplete information is available. An additional assumption is that the agent is more risk averse than the principal, because the principal can spread risk across multiple principal-agent exchanges whereas the agent is fully invested in but one relationship. If valid, these assumptions suggest the potential for a number of agency problems. The first agency problem is goal conflict: to a greater or lesser extent, utility maximization for one party will come at the expense of the other party's interests. The second agency problem is information asymmetry, which refers to the degree to which the principal lacks information on agents' behavior. These problems create two central risks for the principal, namely adverse selection (i.e., the tendency for the agent to misrepresent him or herself to the principal) and moral hazard (i.e., the tendency for the agent to act opportunistically). Agent opportunism involves the agent's pursuit of his or her own goals at the expense of the principal's goals and often is manifested in the agent shirking. The main thrust of agency theory is that agency problems drive the principal's efforts to monitor and control the agent, which, in turn, influence agent compliance.

Principals use two primary mechanisms to respond to agency risks. One is to structure the compensation to the agent so as to better align goals and thereby to limit the probability and/or the severity of the risks. The second approach is to limit the scope and probability of opportunistic or shirking behavior through careful monitoring or hierarchical control. Goal alignment can be accomplished through "outcome-based" compensation. The alternative, behavior-based compensation (e.g., salary, hourly wage, etc.), rewards agents' behavior or efforts in activities presumed to lead to outcomes desired by principals somewhat irrespective of the outcomes. Conversely, outcome-based compensation (e.g., commission, profit sharing) rewards the outcomes of agents' actions somewhat irrespective of the effort or actions themselves. All else being equal, agents are thought to prefer behavior-based compensation because it provides a steady, rather than an uncertain, stream of income (Tosi & Gomez-Mejia, 1994). In consequence, principals must pay a premium to get agents to accept the risk of outcome-based compensation (Stroh, Brett, Baumann, & Reilly, 1996); the cost of this premium is somewhat mitigated by the savings in monitoring or information costs that may be involved in enacting behavior-based contracts. An ideal setting would exist where information is costless, so that principals can offer behavior-based compensation desired by agents while controlling the threat of opportunistic or shirking behavior. However, to the extent that information asymmetry is high, outcome-based compensation is more effective. Information asymmetry reduces the agents' accountability to the principal, thereby increasing the risk that the agent may shirk his or her duty.

In short, outcome-based compensation forces the agent to exert a high level of effort toward the outcomes desired by the principal. However, the efficacy of outcome-based compensation is moderated by several factors including degree of goal conflict, intended length of the exchange relationship, task programmability, outcome uncertainty, and risk propensity of the agent (Eisenhardt, 1989; Gomez-Mejia & Balkin, 1992; Stroh et al. 1996). For example, when outcomes are so uncertain as to preclude a reasonable agent to accept all risks of outcome-based pay, the only alternatives may be either to forgo the exchange or to offer more certain compensation protected only by monitoring, control, or agent bonding.

The second approach to managing agency risk is to employ one or more mechanisms to monitor, control, or bond the actions of the agent. Monitoring mechanisms in an investor-manager context may be specified in advance (e.g., via formal or informal employment contracts) or may evolve at the discretion of the principal. Monitoring mechanisms may be manifested in a variety of ways, including number of outside board members (Daily, Johnson, Ellstrand, & Dalton, 1998), requirements in the timing and frequency of financial reports (Kelly, 1999), a formal information system (Eisenhardt, 1989), and direct observation or involvement of the principal (Sapienza & Gupta, 1994). Similarly, agency risk may be managed through hierarchical control or restriction of the agent's autonomy, which can be accomplished through the terms of the contract, organizational and job design, or through direct supervision (Eccles, 1991; Nilakant & Rao, 1994). Finally, the agent may use bonding costs to reduce agency risk (Jensen & Meckling, 1976). Bonding costs, often voluntarily offered by the agent, are measures included in the contract or employment agreement that make it unattractive or costly for the agent to shirk.

Two main approaches have been employed in agency theory research: the positivist approach and principal-agent approach (Eisenhardt, 1989). The positivist approach focuses on how the exchange relationship should be designed to address agency risk, whereas the principal-agent stream assesses the consequences of various contractual arrangements against the predictions of agency theory. The positivist stream reveals how agency risks affect the actions of the principals in formulating a contract or employment relationship and in managing the relationship on a day-to-day basis. An issue that has received significant empirical support is the relationship between agency risk and the extent to which the agent's compensation is outcome-based. For example, Stroh and colleagues. (1996) found that when their job is difficult to monitor a greater proportion of managers' compensation is likely to be variable pay (i.e., outcome-based). Parks and Conlon (1995) found that principals were more likely to develop outcome-based contracts when they had limited ability to monitor the agent. Research also directly supports the relationship between agency risk and monitoring. For example, Sapienza and Gupta (1994) found that principals are more likely to actively monitor agents when information asymmetry is high and when goal conflict is high. Further, research indicates that agency risk is associated with restricting the autonomy of the agent. For example, research on the contract terms imposed by investors on entrepreneurs indicates that investors specify more control mechanisms (e.g., board control, approval of timing of future investments, noncompete agreements) to the extent that information asymmetry is high and ability to monitor is low (Barney, Busenitz, Fiet, Moesel, 1994; Kelly, 1999).

The principal-agent stream of research is especially pertinent to understanding agent behavior. Specifically, it focuses on agents' responses to principals' efforts to minimize agency risk, responses such as opportunism and expending or withholding effort. Opportunism, which occurs when the agent acts in his or her own interest at the expense of the principal, has been operationalized in a variety of ways, including escalation of commitment to a course of action that is not in the interests of the company (Tosi, Katz, & Gomez-Mejia, 1997), use of unauthorized leave (Kosnick & Bettenhausen, 1992), and greenmail, wherein managers buy back stock at an above-market price (Kosnick, 1987). Research suggests that the principal's efforts to minimize risk through compensation or monitoring are associated with lower incidence of opportunistic behavior. For example, outcome-based compensation has been positively associated with higher firm performance (Gerhart & Milcovich, 1990) and negatively associated with agents' opportunistic behavior (Kosnick & Bettenhausen, 1992; Tosi et al., 1997). The applicable agency theory logic is that outcome-based compensation rewards *only* those results desired by principals thereby forcing agents to attend to principals' goals and exert maximum effort toward their accomplishment. Monitoring has also been associated with less opportunistic behavior (Abrahamson & Park, 1994; Kosnick & Bettenhausen, 1992). Here, the logic is that effective monitoring reduces agents' ability to shirk or to pursue goals in conflict with those of the principals.

TOWARD AN INTEGRATION OF PROCEDURAL JUSTICE AND AGENCY THEORY

On the surface, procedural justice theory and agency theory appear quite divergent; the two have different disciplinary origins and different evolutionary paths. Nonetheless, both have touched upon issues central to the other. For example, though using an agency perspective, Eccles (1991) observed that fairness was mentioned and emphasized heavily by managers. He argued that, due to uncertainty, many aspects of the exchange relationship are left unspecified and evolve over time as conditions change, and as a result, disagreements and perceptions of unfairness are likely. He further argued that both parties evaluate fairness and that agents' perceptions of fairness affect their motivation to comply with the contract. Eccles focused primarily on distributive justice, defining fairness as the fulfillment of the contract (i.e., a fair exchange). The contractual provisions that become the subject of debate, however, suggest that perceptions of *procedural* justice are also relevant. Specifically, Eccles identified three issues of controversy: how to partition decision-making authority between the principal and agent, how to measure the agent's performance, and how to reward performance. These issues clearly involve not only the distribution of outcomes but also the procedures by which the distributions are determined. It is also noteworthy that these three issue correspond to the forms of governance used to manage agency risk: control, monitoring, and compensation, respectively.

In addition to Eccles' (1991) findings, two studies recently addressed the interplay between the theoretical perspectives. Scarpello and Jones (1996) used an agency framework to examine the consequences of pay fairness among supervisory, professional, technical, and clerical employees. Consistent with Eccles (1991), Scarpello and Jones (1996) worked from the assumption that the perception of procedural fairness is necessary to gain agents' compliance with the contract. Based on this assumption, the authors posited and found support for three hypotheses regarding the relationship between perceptions of procedural fairness and attitudes toward pay, supervisory satisfaction, and organizational commitment. Welbourne, Balkin, and Gomez-Mejia (1995) examined procedural justice and agency theory concepts in the context of a gainsharing plan. They argued that, because gainsharing is a group-based compensation plan where each employee relies on the efforts of other employees to achieve an outcome, employees are in the dual role of agent and principal: agents relative to the employer, but principals relative to others in their group. Agency theory suggests that in the role of principal, employees will monitor the efforts of other group members only when the benefits of doing so outweigh the costs. The authors asserted that employees' perceptions of the net benefit to monitoring increases when they perceive the pay plan as procedurally and distributively fair; thus, when perceptions of fairness are high, employees should be more likely to monitor coworkers (i.e., to both note and encourage the performance of coworkers). The findings revealed that procedural justice, but not distributive justice, was related to monitoring coworkers. As they note, the findings suggest that procedural justice enhances the explanatory power of agency theory. The findings also extend the relevance of procedural justice to a new class of behaviors: monitoring and encouraging fellow-employees.

Common Themes

The findings of the research reported above, though limited, suggest an overlap in phenomena explained by procedural justice and agency theories. We suggest three common themes that provide insight into how these theoretical perspectives might be integrated. First, both models focus on exchange relationships. Second, both perspectives address control, or lack thereof, over the actions of the other party. Third, both models recognize the relevance of self-interest. However, the models differ in how each of these themes is approached. These differences, summarized in Table 1, are examined in the following section.[1] We then propose a tentative, integrated model.

The Exchange Relationship

Both theories are concerned with exchange relationships, but they differ in the emphasis placed on process versus outcome. Although outcomes are clearly relevant in procedural justice (Brockner & Wiesenfeld, 1996), the theory places strong emphasis on the form of fair procedures and interactional fairness (Tyler & Lind, 1992). Research suggests that both procedural and interactional justice have an impact on attitudes toward the exchange and the relationship, as well as future exchanges (Tyler & Dawes, 1993; Tyler & Lind, 1992). In contrast, agency theory provides a more static view of the relationship that links pre-existing conditions (agency risks) to the conditions of the contract (e.g., compensation, information systems) and that link contract conditions to agent compliance. As such, agency theory provides insight into the existing and relatively stable conditions that influence the actions of both the principal and agent and the quality of their exchanges. Procedural justice, on the other hand, provides insight into how day-to-day interactions influence the relationship and future exchanges.

TABLE 1
A Summary of Common Themes in Procedural Justice and Agency Theory

Key Theme	Procedural Justice	Agency Theory
Exchange Relationship	• Dynamic view of impact of exchange processes on exchange relationships • Exchange relationship has inherent value • Trust as a determinant of cooperation	• Static view of influence of context on exchange processes • Exchange relationship has no inherent value • Contract as determinant of compliance
Control	• Focus on employees' lack of and need for control over personal outcomes • Managerial control as a threat to employee cooperation	• Focus on manager's vulnerability and need to control employee • Managerial control as a means of ensuring employee compliance
Self-Interest	• Self-interest may be suspended or subjugated • Judgment processes may be nondeliberative • Focus on protection of self-interest	• Self-interest is sole motivation • Assumes rational-calculative processes • Focus on promotion of unconstrained self-interest

The two theories differ in the emphasis placed on exchanges versus the exchange relationship itself. Some perspectives on procedural justice suggest that the exchange relationship itself is highly important (Cropanzano & Ambrose, 2001; Lind, 2001; Tyler & Blader, 2000). For example, the relational model and identity model of procedural justice (Tyler & Lind, 1992; Tyler & Blader, 2000) suggest that persons derive meaning and worth from exchange relationships; therefore the quality of such relationships has inherent value. Consequently, while the outcomes of exchanges are important, the manner in which an exchange occurs (e.g., was the employee treated with dignity and respect) has its own inherent value as a social-emotional reward (Cropanzano & Ambrose, 2001). In contrast, agency theory assumes that neither the relationship nor the exchange process itself has intrinsic value. The best exchange is one where the outcome is favorable and the costs of limiting agency risks are minimized.

The differing views of the value of the exchange relationship have implications for the role of trust and trustworthiness in exchange relationships. Although Eisenhardt (1989) proposed that, over time, exchanges reveal the reliability of an exchange partner, the concept of trust is not explicitly considered in agency theory. Agency theory implicitly assumes that there is no meaningful variation in individuals' propensity to trust or to be opportunistic (i.e., be untrustworthy); risk of opportunism is determined by context and is addressed through governance mechanisms. In contrast, procedural justice theory suggests that there is meaningful variation in trust that is explained by perceptions of procedural justice. That is, the quality of exchanges provides information regarding the character and trustworthiness of the other party. The trust that is built through procedural and interactional fairness in turn promotes cooperative behavior (Tyler & Blader, 2000). Consistent with this theory, research on trust suggests that individuals who trust are more likely to engage in cooperative behavior (Deutsch, 1962; McAllister, 1995; Zand, 1972). Thus, procedural justice provides insight into another source of cooperative behavior.

Control

The second theme is that a central problem in both models is control. Procedural justice focuses on agents' lack of control and their need for control. The importance of control is illustrated in research demonstrating an interaction between procedural justice and outcome control (Tyler, Rasinski, & Spodick, 1985; Korsgaard et al., 1995). The pattern of this interaction is such that procedural justice has a stronger impact when the agent has little control or influence over the outcome. These findings suggest that individuals are concerned with procedures to the extent that they lack direct control. Agency theory is also concerned with control, but it focuses on the principal's need to control the agent's actions through a variety of governance mechanisms.

Viewed together, these issues of control provide insight into when procedural justice is likely to be an especially potent influence on agent attitudes and behavior. The extent and type of control principals exert is likely to affect agents' concern over fair treatment. Specifically, hierarchical control, which involves restricting agents' decision-making authority, limits agents' control over job outcomes. To the extent that agents' decision control is limited and agents' outcomes are dependent on principals' decisions, agents are likely to be sensitive to procedural issues. Further, Eccles (1991) noted that when agents' decision-making authority is limited, principals must rely on behavior-based and subjective forms of evaluation; otherwise, the problem of accountability exceeding authority will occur. Thus, the compensation of agents with limited decision-making authority is dependent on the judgments (and discretion) of principals, which should make salient procedural and interactional justice issues.

A consideration of both perspectives also suggests that agents' fairness has an impact on the principal. As Eccles (1992) observed, fairness is a concern of principals as well as agents: to the extent that agents fulfill their contractual obligations, principals will view the exchange as fair. While Eccles was referring to the fairness of the exchange outcome (i.e., distributive justice), agents' procedural fairness is also relevant. Research in agency theory suggests that agent noncompliance may manifest itself in the form for poor or inaccurate information exchange, rather than in overt violation of exchange agreements. For example, CEOs are more likely to withhold rather than misrepresent information about negative outcomes from shareholders (Abrahamson & Park, 1994). Such tactics, when discovered, influence perceptions of interactional fairness via its informational component (Sapienza & Korsgaard, 1996).

Agency theory also provides insight into how principals, in efforts to minimize agency risk, may unintentionally undermine relational bonds. As noted earlier, the principal may employ a number of governance mechanisms in attempt to control the agent's actions; among these, the most relevant to the current discussion are monitoring and control mechanisms. Principals' efforts to manage agency risk through control and monitoring may have a negative effect on agents' perceptions of both distributive and procedural fairness. Specifically, these governance mechanisms reduce employees' perceptions of control over their jobs and their performance (Smith, Carayon, Sanders, Lim & LeGrande, 1992; Stanton & Barnes-Farrell, 1996) and thus their beliefs about their ability to protect their self-interest. Further, monitoring and a lack of autonomy can also lead to undesirable personal outcomes for employees, such as increased stress and job dissatisfaction (Aiello & Kolb, 1995). Thus, because the imposition of such measures may lead to perceptions of less favorable work and nonwork outcomes for employees, monitoring and control mechanisms have the potential to lower perceptions of distributive justice.

Monitoring and control measures can adversely affect perceptions of procedural justice as well. Some have argued that attempts at close monitoring result in employee-manager interactions that might enhance perceptions of fairness by ensuring evaluations are based on performance data (Niehoff & Moorman, 1993). However, other research suggests that monitoring is likely to undermine procedural justice. For example, close monitoring, which is often viewed as a violation of privacy (Ambrose, Alder, & Noel, 1998), may be viewed as procedurally or interactionally unfair (Bies, 2001) and may pose a threat to employees' sense of self-determination (Stanton & Barnes-Farrell, 1996). Control mechanisms may also be deleterious to perceptions of procedural fairness because they often require lower discretion on the part of employees and less involvement in setting the criteria for measuring success (Lawler, 1976). That is, imposing control results in agents' experiencing less process control or voice. In sum, governance mechanisms designed to address agency risks may unintentionally result in agents' perceptions of unfairness.

Self-interest

The third theme, self-interest, is a significant issue in both models. However, the manner in which each model approaches the motive of self-interest differs in a number of ways. The most apparent difference is that whereas rational self-interest is the sole motive in agency theory, procedural justice theory recognizes additional motivations, such as group identity (Tyler & Blader, 2000) or fairness as a terminal value (Folger, 1998). Moreover, self-interest is unconstrained in agency theory whereas procedural justice theory would suggest that individuals might suspend or perhaps subjugate their self-interest to the interests of the group or organization. That is, the agent is willing to accept suboptimal outcomes and fulfill their obligations of the exchange if procedures suggests that the agent's long-term prospects are favorable (i.e., instrumental model, Lind & Tyler, 1988) and the agent's standing in the relationship is sound (i.e., the heuristic model, Lind, 2001; relational model, Tyler & Blader, 2000). The implication of this difference is that agency theory may have limited predictive power because it overlooks the limits of self-interest as an influence on behavior.

Second, agency theory assumes rational, calculative self-interest, wherein an individual's actions reflect deliberate and systematic reasoning targeted at utility maximization. Theories of procedural justice theory suggest that reactions to exchanges involve processes other than utility maximization. For example, some procedural justice theorists speculate that individuals' reactions to an exchange involve a sense-making process in which the individual assesses the other party's responsibility and intent (Brockner & Wiesenfeld, 1996; Folger & Cropanzano, 2001). Thus, individuals judge the *significance* of a given exchange and the general *character* of the other party rather than reacting to cost-benefit assessments of isolated exchanges. Further, Noorderhaven (1992) argues that, given the bounded rationality assumed in agency theory and the uncertainty in principal-agent relationships, neither party can truly be a utility maximizer. Instead, actors are "utility enhancers" who rely on norms to determine how to act. This argument is consistent with the heuristic model of procedural justice (Lind, 2001), wherein the underlying cognitive process is less calculative. This perspective suggests that individuals may not carefully weigh the costs and benefits of various exchanges but rather make simple, quick evaluations of the exchange process and its implication for future exchanges.

Third and perhaps most significantly, agency theory assumes people are motivated by the *unconstrained pursuit* of self-interest whereas procedural justice assumes individuals are motivated by the protection of their self-interest. Specifically, agency theory focuses on unchecked self-interest on the part of an agent; procedural justice focuses on the protection of self-interest on the part of an agent who lacks power. Self-interest in agency theory translates into the principal's fear of agent opportunism; whereas in procedural justice, the issue is the agent's fear of being exploited by the principal. Moreover, in procedural justice theory the agent is concerned not only with exploitation in the material sense, but in terms of humiliation and loss of dignity.

Although agency theory has been criticized for over-estimating agents' propensity to shirk, which implies agents are averse to work (Nilakant &

Rao, 1994), agency theory's view of self-interest has interesting implications for understanding the actions of both the agent and the principal. Procedural justice has generally viewed the agent's actions solely as a response to the principal's decision making. Noncooperative behavior (such as reduced effort, use of company resources for personal purposes, or stealing office supplies) is considered a response to perceived injustice in procedural justice theory, yet would be viewed as opportunistic in agency theory. Agency theory suggests that agents may *initiate* noncooperative or opportunistic behavior as a means of enhancing their personal outcomes, and not solely in response to injustice. That is, agents are not passive victims, but active participants in an exchange relationship. Further, the emphasis on protection against opportunism in agency theory provides insight into the motives underlying the actions of the principal, which may influence the extent to which the principal appears fair. This insight is significant to procedural justice theory, which is lacking in explanation of the causes of fair behavior (Korsgaard et al., 1998). Agency theory depicts agent opportunism as a primary determinant of the principal's efforts to control the agent's actions.

A Tentative Model

We expand on the three themes discussed above to provide a more powerful explanatory framework for organizational settings than does either

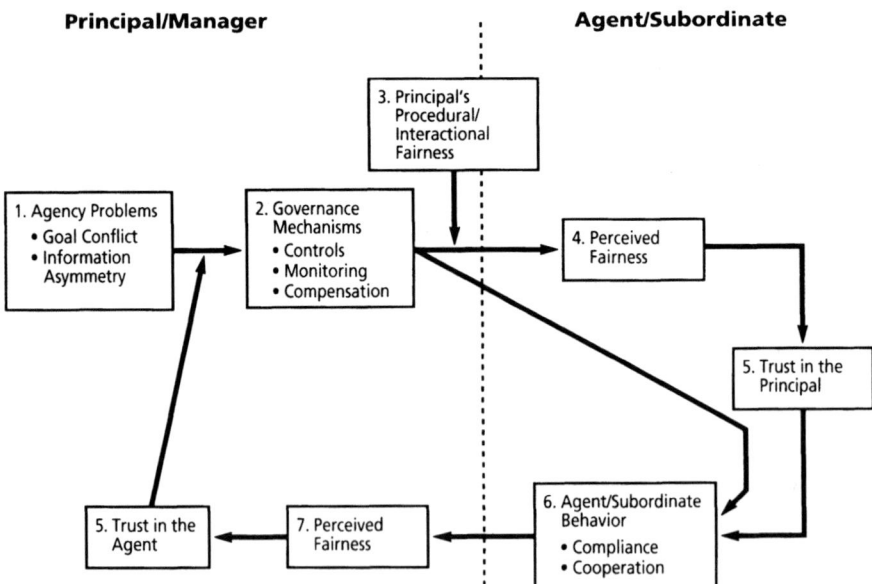

Figure 1. A Tentative Integration of Principal-Agency and Procedural Justice Concept

perspective alone. Figure 1 depicts a model that integrates some of the key constructs from the two theories. The model indicates how principals' efforts to control agents' actions influence agents' behavior, and how these actions in turn affect principals' perceptions and actions. The flow of relationships in the model suggests a cyclical process by which the exchanges between principals and agents are regulated.

The left side of this model depicts the actions of principals and the factors contributing to their behavior; the right side of the model depicts the actions and perceptions of agents. As agency theory suggests, agency problems of information asymmetry and goal conflict (variable 1 in the figure) will influence the type and extent of principals' efforts to control and monitor the agent (2). Such efforts should influence agents' compliance (6). However, these governance mechanisms, which can leave agents feeling vulnerable to exploitation, pose a threat to the agents' standing and can have unintended negative consequences for their attitudes and behavior. Consistent with procedural justice, the model posits that the extent to which principals are procedurally and interactionally fair (3) will mitigate the negative effects of governance mechanisms. That is, the behavior of principals will be evaluated by agents in terms of its fairness (4) and its implications for trustworthiness (5). In consequence, agents will be more or less compliant and cooperative (6).

The agent's behavior influences the principal's perceptions of the agent's fairness (7). We consider compliance with the contract as an indication of distributive justice (i.e., a fair exchange outcome). Additionally, the manner and extent to which the agent shares information with the principal should influence perceptions of the agent's procedural fairness (Sapienza & Korsgaard, 1996). Our model also suggests that the principal's perception of procedural fairness, through its impact on trust in the agent (8), is an important factor in how the principal responds to agency problems. Specifically, the link between agency problems and principals' use of governance mechanisms is moderated by their trust in agents: when trust is high, agency problems have a weaker impact on the imposition of governance mechanisms. In other words, principals' trust in agents influence their willingness to take risks on those agents.

Note that our model is limited in two key ways. First, given our emphasis on procedural issues, we did not explicitly model the role of distributive justice (i.e., the fairness of the exchange outcomes). However, we believe the model has clear implications for distributive justice that are consistent with prior theory and research. Distributive justice concerns enter in at two points in the model, one from agents' perspective and one from the perspective of principals. As noted earlier, monitoring and control can lead to unfavorable job outcomes for agents; these outcomes may be perceived as unfair. Consistent with the empirical evidence of the interaction of distributive and procedural justice (Brockner & Wiesenfeld, 1996), we expect that the negative effects of governance measures on agents' perceptions and attitudes are mitigated by the extent to which such measures are implemented in a procedurally fair manner. Further, we posit that principals' concerns regarding distributive justice, manifested in the extent to which agents fulfill their part of the exchange agreement, directly affect principals' perceptions of fairness.

A second limitation of the model is that we focus on the dyad to the exclusion of the social context. Recent research has suggested that organizations or groups may form a climate for procedural justice (Naumann & Bennett, 2000; Colquitt & Jackson, 2001), one likely to affect both perceived and actual procedures and interactions. Similarly, in their chapter of this volume, Goldman and Thatcher argue that social information can influence fairness judgment and reactions. They identified four forms of social information: explicitly expressed opinions, comments that cue individuals to focus on certain information, comments about the values and motives of management, and post hoc explanations of specific events. Such social information is likely to color an individuals' interpretation of exchanges.

Implications of the Model

Our model provides some interesting insights into the exchange relationship. In this section, we highlight three major implications of our model for future research. First, we examine the implications of agent fairness and trustworthiness in affecting the impact of agency problems on governance procedures. Second, we discuss the impact of agency problems on agents' perceptions of the fairness of governance procedures. Lastly, we discuss competing direct and indirect effects of governance procedures on agents' compliance and cooperation with principals.

Trust, Response to Agency Problems, and Sensitivity to Agent Fairness

The model raises the question of when principals and agents are likely to be most concerned with and affected by attributions of trustworthiness. Agency theory suggests that when agency problems exist (i.e., goal conflict and/or information asymmetry are high), there is a greater risk of agent opportunism. This assertion implies that principals develop an expectation or belief about the likelihood of the agent acting in an unprincipled or opportunistic fashion. In such cases, principals are apt to look for signs indicating agents' (un)trustworthiness and the consequent likelihood of opportunism or exploitation. Our model suggests that principals may view agency problems as less of a threat to the extent that they trust the agent and thus be less prone to impose costly governance mechanisms. In sum:

Proposition 1: When trust is high, agency problems are less likely to motivate the principal to impose governance mechanisms than when trust is low.

Moreover, our model suggests that the extent to which the principal imposes governance mechanisms on future exchanges is affected by the quality of exchange process. Given the strong link between procedural justice and trust (Brockner, Ackerman, & Fairchild, 2001), our model suggests that agents who conduct their transactions with principals in a fair manner are likely to see benefits in terms of less imposition of monitoring and control. Fair interactions between the agent and principal are likely to foster the principal's trust in the agent. As a consequence, the principal will be less prone to impose risk-reducing governance mechanisms. Thus:

Proposition 2: Through its effect on trust, the perceived fairness of the agent is likely to mitigate the impact of agency problems on the principal's imposition of governance mechanisms.

Agency Problems and Agents' Perceptions of Unfairness

Our model provides insight into the contextual factors that motivate principals to engage in actions that may adversely affect agents' perceptions of procedural fairness. Agency theory has typically viewed the effects of agency problems from the perspective of principals. That is, principals are more vulnerable to exploitation to the extent that goal conflict and information uncertainty are high. Our model suggests that agency problems may also adversely affect agents by heightening their sense of vulnerability as well. That is, agency problems are likely to lead to contractual arrangements that are undesirable for the agent. Specifically, the governance procedures that are expected to arise from agency problems—close monitoring and restricted control and discretion—are likely to be viewed as undesirable and potentially unfair to agents. Thus:

Proposition 3: Through their effects on governance mechanisms, agency problems are likely to negatively affect agents' perceptions of fairness.

While harsher governance procedures are generally less desirable for agents, our model suggests that the manner in which these mechanisms are implemented qualifies their effects on agents' perceptions of fairness. For example, one of the reasons monitoring may be related to agents' perceptions of fairness is its implications for violation of their privacy, as well as its impact on perceptions of their self worth (Lawler, 1976). However, research suggests that the link between violation of privacy and procedural justice perceptions may depend on policies regarding the acquisition and sharing of information (Bies, 2001). That is, the manner in which monitoring and control is implemented and enacted may determine whether it is considered procedurally unfair. Thus,

Proposition 4: Governance mechanisms are less likely to adversely affect agents' perceptions of fairness to the extent that their implementation is procedurally fair or they are enacted in a fair manner.

Competing Direct and Indirect Effects of Governance Procedures

The model also highlights the potential dual effects of governance measures used to manage agency risk. Consistent with agency theory, we posit that the imposition of monitoring and/or control should increase *compliance*. That is, given that monitoring and control create disincentives for noncompliance, these measures can directly promote agent compliance and, hence, fair exchanges from principals' perspective. However, we also posit unintended negative effects, particularly when these mechanisms are not implemented in a procedurally just manner. Given that such measures can lead to agents' perceptions of procedural unfairness, governance mechanisms may contribute to a lack of cooperation or, in the extreme, to retaliation. We expect the deleterious effect of governance mechanisms on cooperation to be moderated by the fairness of the policy concerning the implementation of the mechanism and the principal's interactional fairness in carrying out the policy. In short, the policy and/or the principals' style of interacting may undermine governance measures. Thus:

Proposition 5: Governance mechanisms can have competing effects on agent: directly benefiting compliance and, through its effects on agents' fairness perceptions and trust, indirectly harming cooperation.

Proposition 6: The extent to which governance mechanisms have a negative impact on agent cooperation depends on the procedural/interactional fairness of the principal in implementing the governance mechanism.

Agency theory addresses any exchange relationship wherein one party contracts with another party to perform a task or service. As our integrated model illustrates, principals and agents face different concerns and risks, but both parties are likely to be sensitive to fair treatment and procedures. Thus, our model addresses procedural justice from the perspective of both parties and allows for the examination of fairness issues in nonhierarchical relationships as well. The model is thus useful in a broad range of relationships not typically addressed in procedural justice research. In the next section we discuss one such setting as an illustrative example: the case of entrepreneur-venture capitalist relations wherein the relationship is not strictly hierarchical and the effects of fairness are bi-directional.

THE CASE OF ENTREPRENEUR-VENTURE CAPITALIST RELATIONS

Venture capitalists function as intermediaries between institutional and other sources of funding and entrepreneurial firms. Because of their expertise in selecting, monitoring, developing, and exiting investment opportunities in certain industries and phases of new venture startup, venture capital firms (VCFs) attract the funds of limited partners (Berger & Udell, 1998; Sahlman, 1990). Limited partners provide capital to VCFs in exchange for a share of the gains realized from the success of the investees. Entrepreneurs often seek venture capital because their ventures cannot reach or sustain their full potential of growth from internally generated funds and because they possess too little in the way of collateral or too uncertain an income stream to attract bank financing.

Banks ensure that their money is repaid at regular intervals by holding claims against the assets of the venture. Banks place constraints on venture decision making to ensure that their money will be returned regardless of venture outcomes; however, they take little role in the active overseeing of their debtors. They prefer decision making that maximizes the probability that payments are made and are relatively indifferent to huge upside results for the ventures themselves. VCFs, on the other hand, buy a stake in their investees without a guarantee that they will receive any return. A few investees, such as Apple and Digital, experience spectacular growth; however, the majority of investees bring very little return and some fail altogether (Fried & Hisrich, 1994). Consequently, most of the terms in the investment agreements are aimed at protecting venture capitalists' interests by providing VCFs with broad governance rights, including board seats and performance review (Landström, Manigart, Mason, & Sapienza, 1998).

From entrepreneurs' perspective, venture capital is very expensive: returns to VCFs when the venture succeeds are extremely high relative to bank lending rates, and the sharing of decision making authority limits entrepreneurs' autonomy, often a key reason for launching a business. One might argue, however, that when the venture struggles mightily or fails altogether that venture capital is cheap: VCFs receive a very low, zero, or negative return on funds provided. Yet, this fact is little consolation to the failing entrepreneur.

Obtaining venture capital is a struggle. VCFs fund 1 to 2% of business plans they review (Gorman & Sahlman, 1989), and the "due diligence" period is time consuming and often intrusive. Ventures may have to wait well over six months before the deal is completed. When the negotiation of investment terms does occur, the venture capitalist can choose from a variety of provisions that serve as monitoring and control mechanisms, thereby providing some protection against agency risks. These provisions include the creation of a board and the allocation of board seats (the majority of which are typically controlled by VCFs), noncompete agreements that restrict entrepreneurs should they leave the venture, and performance targets that, if missed, may result in additional loss of ownership for the entrepreneurs and/or the removal of the entrepreneurs from leadership positions in the company CEO (Kelly, 1999).

Entrepreneur-venture capitalist exchanges provide a good example of why combining economic and noneconomic theories, such as agency and procedural justice, may be useful. We consider below two phases of the entrepreneur-venture capitalist relationship. First, we examine the pre-investment phase and discuss how our model can help reveal whether the two sides will be likely to reach an agreement and what kind of governance arrangements will evolve. Second, we examine the post-investment phase and how agency and procedural justice conditions influence board of director interactions that comprise the major interface in this phase.

Issues in the Negotiation of the Investment

The preferences of venture capitalists and entrepreneurs regarding the investment contract are divergent and are driven by different factors. From the perspective of the venture capitalist, variations in venture stage and technological innovation are important considerations because they represent different potential agency and business risks (Barney, Busenitz, Fiet, & Moesel, 1989; Sapienza & Gupta, 1994). Besides the business uncertainties associated with early stage and high technology ventures, such venture also pose higher agency risks because the capacities of the entrepreneurial team will not yet be proven, effort-outcome relationships will be very difficult to observe and interpret, and the potential of the core technology will not be well understood by venture capitalists. These considerations will drive VCFs to seek greater equity to compensate for the greater business risk and greater monitoring and control rights to allay agency fears (Landström et al., 1998).

Entrepreneurs are likely to look at the initial contract formation very differently. Their concerns often center on the protection the contract provides against exploitation by the venture capitalist. Unlike investors, their preferences are unlikely to vary significantly with differences in venture stage or level of technology. If anything, the very information asymmetry that drives investors to seek control drives entrepreneurs, not undeservedly, to wish to maintain control. The imposition of control mechanisms deemed necessary on the one side is likely deemed obstructive and suboptimal on the other. In such circumstances, the manner in which decisions are reached are likely to provide powerful signals to both sides regarding not only the goals of their potential exchange partners, but also their character. In sum, the negotiation of investment deals is likely to be marked conflict between venture capitalists' efforts to minimize risk and entrepreneurs' struggle to maintain control and protect their vision of the venture. As evidenced by the fact that more than a few new ventures pass the due diligence phase but fail to obtain funding (Kelly, 1999), it appears that often this conflict is not successfully resolved. The logic of our model may now be applied to this case.

Our model suggests that procedural justice will influence the success of contract negotiations. First, procedural justice on the part of the principal can allay the entrepreneur's concerns regarding oppressive control. Thus, the entrepreneur is influenced by perceptions of the principal's fairness during negotiations; as noted above, principal fairness can help assure the entrepreneur that terms included in the contract will be enacted fairly in the future. Moreover, because of the character assessments that accompany justice judgments, the entrepreneur may also be less fearful of the exploitation from this venture capitalist in the future. For these reasons, entrepreneurs will be more willing to accept provisions that make themselves vulnerable to the venture capitalist when negotiations have proceeded fairly. Additionally, the extent to which the venture capitalist is interpersonally sensitive (i.e., interactionally fair) and preserves the dignity of the entrepreneur, the more willing the entrepreneur will be to accept provisions that cede control to the venture capitalist.

Procedural justice is also likely to influence the extent to which venture capitalists vigorously seek provisions to manage agency risk. The conduct of the entrepreneur during negotiations serves as a signal to the venture capitalist of the entrepreneur's trustworthiness and the venture capitalist's standing in the new venture. If an entrepreneur is perceived as fair and trustworthy, venture capitalists' perceptions of agency risk will be lowered, leading to less reliance on formal governance mechanisms in the contract. Perceptions that the entrepreneur is trustworthy and willing to share decision-making control reduce the perceived need to enact restrictive or intrusive mechanisms. Elements of interactional fairness, such as openness in sharing information and acknowledgement and consideration of venture capitalists' views, are apt to be especially potent influences. Venture capitalists also have relational concerns at stake: venture capitalists view themselves not merely as providers of funds but as partners able to add value beyond the capital invested (Fried & Hisrich, 1994). Thus, they will be affected by the fairness of entrepreneurs' behavior to the extent that it affirms or denies the venture capitalist's standing and worth to the venture. Interpersonal sensitivity during negotiations is therefore likely to be particularly important.

In short, procedural justice facilitates the negotiation of the investment contract by increasing venture capitalists' flexibility on monitoring and control and by increasing entrepreneurs' willingness to accept such provisions. These relationships were proposed and explored by Sapienza, Korsgaard, Folger, Sagrera, and Zhang (1999) in a simulation of investor-entrepreneur negotiations. In this study, the participant's self-report of the extent to which he or she engaged in interactionally fair behavior was positively related to the other party's trust in the participant and the ability of the participant to negotiate provisions that protected the participant's interests. The impact of trust on contract terms was demonstrated in an experiment involving a simulation of investor-entrepreneur negotiations in which mutual trust was manipulated through prior negotiations (Manigart, Korsgaard, Folger, Sapienza, & Baeyens, In Press). In this study, trust led participants acting as entrepreneurs to specify fewer self-protecting provisions and to be more willing to accept provisions that benefited the investors. Together, these findings, while tentative, suggest that contract terms are influenced by the character assessments that each party makes of the other party and that such assessments may be influenced by fair behavior.

If our integrated perspective is correct, the implications are significant for the minimization of agency costs in venture capitalist-entrepreneur contract negotiations. The failure to recognize these effects may result in suboptimal negotiations in which unnecessary or dysfunctional monitoring and control mechanisms loom as impediments. Moreover, the tenor of contract negotiations may have long-ranging effects (Landström et al., 1998). Entrepreneurs' propensity to act opportunistically may be affected by the fairness of the negotiation process. Furthermore, although agency theory does not typically consider the converse situation, venture capitalists' propensity to act opportunistically may also be affected by their perceptions of procedural fairness during negotiations. Our model reveals how the agency concerns of venture capitalists and the negotiation processes themselves interact. It also helps reveal when the damage of procedural unfairness may be greatest. Foreseeing such problems, both sides may be better able to structure both the negotiation procedure and the investment terms themselves.

Issues in Post-Investment Governance

Our framework may also shed light on the appropriate structure and processes of new venture boards in their role as post-investment governance. At post-investment, venture capitalists' efforts to monitor and control the entrepreneur's actions are likely to be manifested in the way the board is structured (e.g., chairing the board or controlling board seats) and through the conduct of board meetings (e.g., control over the agenda, control over strategic and operational decisions). Sapienza, Korsgaard, and Hoogendam (1997) provide a detailed discussion of how agency risks and justice concepts affect the board processes themselves. We summarize some of these points below.

New venture boards, like those of publicly-owned companies, are established to ensure that management takes actions consistent with outside owners' wishes and to determine whether substandard performance may be caused by management opportunism, management incompetence, or outside conditions beyond management control (Walsh & Seward, 1990). However, given the great uncertainty of cause-effect relationships in the volatile context of new ventures, board members may be especially ill-equipped to adequately judge the causes of venture performance. When venture performance is poor, fear of opportunism or incompetence may drive venture capitalists to press board meetings toward a focus on questioning past results and actions. Suspicions of goal conflict between the venture capitalist and entrepreneur may not only cloud interpretation but also make interactions especially contentious. In these conditions, actions such as the replacement of management or extreme tightening of control appear highly justified from the perspective of venture capitalists. As our model suggests, however, the likelihood that such actions would be taken and the perceived meaning of such actions will be affected by venture capitalists' perceptions of procedural justice of board decision making.

First, our model suggests that the propensity of investors to attribute poor performance to opportunism is lowered when entrepreneurs conduct board meetings and strategic decision-making in a procedurally fair manner. Because fairness is related to positive character assessments including honesty, benevolence, and trustworthiness, procedural fairness is likely to offset the tendency to attribute poor firm performance to entrepreneur opportunism. Further, our model suggests that how entrepreneurs react to governance "remedies" will depend in part how fairly they are treated during board meetings. Undoubtedly, managers will not generally be pleased with certain decisions such as replacing some or all of management, even if the argument is that such actions are necessary to take the venture to the next level. However, they are more likely to believe the motives and respect the integrity of the venture capitalists if the venture capitalists have conducted themselves in a procedurally fair manner. In general, our model has suggested that fairness will be especially important when the outcomes are unfavorable in that individuals will be more inclined to accept the decisions and less likely to obstruct or retaliate. These considerations have extreme practical importance for both sides.

CONCLUSION

We set out to develop a framework that integrates concepts from agency theory and procedural justice theory. As an illustration of how this framework might explain organizational relationships, we applied these concepts to entrepreneur-venture capitalist relations. As the above discussion suggests, the integration of these theories has strong potential as an explanatory framework. The entrepreneur-venture capitalist relationship, however, is a unique context wherein the relationship crosses organizational boundaries and is not strictly hierarchical, raising the question of the usefulness of our framework for hierarchical intra-organizational relationships. However, initial research suggests that a perspective that combines agency and procedural justice theories is also effective for exploring hierarchical relationships (Scarpello & Jones, 1996) and even intra-group relations (Welbourne et al., 1995).

Additionally, there are other nonhierarchical settings that have received scant attention from the justice literature that would also benefit from our framework. For example, inter-organizational alliance (Johnson, Korsgaard, & Sapienza, In press) and customer service encounters (Ambrose & Hess, 2001) are two such forms of nonhierarchical exchange relationships in which procedural justice concerns appear to be relevant. Similarly, in their chapter in this volume, Kulik and Holbrook apply the procedural justice framework to explain patients' reactions to encounters with physicians. They propose that patients' perceptions of procedural fairness are likely to affect the extent to which they comply with the prescriptions of their physicians. Our model would suggest that the extent to which the patient is willing to cede control to, and hence cooperate with, the physician is in part determined by their perceptions of fair treatment.

Research on agency theory and procedural justice provide very different views and prescriptions, yet both theories struggle with the question of how to manage cooperative work relationships. While both perspectives have individually impressive theoretical and empirical records, each provides an incomplete view of exchange relationships in organizational settings. Agency theory exaggerates the role of unchecked self-interest and underestimates the role of trust, whereas procedural justice overlooks the role of the principal's or manager's vulnerability—real or imagined—to the opportunistic actions of the agent or employee. By integrating these perspectives, we hope we have developed a more comprehensive explanation of work relationships.

NOTE

1. In the following section, we use the term *principal* to refer to the owner, manager, or superior in the relationship and *agent* for the employee or subordinate in the relationship.

REFERENCES

Abrahamson, E., & Park, C. (1994). Concealment of negative organizational outcomes: An agency theory perspective. *Academy of Management Journal, 37*, 1302-1334.

Aiello, J.R., & Kolb, K. J. (1995). Electronic performance monitoring and social context: Impact on productivity. *Journal of Applied Psychology, 80*, 339-353.

Ambrose, M.L., Alder, G.S., & Noel, T.W. (1998). Electronic performance monitoring: A consideration of rights. In M. Schminke (Ed.), *Managerial ethics: Moral management of people and processes* (pp. 61-80). Mahwah, NJ: Lawrence Erlbaum Associates.

Ambrose, M.L., & Hess, R.L. (2001, August). *Individuals' responses to fairness: A consideration of management and marketing models.* Paper presented at the International Round Table on Innovations in Organizational Justice, Vancouver, British Columbia, Canada.

Barney, J.B., Busenitz, L., Fiet, J., & Moesel, D. (1989). The structure of venture capital governance: An organizational economic analysis of relations between venture capital firms and new ventures. *Academy of Management Proceedings*, 64-68.

Barney, J.B., Busenitz, L., Fiet, J., & Moesel, D. (1994). The relationship between venture capitalists and managers in new firms: Determinants of contractual covenants. *Managerial Finance, 20*, 19-30.

Berger, A.N., & Udell, G.F. (1998). The economics of small business finance: The roles of private equity and debt markets in the financial growth cycle. *Journal of Banking and Finance, 22*(6-8), 613-673.

Bies, R.J. (2001). Interactional (in)justice: The sacred and the profane. In J. Greenberg & R. Cropanzano (Eds.), *Advances in organizational justice* (pp. 89-118). Stanford, CA: Stanford University Press.

Brockner, J., Ackerman, G., & Fairchild, G. (2001). When do elements of procedural fairness make a difference? A classification of moderating differences. In J. Greenberg & R. Cropanzano (Eds.), *Advances in organizational justice* (pp. 179-212). Stanford, CA: Stanford University Press.

Brockner, J., & Wiesenfeld, B.M. (1996). An integrative framework for explaining reactions to decisions: Interactive effects of outcomes and procedures. *Psychological Bulletin, 120*, 189-208.

Colquitt, J., Noe, R.A., & Jackson, C.L. (2001, August). *Justice in teams: Antecedents and consequences of procedural justice climate.* Paper presented at the International Round Table on Innovations in Organizational Justice, Vancouver, British Columbia, Canada.

Cropanzano, R., & Ambrose, M.L. (2001). Procedural and distributive justice are more similar than you think: A monistic perspective and a research agenda. In J. Greenberg & R. Cropanzano (Eds.), *Advances in organizational justice* (pp. 119-151). Stanford, CA: Stanford University Press.

Daily, C.M., Johnson, J.L., Ellstrand, A.E., & Dalton, D.R. (1998). Compensation committee composition as a determinant of CEO compensation. *Academy of Management Journal, 41*, 209-220.

Deaux, K. (1996). Social identification. In E. T. Higgins & A. W. Kruglanski (Eds)., *Social psychology: Handbook of basic principles* (pp. 777-798). New York: Guilford Press.

Deutsch, M. (1962). Cooperation and trust: Some theoretical notes. In M.R. Jones (Ed.), *Nebraska symposium on motivation* (pp. 275-317). Lincoln: University of Nebraska Press.

Eccles. R.G. (1991). Transfer pricing as a problem of agency. In J. W. Pratt, & R.J. Zeckhauser (Eds.), *Principals and agents: The structure of business* (pp. 151-186). Boston, MA: Harvard Business School Press.

Eisenhardt, K.M. (1989). Agency theory: An assessment and review. *Academy of Management Review, 14,* 57-74.

Folger, R. (1993, August). *The "Churchill Paradox" in managing hard times.* Paper presented at the Academy of Management Meetings, Atlanta, GA.

Folger, R. (1998). Fairness as a moral virtue. In M. Schminke. (Ed.), *Managerial ethics: Moral management of people and processes* (pp. 13-34). Mahwah, NJ: Lawrence Erlbaum Associates.

Folger, R., & Cropanzano, R. (2001). Fairness theory: Justice as accountability. In J. Greenberg & R. Cropanzano (Eds.), *Advances in organizational justice* (pp. 1-55). Stanford, CA: Stanford University Press.

Folger, R., & Konovsky, M.K. (1989). Effects of procedural and distributive justice on reactions to pay raise decisions. *Academy of Management Journal, 32,* 115-130.

Folger, R., Konovsky, M.A., & Cropanzano, R. (1992). A due process metaphor for performance appraisal. In B.M. Staw & L.L. Cummings (Eds.), *Research in organizational behavior* (vol. 14, pp. 129-177). Greenwich, CT: JAI Press.

Folger, R., & Skarlicki, D.P. (2001). Fairness as a dependent variable: Why tough times can lead to bad management. In R. Cropanzano (Ed.), *Justice in the workplace: From theory to practice* (vol. 2, pp. 97-120). Mahwah, NJ:Lawrence Erlbaum Associates.

Fried, V.H., & Hisrich, R.D. (1994). Toward a model of venture capital investment decision making. *Financial Management, 23*(3), 28-37.

Gerhart, B., & Milkovich, G.T. (1990). Organizational differences in managerial compensation and financial performance. *Academy of Management Journal, 33,* 663-691.

Gomez-Mejia, L.R., & Balkin, D.B. (1992). Determinants of faculty pay: An agency theory perspective. *Academy of Management Journal, 35,* 921-955.

Gorman, M., & Sahlman, W.A. (1989). What do venture capitalists do? *Journal of Business Venturing, 4,* 231-238.

Greenberg, J. (1990). Employee thefts as a reaction to underpayment inequity: The hidden cost of pay cuts. *Journal of Applied Psychology, 75,* 561-568.

Greenberg, J. (1993). The social side of fairness: Interpersonal and informational classes of organizational justice. In R. Cropanzano (Ed.), *Justice in the workplace: Approaching justice in human resource management* (pp. 79-103). Hillsdale, NJ: Lawrence-Erlbaum.

Greenberg, J., & Cropanzano, R. (1997). Progress in organizational justice: Tunneling through the maze. In C. L. Cooper & I.T. Robertson (Eds.), *International review of industrial and organizational psychology.* New York: John Wiley & Sons.

Hogg, M.A., & Terry, D.J. (2000). Social identity and self-categorization processes in organizational contexts. *Academy of Management Review, 25,* 121-140.

Jensen, M.C., & Meckling, W.H. (1976). Theory of the firm: Managerial behavior, agency costs and ownership structure. *Journal of Financial Economics, 3,* 305-360.

Johnson, J.P., Korsgaard, M.A., & Sapienza, H.J. (In press). Perceived fairness, decision control, and commitment in IJV management teams. *Strategic Management Journal.*

Kelly, P. (1999). *Private investors and entrepreneurs: How context shapes their relationship.* Unpublished Doctoral Dissertation, London Business School.

Kim, W.C., & Mauborgne, R.A. (1991). Implementing global strategies: The role of procedural justice. *Strategic Management Journal, 12,* 125-143.

Kim, W.C., & Mauborgne, R.A. (1993). Procedural justice, attitudes, and subsidiary top management compliance with multinationals' corporate strategic decisions. *Academy of Management Journal, 26,* 502-506.

Konovsky, M.A., & Cropanzano, R. (1991). Perceived fairness of employee drug testing as a predictor of employee attitudes and job performance. *Journal of Applied Psychology, 78,* 698-707.

Konovsky, M.A., & Pugh, S.D. (1994). Citizenship behavior and social exchange. *Academy of Management Journal, 37,* 656-669.

Korsgaard, M.A., Roberson, L. & Rymph, D. (1998). What motivates fairness? The role of subordinate assertive behavior on manager's interactional fairness. *Journal of Applied Psychology, 83,* 731-744

Korsgaard, M.A., Schweiger, D.M., & Sapienza, H.J. (1995). The role of procedural justice in building commitment, attachment, and trust in strategic decision-making teams. *Academy of Management Journal, 38,* 60-84.

Kosnick, R.D. (1987). Greenmail: A study of board performance in corporate governance. *Administrative Science Quarterly, 32,* 163-195.

Kosnick, R.D., & Bettenhausen, K.L. (1992) Agency theory and the motivational effect of management compensation: An experimental-contingency study. *Group and Organization Management, 17,* 309-322.

Landström, H., Manigart, S., Mason, C., & Sapienza, H. (1998). Contracts between entrepreneurs and investors: Terms and negotiation processes. *Frontiers of entrepreneurship research* (pp. 571-585). Wellesley, MA: Babson College.

Lawler, III, E.E. (1976). Control systems in organizations. In M.D. Dunnette (Ed.) *Handbook of industrial and organizational psychology* (pp. 1247-1291). Rand-McNally Publishing.

Leventhal, G.S. (1980). What should be done with equity theory? In K.J. Gergen, M.S. Greenberg, & H.R. Willis (Eds.), *Social exchange: Advances in theory and research* (pp. 27-55). New York: Plenum Press.

Lind, E.A. (2001). Fairness heuristic theory: Justice judgments as pivotal cognitions in organizational relations. In J. Greenberg & R. Cropanzano (Eds.), *Advances in organizational justice* (pp. 56-88). Stanford, CA: Stanford University Press.

Lind, E. A., Kulik, C. T. Ambrose, M. & de Vera-Park, M. W. (1993). Individual and corporate dispute resolution: Using procedural fairness as a decision heuristic. *Administrative Science Quarterly, 38,* 224-251.

Lind, E.A., & Tyler, T.R. (1988). *The social psychology of procedural justice.* New York: Plenum.

Manigart, S., Korsgaard, M.A., Folger, R., Sapienza, H.J., & Baeyens, K. (2001). The impact of trust on private equity contracts. *Frontiers of entrepreneurship research.* Wellesley, MA: Babson College. 494-502

McAllister, D.J. (1995). Affect- and cognition-based trust as foundations for interpersonal cooperation in organizations. *Academy of Management Journal, 38,* 24-59.

Mikula, G. (1998). Division of household labor and perceived justice: A growing field of research. *Social Justice Research, 11,* 215-241.

Moorman, R.H. (1991). Relationship between organizational justice and organizational citizenship behaviors: Do fairness perceptions influence employee citizenship? *Journal of Applied Psychology, 76,* 845-855.

Naumann, S.E., & Bennett, N. (2000). A case for procedural justice climate: Development and test of a multilevel model. *Academy of Management Journal, 43,* 881-889.

Niehoff, B.P., & Moorman, R.H. (1993). Justice as a mediator of the relationship between methods of monitoring and organizational citizenship behavior. *Academy of Management Journal, 36,* 527-556.

Nilakant, V., & Rao, H. (1994). Agency theory and uncertainty in organizations: An evaluation. *Organization Studies, 15,* 649-672.

Noorderhaven, N. . (1992). The problem of contract enforcement in economic organization theory. *Organization Studies, 13,* 292-243.

Parks, J.M., & Conlon E.J. (1995). Compensation contracts: do agency theory assumptions predict negotiated agreements? *Academy of Management Journal, 38,* 821-838.

Perrow, C. (1986). *Complex organization: A critical essay.* Glenview, IL: Scott Foresman.

Pratt, J.W., & Zeckhauser, R.J. (1991). Principals and agents: An overview. In J.W. Pratt & R.J. Zeckhauser (Eds.), *Principals and agents: The structure of business* (pp. 1-35). Boston, MA: Harvard Business School Press

Sahlman, W.A. (1990). The structure and governance of venture-capital organizations. *Journal of Financial Economics, 27,* 473-521.

Sapienza, H.J., & Gupta, A.K. (1994). Impact of agency risks and task uncertainty on venture capitalist-entrepreneur relations. *Academy of Management Journal, 37,* 1618-1632.

Sapienza, H.J., & Korsgaard, M.A. (1996). Managing investor relations: The impact of procedural justice in establishing and sustaining investor support. *Academy of Management Journal, 39,* 544-574.

Sapienza, H.J., Korsgaard, M.A., Folger, R., Sagrera, C., & Zhang, C. (1999, May). *A behavioral view of partnership formation in investor-entrepreneur dyads.* Paper presented at the Babson/Kauffman Entrepreneurship Research Conference, Columbia, SC.

Sapienza, H.J., Korsgaard, M.A., & Hoogendam, J. (1997). What do new venture boards do? *Frontiers of entrepreneurship research* (pp. 118-130). Wellesley, MA: Babson College.

Scarpello, V., & Jones, F.F. (1996). Why justice matters in compensation decision making. *Journal of Organizational Behavior, 17,* 285-299.

Schaubroeck, J., May, D.R., & Brown, F.W. (1994). Procedural justice explanations and employee reactions to economic hardship: A field experiment. *Journal of Applied Psychology, 79,* 455-460.

Skarlicki, D.P., & Folger, R. (1997). Retaliation in the workplace: The roles of distributive, procedural, and interactional justice. *Journal of Applied Psychology, 82,* 434-443.

Smith, M.J. Carayon, P., Sanders, K. J., Lim, S.Y., & LeGrande, D. (1992). Employee stress and health complaints in jobs with and without electronic performance monitoring. *Applied Ergonomics, 23,* 17-27.

Stanton, J.M., & Barnes-Farrell, J.L. (1996). Effects of electronic performance monitoring on personal control, task satisfaction, and task performance. *Journal of Applied Psychology, 81,* 738-745.

Stroh, L.K., Brett, J.M., Baumann, J.P., & Reilly, A.H. (1996). Agency theory and variable pay compensation strategies. *Academy of Management Journal, 39,* 751-767.

Thibaut, J., & Walker, J. (1975). *Procedural justice: A psychological analysis.* Hillsdale, NJ: Lawrence Erlbaum Associates.

Tosi, H.L., & Gomez-Mejia, L.R. (1994). CEO compensation monitoring and firm performance. *Academy of Management Journal, 37,*1002-1016.

Tosi, H.L., Katz, J.P., & Gomez-Mejia, L.R. (1997). Disaggregating the agency contract: The effects of monitoring, incentive alignment, and term in office on agent decision making. *Academy of Management Journal, 40,* 584-602.

Turner, J.C., & Onorato, R.S. (1999). Social identity, personality, and the self-concept: A self-categorization perspective. In T.R. Tyler, R.M. Kramer, & O.P. John (Eds.), *The psychology of the social self* (pp. 11-46). Mahwah, NJ: Lawrence Erlbaum Associates.

Tyler, T.R., & Bies, R.J. (1990). Beyond formal procedures: The interpersonal context of procedural justice. In J. Carroll (Ed.), *Applied social psychology and organizational settings* (pp. 77-98). Hillsdale, NJ: Lawrence Erlbaum Associates.

Tyler, T., & Blader, S.L. (2000). *Cooperation in groups: Procedural justice, social identity, and behavioral engagement.* Philadelphia: Psychology Press.

Tyler, T., & Dawes, R.M. (1993). Fairness in groups: Comparing the self-interest and social identity perspectives. In B.A. Mellers & J. Baron (Eds.), *Psychological perspectives on justice: Theory and applications* (pp. 87-108). Cambridge: Cambridge University Press.

Tyler, T.R., & Lind, E.A. (1992). A relational model of authority in groups. In M. Zanna (Ed.), *Advances in experimental social psychology* (vol. 25, pp. 115-191). New York: Academic Press.

Tyler, T.R., Rasinski, K.A., & Spodick, N. (1985). Influence of voice on satisfaction with leaders: Exploring the meaning of process control. *Journal of Personality and Social Psychology, 48,* 72-81.

Walsh, J.P., & Seward, J.K. (1990). On the efficiency of internal and external corporate control mechanisms. *Academy of Management Review, 15,* 421-458.

Welbourne, T.M., Balkin, D.B., & Gomez-Mejia, L.R. (1995). Gainsharing and mutual monitoring: A combined agency-organizational justice interpretation. *Academy of Management Journal, 38,* 881-889.

Zand, D.E. (1972). Trust and managerial problem solving. *Administrative Science Quarterly, 17,* 229-239.

CHAPTER 2

THE RELIGIOUS UNDERPINNINGS OF SOCIAL JUSTICE CONCEPTIONS

Dianna L. Stone and Eugene F. Stone-Romero

ABSTRACT

Cross-cultural conceptions of social justice are considered, relying on religious and moral teachings that are common in Eastern nations (e.g., China, Japan) and Western nations (e.g., the United States). Whereas Western conceptions of social justice have been influenced largely by the teachings of Christianity (Catholicism and Protestantism) and Judaism, Eastern conceptions of justice have stemmed mainly from the teachings of Buddhism and Confucianism. For each of these religions, we offer examples of various justice-related teachings. In addition, we specify how these teachings have influenced views about justice among people from Western and Eastern nations. We conclude by arguing that a consideration of the differing conceptions that people from different cultures have about justice will facilitate our understanding of individuals' views about the fairness of procedures for allocating outcomes in organizations and the fairness of experienced outcomes. As organizations become more diverse, it is increasingly important to adopt a multicultural perspective on social justice.

Justice is a central moral standard in social life. . . . In a formal sense, justice concerns ensuring that each person receives what she or he is due. But what is each due? In virtue of what condition, conduct or characteristic is this to be established and how? (Cohen, 1986, p. 1).

Social theorists (e.g., Cohen, 1986) have long argued that there are differing theories of social justice in world societies, and these theories of justice play a pivotal role in determining the social order. The same justice theories determine what each person deserves, and ultimately define how scarce resources are allocated among members of the society. Interestingly, sociologists and religious scholars (e.g., Smith, 1995; Tawney, 1958; Weber, 1958) also claim that religious values have a profound influence on views of social justice and affect beliefs about the type of social order that will maximize societal well-being. In particular, Smith (1994) maintains that "the surest way to [understanding] the heart of a people is through their faith" (p. 13).

We believe that religious and moral values play a key role in the development of justice ideologies and determine how outcomes are allocated in a society. *Ideologies* are sets of shared, interrelated beliefs about how things work; they are values that indicate what's worth having or doing, and norms that tell people how they should behave (Trice & Beyer, 1993). The classic work of Weber (1958) provides a vivid illustration of the way in which religious beliefs, values, and norms (e.g., the Protestant Ethic) have influenced behavior over time. For example, the Protestant doctrine of Calvinism taught that peoples' impulses must be subordinated to God's will in order for them to attain salvation (see Stone-Romero & Stone, 1998). The only way to demonstrate that each individual was chosen by God was to accumulate tangible evidence of God's favor through hard work in a worldly calling. Furthermore, the religious belief in hard work compelled people to action because the Calvinists cared very deeply about attaining salvation and wanted to believe that hard work would ensure that they would reach their goal. In addition, the requirements for hard work and the accumulation of wealth were made more acceptable because they were based on moral justification of the will of God. Finally, according to Weber (1958) the belief in the Protestant Ethic inspired the development of the capitalistic social and economic system in the Western world. Thus, just as Calvinist beliefs and values influenced the Protestant Work Ethic, we believe that religious beliefs and values have played a critical role in the development of both conceptions of social justice and the moral justification for systems of justice in varying societies. Similarly, religious beliefs and values are often embodied in justice ideologies, and therefore influence the actions that individuals take in response to feelings of injustice. Likewise, the fact that views about social justice often stem from religious beliefs and values leads people to have very strong emotional feelings about justice in a society.

Recently, social psychologists have argued that moral, ethical, and normative concepts influence perceptions of fairness (e.g., Deutsch, 1975; Rasinski, 1987). In particular, Deutsch (1975) claimed that judgments of "what is fair" are determined primarily by the normative goals of society, not by individual concerns. Furthermore, he maintained that allocations based on the principles of equity, equality, or need will be labeled as fair depending on whether the society emphasizes productivity, social harmony, or humanitarianism (Deutsch, 1975). Interestingly, empirical research by Rasinski (1987) provides support for Deutsch's arguments. Rasinski's research revealed that there was a relationship (albeit weak) between one's value orientation and perceptions of distributive fairness.

Recently, Furby (1986) argued that psychologists have paid relatively little attention to the notion of rights or entitlements in our society, and have not examined the origins of the concept of rights or justice. Thus, in this chapter we consider moral and religious beliefs and values as underlying bases for views on justice. Despite the importance that such beliefs and values may have for understanding social justice, we know of no previous work in Industrial and Organizational Psychology, Organizational Behavior, or closely-related fields that has directly addressed this issue. This is unfortunate because an understanding of the religious underpinnings of social justice may provide social and organizational researchers with a means of gaining greater insight than we now have about cross-cultural views of social justice, and help theorists develop broad, culturally inclusive theories of social justice.

Given that religious and moral values play a key role in determining views of social justice and the way that outcomes are allocated in a society, the primary purpose of the present chapter is to consider the influence that Western religions and Eastern belief systems have had on conceptions of distributive justice (i.e., outcome fairness). A secondary purpose is to consider how such conceptions influence views about justice in Western versus Eastern cultures. As noted above, religion often has a profound effect in shaping culture in a society. For example, Weber (1958) indicated that religious forces have "decisive influences in the formation of national character" (p. 155). Although we argue that religious beliefs and philosophy influence cultural values and conceptions of social justice, we recognize that a number of other factors affect culture, including history, government, natural resources, and economic forces. However, because religious beliefs are totally intertwined with culture it is impossible to determine whether religion causes culture or culture causes religion. Furthermore, the causal link between religion and culture is not really the issue because it is evident that both religious beliefs and culture influence basic values and justice ideologies. However, consistent with Weber (1958) we assume that religious teachings and beliefs are a cause of values and justice ideologies. Thus, in the following sections we consider the presumed effects of religious values on justice conceptions. In addition, we present several propositions regarding religion and social justice that can be used to guide future research on the topic. However, before discussing the influence of religion on social justice conceptions we define the construct of religion. In addition, we specify several criteria that can be used to assess the fairness of outcome allocations.

RELIGION

As noted above, a major premise of this paper is that views about social justice, particularly outcome allocation principles, are heavily influenced by religious beliefs and values. Thus, it is important to consider the meaning of the concept of religion. Although most religious scholars argue that there is no generally accepted definition of the term religion (Nigosian, 1994), others suggest that *religion* can be defined in terms of the values, beliefs, attitudes, behaviors (e.g., rituals), and habits of people who are religious (Gaer, 1963). Furthermore, Smith (1994) argues that there are at least six characteristics that can be used to define a religion including: (a) authority, (b) ritual, (c) explanation, (d) tradition, or code of conduct, (e) grace, and (f) mystery. Most religions make use of some authority or talented person that will lift individuals above the masses in matters of the spirit. In addition, most religions utilize some form of ritual or collective expression of the joys or sorrows of people. Moreover, most religions have traditions and codes of conduct that specify the basic norms that ought to govern human conduct. For example, Christianity and Judaism have the Ten Commandments, and almost "all religions have some version of Golden Rule" (Smith, 1994, p. 245). Likewise, religions typically provide individuals with some form of grace or assurance that God and reality are on their side. Moreover, almost all religions involve some elements of mystery. The latter characteristic suggests that being finite, the human mind cannot fathom the infinite that envelops it (Smith, 1994).

It merits noting that the term religion often has little or no meaning among people in Eastern cultures (e.g., Japan, China, Vietnam; see Nigosian, 1994). Some religious scholars suggest that many Eastern belief systems (e.g., Buddhism, Confucianism) are not actually religions, but a set of interrelated beliefs whose characteristics are not fully consistent with those specified above. For example, Buddhism is devoid of authority, ritual, tradition, grace or the supernatural. As a result, many scholars refer to Eastern belief systems as opposed to Eastern religions (e.g., Nigosian, 1994). In spite of this, the literature on religion reveals a common tendency to label belief systems such as Buddhism and Confucianism as religions. Thus we follow this convention here.

Although there are a great many religions (e.g., Judaism, Hinduism, Islam, Christianity, Taoism, Shintoism, Primal Religions of indigenous peoples), our review considers only a subset of them: We offer in-depth treatments of conceptions of justice stemming from Judaism, Christianity, Confucianism, and Buddhism. We also offer a very brief analysis of the connection between Islam and Judaism. There are two principal reasons for limiting our coverage of religions. First, space limitations preclude a review of all religions here. Second, the basic beliefs of some religions serve as the foundation for those of others (see Smith, 1994). For example, Judaism serves as the foundation for both Christianity and Islam, and Confucianism is considered the founding belief system for many Eastern belief systems (cf. Smith, 1994). For example, Confucianism and Buddhism laid the foundation for Shintoism, and many Taoist beliefs are related to Confucian principles. Furthermore, as noted in a subsequent section, Buddhism is inextricably related to Hinduism, and was chosen for this chapter because it highlights an alternative set of beliefs that have important implications for social justice.

JUSTICE ALLOCATION RULES OR PRINCIPLES

Philosophers and psychologists have traditionally assumed that conceptions of fairness are based on three primary values, i.e., proportionality, egalitarianism, and need (Buchanan & Mathieu, 1986; Leventhal, 1980). *Proportionality* refers to the extent to which rewards or punishments are distributed in proportion to one's contributions. According to a proportionality or equity criterion, people who make the greatest contributions should receive the greatest level of outcomes. Alternatively, an *egalitarianism* or *equality* criterion defines a fair situation as one in which everyone receives either the same or very similar outcomes, regardless of their needs or contributions. A *Needs Rule* dictates that people with the greatest needs should receive the highest level of outcomes.

Leventhal (1980) identified five other important distributive justice rules, including (a) the Rule of Justified Self-Interest, (b) the Rule of Adhering Commitments, (c) the Ownership Rule, (d) the Legality Rule, and (e) the Status Rule. The *Rule of Justified Self-Interest* dictates that, in some circumstances, it is fair for an individual to take as much for himself as possible (Lerner, 1971). The *Rule of Adhering Commitments* indicates that fairness is violated unless people receive that which has been promised them (Leventhal, 1976). The *Legality Rule* specifies that fairness is violated if the distribution of rewards and punishments is inconsistent with existing laws and regulations (Berkowitz & Walker, 1967). The *Ownership Rule* mandates that it is fair for individuals to continue to possess rewards and resources that already belong to them, and it is unfair to take these resources away from them. Finally, the *Status Rule* dictates that it is fair for persons of high social rank to receive greater levels of outcomes than those of lower social rank. Interestingly, equity theory treats such characteristics as gender, ethnicity, race, and social position as possible inputs that may merit differential levels of outcomes (e.g., Leventhal, 1980).

Not surprisingly, the just considered distribution principles are based largely on Western beliefs and values. Thus, it merits emphasis that some of the allocation rules are not directly applicable to non-Western cultures. Nevertheless, we offer comparisons of religions in terms of all of Leventhal's distributive justice rules. In addition, we provide a summary of the

TABLE 1
Strength of Commitment of Major Religions to Justice Rules

	Religion			
Justice Rule	Buddhism	Christianity	Confucianism	Judaism
Proportionality	Moderate	Strong	Weak	Strong
Equality	Strong	Weak	Moderate	Weak
Need	Strong	Weak	Strong	Weak
Justified Self-Interest	None	Strong	None	Strong
Adhering Commitments	None	Strong	Strong	Strong
Legality	None	Strong	Weak	Strong
Ownership	None	Strong	Moderate	Strong
Status	None	Strong	Moderate	Strong

positions taken by various religions on various distributive justice principles in Table 1.

We recognize that many of the religious beliefs reviewed in this chapter have implications for values regarding not only distributive justice, but also procedural justice. However, a treatment of both the distributive justice and procedural justice principles is beyond the scope of the chapter. Therefore, we leave the discussion of the influence of religion on procedural justice conceptions to a subsequent paper.

As noted above, in the present chapter we consider only a subset of religious belief systems that have influenced views about social justice. In particular, we focus on two primary categories of religious beliefs, i.e., Western religions (e.g., Judaism, Christianity) and Eastern religions or belief systems (e.g., Confucianism and Buddhism). Thus, in the following sections, we summarize the major teachings of each of these religions and consider the implications of such teachings for beliefs about distributive justice in work organizations.

WESTERN RELIGIONS

Judaism

Some estimates suggest that there are approximately 13 million followers of Judaism in the world, and over one third of the people in the West have Jewish ancestry (Smith, 1994). Thus, it is not surprising that Judaism has played a pivotal role in defining Western culture and values (Smith, 1994). Some of the basic belief systems of Judaism and the implications of these beliefs for social justice in Western organizations are outlined below.

Basic Beliefs of Judaism

The followers of Judaism believe in one God who is simultaneously loving, merciful, caring, and the arbiter of rewards, punishments, and one's ultimate destiny. According to Judaism, God is thought to have very high standards for man, and is intolerant of injustice, exploitation, corruption, and mediocrity (Gaer, 1963). He is also thought to execute final justice. Those who love him and keep his commandments benefit from his love and grace. However, those who disobey his commandments reap only his anger or punishment (Nigosian, 1994).

Apart from the belief in a single God, Jews share a number of basic beliefs about men and women and their relationship to God (Gaer, 1963; Nigosian, 1994). First, people are regarded as God's beloved children, and are thought to have rights that even kings must respect (Smith, 1994). In addition, they believe that man is born innocent and possesses free will or the capacity to choose between good and evil (Gaer, 1963). Thus, Jews fervently value individual rights and freedom. In addition, they maintain that the infinite worth of each individual derives, in part, from the fact that everyone is unique and thus irreplaceable (Smith, 1994).

Given that the West has a strong Jewish heritage, it is not surprising that Western organizations have been heavily influenced by the teachings of Judaism. As a result, Western culture and organizations have fostered policies and practices that are fairly individualistic in nature, including rewards based on principles of equity (proportionality), and recognition systems that foster competitive achievement rather than cooperation and teamwork (Stone-Romero & Stone, 1998).

Second, Jews believe that people have a life span that is brief and finite. As Smith (1994) has noted, all pursuits of human beings are transitory and "their earthly span is brief as grass...and troubled like a sigh" (p. 185). Consequently, Western cultures have stressed a relatively short-term time perspective, and believe that one should maximize short-term gains and pleasures. In addition, time is thought to be linear like an irreversible arrow, which has an origin, a direction, and a destination (Smith, 1992). Furthermore, many Western organizations have adopted these short-term, linearly-oriented philosophies of time. As a result, they often embrace management practices that stress rapid decision making and an emphasis on short-term profits (Stone-Romero & Stone, 1998).

Although life is short in duration, Jews also regard it as having an unspeakable grandeur, and believe that a person should love the world, hallow in daily pleasures such as eating, drinking, working, and treat these activities as if every act were sacred. As a result, Western culture has stressed materialism, and some religious scholars have lamented that Western culture has become obsessed with physical and material possessions. In addition, religious scholars have argued that the heavy emphasis on material wealth in the West has created an imbalanced world which is composed of "islands of affluence off the mainland of misery" (Smith, 1992, p. 231).

Third, the followers of Judaism have well-documented moral standards that regulate social relations and institutions. More specifically, they believe that absolute loyalty and obedience to God's laws will result in the redemption of humanity. In particular, the Ten Commandments were designed to control four danger zones in human relations, i.e., force, wealth, sex, and speech. In addition, Rabbinic Law contains 613 commandments, and the *Torah*, the first five books of the Bible, outlines minimum standards that make collective life possible. For example, the *Torah* states that people should not murder, commit adultery, steal, or bear false witness against neighbors. Not surprisingly, this Judaic emphasis on laws and written rules has influenced Western culture and organizations. Thus, in the West there is an emphasis on legal or written contracts, and organizations often have formalistic rules and procedures that are designed to achieve social control over workers (Stone-Romero & Stone, 1998).

Fourth and finally, followers of Judaism place great value on knowledge and change. As a result, some scholars argue that Jews have helped foster the emergence of science and change, and these values have become the hallmarks of Western civilization (Smith, 1994).

Apart from the just-noted beliefs, Jews have developed a passion for justice and freedom that has spread throughout the Western world. This emphasis on justice and freedom is, in part, due to the fact that, throughout history, Jews have continuously experienced suffering, exile, enslavement, and oppression. In fact, Jews believe that there are lessons and insights that suffering illuminates as nothing else can. Exile and defeat taught them the importance of freedom, and oppression revealed the true value of justice (Smith, 1994).

Not surprisingly, justice is one of the common themes in the Old Testament of the Bible. One notable example is: "What doth the Lord require of thee but to do justice, love, and mercy." Another example is the story of Naboth which emphasizes the importance of justice in maintaining the social order (*1 Kings* 21:1-13). Naboth owned a family vineyard and King Ahab, King of Samaria, wanted Naboth to relinquish his vineyard. When Naboth refused, he was framed on false charges of blasphemy against God and the King, and ultimately stoned to death. Upon Naboth's death the King took possession of the vineyard. The news of the incident spread, and when it reached Elijah, a common man, the word of God came to him, saying, "go down to meet King Ahab and say to him, you have killed and taken possession. In the place where dogs licked up the blood of Naboth shall dogs lick thy blood, even thine" (*1 Kings* 21:19). The story is significant because it reveals how someone "without official position can take the side of a wronged man and denounce the king on grounds of injustice" (Smith, 1994, p. 189). It also underscores the importance of two Judaic convictions: (a) that the future of any people depends in large part on the justice of its social order, and (b) that individuals are accountable for the social structure of their society (Smith, 1994).

Implications of Judaism for Social Justice

It is evident from our description of Judaism above that Western conceptions of social justice have been influenced greatly by Judaic beliefs. In fact, many of Leventhal's (1980) principles of justice are derived almost directly from Jewish teachings and traditions. Furthermore, the word "just or justice" appears in the Old Testament of the Bible over 104 times, and the related word "righteous" occurs hundreds of times in the Bible (King, 1995). For example, the Bible states "God's work is perfect[, is]...without iniquity, just, and right" (*Deuteronomy* 32:4). Interestingly, the Jewish belief that "individuals have rights that even kings must respect" set the stage for our current views of justice, and led people in the West to expect that they have individual rights given to them by God. Some authors (e.g., Crosby, Muehrer & Loewenstein, 1984; Stone-Romero & Stone, 1998) have interpreted this expectation to mean that people believe they are entitled to fair treatment in their interactions with organizations and others in society.

Proportionality or Equity. It is clear that the notions of proportionality or equity have been influenced greatly by Jewish teachings. As noted above, views of equity are based on the fact that justice is the essential perfection of God, and God doles out rewards and punishments depending on one's contributions or behaviors on earth (Smith, 1994). If a person keeps God's commandments, they benefit from his love. However, if they disobey his commandments they reap his wrath and punishment. In essence, one receives what one deserves in life, and a final authority, God, enforces or upholds what is just. This belief in justice has had a profound impact on Western culture, and the behavior of people in the Western world. In particular, these teachings have fostered a strong belief in individualism and self-reliance. The same beliefs have also served as the foundation of much of utilitarian philosophy, and are highly consistent with many Western theories of motivation (e.g., reward theory, equity theory).

Although the Bible stresses equity and justice, there is one notable exception to the notion of equity in the story of Job (King, 1995). He was a prosperous man of impeccable character, and he treated everyone (i.e., servant, friend, stranger, rich, poor) justly and humanely. Job was also generous, and no one was ever turned away from his door empty handed. He atoned daily for any wrong his children might have committed and offered many sacrifices to God. Despite his virtuous behavior, Job was struck with calamity after calamity until all his wealth was lost. In addition, his children were killed in accidents, and he became seriously ill. His wife urged him to curse God and die. Subsequently, he cursed the day he was born and berated God. This story stresses the notion that even though one follows

God's teachings, there is no assurance that he or she will experience only positive outcomes in life. This seems quite inconsistent with the view that one's rewards will be consistent with one's contributions.

Equality. Judaic beliefs do not typically stress that rewards should be handed out equally regardless of need or merit. However, one notable exception to this is that of the Jewish Kibbutzim which was founded as a collective. In the Kibbutzim, outcomes are generally distributed equally to all members. Interestingly, Erez and Earley (1993) argue that the Israeli Kibbutzim is a unique collective that does not emphasize in-group harmony like collectives in Asian cultures. In the Israeli Kibbutzim, members stress a level of frankness in dealings with others that might seem harsh to Asians or Americans. A principal reason for such frankness is that it is viewed as being conducive to in-group longevity (Erez & Earley, 1993). However, it merits adding that the Israeli Kibbutzim is a unique or exceptional social institution.

Need. Even though followers of Judaism believe that people should help the needy, they do not believe that most outcomes should be allocated on the basis of need. One reason for this is that in the Jewish tradition, suffering is always based on one's conduct. If there appears to be unmerited suffering, sin lies at the door somehow (Smith, 1994). Thus, people are viewed as somewhat responsible for their suffering or need. Not surprisingly, this belief may have served as the basis for the *just world hypothesis* (Lerner, 1980) which suggests that individuals want to believe in a world that is good and just, a world where people get what they deserve, and good things happen to good people and bad things happen to bad people. Thus, the presence of a person in need threatens the belief that the world is fair, and individuals employ a number of strategies to interpret the cause of the person's need (e.g., inferring that the person must have done something wrong and, thus, deserves his or her fate).

Rule of Justified Self-Interest. As noted previously, Judaism places a great deal of emphasis on individualism and individual rights. Thus, there is a strong belief in justified self-interest (i.e., the principle that it is fair for an individual to take as much for himself as possible) (see Leventhal, 1980). For example, consistent with the Proportionality Rule, followers of Judaism believe that self-interest is justified when it is based on labor or hard work. However, it is not justified when it is based on vanity. For example, the Old Testament of the Bible states that "Wealth [gotten] by vanity shall be diminished but he that gathereth by labour shall increase" (*Proverbs* 13:11), and "Withhold not good from them to whom it is due, when it is in the power of thine hand to do [it]" (*Proverbs* 3:27). In addition, "And, the labourer is worthy of his reward" (*1 Timothy* 5:18), "Wealth and riches shall be in his house and his righteousness shall endureth for ever" (*Psalms* 112:3), and "The rich man's wealth is his strong city" (*Proverbs* 18:11).

Rule of Adhering Commitments. As noted previously, the Rule of Adhering Commitments states that fairness is violated unless people receive that which has been promised (Leventhal, 1980). It is clear from the Old Testament of the Bible that followers of Judaism strongly believe in the Rule of Adhering Commitments. In fact, the principle of adhering to commitments is stressed all throughout the Old Testament of the Bible. For instance, Judaism argues that when individuals keep their commitments and promises, they are just and are emulating God. Furthermore, God keeps his promises, and people should also keep their promises in order to be valued in the eyes of God. For example, the Bible states that "If a man vow a vow unto the Lord, or swear an oath to bind his soul with a bond, he shall not break his word, he shall do according to all that proceedeth out of his mouth" (*Numbers* 30:2). In addition, "When thou shalt vow a vow unto the Lord thy God, thou shalt not slack to pay it, for the Lord thy God will surely require it of thee, and it would be a sin of thee" (*Deuteronomy* 23:21).

Ownership Rule. As noted previously, Jewish tradition stresses that ownership is a right of individuals. For example, the Bible states, "that which is altogether just shalt thou follow, that thou mayest live, and inherit the land which the Lord thy God giveth thee" (*Deuteronomy* 16:20). In fact, during the past century we have witnessed a great deal of conflict over the ownership of the Jewish homeland (e.g., Israel and Palestine), assumed to be given to the Jewish people by God. Likewise, the concept of the right of ownership was explicit in the story of Naboth, described above. The same story teaches that leaders and others cannot take land away from its owners. Such a belief system appears to have been codified in the Western world. More specifically, the right to own property was spelled out in the first 10 Amendments to the U.S. Constitution, and by a number of political theorists in the seventeenth and eighteenth centuries (e.g., John Locke, Thomas Jefferson). Interestingly, the story of Naboth also appears to be consistent with several principles of procedural justice including (a) the right of individuals to speak out about injustices (e.g., voice), and (b) the right of individuals to be judged on accurate, not false, information (noted as bearing false witness in the Bible).

Legality Rule. As noted above, Judaism has a very formal legal system and code of ethics. This legal system is epitomized by the Biblical figure, Moses, the lawgiver, and followed by judges and kings who were all assumed to be enforcers and upholders of the law or justice (King, 1995). For example, the Ten Commandments, the Rabbinic law, and the *Torah* set the stage for formal laws of conduct in the West. In Western democracies, for example, laws are presumed to apply to everyone in the same way at the same time. The concept of equal justice under the law is not based on the whims of officials, and all citizens are subject to the same law. Consistent with Jewish teachings, Western cultures and Western organizations often have very formalistic legal codes and policies to govern the conduct of people. It merits noting that this same point was recently emphasized by McFarlin and Sweeney (2001) when discussing cross-cultural views of justice.

Status Rule. Judaism stresses that persons of higher status should receive greater outcomes. In fact, religious scholars (Smith, 1994) have long maintained that Judaism emphasizes status differences and distinctions between people. As noted above, Jews believe that every person is unique and irreplaceable, and followers of Judaism maintain that the Jews are the chosen people in the eyes of God. Although this belief appears as favoritism on the surface, some religious scholars have asserted that the notion of the Jews as the chosen people is often misunderstood. For example, Smith (1994) argues that Jews believe that they were chosen to receive unique commissions, not singled out to receive special advantages: They singled themselves out for responsibilities rather than privileges, and this imposed on them a far more demanding morality than was expected of their peers. They were also elected to shoulder tremendous levels of suffering, and there is nothing innately special about them as human beings, the specialness derives from God (Smith, 1994).

Not surprisingly, there has been a great deal of controversy surrounding the use of the Status Rule in the West, and religious scholars have argued that the emphasis on distinctions and differences between people has sparked much of the world's conflict (Smith, 1994). As noted above, equity theory stresses that race, gender, ethnicity, and social status may be viewed as relevant inputs (Leventhal, 1980). Thus, the use of the Status Rule in the United States has often been interpreted to mean that many racial minorities, women, and other low socioeconomic status individuals are less deserving of outcomes than their higher status counterparts. Furthermore, attempts to equate minority or low status individuals in terms of inputs through affirmative action have often been opposed on the grounds that they violate norms of meritocracy and fairness (Peterson, 1994).

Christianity

Basic Beliefs of Christianity

Christianity is currently the most widespread religion in the world, and it is the predominant religion in the United States with 64 percent of residents being Protestant and 25 percent being Roman Catholic (*Comptons Encyclopedia*, 1998). The Christian belief system is based on the teachings of

Jesus of Nazareth (Smith, 1994). Over the last two centuries Christianity has split into three major divisions, Roman Catholicism, Eastern Orthodoxy, and Protestantism. As might be expected, there are considerable differences in the beliefs and values associated with these three divisions. Despite these differences, there are some common strands that unite branches of the Christian religion. These common values and beliefs are considered below.

First, Christianity teaches that people should love and have mutual regard for others including those who are enemies, outcasts, and thieves. A number of religious scholars (e.g., Little & Twiss, 1978; Nigosian, 1994; Smith, 1994) have argued that this belief stems from the fact that God has unconditional love for humans, and humanity should emulate that love by caring and serving others. This norm of mutual regard for others is reflected in the biblical prescription, "Thou shalt love your neighbor as yourself" (*Matthew* 22:39). Furthermore, some authors have noted that Christians believe that the deepest impulse in the human self is to be lovingly related to others (Smith, 1994), and that love is the primary cause of joy and inner peace.

Second, Christianity teaches that people's interactions with others should be guided by the Golden Rule: "Do unto others as you would have them do unto you." This implies that people should show mercy and forgiveness toward others, refrain from judging others, and demonstrate kindness and benevolence toward the needy or one's enemies. Christians believe that they serve God by engaging in kindness and mercy.

Third, Christian teachings maintain that God is the ultimate authority, and that people should acquiesce to his will. They also believe that God has the power to reward the faithful and punish those who lack faith. In fact, the Bible indicates that "Whoso despiseth the word [of the Lord] shall be destroyed, but he that feareth the commandment shall be rewarded" (*Proverbs* 13:13). In addition, the Bible indicates that those who are faithful to the "will of the Father" will be granted eternal life, whereas those who are sinful will be thrown into the furnace of fire (*Proverbs* 10:24). Furthermore, Christians believe that people have an immortal soul and God controls its ultimate fate (i.e., regulates salvation). Salvation is an essential part of the Christian belief system because people are thought to be born of sin and are in need of redemption or salvation. According to Christian beliefs, when Adam and Eve ate the forbidden fruit in the Garden of Eden, people became estranged or separated from God. Thus, sin is broadly defined as disconnectedness or estrangement from God, and salvation or atonement allows for humanity to be rejoined with God.

Fourth, early Christian principles stressed that everyone was equal in the eyes of God. In fact, Jesus was said to have hated injustice and the artificial social barriers created by one of the movements of the Jewish religion, the Pharisaic Holiness program (Smith, 1994). While the Jews were under Roman domination, the Pharises sought to remain within society and revitalize Judaism through strict adherence to Mosaic law (Smith, 1994). The Holiness program drew lines of distinction between people because the Pharises believed that God selected the Jews as the people chosen to receive his holiness code on earth. As a result, the Holiness program created a social structure that divided people into the clean and unclean, pure and defiled, sacred and profane, Jew and gentile (Smith, 1994). Jesus saw the social barriers and distinctions between people as an affront to God's compassion. For example, Jesus said, "For he maketh his sun to rise on the evil and on the good, and sendeth rain on the just and the unjust" (*Matthew* 5:45). In addition, "We are told that outcasts and harlots enter the kingdom of God before many who are perfunctorily righteous" (Smith, 1994, p. 212). When Jesus voiced these egalitarian views he became a catalyst for social change, challenging the existing social order, and advocating a more compassionate view of the human community (Smith, 1994). Although his convictions did not prevail, his views put him at odds with the Pharises, and alarmed the Roman authorities of the time. This ultimately led to his arrest, conviction, and crucifixion.

Interestingly, Christian sects differ greatly on the extent to which they accept or adopt Jesus' egalitarian values (see Weber, 1958). The differences in beliefs among the Christian denominations are discussed in the sections that follow on Catholicism and Protestantism. However, it merits noting that a review of all Christian denominations is beyond the scope of this chapter. As a result, we consider the views of only Roman Catholicism and the major Protestant sects.

Roman Catholicism

The Roman Catholic Church was founded in 331 A.D., and has the largest following of all the world's formal religions. Catholicism is characterized by, at least, three fundamental beliefs (Nigosian, 1994). First, Catholics assert that there is one God that takes the form of the Holy Trinity (i.e., Father, Son, and Holy Ghost). Although the Holy Trinity is sometimes difficult for non-Catholics to comprehend, it is often seen as analogous to viewing water in three forms (i.e., liquid, solid or ice, and vapor or steam). Second, Catholics believe in incarnation, that is in Christ, God assumed a human body and Jesus' life provides the perfect model for all of humanity. In addition, Catholics assume that God was concerned enough about humanity that he was willing to assume the limitations of human life and suffer in its behalf (Smith, 1994). Third, and finally, Catholics accept the doctrine of reconciliation or atonement. Jesus' death is viewed as self-sacrifice or atonement for the original sin of Adam and Eve, and Jesus' resurrection is interpreted as proof of universal atonement or triumph over death.

Followers of Catholicism also believe in the teaching authority or infallibility of the Pope, their moral leader. Given the Pope's authority, in terms of faith and moral affairs, the Church established an elaborate hierarchical structure, and developed a complex bureaucracy for the administration of its affairs (i.e., the Curia). The Catholic Church also advocated the acceptance of power inequality among individuals. Subordinates were expected to accept the authority of their superiors.

Apart from the teaching authority of the Church, Catholics also adopt the view that the Church is a *sacramental agent*. As such, the Church helps transfuse energy from God to the human soul (Smith, 1994). Sacraments mark the important moments in human life: Baptism, Confirmation, Holy Matrimony, Sacrament of the sick (death), reconciliation, and communion. Although the sacramental and other religious ceremonies of the Catholic Church are very ritualistic and formalistic, the day to day activities of Catholics do not seem to be marked by high levels of either formalism or legalism (Stone-Romero & Stone, 1998).

Protestantism

The Protestant Reformation, or break with the Roman Catholic Church, occurred in the sixteenth century A.D. (Smith, 1994). As noted above, the Protestant religion consists of a large number of denominations or sects which can be categorized into several basic traditions, such as, Lutheran, Calvinist, Anabaptist, and Anglican (Nigosian, 1994). Among the sects, four are considered to have ascetic beliefs: Calvinists, Pietists, Methodists, and Baptists (Weber, 1958). (See Weber, 1958, for a more detailed description of these sects.) *Asceticism* is a philosophy that stresses the importance of fundamentals such as self-denial of pleasure and material goods, intense work as a calling, and unemotional or rational behavior (Stone-Romero & Stone, 1998).

Although there are clearly differences between denominations, there are two central features of all Protestant belief systems: (a) justification by faith, and (b) The Protestant Principle (Smith, 1994). The Protestant belief in *justification by faith* means that one should respond to one's faith with the entire self (i.e., mind, heart, and will) and by doing rather than merely saying. The *Protestant Principle* warns people against idolatry which means giving one's life first and foremost to something in the finite world. Protestants view everything in life as finite and limited, and maintain that sex and success are merely idols. They also believe that religious experience is private, and reject the notion that the Church or clerics mediate the relationship between any individual and God. To followers of the Protestant faiths, salvation is a personal matter and the Church plays no meaningful role as a sacramental agent.

Specific Protestant Beliefs

As noted above, each Protestant sect or denomination has a specific set of beliefs about rewards and punishments, the value of work, asceticism, and the distribution of resources. It is beyond the scope of this chapter to review all of the beliefs of all the sects. Thus, we consider some of the basic beliefs (e.g., use of rewards and punishments, distribution of resources) of various Protestant sects below.

First, Protestants believe that the Bible should be used as the principal moral and spiritual guide for people. Consistent with a reliance on written principles as guides for behavior, many ascetic Protestants (e.g., Puritans) stress that formalism and legalism in business and organizational affairs is a way of pleasing God (Stone-Romero & Stone, 1998). Second, almost all Protestant sects believe in the use of rewards and punishments as a means of controlling the behavior of others. In fact, God is viewed as the ultimate source of rewards and punishments, and the Bible states, "Thou shalt beat him [i.e., the child] with the rod and shalt deliver his soul from hell" (*Proverbs* 23:14). Interestingly, the Protestant view of rewards and punishments appears quite consistent with most of the motivational theories that are popular in Western culture (e.g., Expectancy Theory, Reinforcement Theory). The same belief system also appears to be the foundation of the utilitarianism-based view that the behaviors and traits of individuals (e.g., conscientiousness, honesty) are considered virtuous largely because they lead to desired outcomes (e.g., succeeding in business, gaining wealth).

Third, as noted above, some Protestant denominations believe in *asceticism*, a philosophy that supports a lifestyle involving religiously inspired hard work and self-denial of material and pleasureful activities (Nigosian, 1994). The ascetic sects typically include Puritans, Calvinists, Baptists, Mennonites, and Quakers (Weber, 1958). These sects view intense work as a calling, and a means of fulfilling one's moral duty to God. They also view the "unwillingness to work as symptomatic of lack of grace" (Weber, 1958, p. 159). In addition, the ascetic sects emphasize rational behavior, lack of emotionality, and the elimination of all forms of spontaneous enjoyment (Weber, 1958). Furthermore, they believe that individuals should use self-denial when it comes to material goods and pleasures, especially "pleasures of the flesh." Although the ascetic sects typically believe in self-denial of material goods, other Protestant sects (e.g., Methodists) view the accumulation of wealth as a moral necessity or a sign of God's blessing (Weber, 1958). In fact, John Wesley, the founder of Methodism, argued that "we must exhort all Christians to gain all they can, that is, to grow rich" (cited in Weber, 1958, p. 175). As a result, many Protestants see the pursuit of wealth as a religious or moral duty (Tawney, 1958).

Fourth, and finally, many Protestant denominations view the unequal distribution of resources stemming from work (e.g., pay, status) as not only desirable, but justifiable (Stone-Romero & Stone, 1998). For example, the Bible advises, "For even when we were with you, this we commanded of you, that if any would not work, neither should he eat" (*2 Thessalonians*, 3:10). They also believe that the unequal distribution of outcomes is consistent with the view that one's actions should be guided by self-interest. In particular, John Wesley and other Methodists saw the unequal distribution of goods as a product of "divine providence" (Weber, 1958). This led to the endorsement of beliefs that were supportive of rugged individualism and economic Darwinism. Weber (1958) wrote that "the capitalism of today educates and selects the economic subjects which it needs through a process of economic survival of the fittest" (p. 55).

Not surprisingly, Protestantism has had a profound influence on Western culture and Western organizations, especially in the United States which is considered to be a predominantly Protestant nation (Stone-Romero & Stone, 1998). In particular, Protestantism appears to have influenced many of the basic American values, including competitive achievement, individualism, self-reliance, materialism, group superiority, and the value of work as a central life interest (Trice & Beyer, 1993; Weber, 1958). It is also evident that Protestant beliefs have played a large part in shaping the values of many U.S. organizations which often emphasize rationality, formalistic rules and procedures, hierarchical differences in authority, authoritarian control of employees, and social Darwinism via an intolerance of poor performance (Trice & Beyer, 1993).

Implications of Christianity for Social Justice

Given that Christianity was originally based in Jewish belief systems, it is not surprising that Christian norms and values regarding justice are somewhat similar to those of Judaism. In fact, the New Testament of the Bible states "Masters, give unto your servants that which is just and equal knowing that you also have a Master in heaven" (*Colossians* 4:1). Furthermore, St. Paul wrote, "Therefore, whosoever resisteth the power, resisteth the ordinance of God: and they that resist shall receive themselves to damnation" (*Romans* 13:2).

Proportionality or Equity. Consistent with Judaism, Christians believe in the concept of equity or proportionality. In particular, Protestants believe that the unequal distribution of resources stemming from work is justified in the eyes of God (Stone-Romero & Stone, 1998; Weber, 1958). They also emphasize that one's outcomes should be based on individual contributions. For example, they often asserted "that if any [person] would not work, neither shall he eat" (2 *Thessalonians* 3:10). As noted above, the concept of equity was also closely tied to the notion of justified self-interest. In fact, some Protestant denominations believe that the unequal distribution of goods is a sign of "divine providence," and that the accumulation of wealth is both a duty to God and a sign of his blessing (Weber, 1958). As a result, some religious scholars (Nigosian, 1994; Smith, 1994) have criticized the Christian belief in maximization of individual wealth because they feel that it has led the Western culture to become the most materialistic and competitive culture on earth.

Equality. Most Christian sects do not believe that outcomes should be allocated equally among people. However, there are some exceptions to this rule in the teachings of Jesus. These are discussed in the subsection on the Status Rule below.

Need. There are clearly inconsistencies in the Christian belief systems regarding the distribution of outcomes based on need. As noted previously, many Protestant sects believe that the unequal distribution of resources is a sign of "divine providence." Thus, those in need are *not* viewed as deserving in the eyes of God, and an unwillingness to work is thought to merit God's disapproval. However, Jesus taught that people should show mercy, kindness, and benevolence toward the needy. In fact, he repeatedly argued that the meek will inherit the earth, and God loves all human beings absolutely without pausing to calculate their worth. He also maintained that we should give "our coat" to the needy because God has ministered far more importantly to our needs (Smith, 1994). In addition, Jesus taught that "It is easier for a camel to go through the eye of a needle than for a rich man to enter the kingdom of God" (*Matthew* 19:24).

As a result of the teachings of Jesus, many Christians espouse the humanitarian values of assisting and helping those in need. However, despite these beliefs some Christian denominations do not advocate allocating outcomes based on need. As noted above, several ascetic Protestant sects place a great deal of emphasis on self-reliance and rugged individualism. Furthermore, some anthropologists contend that one of the greatest fears in American life is that of becoming dependent on others (e.g., Hsu, 1961, cited in Trice and Beyer, 1993). Hsu maintains that the fear of dependence is so great in American culture that an individual who is not self-reliant is an object of hostility and is stigmatized (Hsu, 1961, cited in Trice & Beyer, 1993). Interestingly, Trice and Beyer (1993) argue that there is an inherit conflict in U.S. culture regarding the allocation of resources based on need: It favors helping others in need rather than letting them fend for themselves, yet the same culture often resents those who are dependent or in need. These inherent contradictions in the culture may stem from the many inconsistencies in beliefs of varying Christian sects. As a result of these belief systems, some religious scholars (Smith, 1994) have argued that the world has become more imbalanced in terms of wealth and power, and those in need are often forgotten in Western societies.

Rule of Justified Self-Interest. As noted above, the Rule of Justified Self-Interest is a key element of Christianity, especially some Protestant sects. For example, as noted above, some Protestant sects (e.g., Calvinism) believe that certain individuals are chosen in the eyes of God. Thus, the accumulation of wealth is justified because it is a sign of God's blessing. For example, Weber (1958) noted that in Calvinism and other Protestant sects, "Above all, in practice the most important criterion is private profitableness" (p. 39), and although "Asceticism looked upon the pursuit of wealth as an end itself as highly reprehensible; the attainment of it as a fruit of labour in a calling was a sign of God's blessing" (p. 172). He also noted that "The faithful Christian must follow the call [of private profitableness] by taking advantage of the opportunity" (p. 162). Further, "If God shows you a way in which you may lawfully get more in another way (without wrong to your soul or any other), if you refuse this, and choose the less gainful way, you cross one of the ends of your calling, and you refuse to be God's steward" (p. 162). Thus, if you are among the small proportion of men chosen for eternal grace, it is your obligation to God to gain as much as you can.

Similarly, the new testament of the Bible stresses that self-interest is justified in the eyes of God. For example, in *Ecclesiastes* it is stated that "Every man also to whom God hath given riches and wealth, and hath given him power to eat thereof, and to take his portion and to rejoice in his labour, this [is] the gift of God" (*Ecclesiastes* 5:19). Similarly, the Bible states that "And whatsoever mine eyes desired I kept not from them, I withheld not my heart from any joy, for my heart rejoiced in all my labour and this was my portion of all my labour" (*Ecclesiastes* 2:10). It is clear from the Bible and Weber's (1958) compelling analysis that Christianity provides a providential interpretation to the Rule of Justified Self-Interest.

Rule of Adhering Commitments. In view of the fact that Christianity is based in the Judaic belief system, it is clear that Christians, like Jews, believe that fairness is violated unless people receive what they have been promised. Furthermore, consistent with Judaism, Christians believe that keeping one's promises is Godlike. For example, the Bible states, "But whoso keepeth his word, in him, verily is the love of God perfected; hereby know we that we are in him" (*1 John* 2:5).

Ownership and Legality Rule. The Christian views of the Ownership Rule and Legality Rule are similar to the Judaic beliefs. Thus, these views are not repeated here.

Status Rule. Interestingly, there are contradictory views on the Status Rule in Christianity. As noted above, Jesus was an egalitarian and stressed that everyone was equal in the eyes of God. He hated the social barriers that divided people into artificial categories, and argued that status based on economic differences had no meaning to God (Smith, 1994). Despite these teachings, some Protestant sects strongly support the Status Rule in allocating outcomes because status and wealth are often thought of as signs of approval in the eyes of God (Stone-Romero & Stone, 1998; Weber, 1958). Thus, members of such sects firmly believe that those who are of higher economic status should receive greater outcomes. Furthermore, the Catholic Church believes that there are justifiable status differences between lay persons and the clergy. For example, Catholics believe in the supreme authority and infallibility of the Pope. As noted in the preceding section on Judaism, the belief in the Status Rule has resulted in serious levels of intergroup conflict in the United States and other countries.

Islam

Although page limitations preclude a complete consideration of Islam and social justice conceptions, we provide a brief overview of Islamic beliefs about justice in this subsection. At the outset, it merits noting that religious scholars (e.g., Smith, 1994) classify Islam as a Western religion. The primary reason for this is that Islam is based in Judaism, and many basic Islamic beliefs are similar to the beliefs of Judaism. For example, the first part of the *Koran*, the holy book of Islam, is the same as the Bible because the founder of Islam, Ishmael, was the son of Abraham, the Israelite (Smith, 1994). The Bible provides the history of Abraham and Ishmael, and indicates that Abraham's wife Sara was unable to bear him a child so Abraham took a second wife, Hagar. Hagar and Abraham had a son named Ishmael. Once Ishmael was born, Sara became pregnant very late in life, and bore Abraham another son named Isaac. When Isaac was born Sara demanded that Abraham banish Hagar and Ishmael from the tribe. Subsequently, Ishmael went to Mecca and became the founder of Islam.

Given that Islam is rooted in Judaism, the five principles of Islam share many similarities with Judaic beliefs (cf. Smith, 1994). For example, the five Islamic principles are: (1) there is no God, but Allah, (2) canonical prayer is needed to keep human life in perspective, and express gratitude to Allah, (3) two and one half percent of earnings should be distributed to the poor, especially those in immediate need, (4) one should observe Ramadan (the Holy Month), and (5) one should heighten commitment to God by observing a pilgrimage to the holy city at least once in a lifetime (cf. Smith, 1994).

Followers of Islam believe that wealth should be in vigorous circulation, and they value competition and the profit motive. In addition, Islamic principles specify a number of proscribed activities, including gambling, lying, thieving, eating pork, drinking intoxicants, and being sexually promiscuous. Furthermore, Islam stresses racial equality. It also permits a plurality of wives, probably because Abraham had multiple wives (i.e., Sara and Hagar). Islam also stresses that wrongdoers should be punished to the full extent of the wrong they have committed. Thus, if someone does you an injustice, it is justifiable for you to repay them in kind (e.g., retribution is acceptable) (see Smith, 1994). Unlike some forms of Christianity, it does *not* endorse pacifism or turning the other cheek. However, Islam does allow for forgiveness. It follows from this brief review that many Islamic conceptions of distributive justice are likely to be quite similar to Judaic or other Western views.

EASTERN BELIEF SYSTEMS

Confucianism

Confucianism is based in the teachings of K'ung Fu Tzu, also known as Confucius, who was born around 551 B.C. His mission was the revitalization of the entire Chinese society, and he was thought to have championed the cause of the common people against the oppressive nobility of the day. The Confucian belief system is based on teachings contained in the *Five Classics* or *Wu Chung*.

Interestingly, Confucius wanted to eliminate many of the problems inherent in the society of his time. In particular, he wanted to guard against the selfish interests of individuals and clans because he thought that selfishness would be fatal to the state (Fitzgerald, 1966). As a result, he made loyalty and public service virtues in his new social order. In addition, Confucius felt that people had a detached indifference to the affairs of others beyond their family circle, and he believed that such indifference would ultimately be harmful to society (Fitzgerald, 1966). Thus, he promoted collectivism and concern for others by valuing benevolence, submission to authority, and loyalty to the prince. Confucius also assumed people are naturally lustful, greedy and jealous, and these base impulses predominate over more noble motives (Smith, 1994). As a result, he believed that as a consequences of peoples' desires for greed and personal gain, strife and conflict would result, and courtesy would die in society. Thus, he stressed that the superior or ideal person must be respectful, faithful, and concerned with others before himself. Apart from his other concerns, Confucius feared that the youth of his day were being corrupted by the kindly indulgence of their parents (Fitzgerald, 1966). Thus, he insisted on filial duty and the strict training of children. He also assumed that people are inherently short-sighted and rulers must envision long-range goals because their subjects are incapable of long-range thinking. As is evident from the values noted above, the ideals of Confucius' ideal society were social harmony, duty, and benevolence.

Given the goals just noted, the Confucian belief system was structured on the basis of five ideals or primary virtues (Smith, 1994). The first ideal was *jên*, variously translated as benevolence, kindness, and human-heartedness in dealing with others. In public life, *jên* was thought to elicit untiring diligence. In private life, *jên* was thought to evoke courtesy, unselfishness and empathy or the capacity to measure the feelings of others by one's own feelings. Confucius believed that the ultimate objective of moral development was to acquire affection for all people. For example, the *Analects* of Confucius advised that "a gentleman never discards his kinsmen. He does not expect one man to be capable of everything" (*Analects*, XVIII-10).

The second ideal in Confucianism was *chün-tzu*, which refers to respect in relationships with others. *Chün-tzu* is the opposite of the petty person, and Confucius taught that civilizations are built with such large-hearted people (Smith, 1994). He argued "If there is righteousness in the heart, there will be beauty in the character. If there is beauty in the character, there will be harmony in the home. If there be harmony in the home, there will be order in the nation. If there be order in the nation, there will be peace in the world" (Smith, 1994, p. 10).

According to Confucius, the third ideal was *li* which means propriety, ritual, or doing things in the right or proper way. The right way takes a number of factors in account, including (a) norms relevant to the conduct of individuals in specific roles (e.g., father, ruler), (b) the middle course or behavior that is not extreme or excessive which yields harmony, balance, and compromise, (c) relationships that are constant between parent and child, husband and wife, ruler and subject, and (d) respect for family and age. Doing things in the proper way implies that one should not allow one's efforts to be diverted by such considerations as personal gain and impatience. In particular, Confucius wrote that "Any thought of accepting wealth and rank by means that I know to be wrong is as remote from me as the clouds that float above me" (*Analects*, VII-15). In addition, he believed that "The duty of children to their parents is the fountain from which all virtues spring" (Smith, 1994, p. 111).

The fourth ideal of Confucius is *tê*, meaning the power by which men are ruled. He believed that rulers need the voluntary cooperation of subjects, and cooperation will emerge only when people believe that their leaders merit it. To merit such cooperation, leaders must be persons of character, sincerely devoted to the common good, and they must possess a character that compels respect from their followers. Thus, *tê* is the power of moral leadership, and Confucius argued that "If the ruler himself is upright, all will go well even though he does not give orders. But if he himself is not upright, even though he gives orders they will not be obeyed (*Analects*, XIII-6).

Similar to the ideal of *tê*, Confucius believed in the virtue of justice, that is *i*, in social systems, especially in the government. When asked if there is any single saying that one can dwell on all day, he said: "Never do to others what you would not like them to do to you" (*Analects*, XV-23). In addition, he argued that "he who is just is the joy [of the people]" (*Analects*, XX-1).

Fifth and finally, Confucius valued knowledge (*chi*) and learning. He believed in carefully evaluating the truth of what one is told, and in using self-awareness that one lacked knowledge as a basis for self-improvement. For example, he advised, "Learn as if you were following someone whom you could not catch up, as though it were someone you were frightened of losing" (*Analects*, VIII-17). He also argued that "if you have made a mistake, do not be afraid of admitting the fact and amending your ways" (*Analects*, IX-24). He also instructed that "To have faults and to be making no effort to amend them is to have faults indeed" (*Analects*, XV-29).

Apart from the just-noted ethical principles, Confucianism also has a transcendent or spiritual dimension. Confucius viewed the world as divided into Heaven and Earth, and though distinct, the two dimensions were tightly intertwined (Smith, 1994). Heaven was the abode of the ancestors (*ti*) as presided over by the supreme ancestor, *Shan Ti*. Earth was inhabited by mortals. The whole was one unbroken procession in which death spelled no more than transition from the body to the more honorable state of ancestor. The two populations were thought to be in constant contact. Ancestors watched over their offspring while counting on them to supply some of their needs through offerings. Heaven was also thought to be the more powerful, august, and important of the two realms. However, Confucius argued that the concerns of the mortals should take precedence over the claims of ancestors. In particular, he noted, "Till you have learnt to serve men, how can you serve ghosts [spirits]?" (*Analects*, XI-11). He also believed that somewhere in the universe there was a power that was on the side of right. He taught that the spread of righteousness is a heavenly demand, and he believed that the "will of Heaven is the first thing a *chün-tzu* should respect" (Smith, 1994, p. 117). Confucius also taught that the task of becoming fully human involved sequentially transcending egoism, nepotism, parochialism, and ethnocentrism.

Not surprisingly, for over two thousand years Confucianism has had a profound effect on values and norms in Eastern societies (e.g., China, Japan, Korea). The Confucian texts became the basic discipline for training government officials, and also served as the basis for China's famous civil service examination system which helped create the Chinese Empire (Smith, 1994). In addition, Confucianism was based on the assumption that competitiveness was divisive. As a result, Confucius created a religion that served the needs of everyone, and viewed the extended family as its most important element (Smith, 1994).

Implications of Confucianism for Social Justice

It is evident from the above that Confucian views of social justice are quite different from those that are common in Western nations. In Western nations, Judaism laid the foundation of individualism and individual rights based on the assumption that individuals had rights that even kings must respect. Furthermore, Protestantism extended these beliefs to include the maximization of personal wealth as a virtue. However, the Confucian belief system stressed that individuals had duties or obligations to others, and individuals should not be diverted by motives of personal gain or self-interest. Thus, justice according to Confucius is concerned with others not oneself, and is based on eliminating selfishness, envy, and greed. In particular, Confucius taught that the true gentleman ". . .is not concerned lest his people should be poor, but only lest what they have should be ill-apportioned. And indeed, if all is well-apportioned, there will be no poverty; if they are not divided against one another, there will be no lack of men. . . . And where there is contentment there will be no upheavals" (*Analects*, XVI-8-9).

Proportionality or Equity. It is apparent from the above that Confucianism does not emphasize proportionality or equity in the allocation of outcomes. The primary reason for this is that Confucius believed that the concept of proportionality encouraged invidious comparisons between people, and fostered competition, greed or anger among individuals. Given his goal of harmony in society, he believed that the social structure should be designed in such a way as to avoid competition or conflict between individuals. As a result, the Confucian belief system stresses that an individual should be concerned with his/her duty, loyalty and benevolence toward others rather than being concerned with the self and with what he/she deserves relative to others. He also emphasized that people should not be envious, resentful of others or presumptuous. In particular, he stated when one sees people who are better than oneself, one should turn one's attention to equalling them (*Analects*, IV-17). Likewise, he argued that the good man does not grieve that other people do not recognize his merits. His only anxiety is lest he should fail to recognize theirs" (*Analects*, I-16). Similarly, he maintained that "To be poor and not resent it is far harder than to be rich, yet not presumptuous" (*Analects*, XIV-10, 11). Confucius also stressed that people should not pursue personal gain at the expense of their ethics or integrity. In fact, he argued that when one sees a chance of gain, one should divert one's attention to whether it can be pursued without violation of what is right (*Analects*, XIV-13).

Although Confucius did not generally advocate a philosophy of proportionality when allocating outcomes, he did stress merit in promotion to positions in the government or civil service. In a Confucian society, learning and knowledge are honored above birth and wealth (Fitzgerald, 1966). As a result, scholars were examined for positions in public service, and promotions to these positions were based on the person's knowledge or merit. Confucius argued "promote those who are worthy, train those who are incompetent, that is the best form of encouragement" (*Analects*, II-20).

Thus, in one sense Confucianism did advocate that promotions to public service positions should be proportional to one's knowledge or merit.

Equality. It is clear from the above that the Confucian belief system generally stresses equality in the allocation of outcomes. Confucius believed that one could eliminate poverty and strife by making sure that all people received an equal share of available outcomes. Moreover, he argued that "In his private conduct he [the good man] was courteous, in serving his master he was punctilious, in providing for the needs of people he gave them even more than their due, in exacting service from the people, he was just" (*Analects*,V-15). He also noted that "He who devotes himself to securing for his subjects what is right . . . may be termed wise" (*Analects*, VI-20).

Need. As noted above, Confucius stressed sympathy, and benevolence toward others. Thus, he strongly believed that outcomes should be allocated on the basis of need. In fact, Confucius taught that the good of the entire community comes before the good of the individual, and a *chün-tzu* (a true gentleman) is guided through life by altruism and refrains from doing to others what de does not wish them to do to him (*Analects*, V-11). As a result, some authors maintain that the Chinese concept of justice is not a "cold intellectual principle, but a kind of compassionate wisdom" (Shafer, 1997, p. 3). For example, Confucius stated that "A gentleman helps out the necessitous, he does not make the rich, richer still" (*Analects*, VI-3). Confucianism also stresses that generosity and helpfulness are virtues. In particular, Confucius argued that "When gentlemen deal generously with their own kin, the common people are incited to goodness" (*Analects*, VIII-2).

Rule of Justified Self-Interest. Given the tenets of Confucianism outlined above, it is evident that justified self-interest is *not* endorsed by Confucianism. In fact, Confucianism emphasizes an opposite principle, that individuals have duties or obligations to others, and one should elevate the welfare of the community rather than focusing on the self. Confucius believed that people have a natural tendency to seek personal gain and that the selfish interests of individuals and clans would result in strife and would prove fatal to the community. Thus, he made loyalty, altruism, and benevolence toward others virtues and guiding moral principles. In fact, the demands of morality indicated that, if need be, one must sacrifice one's life to do what is right (Smith, 1994).

Furthermore, the maintenance of peace and harmony were viewed as more important than individual rights, and Confucius seemed to have been opposed to the pursuit of individual profit (Smith, 1994). For example, in the *Analects* it is noted that when one sees a chance to gain, one should divert one's attention to whether it can be pursued without violation of what is right (*Analects*, XIV-13). Confucius also argued that when one is guided by mere profits rather than devotion to the task he or she will incur much ill will. In addition, "A gentleman helps out the necessitous, he does not make the rich richer still" (*Analects*, VI-3). And, "As for goodness—you yourself desire rank and standing, and then [you should] help others get rank and standing. You want to turn your own merits to account; then help others to turn theirs to account" (*Analects*, VI-28).

Rule of Adhering Commitments. In establishing a social order, Confucius stressed that individuals should keep their word or promises to others. Thus, the Rule of Adhering Commitments is consistent with the basic values of Confucianism. Not surprisingly, there are numerous examples of this rule in the *Analects*. For example, "In your promises cleave to what is right and you will be able to fulfill your word. In your obeisances cleave to ritual and you will keep dishonour at bay" (*Analects*, I-13). In addition, Confucius said, "A young man's duty is to behave well to his parents at home and to his elders abroad, to be cautious in giving promises and punctual in keeping them" (*Analects*, I-6), and "He who is broad wins the multitude, he who keeps his word is trusted by the people, he who is diligent succeeds in all he undertakes, he who is just is the joy [of all the people]" (*Analects*, XX-1).

Legality Rule. Interestingly, Confucius was opposed to the idea of the law, and therefore, did not subscribe to the Legality Rule as we know it in the West. In particular, he based his social order on moral authority rather than legal sanctions or penalties. He did not want people constrained by fear of penalties, but charmed by the sheen of virtue (Fitzgerald, 1966).

The legal system in the early Confucian era was applied only to those who were ignorant and unlearned. The primary foundation of the Confucian legal system was the Doctrine of the Mean, or middle way. As a result, Chinese people still typically prefer negotiation, mediation, and the use of a "middle man" rather than impersonal courts of law (Smith, 1994). Until recently, legal action has been regarded as something of a disgrace, a confession of the person's inability to work things out through compromise.

Status Rule. It is apparent from the foregoing that although the Confucian belief system is hierarchical, it does stress the need for status differences. However, the Confucian view of hierarchy is linked to a social view of humanity, and emphasizes interrelationships and mutual regard for others. Interestingly, the Status Rule as we know it in the West is not directly applicable to Confucianism. Confucius believed that those of higher status were not expected to receive higher outcomes, rather those of higher status had greater duties or obligations to others. As noted above, Asian societies under Confucianism were states based on the rule of moral authority, and the scholar leaders were expected to be role models of virtue for ordinary people. In addition, there were five relationships in Confucian society, and there were different duties and obligations or "right actions" associated with each relationship (Shafer, 1997). For example, in the ruler-subject relationship, the subject was expected to be loyal to the ruler, and the ruler had a duty to be benevolent toward the subject. In the father-son relationship, the son was expected to exhibit filial piety, and the father had an obligation to be kind to his son. Confucianism taught, "A gentleman can be bounteous without extravagance, can get work out of people without arousing resentment, has longings but is never covetous" (*Analects*, XX-2).

Buddhism

Siddhartha Gautama, or Buddha, was born in 563 B.C., and during his early years lived a lavish life as a prince. His father sheltered him from all worldly problems, and would not let him see those who were sick and dying. However, once he learned the truth about the body's inescapable involvement with disease, decrepitude, and death he gave up on the physical plane as a means of finding personal fulfillment. He then joined a band of ascetics from whom he learned the futility of asceticism and importance of the Middle Way between indulgence and asceticism. Gautama devoted the final phase of his quest to a combination of rigorous thought and mystic concentration which lead to his "Great Awakening" and the four Noble Truths.

Buddhism developed out of Guatama's dissatisfaction with various aspects of Hinduism, including its caste system, and the notion that the soul undergoes many cycles of reincarnation (Gaer, 1963). Buddhism is a belief system that is based on infinite compassion and charity, and most of its followers reject materialism. As noted above, Buddhists believe in the four Noble Truths. The first Noble Truth is that life, as it is typically lived, is based on suffering. This enormous suffering blocks creativity, restricts movement, and causes interpersonal conflict.

The second Noble Truth addresses the question, "What causes life's suffering?" According to Buddha, the desire for private fulfillment or ego is the cause of suffering. Buddha asked his followers these questions: "Where is the man that is as concerned that no children go hungry as that his own child have food? Where is the woman who rejoices in her colleague's promotion as much as her own?" He believed that the ego strangles people and keeps them from happiness.

The third Noble Truth is that if the cause of life's dislocation is selfish craving, then its cure lies in overcoming such craving. If one is released from the narrow limits of self-interest into the vast expanse of universal life, then he or she will also be released from torment.

The fourth, and final, Noble Truth is that suffering can be overcome with the complete annihilation of desire, separating oneself from it and completely expelling it. The annihilation of desire can be gained by following the Eightfold Path (see Gaer, 1963), which can be viewed as the code of conduct in the Buddhist belief system. Buddhists believe that one will achieve Nirvana or enlightenment by adhering to the Eightfold Path.

The elements of the Eightfold Path are as follows: (a) *Right Knowledge* reflects knowledge of what life is about; (b) *Right Aspiration* means a clear devotion to being on the Path toward enlightenment; (c) *Right Speech* implies that one should be attentive to what speech reveals about his or her character. One should not belittle others, be tactless in speech or engage in lies, slander, or gossip; (d) *Right Behavior* involves five basic laws of behavior (not to kill, steal, lie, drink intoxicants, or commit sexual offenses); (e) *Right Livelihood* dictates that one should do work that promotes life and does not harm other beings (e.g., human or infra-human). Thus, such occupations as butcher, soldier, slave trader or prostitute are not right livelihoods; (f) *Right Endeavor* means being earnest and steadfast in preserving the Way (i.e., doing what is good, not what is bad or evil); (g) *Right Mindfulness* implies an ongoing self-examination and awareness; and (h) *Right Concentration* means controlling the mind through meditation so that is completely subject to one's will.

Although the followers of Buddhism subscribe to the notion of Karma (i.e., the moral law that relates causes to effects), they do not believe in the Hindu view that the soul is reincarnated. Contrary to the Hindu view, Buddhists believe that when a being dies it reappears in an altered state of renewed existence. In addition, Buddhists believe that when a being experiences a renewed existence, it is a product of what the being has wanted or done in a past life. Karma, for example, is thought to influence such factors as the being's form at the time of rebirth (e.g., human or subhuman), its intelligence, attractiveness, wealth, and social status. Thus, Karma functions as a process that provides for *ultimate justice* in the world. As a result of Karma, one pays the consequences or reaps the benefits of one's actions in the next life. Note, however, that in Buddhism there is no God or authority figure that judges one's life and metes out rewards and punishments. Moreover, Karma allows for no psychological projection (e.g., blaming others) or appeals to bad luck. It decrees that although every decision is arrived at freely by the person, it will have its consequences.

Interestingly, Buddhists believe in the idea that people should not identify too strongly with their own personal existence in any one life. An individual's release from the process of birth, death, and rebirth, and an end to suffering come about when the person reaches the enlightened state of Nirvana. This is a state of ultimate consciousness in which self-interest, hatred, and ignorance are extinguished. It is reached through the development of the virtuous attitudes of loving kindness, compassion, sympathetic joy, and equanimity (Smith, 1994). The duty of the true Buddhist is to purify the heart, then to practice charity, and arrive at universal benevolence (Fitzgerald, 1966). Not surprisingly, Buddhism has had a profound effect on the culture and moral values of people in many Asian societies (e.g., Mongolia, Tibet, China, Japan, Korea, Vietnam and Nepal). However, Buddhism has generally not focused on changing the social order in a society as have other religious belief systems (e.g., Catholicism, Confucianism, Judaism). The reasons for the Buddhist indifference to societal issues are discussed in the following section.

Implications of Buddhism for Justice

Justice is a rare and almost nonexistent word in the Buddhist belief system (King, 1995). In fact, Buddhists are generally uncomfortable with the ideals and principles of justice that are common to the Western world. The reason for this is that Buddhism focuses primarily on inner-states and Buddhists are not typically concerned with the samsaric or social world which is thought to be driven by greed and hatred, and ruled by desires for power, wealth, fame and sensual enjoyment (King, 1995). Furthermore, as noted above, Buddhists believe that suffering in the social world can only be escaped by detachment from worldly desires. They also believe that some Western views of justice are based on a revengeful "quid pro quo" quality, and an endless balancing of rival claims and rights structured by human pride, jealousy, competition, and anger (King, 1995). This belief is represented in the following from the *Dhammapada*: "He abused me, he beat me, he defeated me, he robbed me, the hatred of those who do not harbor such thoughts is appeased. Hatreds never cease by hatred in this world, by love alone they cease" (Thera, 1954, pp. 15-16).

Until recently, Buddhists also believed that human beings should not think that they can do anything to alleviate "unjust" situations in society because Karma will ensure that all actions will have their ultimate consequences. As noted above, the principle of Karma is a form of social justice, and all sentient beings are thought to experience consequences for their actions in the next life. The only general escape from Karmic justice is not into a better life in this world or the next, but Nirvana or enlightenment. Interestingly, over the years, some Buddhists have become concerned with societal values and improving the social order (King, 1995). These Buddhist concerns and solutions to social problems are discussed in the subsections that follow.

Proportionality or Equity. It is clear from the above that Buddhists do not generally believe in principles of proportionality or outcomes based on inputs or contributions. The primary reason for this is that they believe that the allocation of outcomes based on the proportionality principle results in competition, jealousy, and hatred among individuals. Thus, proportionality is thought to foster worldly desires and lead to endless emotional suffering. In fact, some Buddhists believe that concern with equity encourages individuals to become *addicted* to worldly outcomes, and diverts their attention from the more important goals of wisdom and compassion.

Despite these general beliefs about proportionality, it appears that there are two elements of proportionality in the Buddhist belief system. The first element is found in the concept of Karma which is based on the principle that every state of renewed existence is caused by ethically good or evil deeds in a former life. Thus, individuals experience a renewed existence that is a direct consequence of their deeds in a former life. In some respects this is a belief in proportionality or equity, but the outcomes are distributed in a future existence, not in one's present life.

In addition, the concept of proportionality is embedded in the Buddhist view that the relationships between varying social groups should be balanced, and based on rights. In general, Buddhists believe that the societal world is divided into six directions of relationships, including the relationship among the individual and his or her (a) mother and father, (b) teachers, (c) spouse and child, (d) friends and companions, (e) workers and helpers, and (f) ascetics. An example of the Buddhist belief in balanced relationships is provided by a passage from the *Sigalovada Suutra*: "There are five ways in which a master should minister to his servants, and workpeople . . . by arranging their work according to their strength, by supplying them with food and wages, by looking after them when they are ill, by sharing special delicacies with them, and by letting them off work at the right time" (Walsh, 1995, p. 468).

Equality. As noted previously, Buddhists were slow to embrace the importance of creating a social order based on their own values and principles. However, once Buddhist leaders built their social systems, they chose the principle of equality as the primary basis for allocating outcomes. In particular, Asoka, a Mauryan Indian monarch, who lived about 270–230 B.C. was one of the first rulers to build a social structure on Buddhist principles. He dealt with social problems (e.g., theft, violence, aggression) by means of a system of benevolent social welfare that removed the social and economic causes of such problems: In Asoka's state, basic physical necessities were provided to all people in order to generate a climate of tolerance, kindness, and regard for others (King, 1995). Justice in Asoka's state was achieved through preventive benevolence. In fact, the *Dharma* or teaching of the *Wheel Turning Monarch* was based on a portrait of a ruler who embodied the Five Precepts (no killing, stealing, lying, sexual immorality or use of intoxicants), and argued that a ruler should be one who leans on the Norm (the Law of Truth and Righteousness), honoring, respecting, and revering it: "Throughout the Kingdom let no wrongdoing prevail, and whosoever in the Kingdom is poor, to let wealth be given" (Rhys David & Rhys David, 1965).

According to Buddhist teachings, the era of peace and righteousness fostered by the values in the *Wheel Turning Monarch* were thought to have lasted several hundred years. Then the seventh King, a war-lord, Kshatriya, came to power. Upon assuming power, Kshatriya was informed that the Dharma-wheel had slipped from its dominating height, and he was not performing his job as King. Then the King ceased bestowing goods on the poor, and violence and thievery erupted in the Kingdom. In order to deal with the problems, the King instituted a justice-punishment system similar to that used in the West. This system sparked an era of violence, stealing, murder and immorality that had never been seen before. Thus, through this story, followers of Buddhism are taught that when outcomes are not allocated equally, then the whole social order deteriorates and immorality prevails.

Need. One of the foundations of Buddhism is the principle of compassion or benevolence toward all living things. As a result, Buddhists strongly believe that need should be considered when distributing outcomes. The primary reason for this is that benevolence and charity are among the most important ideals for Buddhists, and some Buddhist sects (e.g., Amida Buddhism) believe that showing true compassion to all living creatures on earth allows them to enter the Buddhahood (Fitzgerald, 1966). To these same individuals, the goal is not Nirvana, the extinction of desire and relief from suffering, but it is to achieve the altruistic aspiration of Buddhahood, called *bodhichitta* (The Dalai Lama, 1997). Thus, many Buddhists believe that they should not be content with working for their own personal benefit, but should primarily work for the benefit of others (The Dalai Lama, 1997). The Dalai Lama (1997) argues that "If we see suffering and helplessness in others, and we still work for our own benefit, we will not only be acting unfairly, but extremely ungratefully" (p. 197). Other Buddhists known as *Bodhisattvas* devote their entire existence to alleviating the suffering of sentient beings on earth. In fact, stories recount tales of Buddhists (e.g., Kuan Shuh Yin, known as the compassionate *Bodhisattva*) who postponed Buddhahood because they heard the cry of suffering from the earth, and vowed to work until they could alleviate the suffering of all of those in need (Fitzgerald, 1966).

As noted above, for many years Buddhists did not believe in human intervention in society. However, recently some have argued for active participation in creating a new social order based on their beliefs of wisdom and compassion (e.g., Ives, cited in King, 1995). More specifically, Ives (cited in King, 1995) argues that modern Buddhists should advocate a social order based on participative and compassionate justice that prevents the weak from being ground into poverty, sets an upper boundary on wealth, and seeks to achieve an environmentally sustainable way of life. This latter principle is based on the Buddhist belief that all beings are biologically interdependent, and there is an interrelationship among all elements on earth.

Rule of Justified Self-Interest. As is evident from the foregoing, followers of Buddhism are opposed to the concept of justified self-interest. In fact, the basic tenets of Buddhism emphasize that enlightenment, or Nirvana, exists only when self-interest is extinguished and replaced with the virtuous attitudes of compassion, loving kindness, sympathetic joy, and equanimity. As noted above, Buddhists believe that people should not be consumed with personal self-interest or gain, and one's suffering can only be overcome by annihilating desire or self-interest (i.e., the Fourth Noble Truth). Furthermore, one's duty is to purify the heart and arrive at universal benevolence, and charity toward others. For example, the Dalai Lama (1997) noted that "The unique feature of human beings is that they work for the benefit of others, not being concerned with their own welfare alone. That is the beauty and the specialty of a human being" (p. 132). In addition, he stated that "People like the American president Abraham Lincoln and the Indian Leader Mahatma Gandhi are regarded as really great men because they did not think of themselves alone but worked for the benefit of the people. They thought of the entire human society, and they struggled and fought for the rights of the poor" (p. 132).

Rule of Adhering Commitments. As noted above, followers of Buddhism believe that individuals should adhere to the Eightfold Path, but the type of commitment emphasized by Buddhism is not the same as the Rule of Adhering Commitments noted by Leventhal (1980). Buddhism focuses primarily on inner states and has not been concerned with the social world or material outcomes. Thus, the Rule of Adhering Commitments is not directly applicable to the Buddhist belief system.

Ownership Rule and Legality Rule. As noted above, the Buddhist belief system does not stress justice as we know it in the samsaric or social world. Thus, in Buddhist writings there is almost no consideration of such matters as principles of ownership and the legal rights of individuals. In fact, Buddhists have generally been socially and politically conforming because they have focused on inner states rather than material or external possessions. Furthermore, no ethical judgments are made about the worth of governmental authorities or rulers. Rulers are presumed to be rulers because of their Karmic destiny, and the word "deserve" means no more than "decreed by the sovereign's law" (King, 1995).

Status Rule. The Status Rule, as defined by Leventhal (1980), is also not directly applicable to the Buddhist belief system. In fact, Buddha was an egalitarian who developed his belief system in response to the problems with the Hindu religious system (Smith, 1994). More specifically, he rejected the Hindu caste system, and challenged the Hindu view that authority and aptitudes should be based on hereditary. In Buddha's era the Hindu Brahmins (i.e., upper class members) believed that their birth gave them special authority and knowledge about religion. As a result, they exploited others by hoarding religious secrets and charging exorbitant fees for teaching religious principles (Smith, 1994). Interestingly, Buddha argued that surface distinctions meant little in terms of enlightenment, and insisted that women were as capable of enlightenment as men. It is important to note that his views about women and egalitarianism were unparalleled in his age.

IMPLICATIONS OF RELIGIOUS IDEOLOGIES FOR ORGANIZATIONS IN WESTERN AND EASTERN CULTURES

Our review of the religious underpinnings of conceptions of social justice suggests that religious beliefs and values play a central role in the formation and justification of social justice ideologies. Furthermore, it is clear from our review that there are dramatic differences in justice ideologies across Western and Eastern cultures. Some of these differences are considered below.

Western Justice Ideologies

Western religions (e.g., Judaism and Christianity) stress three fundamental beliefs and values about social justice. First, they generally advocate that outcomes should be allocated on the basis of proportionality or equity rather than need or equality. Second, they place a great deal of emphasis on the belief that individuals are entitled to varying rights, and that individuals have rights that even Kings must respect. Third, Protestantism stressed that people should maximize their own outcomes because wealth was a sign of divine providence. As a result of these basic beliefs, a number of authors have noted that the Western cultures are highly individualistic (Hofstede, 1980), and motivated primarily by self-interest or personal gain (Weber, 1958).

In view of the foregoing, we believe that the fundamental beliefs and values of Western religions have a number of important implications for individuals' attitudes and behaviors in organizational settings. As a result, we present several propositions that can be used to guide future research on justice. For example, given that Western religions stress individualism and proportionality, we propose the following:

Proposition 1. The more individuals adhere to the basic teachings of Western religions (e.g., Judaism, Christianity), the more they will believe that organizational outcomes should be allocated on the basis of equity or proportionality.

Furthermore, as noted above, Western religions and cultures are more likely to emphasize Leventhal's (1980) other distributive justice rules than Eastern religions or cultures. Thus we present several propositions regarding these principles below:

Proposition 2. The more individuals adhere to the basic teachings of Western religions (e.g., Judaism, Christianity), the more they will believe in the principle of justified self-interest.

Proposition 3. Individuals who subscribe to the basic teachings of Protestantism (especially Calvinism) will be more likely to believe in the principle of justified self-interest than those who subscribe to the beliefs of Judaism or Catholicism.

Proposition 4. The more individuals adhere to the basic teachings of Western religions (e.g., Judaism, Christianity), the more they will believe in (a) the Rule of Adhering Commitments, (b) the Ownership Rule, (c) the Legality Rule, and (d) the Status Rule.

Although there may be a number of positive consequences (i.e., productivity, material gain) associated with the Western emphasis on individualism and the maximization of individual outcomes, the same beliefs may also lead to negative outcomes in organizations. For example, when individuals emphasize the maximization of individual outcomes and justified self-interest, they may perceive that their inputs or contributions are the most important inputs in an organization. These perceptions may serve as an expectation of high levels of positively valent outcomes and the view that such outcomes are deserved. Consequently, in social exchange, people may experience inequity because others fail to (a) recognize their inputs or (b) view them as relevant. Unfortunately, when proportionality or equity criteria are used to allocate outcomes, only a few people can get the most positively valent outcomes: Of necessity, many individuals will feel that they have received less than they deserve, and in order to deal with this perceived inequity they may argue that the allocation system is unfair. Furthermore, in an effort to resolve their perceptions of inequity, individuals may argue that the system should be changed so as to insure that their inputs are recognized and viewed as relevant. To the degree that the system remains unchanged, the same individuals may feel chronic dissatisfaction with it. For example, they may disagree with the outcomes they experienced from performance evaluation processes. As a result of their chronic dissatisfaction, individuals may be unwilling to work for the good of the organization. Moreover, they may be prone to withdraw from organizations through such means as absenteeism, turnover, or withholding inputs. As a result, we offer the following proposition:

Proposition 5. The greater the degree to which people subscribe to the norm of proportionality, the less satisfied they will be with outcomes (e.g., raises, promotions, performance appraisals) received in organizational contexts.

As a result of the emphasis on proportionality and the maximization of individual outcomes stressed in Western cultures, there is often an overemphasis on the self; thus, it is rare for people in such cultures (e.g., the United States) to scale down their expectations or perceive that they deserve less. As noted above, one reason for this is that many of the ascetic Protestant sects stress that people should gain all they can while they are on earth. For example, John Wesley, the founder of the Methodism, argued that "we must exhort all Christians to gain all they can, that is, to grow rich." (cited in Weber, 1958, p. 175). Thus, many Protestants see the pursuit of individual wealth as a moral and religious duty. These beliefs have led some religious scholars (Smith, 1994) to argue that although Western cultures are the most well-developed progressive social systems in the world, they are also the most materialistic, divisive, alienated, and spiritually unfulfilled cultures on earth.

Another consequence of the adherence to beliefs in proportionality and maximization of individual outcomes is that when rewards are scarce, systems are often set up to ensure that individuals compete for them (i.e., economic Darwinism). Not surprisingly, one consequence of such systems is that there is often chronic conflict between individuals or groups within the system. For example, unions have long fought with management over controlling allocation processes in organizations, and in many organizations unionized workers constantly file grievances. Thus, we propose that:

Proposition 6. The greater the degree to which members of organizations subscribe to the teachings of Western religions, the greater the level of interpersonal conflict in organizations.

There is also a high level of distrust of systems in the Western world, and some authors have noted that we have an "ecosystem of distrust" in Western nations (e.g., Stone-Romero & Stone, 1998). As a result of this distrust, people typically tend to view allocation systems as unfair, and as a consequence they are unwilling to exhibit good citizenship behaviors in organizations (McFarlin & Sweeney, 2001). Likewise, when the system is highly competitive, individuals often try to subvert it by using political means to ensure they will get the outcomes they want. In addition, they often resort to legalistic systems or formalistic rules and procedures (McFarlin & Sweeney, 2001) to achieve process control. Thus, one rather dysfunctional byproduct of Western belief systems is that in Western organizations a great deal of energy is diverted from task accomplishment to the management of conflict. Thus, we propose that:

Proposition 7. The greater the degree to which individuals subscribe to Western religious teachings, the greater will be the organization's need to deal with worker grievances and complaints.

Eastern Justice Ideologies

As should be apparent from our review, Eastern religious norms and values about justice are quite different from those that stem from Western-based ideologies. First, Eastern belief systems do *not* stress the maximization of individual outcomes; rather, individuals are thought to have obligations and duties to others including their families and workgroups. As a result, people in Eastern cultures are not as chronically concerned with the self as are people in Western cultures, and are not preoccupied with gaining all that they can while on earth (Markus & Kitayama, 1991a, 1991b). Consequently, when individuals in Eastern cultures do not receive higher levels of rewards than others their motivation does not decrease and they do not experience chronic unhappiness. In view of this we propose:

Proposition 8. Compared to individuals who subscribe to Western religious teachings, individuals who adhere to the teachings of Eastern belief systems (e.g., Confucianism, Buddhism) will be less concerned with issues of individual justice and more concerned with collective justice (i.e., justice for the group or community as a whole).

Second, because of extant values, in Eastern cultures rewards are typically allocated on the basis of equality or need. In addition, significant rewards come from social ties or doing things that benefit the group (Markus & Kitayama, 1991a, 1991b). Thus, we propose the following:

Proposition 9. The more individuals adhere to the basic teachings of Eastern belief systems (e.g., Confucianism, Buddhism), the more they will believe that outcomes should be allocated on the basis of either equality or need.

In Eastern societies, individuals are recognized when they make a contribution to the collective good, indicating that they are a good group member. The ultimate reward is social acceptance and belonging to a group. As a result, there is less conflict, anger, resentment, and envy in Eastern than in Western cultures. Furthermore, there is more trust in the overall system in Eastern cultures than in Western cultures and individuals often cede process control to others (McFarlin & Sweeney, 2001). Thus, some religious scholars have argued that all Chinese philosophy is the study of how men can best be helped to live and work together in harmony and good order (Waley, cited in Smith, 1994). Moreover, China's emphasis on social harmony has helped the Chinese culture develop the most long lasting civilization humankind has ever known (Smith, 1994). Many of the warriors who conquered the Chinese Empire over a two thousand year period were themselves later conquered by the wisdom and compassion of the Chinese culture (Smith, 1994).

Third, Eastern religions place a great deal of emphasis on the inner-self and inner-freedom rather than external rewards and punishments. In particular, Buddhism stresses that most of life is dislocated or "out of joint" because of the preoccupation with individual fulfillment or personal desires. As a result, Eastern belief systems highlight the importance of continuous self-improvement, and the individual's internal capacity to revitalize or renew oneself (Markus & Kitayama, 1991a, 1991b; Stone-Romero & Stone, 1998). Thus, in Eastern cultures, internal processes rather than external systems serve to control the behavior of individuals. Moreover, individuals in Eastern cultures are more likely to accept responsibility for their actions, and less likely to blame "the system" when they do not receive rewards. Given these differences, we hypothesize that:

Proposition 10. People in Eastern cultures will be less concerned with (a) the principle of justified self-interest, (b) the principle of adhering commitments, (c) the Ownership Rule, (d) the Legality Rule, and (e) procedural justice or process control than people in Western cultures.

Interestingly, religious scholars have argued that Eastern cultures are far superior to those of the West in terms of social wisdom and psychological insight (e.g., Smith, 1994). At the same time, however, such scholars (e.g., Smith, 1994) have noted that the standard of living remains considerably lower in the East than in the West because many Eastern cultures have not paid as much attention to science and material progress as have Western cultures.

Finally, the Confucian-based system emphasizes status differences between scholar-leaders and others. As a result, individuals in Eastern cultures expect status differences and accept them. In exchange, individuals with higher status have a great sense of obligation to their followers. In fact, in Confucian cultures leaders are expected to be generous and hold the society together through the power of moral example. Such moral example and benevolence was thought to inspire the populace to live together in harmony and decency, and to deter greed and self-interest on the part of individuals. In addition, the Confucian belief system stresses that knowledge is a virtue. Thus, centuries ago the Chinese designed a civil-service examining system to ensure that promotions would be based on a person's knowledge rather than on friendship or politics. Interestingly, the United States adopted the same (meritocracy-based) system and has long used examinations to hire and promote individuals in public- and private-sector organizations.

As noted above, the Buddhist belief system does not stress status differences. Instead, followers of Buddhism strongly believe in egalitarianism and emphasize that all living beings are interrelated. Thus, the various Eastern religions have quite different beliefs about status. As a result, we propose:

Proposition 11. Individuals who adhere to the basic teachings of Buddhism will be less likely to believe in the Status Rule than those who adhere to the basic teachings of either Confucianism or Christianity.

CONCLUSION

In order to gain a better understanding of justice ideologies, we reviewed literature germane to the proposition that conceptions of social justice have religious and moral underpinnings. We hope that our review will: (a) provide justice scholars with additional insight into the bases for views of social justice and (b) motivate them to consider broader views about social justice than are common in the Western literature. In addition, we believe that our review has a number of important implications for theory and research on social justice in organizational settings.

First, it seems clear that each of the religious or moral belief systems considered in this chapter has something to contribute to our understanding of social justice. In particular, Western belief systems have resulted in a passion for individual freedom and individual rights, and Eastern belief systems have inspired a value system based on compassionate justice, self-insight, and social harmony. Each religion or belief system offers a unique perspective on justice. An appreciation of these perspectives should enable us to better explain why any given outcome (e.g., reward) allocation system is likely to evoke different views about fairness among individuals from diverse cultural backgrounds. Furthermore, our analysis of the religious underpinnings of social justice suggests that current theoretical views of distributive justice (e.g., Leventhal, 1980) are heavily influenced by Western value systems, especially those of Judaism and Christianity. As a result, our Western theories may not apply to individuals from many Eastern cultures, because the underlying value systems are quite different in these cultures. Thus, we argue, as do others (e.g., Leung, Su, & Morris, 2001;

McFarlin & Sweeney, 2001; Shapiro & Tinsley, 2001; Steiner, 2001), that current theories of social justice should be modified or expanded to include the value systems of other cultures.

Second, as do others (Weber, 1958), we believe that religious beliefs influence cultural values, and the same values affect the extent to which allocation systems are viewed as fair. For example, as noted above, individuals from Western cultures may see allocations based on proportionality as fair, while those from Eastern cultures may view allocations based on equality or need as fair. Thus, consistent with previous research on cross-cultural views of social justice (e.g., Leung, 1997; Leung et al., 2001; McFarlin & Sweeney, 2001; Steiner, 2001), we maintain that multinational or multicultural organizations should consider differences in cultural values when designing organizational policies regarding allocation systems. Interestingly, our review also suggests that organizations should set flexible policies or, at least, establish policies that do not favor one cultural group over the other. As noted above, we also believe that the current focus on Western equity-based systems may result in a number of dysfunctional consequences in organizations including chronic dissatisfaction, withdrawal behaviors, distrust, and conflict in organizations. Thus, the use of a broader set of allocation principles may enable organizations to minimize dissatisfaction or conflict, and divert more of their energies to task accomplishment. However, research is needed to determine the consequences of culturally sensitive allocation principles in organizations.

Third, and finally, although our review suggests that religious values affect justice ideologies, it is important to recognize that within any given religion there will be variability in the degree to which people adhere to the teachings of that religion. Thus, the more fundamental the individual's beliefs, the greater will be the difference in values regarding the distribution of outcomes. For example, those individuals who adhere more strictly to the teachings of Protestantism will be more likely to endorse the principles of proportionality and justified self interest than those who adhere less strictly to the same teachings. Likewise, although religious values may affect the culture of a society there will certainly be variability within that culture regarding beliefs about social justice. Furthermore, as noted above, factors other than religious beliefs (e.g., history, government, the ethnic background of the people, the economy, national resources, climate) may influence cultural values. For example, although most individuals from Latin American countries are Christian (e.g., Catholic), many of their beliefs (especially those of indigenous people) are consistent with the Eastern values of collectivism (Hofstede, 1980). The primary reason for this is that people in many Latin American nations have been influenced by the indigenous (Native or Indian) people of those countries. Interestingly, some Latin American countries (e.g., Columbia, Ecuador, Mexico, Peru, Venezuela) are predominantly made up of individuals who are Indian or those who are of mixed ethnicity (e.g., Mestizos represent a mixture of

Indian and White European ancestry) (www.worldpop.org/prbdata.htlm, 2001). As a result, both the ethnic background of the people and their religious values may play a pivotal role in determining cultural values and justice ideologies.

Theory and research on justice in organizational settings has contributed much to the understanding of behavior in organizational settings. Regrettably, the same theory and research has approached justice from a highly Western perspective. As a result, our understanding of justice in organizations is less complete than it would be if broader perspectives on justice were considered. Thus, we hope that future research and theory will consider more comprehensive views of social justice.

REFERENCES

Buchanan, A., & Mathieu, D. (1986). Philosophy and justice. In R. Cohen (Ed.), *Justice: Views from the social sciences* (pp. 11-46). New York: Plenum Publishing.

Cohen, R. (1986). Introduction. In R. Cohen (Ed.), *Justice: Views from the social sciences.* (pp. 1-10). New York: Plenum Publishing.

Deutsch, M. (1975). Equity, equality, and need: What determines which value will be used as the basis of distributive justice? *Journal of Social Issues, 31,* 137-150.

Erez, M., & Earley, C. (1993). *Culture, self-identity, and work.* New York: Oxford University Press.

Fitzgerald, C.P. (1966). *China: A short cultural history* (3rd ed.). New York: Praeger Publishers.

Gaer, J. (1963). *What the great religions believe.* New York: Dodd, Mead & Company.

Hofstede, G. (1980). *Culture's consequences: International differences in work-related values.* Beverly Hills: Sage Publications.

King, W. (1995). Judeo-Christian and Buddhist justice. *Journal of Buddhist Ethics, 2,* 1-14.

Lenski, G. (1963). *The religious factor: A sociologist's inquiry.* Garden City, NY: Anchor Books.

Lerner, M.J. (1980). *The belief in a just world: A fundamental delusion.* New York: Plenum Press.

Leung, K. (1997). Negotiation and reward allocation across cultures. In P. C. Earley & M. Erez (Eds.), *New perspectives in international Industrial and Organizational Psychology* (pp. 640-675). San Francisco: The New Lexington Press.

Leung, K., Su, S.K., & Morris, M.W. (2001). Justice in the culturally diverse workplace: The problems of over and under emphasis of cultural differences. In S. Gilliland, D. Steiner, & D. Skarlicki (Eds.), *Theoretical and cultural perspectives on organizational justice* (pp. 161-185). Greenwich, CT: Information Age.

Leventhal, G.S. (1980). What should be done with equity theory: New approaches to the study of fairness in social relationships. In K.J. Gergen, M.S. Greenberg, & R.H. Wills (Eds.), *Social exchange: Advances in theory and research* (pp. 27-55). New York: Plenum.

Little, D., & Twiss, S. B. (1965). *Comparative religious ethics.* New York: Harper & Row

Markus, H.R., & Kitayama, S. (1991a). Culture and the self: Implications for cognition, emotion, and motivation. *Psychological Review, 98*, 224-253.

Markus, H.R., & Kitayama, S. (1991b). Cultural variation and self-concept. In G.R. Goethals & J. Strauss (Eds.), *Multidisciplinary perspectives on the self* (pp. 18-48). New York: Springer-Verlag.

McFarlin, D.B., & Sweeney, P.D. (2001). Cross-cultural applications of organizational justice. In R. Cropanzano (Ed.), *Justice in the workplace* (vol. 2, pp. 67-95). Hillsdale, NJ: Lawrence Erlbaum.

Nigosian, S.A. (1994). *World faiths* (2nd ed). New York: St. Martin's Press.

Peterson, R.S. (1994). The role of values in predicting fairness judgments and support of affirmative action. *Journal of Social Issues, 50*(4), 95-115.

Rasinski, K.A. (1987). What's fair is fair—Or is it? Value differences underlying public views about social justice. *Journal of Personality and Social Psychology, 53*, 201-211.

Rhys David, I.W., & Rhys David, C.A.F. (1965). *Dialogues of the Buddha.* London: Luzac & Co.

Shafer, L. H. (1997). *Confucianism.* http://www.usao.edu/-usao-ids 3313/html confucianism.html.

Shapiro, D.L., & Tinsley, C.H. (2001). Intervening "fairly" in disputes among nationally-different employees: Is this possible? In S. Gilliland, D. Steiner, & D. Skarlicki (Eds.). *Theoretical and cultural perspectives on organizational justice* (pp. 187-216). Greenwich, CT: Information Age.

Smith, H. (1994). *The illustrated world's religions: A guide to our wisdom traditions.* San Francisco: Harper.

Smith, H. (1995). *Essays on world religions.* New York: Paragon House.

Steiner, D.D. (2001). Cultural influences on perceptions of distributive and procedural justice. In S. Gilliland, D. Steiner, & D. Skarlicki (Eds.), *Theoretical and cultural perspectives on organizational justice* (pp. 111-138). Greenwich, CT: Information Age.

Stone-Romero, E.F., & Stone, D.L. (1998). Religious and moral influences on work-related values and work quality. In D. Fedor & S. Ganoush (Eds.) *Advances in the management of organizational quality* (vol. 3, pp. 185-285). Greenwich, CT: JAI Press.

Tawney, R.H. (1958). Foreword. In M. Weber (Ed.), *The Protestant ethic and the spirit of capitalism* (pp. 1-11). New York: Charles Scribner's Sons.

The Dalai Lama. (1995). *Awakening the mind, lightening the heart: Core teachings of Tibetan Buddhism.* San Francisco: Harper Collins.

Thera, N. (1954). *Dhammapada.* London: John Murray.

Trice, H.M., & Beyer, J.M. (1993). *The cultures of work organizations.* Englewood Cliffs, NJ: Prentice-Hall.

Waley, A. (1989). *The Analects of Confucius.* (A. Waley, Trans. & Annotated). New York: Random House.

Walsh, M. (1995). *Thus I have heard (Diigha-Nikaaya).* London: Wisdom Publishers.

Weber, M. (1958). *The Protestant ethic and the spirit of capitalism.* (T. Parsons, Trans.) New York: Charles Scribner's Sons (Original work published 1904-1905).

www.worldpop.org/prbdata.htlm (2001).

CHAPTER 3

PATIENTS AND PHYSICIANS AS STAKEHOLDERS:

Justice in the Medical Context

Carol T. Kulik and Robert L. Holbrook, Jr.

ABSTRACT

One of the most important problems in the physician-patient relationship is the failure of patients to follow through on physicians' recommended treatments. We draw on the justice literature to frame patient adherence to treatment regimens as one example of a common organizational dilemma—how can authorities achieve compliance with their directives? This authority dilemma has received extensive attention in the justice literature, but justice concepts have rarely been applied to the medical domain. In this chapter, we present a model that explores how characteristics of a patient-physician encounter influence patient reactions and physician outcomes. We use fairness judgments as a central, mediating variable to understand how patients interpret their physician's behavior, decide whether to follow through on the physician's recommended treatment, and ultimately manage the uncertainty inherent in the medical context. We use the medical and the justice literatures to suggest avenues for future research in both medical and nonmedical domains.

The health care industry has been rocked by dramatic changes over the last decade. As more and more companies try to gain control over the rising cost of benefits, Americans increasingly find themselves participants in managed care programs and adjusting to new policies and constraints. For example, a patient's choice of physician may be limited by the health plans offered by his or her employer. Continuity with the patient's usual physician may be lost because of changes in plans offered by the patient's employer or changes in the plans in which the physician participates. In addition, pressures on physicians to increase their cost effectiveness may result in shorter appointment times and more limited hours (Thom & Campbell, 1997). All of these changes have the potential to profoundly change the patient-physician relationship (Kao, Green, Davis, Koplan, & Cleary, 1998) and introduce greater uncertainty for the patient. Yet the relationship between the physician and the patient is understudied (Thom & Campbell, 1997).

To date, justice researchers have largely ignored the medical context. While justice research has increasingly moved outside of the legal realm to explain individuals' reactions to authority in contexts as varied as business settings (Konovsky & Folger, 1991), police encounters (Tyler & Folger, 1980), and classrooms (Tyler & Caine, 1981, Study 2; Tyler, Rasinski & Spodick, 1985, Study 2), the patient's reaction to encounters with his or her physician has received surprisingly little attention. We identified only four studies that tried to apply justice concepts to a medical encounter (Hughes & Larson, 1991; Lence & Smith, 1987; Miles & Dansky, 1998; Swan, Sawyer, Van Matre, & McGee, 1985). Medical researchers note that justice research has not included the medical setting even when the research addresses concepts such as interpersonal trust that are clearly relevant to the medical setting (Thom & Campbell, 1997).

This lack of attention is unfortunate because complaints by both patients and physicians clearly reflect fairness concerns. Polls indicate that patients are dissatisfied with physicians' behavior and frequently switch medical providers because of it (Nazario, 1992). Patients complain that their physicians are not friendly, do not answer questions honestly, and are too interested in making money (Nazario, 1992). At the same time, physicians complain that the lack of patient adherence to recommended treatment interferes with their ability to successfully treat patient conditions (Tanouye, 1992). Fairness perceptions may be a central, mediating variable in understanding the patient's decision about whether to follow through on the physician's recommended treatment. A fairness model may provide guidance to physicians about the factors that contribute to patient commitment.

The medical context is one where patients may experience a high degree of uncertainty. Individuals who face uncertainty, particularly as it pertains to their own mortality, have a greater need for fairness and focus greater attention on factors related to fairness than individuals who are more sure about their future (Van den Bos & Miedema, 2000). In medical situations, many uncertainty issues arise. For example, patients experience uncertainty with respect to whether their physicians are trustworthy and are providing good advice. Most patients will not have the medical background or training to fully understand the causes or consequences of their medical condition and therefore need to take their physicians' advice on faith (Koehler, Fottler, & Swan, 1992). There is also considerable uncertainty related to outcomes associated with the medical encounter. Unknown factors may impact the recovery process, making it difficult to predict whether a selected treatment will solve the problem experienced by the patient. We believe uncertainty underscores the need for a model identifying antecedents of fairness in the patient-physician encounter.

In this chapter, we present a model that explores how characteristics of a physician visit influence patient and physician outcomes. Quality health care is the result of a series of exchanges between a physician and a patient, and the basic unit of service delivery is the physician visit (Koehler et al., 1992). During these visits, the patient and the physician jointly contribute to the patient's recovery (Given, Given, & Simoni, 1979). While the patient is dependent on the physician's expertise (Hughes & Larson, 1991), the patient also brings to the relationship personal knowledge about his or her symptoms and his or her ability and willingness to commit to a treatment regimen (DiMatteo, 1994a). Patient adherence to a treatment regimen has implications for the patient's recovery, the patient's satisfaction with the physician, and the physician's ability to build a stable customer base. Therefore, both the patient and the physician are stakeholders with a vested interest in the outcomes of their encounter (Koehler et al., 1992; Linn, Yager, Cope, & Leake, 1985; Rashid, Forman, Jagger, & Mann, 1989).

The model we present focuses on the psychological mechanisms operating in the patient-physician encounter. Therefore, the model does not consider a variety of demographic (e.g., patient age) or structural (e.g., size of the medical practice) variables that might also influence patient and physician outcomes. We draw upon traditional justice research as well as medical research to describe the role of traditional justice mechanisms (e.g., opportunity for voice, interpersonal treatment) in this context. However, we also note that the medical context identifies important variables that have not received much attention in the justice literature (e.g., the importance of the "stakes," physician expertise). Finally, we suggest some additional justice interventions (e.g., causal accounts) that have not been addressed in the medical literature. While the model is probably most appropriate for describing first time encounters between a physician and a new patient, it also has implications for the future of the relationship between the physician and patient.

THE CENTRAL ROLE OF FAIRNESS PERCEPTIONS

Imagine the following scenario: a patient comes to a physician's office for the first time. She describes several symptoms, none of which are immediately life threatening, but the combined effects of which are causing considerable discomfort. After additional discussion, and some clinical tests, the physician tells the patient that her condition is treatable through a combination of daily medication, a restricted diet, and regular exercise. The patient hesitates. Will she agree to the treatment regimen? More importantly, if she does agree, will she follow the physician's instructions and complete the regimen in full?

One of the biggest concerns in the medical literature is the increasing body of evidence demonstrating that patients frequently do not adhere to treatment regimens. While a physician's diagnosis and treatment are essential components of the health care process, these activities alone may not be sufficient to achieve the desired outcomes (Given et al., 1979). Controlling a chronic medical condition (e.g., hypertension, asthma) may require considerable effort on the patient's part (Barsky, 1976) and the failure of the patient to adhere to treatment recommendations can significantly limit the effectiveness of medical care (DiMatteo et al., 1993). Unfortunately, a meta-analysis of 537 medical studies covering a full range of patient adherence-related behaviors (e.g., appointment keeping, short-term medication, long-term medication, diets) found that adherence rates converged around 50% (Sackett & Snow, 1979). Another review found that the amount of noncompliance ranged from 19% to a high of 72% (Stimson, 1974). At least 38% of patients fail to follow short-term treatment plans (e.g., completing an antibiotic course) and at least 43% do not adhere to recommendations for long term treatment (e.g., taking anti-hypertensive medication) (Epstein & Cluss, 1982). More than 75% of patients are unwilling or unable to follow recommended lifestyle changes such as exercising or eating a low-fat diet (Brownell, Marlatt, Lichtenstein, & Wilson, 1986).

Patient satisfaction frequently receives attention in the medical literature. Medical theorists posit patient satisfaction as a mediator between characteristics of the patient-physician encounter and the patient's subsequent adherence to a treatment regimen (e.g., Bartlett et al., 1984; Becker, Drachman, & Kirscht, 1972; DiMatteo, Taranta, Friedman, & Prince, 1980; Hulka, Cassel, Kupper, & Burdette, 1976; Kincey, Bradshaw, & Ley, 1975; Koehler et al., 1992; Ley, Bradshaw, Kincey, & Atherton, 1976; Linn, Linn, & Stein, 1982; Ware, Davies-Avery, & Stewart, 1978). A fundamental assumption in the medical literature is that patients who are satisfied (with the physician and with the medical process) will be more likely to follow the physician's recommendations and complete the treatment regimen (Bartlett et al., 1984; DiMatteo et al., 1993; Korsch, Gozzi, & Francis, 1968; Roter, 1977). Empirical research, however, finds that the level of association between patient satisfaction and patient adherence is modest, suggesting that other variables may predict a larger proportion of the variance in compliance (Linn et al., 1982). In addition, the causal relationships among characteristics of the patient-physician encounter, patient satisfaction, and patient adherence to a treatment regimen are difficult to untangle. Self-reports of patient satisfaction and patient adherence are frequently collected in the same interview (e.g., Bartlett et al., 1984; Given et al., 1979) and measures of satisfaction frequently confound descriptions of the encounter (e.g., "treated with respect," "seemed to have a genuine interest in me as a person") with measures of overall satisfaction (e.g., Bartlett et al., 1984; Brody et al., 1989; Putnam, Stiles, Jacob, & James, 1985). As a result, researchers in the medical field have concluded that while characteristics of the patient-physician relationship clearly influence patient adherence to a treatment regimen, "the actual mechanisms by which these influences occur remain obscure" (Becker, 1985, p. 547).

The justice literature is uniquely situated to cast light on these mechanisms. Research in a variety of domains has demonstrated that individuals' perceptions of justice influence their willingness to comply with authorities of various kinds. Procedural justice judgments have been found to influence litigants' acceptance of awards from court-ordered arbitration (Lind, Kulik, Ambrose, & de Vera Park, 1993), workers' acceptance of task assignments and work goals (Earley & Lind, 1987; Lind, Kanfer, & Earley, 1990), citizens' willingness to obey traffic laws and other everyday legal rules (Tyler, 1990), and managers' compliance with strategic directives in multinational firms (Kim & Mauborgne, 1993).

Figure 1 presents a model describing the patient's reaction to a medical encounter with a physician. As shown in the figure, we present fairness judgments as a central mediating variable. Medical encounters are filled with uncertainty and heighten the patient's sensitivity to fairness. We suggest that fairness judgments play an important role in facilitating patient adherence to the prescribed regimen, the ultimate recovery of the patient, and other important patient responses and physician outcomes. In developing this model, we draw upon Lind and Tyler's concept of a "fairness heuristic" (Lind & Tyler, 1988; Tyler & Lind, 1992).

Lind and Tyler (1988, pp. 209-214) point out that decisions about whether to accept an authority's directives present some of the same basic problems regardless of whether the authority is a legal figure, an organizational supervisor, or, in our context, a medical doctor. It is often difficult for a person to determine whether a directive presented by an authority is legitimate or appropriate, and therefore some kind of rule-of-thumb must be used in deciding whether or not to accept the authority's directive. Uncertainty about the authority's directive is especially evident in the patient-physician encounter. Patients generally know very little about the specifics of medical care and therefore the acceptance of a treatment regimen requires placing their faith in the physician's expertise (Koehler et al., 1992).

Since the quality of the authority's directive cannot be directly evaluated, how can a patient decide whether the physician's recommended treatment should be accepted? Lind and Tyler (Lind & Tyler, 1988; Tyler &

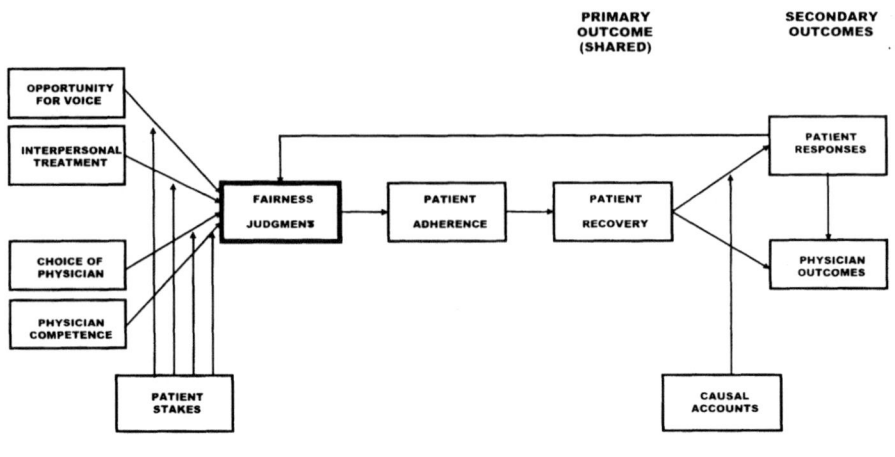

Lind, 1992) suggest that people solve these authority dilemmas by using their evaluations of the process to generate a global impression of the procedural fairness of an authority, which is then used to determine whether or not the authority should be obeyed. Since impressions of the process and procedures used by authorities are usually available prior to impressions of the outcomes they generate, judgments of the fairness of process and procedures form the heart of the fairness heuristic. The fairness heuristic is clearly applicable to the medical encounter. The patient must decide whether to accept the physician's treatment recommendation before any observable outcomes are available.

As shown in Figure 1, fairness judgments have an indirect effect on both primary and secondary outcomes. The patient's adherence to the treatment regimen has a direct effect on the primary outcome—the patient's ultimate recovery (Given et al., 1979). In turn, a successful treatment may also lead to other positive patient reactions. Research demonstrates a positive association between patients' health and patient satisfaction (Greenley, Young, & Schoenherr, 1982; Hall, Feldstein, Fretwell, Rowe & Epstein, 1990; Hall, Roter, & Katz, 1988; Stewart & Wanklin, 1978). In addition, patient satisfaction is associated with intentions to return to the same medical facility (Lence & Smith, 1987), and to maintain a relationship with the same physician (Breslau & Mortimer, 1981; DiMatteo, Prince, & Taranta, 1979; Doyle & Ware, 1977; Kasteller, Kane, Olsen, & Thetford, 1976; Marquis, Davies, & Ware, 1983; Ware, Wright, Snyder, & Chu, 1975).

Positive patient reactions have an impact on physician outcomes. For example, Koehler et al. (1992) suggest that patient satisfaction leads to and enhances physician satisfaction. In fact, Swan et al. (1985) suggest that one way health organizations can increase *physician* satisfaction is by improving their patients' perceptions of fair treatment. Satisfied patients are more likely to return to the same physician—an important outcome for physicians who wish to enhance their practices, since return business saves the physician time in learning the medical history of new patients (Koehler et al., 1992). In contrast, dissatisfied patients are more likely to file malpractice claims (Beckman, Markakis, Suchman, & Frankel, 1994; Hickson, Clayton, Githens, & Sloan, 1992; Shapiro et al., 1989; Vaccarino, 1977), increasing the physician's cost of doing business.

Figure 1 also includes a feedback loop from the patient's responses to fairness judgments. The fairness heuristic explanation suggests that the outcomes resulting from a specific encounter with an authority are integrated into subsequent procedural justice judgments (Lind et al., 1993; Van den Bos, Lind, Vermunt, & Wilke, 1997; Van den Bos, Vermunt & Wilke, 1997; Van den Bos, Wilke, Lind, & Vermunt, 1998). Because process evaluations have already been used to form a first impression of fairness and because people tend to hold onto these early impressions of fairness, the impact of outcomes is not as strong as the effect of process (Lind & Tyler, 1988, p. 228).

Figure 1 presents four antecedents of fairness judgments in the medical context. The first two, opportunity for voice and interpersonal treatment, are characteristics of interactions with authorities that have consistently been found to influence perceptions of fairness. The other two antecedents, choice of physician and physician competence, have received little attention in the justice literature although they are frequently discussed in the medical context. These two antecedents represent characteristics of the broader organizational context (how authorities are allocated, how competent those authorities are perceived to be) that have implications for the perceived fairness of subsequent encounters with these authorities. The two pairs of antecedents are conceptually distinct, but we believe a model of fairness in the patient-physician relationship must consider the characteristics of both the specific encounter and the broader context in order to understand the role that perceived fairness plays in patient adherence to treatment regimens. Individuals facing the ambiguities associated with medical problems and treatment are likely to consider both sets of antecedents in an effort to feel a sense of control and reduce their subjective uncertainty (Van den Bos & Lind, in press). In the next two sections, we describe these antecedents in greater detail and outline their effects on fairness perceptions.

TRADITIONAL ANTECEDENTS OF FAIRNESS PERCEPTIONS: OPPORTUNITY FOR VOICE AND INTERPERSONAL TREATMENT

Having established that uncertainty in the medical context exacerbates the need for fairness and patients' fairness judgments are likely to play an important role in determining patient adherence to treatment regimens, patient recovery, and other outcomes important to both patients and physicians, we now turn our attention to the antecedents of these judgments. Figure 1 illustrates the effects of two variables (opportunity for voice and interpersonal treatment) that have received extensive attention in both the justice and medical literatures.

Procedures vary in terms of structural components (e.g., the degree to which decision recipients can contribute to the decision process) and social components (e.g., the quality of interpersonal treatment received from the decision maker) (Cropanzano & Greenberg, 1997). Both of these components have been found to influence people's reactions to authorities in nonmedical contexts.

The opportunity to contribute information into an authority's decision has been labeled "voice" (Folger, 1977). When the trustworthiness of an authority is unknown, individuals infer trustworthiness by observing opportunities for input (Van den Bos, Wilke, & Lind, 1998). Opportunities for voice may indirectly influence the authority's decision by providing relevant information to the authority (decision control). However, even in the absence of direct influence on the decision, people who have an opportunity to provide input to a decision consistently report higher perceptions of justice (Bies & Shapiro, 1988; Lind et al., 1990; Tyler et al., 1985). Further, recipients report more positive evaluations of decision authorities who offer voice, regardless of whether the decision-maker is a court authority (Tyler et al., 1985, Study 1), a supervisor (Korsgaard & Roberson, 1995), or a teacher (Tyler et al., 1985, Study 2).

Decision recipients also respond to the quality of interpersonal treatment received from authorities (Greenberg, 1993). Interpersonal treatment during social interactions reflects the decision maker's concern for the recipient. In particular, politeness and respect signal greater concern than undignified, disrespectful, or impolite treatment (Bies & Moag, 1986; Tyler, Degoey, & Smith, 1996). Interpersonal treatment has been found to influence recipients' reactions to decisions in a variety of nonmedical contexts. Tyler (1994) analyzed data from two field studies examining citizen encounters with legal authorities and supervisors' handling of employee problems. Structural equation modeling suggested that relational concerns (e.g., polite treatment, honesty) dominated justice perceptions, affective reactions, and acceptance of decisions. In a field study of hospital employees, Aquino and colleagues found that better interpersonal treatment from supervisors led to higher satisfaction with the supervisors (Aquino, Griffeth, Allen, & Hom, 1997).

In the medical context, a great deal of research attention has been devoted to the physician's interpersonal behavior as a factor in patient satisfaction. Unfortunately, this research does not always distinguish between voice (opportunity for the patient to provide input to the decision) and interpersonal treatment (the physician's interpersonal sensitivity). For example, a field study examining the communication skills of primary care physicians measured interpersonal skills using items indicative of both voice (e.g., "allows expression of feelings") and interpersonal treatment (e.g., "conveys understanding and/or empathy") (Bartlett et al., 1984). Roter (1977) used a composite measure called "indirect satisfaction" that included items related to both voice (e.g., "I think my doctor forgets to ask about the problems I've had in the past") and interpersonal treatment (e.g., "Sometimes doctors make the patient feel foolish"). Nonetheless, there has been sufficient attention to both of these variables in the medical literature to draw firm conclusions that both opportunity for voice and interpersonal treatment positively influence patient reactions in medical encounters. This research is described below.

Opportunity for Voice

In a now classic study, Korsch and colleagues (1968) taped 800 pediatric emergency room visits, performed a content analysis on the verbal exchanges, and related the coded verbal behaviors to mothers' reactions to the encounter. The results of this study suggested that mothers were more satisfied when the physician attending to their child gave mothers the opportunity to express their "main worries" about the child's illness. An extensive meta-analysis of studies using this paradigm (in which aspects of the exchange are coded by observers and related to patient satisfaction) concluded that "partnership building" behaviors (behaviors in which the physician tries to increase the likelihood of patient participation by requesting questions from the patient, agreeing to suggestions from the patient, or using "we" as a sentence stem) were clearly and positively related to patient satisfaction (Hall et al., 1988). Older patients were more satisfied with physician encounters in which they were questioned about and given an opportunity to provide information about their own agenda items (Greene, Adelman, Friedmann, & Charon, 1994). Patients reported greater satisfaction when their physicians displayed more of a "customer approach," in which they allowed the patients to express their opinions and thoughts about an appropriate treatment plan even if patients didn't get the treatment they wanted (Eisenthal & Lazare, 1976).

Opportunity for voice also appears to have a positive association with other patient outcomes besides satisfaction. Using a scenario methodology, Hughes and Larson (1991) found that vignettes describing patients who had input into the selection of a prescription medication to treat an asthma condition resulted in higher perceptions of procedural fairness. Patients who perceived themselves as actively participating in the therapeutic process reported greater adherence to a hypertension regimen (Given et al., 1979). After controlling for baseline illness severity, patients who had played an active role in an initial physician visit reported less physical discomfort from their symptoms a week later than patients who had played a passive role (Brody, Miller, Lerman, Smith, & Caputo, 1989). Levinson, Roter, Mullooly, Dull, and Frankel (1997) found that physicians who had no malpractice claims filed against them engaged in more facilitation behavior (solicitation, checking understanding, and encouraging patients to talk) than physicians who had had claims filed against them.

Interpersonal Treatment

In addition to research on opportunity for voice, research in the medical domain has demonstrated that patients respond positively to other aspects of physician interpersonal behavior. Interpersonal behavior shows strong associations with patient satisfaction. In one study, trained observers watching through a oneway mirror rated physicians on a checklist as they interviewed a patient. Patient satisfaction was highly correlated with physician courtesy (formally greeting and discharging the patient) (Comstock, Hooper, Goodwin, & Goodwin, 1982). DiMatteo and Hays (1980) found that patients' overall satisfaction with family practice residents was very highly correlated with their perceptions of the residents' kindness and considerateness, concern about patient feelings, ability to relieve patient worries, and ability to treat the patient with respect without "talking down." Similar results were reported by DiMatteo et al. (1979), who found that patient satisfaction was most highly correlated with perceptions that the physicians cared for the patients as persons.

Interpersonal treatment also has implications for outcomes other than patient satisfaction. Korsch and colleagues (Freemon, Negrette, Davis, & Korsch, 1971; Korsch et al., 1968) have found that, in general, the greater the friendship and warmth expressed by the physician, the greater the patient's commitment to a treatment regimen. Hall and colleagues found that the communication of affect between the physician and the patient influenced whether the patient kept subsequent appointments (Hall, Roter, & Rand, 1981). Thom and Campbell (1997) found that focus group participants' trust in their physicians was associated with several categories of interpersonal treatment (e.g., expressing caring and demonstrating honesty/respect for the patient). Finally, while 71% of a sample of sued physicians reported a relatively high level of respect for their patients, only 45% of suing patients believed that their physician had such a high level of respect for them (Shapiro et al., 1989).

In general, research in both nonmedical and medical contexts strongly suggests that opportunity for voice and interpersonal treatment will influence patients' perceptions of fairness in the medical encounter and, indirectly, influence other patient reactions and physician outcomes.

OTHER ANTECEDENTS OF FAIRNESS PERCEPTIONS: CHOICE OF PHYSICIAN AND PHYSICIAN COMPETENCE

Figure 1 indicates that there are two additional antecedents that may contribute to perceived fairness in the medical encounter. We include these antecedents because they have been extensively discussed in the medical literature. However, these variables have received little attention in the justice literature and may represent interesting areas for future research.

Choice of Physician

In the traditional model of health service, patients generally had free choice of physicians. However, in some current health maintenance organizations (HMOs), patients may find their physician choices to be severely limited. The patient may be given a choice of physicians, but the choice is meaningless since the patient is unfamiliar with any of the HMO's personnel. In other HMOs, the organization may directly assign a physician to the patient's case (Schmittdiel, Selby, Grumbach, & Quesenberry, 1997).

A few studies in the medical literature have suggested that physician choice may be linked to patient satisfaction. For example, in a large-scale survey of HMO members, Schmittdiel et al. (1997) found that patients who chose their personal physicians were far more satisfied than patients who had their physicians assigned to them by the HMO. Weyrauch (1996) found that patients reported more satisfaction with HMO visits when they were given access to the physician they wished to see. Finally, patients who reported that they had had "enough choice" of physicians were more likely to trust their physicians (Kao et al., 1998).

These findings, while based on only a few studies, suggest that choice of physician may contribute to the patient's perceived fairness of the medical encounter. When the patient evaluates the fairness of his or her medical encounter, the patient may consider not just the behavior of his or her own physician, but the behavior of the larger medical organization as well. Assigning patients to physicians without regard for their personal preferences may convey a cold, impersonal, uncaring attitude about the patient's well-being. Alternatively, the assignment may evoke doubt in the patient's mind about the physician's capabilities or trustworthiness. The relation between physician choice and patient perceptions of fairness seems to warrant additional research.

Research in the justice literature has sometimes used participant choice as a voice operationalization. For example, Earley and Lind (1987) found that procedures that permitted employees to choose their own task assignments resulted in more perceived fairness than procedures that did not permit choice. Cropanzano and Folger (1989) found that participants who had been permitted to choose which of two tasks would be used as a basis for performance-based compensation perceived less unfairness with low compensation than participants who were not permitted choice. Similarly, research in the medical literature suggests that patients who are permitted a choice among treatment plans are more likely to adhere to the plan (Eisenthal, Emery, Lazare, & Udin, 1979).

However, we could find no research in the justice literature that specifically examined how a participant's choice *of an authority* might influence fairness perceptions. This is an interesting area for future study, especially since there are procedures in nonmedical domains that vary in the amount of authority choice they permit participants. For example, some nonunion organization dispute resolution procedures use a "open-door" policy in which employees with a grievance can approach *anyone* in upper management with their complaint, while other procedures use a third-party decision-maker appointed by the organization (Cascio, 1995, pp. 496-497).

Physician Competence

Figure 1 also suggests that physician competence contributes to patient perceptions of fairness. Physician competence appears to contribute to patient reactions above and beyond the physician's interpersonal behavior (e.g., opportunity for voice and interpersonal treatment): "A provider's merely being nice or caring, in the absence of positive or negative indications of task performance, does not supply the evidence on competence that a patient needs in order to decide whether to attend to information, stick to a regimen, and generally have confidence in the quality of medical care received" (Hall et al., 1988, p. 668). In their meta-analysis, Hall et al. (1988) examined studies in which physician technical competence was evaluated by observers other than the patient (either through multi-item checklists or global ratings) and concluded that greater physician competence is associated with patient satisfaction and adherence to treatment regimens.

Patients rarely have access to direct information about physician competence and therefore competence must be inferred from observable behavior. However, perceptions of physician competence seem to be inferred from different aspects of physician behavior than perceptions of physician interpersonal skills (Willson & McNamara, 1982). For example, research has suggested that physician behaviors such as providing more information to the patient (Comstock et al., 1982), ordering more medical tests (DiMatteo et al., 1993), spending more time on the physical examination (Robbins et al., 1993), and acting with certainty (Johnson, Levenkron, Suchman, & Manchester, 1988) all contribute to perceptions of competence and correlate highly with patient satisfaction and/or adherence to medical treatments. DiMatteo et al. (1979) found patients' satisfaction was significantly positively correlated with perceptions of their physicians' intelligence.

Only a handful of justice studies have directly measured authority competence. Barclay and Harland (1995) investigated the perceived fairness of a peer performance appraisal system. Manipulating the peer rater's education and experience influenced perceptions of rater competence as well as perceptions of fairness and overall satisfaction with the procedure. Despite the lack of direct research attention, competence appears to be a key element contributing to perceptions of an authority figure (Folger & Cropanzano, 1998). Following a tax audit, Stalans and Lind (1997) asked taxpayers and their representatives to describe their impressions of the auditor. One of the categories of comments that emerged with some frequency involved comments about the auditor's competence (e.g., references to the auditor's knowledge and skill in understanding tax law, facts, and accounting procedures).

Tyler and Lind (1992, p. 156) contrast associations between ratings of authority competence and perceptions of justice in a management and a legal setting. In both studies, competence was less important than other authority behaviors (ethicality, honesty, consistency) but competence was more related to fairness perceptions in the management setting than in the legal setting. It is interesting to note that the questions used in this research (e.g., "How hard did authority try to solve problem? How hard did authority try to find satisfactory solution?") seem to be conceptually similar to the measures of authority effort (e.g., number of medical tests, amount of time spent on the physical examination) used in the medical literature. More research on perceptions of authority competence seems warranted, especially in settings where participants have the opportunity to choose among authorities (e.g., in choosing between jobs reporting to different bosses, in choosing among teachers in elective courses).

MODERATING VARIABLES IN THE PHYSICIAN-PATIENT ENCOUNTER

Figure 1 indicates that there are two variables that act as moderators in our model. The moderators represent opportunities for these two disparate literatures (justice and medical) to contribute to one another.

Stakes

In earlier sections of this chapter, we presented a series of antecedent factors that we believe contributes to a patient's fairness perceptions in a medical encounter. These antecedent factors, especially the procedural ones (opportunity for voice, interpersonal treatment, choice of physician) are likely to have strong effects on fairness perceptions and other important patient reactions. In a review of the medical literature, Lochman (1983, p. 103) concluded that "physicians' conduct and interaction with their patients was a more powerful source of influence on patient satisfaction than ... physicians' perceived competence...." This conclusion is certainly consistent with the justice literature, which has consistently replicated procedural effects on participant reactions.

However, we question whether these procedural factors will always exercise the same strength in influencing patient perceptions of fairness. Figure 1 presents "stakes" (i.e., the severity of the patient's condition) as a moderator variable, interacting with each of the antecedent variables (opportunity for voice, interpersonal treatment, choice of physician, and physician competence) to influence fairness judgments. Specifically, we suggest that patients will be *more* sensitive to physician competence and interpersonal treatment, and *less* sensitive to choice and voice opportunities, when their medical condition is more severe.

This prediction is based on findings in the medical literature that patients suffering from more severe illnesses express less interest in being active participants in their treatment decisions (Benbassat, Pilpel, & Tidhar, 1998). These findings have been replicated with a variety of methodologies. For example, Degner and Sloan (1992) found that as many as 91% of their healthy respondents, but only 41% of their cancer patients, expressed a preference for active involvement in clinical decision making. Krantz, Baum, and Wideman (1980) reported a 42.1% score on an instrument measuring the desire for participation in decision making among healthy college students, but Pendelton and House (1984) found that the score for older diabetics on the same instrument was only 15.4%. Using a scenario methodology, Ende, Kazis, Ash, and Moskowitz (1989) found that the more serious the hypothetical disease situation they presented to respondents, the less the patients wanted to be involved in decisions. Finally, DiMatteo et al. (1979) found that patient reactions to physician behavior depended on the severity of their conditions. For patients with less serious illnesses, satisfaction was highly correlated with physician communication behaviors. These patients were more concerned that the physician had listened to what they had to say (i.e., voice). However, the satisfaction of patients with more serious illnesses was more closely associated with perceptions of whether the physicians cared about them as persons (i.e., interpersonal treatment) (DiMatteo et al., 1979).

Some authors (e.g., Lind, 1990) have suggested that it is time to examine boundary conditions that set limits on justice-related phenomena, and several commentators (Greenberg, 1990; Tyler, 1987) have asked whether justice matters less as outcomes become more important. To date, research examining the effects of stakes has failed to find a moderating effect. Tyler (1987) examined citizens' ratings of the fairness of the police and other public officials. He found that the positive effects of fair procedures influenced evaluations of the authorities for both important and unimportant outcomes. Lind (1990) found that the amount of money involved in cases sent to a court-annexed arbitration program did not influence the impact of fairness perceptions on subsequent evaluations of the experience. However, it is important to note that these authors have tested a different moderating effect than the one we are proposing here. Tyler (1987) and Lind (1990) were suggesting that the size of the stakes would moderate the effect of fairness perceptions on subsequent evaluations (i.e., perceptions of procedural fairness are less important when the stakes are high); we are suggesting that the antecedent factors are weighted differently depending on the size of the stakes.

Why would voice and choice effects matter less when the patient's condition is more severe? We suggest that these moderating effects reflect the different kinds and amounts of expertise that the patient and physician bring to the medical encounter. When the physical complaint is not severe (e.g., a minor rash, or a psoriasis condition that flares up only infrequently), the patient may see the kinds of knowledge that he or she brings to the encounter (e.g., about the patient's lifestyle or treatment preferences) as nearly as important as the physician's expertise in diagnosis and treatment. However, as the physical complaint becomes more severe, perhaps even life threatening, the patient's interest is in maximizing the probability of solving the problem. That doesn't mean that the patient no longer wants to be treated fairly, but it does suggest that opportunity for voice may be a less essential component of fairness perceptions.

Causal Accounts

Figure 1 also presents causal accounts as a moderating variable operating between the patient recovery and subsequent responses (e.g., overall satisfaction, intention to maintain the relationship with the physician). The prediction is derived directly from the justice literature. Causal accounts are explanations that provide a rationale, after the fact, for decisions/outcomes in an attempt to mitigate the harmdoer's responsibility (Bies, 1987). In a variety of contexts, research finds that causal accounts mitigate negative reactions of decision recipients to unfavorable outcomes (Folger & Cropanzano, 1998). For example, causal accounts have been found to "soften the blow" of an organizational pay freeze (Schaubroeck, May, & Brown, 1994), job relocations (Daly, 1995), sex-based promotion systems (Bobocel & Farrell, 1996), and layoffs (Brockner, DeWitt, Grover, & Reed, 1990). In addition, research has identified a variety of causal accounts that are effective in different situations, including ideological accounts (e.g., appeals to superordinate goals), referential accounts (i.e., comparisons to others), reputational accounts, and intimidation (Bies, 1987; Greenberg, 1991).

There has been little direct empirical attention to the causal accounts provided by physicians to their patients. In the medical literature, the physician's ability to provide explanations about the diagnosis and the treatment is cited as one factor contributing to patient satisfaction (e.g., Bartlett et al., 1984; Ross & Duff, 1982). However, our concern here is with accounts that occur later in the relationship—after patients have participated in the treatment and experienced unfavorable outcomes.

In our review of the medical literature, we were struck by the number of articles that sought to explain why patients file malpractice suits against their physicians. Negative outcomes alone do not predict litigation behavior (Brennan, Localio, Laird,1989; Brennan et al., 1990); rather, it is the combined effects of negative outcomes and patient dissatisfaction with physician behavior that results in the patient filing a lawsuit (Levinson, 1994).

One investigation of families who had brought malpractice claims after their infants had experienced permanent injuries or deaths reported that 24% of the respondents had filed "when they realized that physicians had failed to be completely honest with them about what had happened," and 20% of the respondents filed "when they decided that the courtroom was the only forum in which they could find out what happened from the physicians who provided care" (Hickson et al., 1992). In other words, they had filed claims in an attempt to get an explanation. Similarly, Burg (1996) reported that a widow sued a physician after requesting and failing to receive an explanation about why her husband died. Patients are less satisfied with the amount of explanations provided by their physicians than with any other aspect of their care (Adamson, Tschann, Gullion, & Oppenberg, 1989).

These examples suggest that causal accounts may be useful in mitigating patients' (and patients' families') responses to unfavorable medical outcomes. Future research should examine the type and timing of causal accounts that are beneficial in the medical context.

CONCLUSIONS

The model presented in Figure 1 accomplishes three different purposes. First, our efforts to organize and interpret the medical research suggest this is a viable context for justice investigations. Uncertainty is inherent in the medical context and this focuses the patient's attention on justice issues. Our review suggests that antecedent factors traditionally studied in the justice literature may also be effective in producing positive perceptions of fairness in medical encounters.

Second, our integration of the medical and justice literatures has identified possible avenues for future research which are not yet addressed. For example, the medical literature suggests that the main effects of choice of authority and authority competence might be usefully investigated in nonmedical domains. In addition, the medical literature suggests that the size of stakes might be pursued as a moderator variable. In contrast, the medical research has given little systematic attention to the value of causal accounts following negative outcomes.

Finally, and perhaps most importantly, our model suggests some ways in which medical providers can improve patient adherence and subsequently result in positive outcomes for both the patient and the attending physician. While there is no question that patient adherence is an important variable, commentators in the medical literature have complained that the advice they receive from researchers is not usually helpful (Levinson, 1994). Specifically, global suggestions to physicians, such as "improve your communication skills" are unlikely to produce dramatic change. However, the justice literature could be used to develop training programs and other interventions focused on improving specific physician skills in providing explanations, presenting opportunities for patient voice, and treating patients with respect and dignity.

We emphasize that the burden for enhancing most of the procedural antecedents falls on the shoulders of the physicians, because they control the intensity, quality, and cost of health services delivery (Koehler et al., 1992). Some researchers have attempted to develop interventions directed at the patients, and this research suggests that patients can be trained to discuss concerns with their physicians (Greenfield, Kaplan, & Ware, 1985; Greenfield, Kaplan, Ware, Yano, & Frank, 1988; Roter, 1977). However, while these interventions may increase participation, the results indicate that voice opportunity that is created by the patient does not enhance patient satisfaction with the encounter (Greenfield et al., 1985). In fact, one study found that patients who were encouraged to ask their physicians questions were *less* satisfied than patients who were not so encouraged (Roter, 1977). This finding can be interpreted within the framework of the justice heuristic. Recall that patients use the authority's behavior to decide whether they should adhere to the authority's directives. When the patient realizes that he or she is creating opportunity for voice instead of the authority, the patient may interpret this as a failure on the part of the authority—resulting in lower perceptions of fairness, and a lower likelihood of adherence to the authority's recommended treatment.

Unfortunately, there are significant barriers constraining physician behavioral change. Physicians are largely unaware of noncompliance problems and think that the statistics result from other people's patients (DiMatteo, 1994a). Some physicians may believe that sharing control of decision making with patients will make them appear less competent (Lerman et al., 1990). In addition, some structural aspects of health organizations may place significant pressure on physicians to see many patients in a brief period. As a result, physicians are able to spend very little time listening to patients and tend to limit patients' communication of information (DiMatteo, 1994b; Freemon et al., 1971; Putnam et al., 1985; Kaplan, Greenfield, Gandek, Rogers, & Ware, 1996).

ACKNOWLEDGEMENTS

We thank Donna Blancero, Allan Lind, and the participants in the 1999 International Roundtable on Organizational Justice for their helpful comments on our model.

REFERENCES

Adamson, T.E., Tschann, J.M., Gullion, D.S., & Oppenberg, A.A. (1989). Physician communication skills and malpractice claims: A complex relationship. *The Western Journal of Medicine, 150,* 356-360.

Aquino, K., Griffeth, R.W., Allen, D.G., & Hom, P.W. (1997). Integrating justice constructs into the turnover process: A test of a referent cognitions model. *Academy of Management Journal, 40,* 1208-1227.

Barclay, J.H., & Harland, L.K. (1995). Peer performance appraisals: The impact of rater competence, rater location, and rating correctability on fairness perceptions. *Group and Organization Management, 20,* 39-60.

Barsky, A.J., III (1976). Patient heal thyself: Activating the ambulatory medical patient. *Journal of Chronic Diseases, 29,* 585-597.

Bartlett, E.E., Grayson, M., Barker, R., Levine, D.M., Golden, A., & Libber, S. (1984). The effects of physician communications skills on patient satisfaction, recall, and adherence. *Journal of Chronic Diseases, 37,* 755-764.

Becker, M.H. (1985). Patient adherence to prescribed therapies. *Medical Care, 23,* 539-555.

Becker, M.H., Drachman, R.H., & Kirscht, J.P. (1972). Motivations as predictors of health behavior. *Health Services Reports, 87,* 852-862.

Beckman, H.B., Markakis, K.M., Suchman, A.L., & Frankel, R.M. (1994). The doctor-patient relationship and malpractice. *Archives of Internal Medicine, 154,* 1365-1370.

Benbassat, J., Pilpel, D., & Tidhar, M. (1988). Patients' preferences for participation in clinical decision making: A review of published surveys. *Behavioral Medicine, 24(2),* 81-88.

Bies, R.J. (1987). The predicament of injustice: The management of moral outrage. In L.L. Cummings & B. M. Staw (Eds.), *Research in organizational behavior* (Vol. 9, pp. 289-319). Greenwich, CT: JAI Press.

Bies, R.J., & Moag, J.S. (1986). Interactional justice: Communication criteria for fairness. In B. Sheppard (Ed.), *Research on negotiation in organizations* (Vol. 1, pp. 43-55). Greenwich, CT: JAI Press.

Bies, R.J., & Shapiro, D.L. (1988). Voice and justification: Their influence on procedural fairness judgments. *Academy of Management Journal, 31,* 66-685.

Bobocel, D.R., & Farrell, A.C. (1996). Sex-based promotion decisions and interactional fairness: Investigating the influence of managerial accounts. *Journal of Applied Psychology, 81,* 22-35.

Brennan, T.A., Localio, R.J., & Laird, N.L. (1989). Reliability and validity of judgments concerning adverse events suffered by hospitalized patients. *Medical Care, 27,* 1148-1158.

Brennan, T.A., Localio, R.J., Leape, L.L., Laird, N.M., Peterson, L., Hiatt, H.H., & Barnes, B.A. (1990). Identification of adverse events occurring during hospitalization: A cross-sectional study of litigation, quality assurance, and medical records at two teaching hospitals. *Annals of Internal Medicine, 112(3),* 221-226.

Breslau, N., & Mortimer, E. A. (1981). Seeing the same doctor: Determinants of satisfaction with specialty care for disabled children. *Medical Care, 19,* 741-758.

Brockner, J., Dewitt, R.L., Grover, S., & Reed, T. (1990). When it is especially important to explain why: Factors affecting the relationship between managers' explanations of a layoff and survivors' reactions to the layoff. *Journal of Experimental Social Psychology, 26,* 389-407.

Brody, D.S., Miller, S.M., Lerman, C.E., Smith, D.G., & Caputo, G.C. (1989). Patient perception of involvement in medical care: Relationship to illness attitudes and outcomes. *Journal of General Internal Medicine, 4,* 506-511.

Brody, D.S., Miller, S.M., Lerman, C.E., Smith, D.G., Lazaro, C.G., & Blum, M.J. (1989). The relationship between patients' satisfaction with their physicians and perceptions about interventions they desired and received. *Medical Care, 27,* 1027-1035.

Brownell, K.D., Marlatt, G.A., Lichtenstein, E., & Wilson, G.T. (1986). Understanding and preventing relapse. *American Psychologist, 41,* 765-782.

Burg, B. (1997, February 12). Malpractice: Doctor's six fatal mistakes. *Medical Economics,* 226-236.

Cascio, W.F. (1995). *Managing human resources* (4th ed.). New York: McGraw-Hill.

Comstock, L.M., Hooper, E.M., Goodwin, J.M., & Goodwin, J.S. (1982). Physician behaviors that correlate with patient satisfaction. *Journal of Medical Education, 57,* 105-112.

Cropanzano, R., & Folger, R. (1989). Referent cognitions and task decision autonomy: Beyond equity theory. *Journal of Applied Psychology, 74,* 293-299.

Cropanzano, R., & Greenberg, J. (1997). Progress in organizational justice: Tunneling through the maze. In C.L. Cooper & I.T. Robertson (Eds.), *International review of industrial and organizational psychology* (pp. 317-372). New York: Wiley.

Daly, J.P. (1995). Explaining changes to employees: The influence of justifications and change outcomes on employees' fairness judgments. *Journal of Applied Behavioral Science, 31,* 415-428.

Degner, L.F., & Sloan, J.A. (1992). Decision making during serious illness: What role do patients really want to play? *Journal of Clinical Epidemiology, 45,* 941-950.

DiMatteo, M.R. (1994a). Enhancing patient adherence to medical recommendations. *Journal of the American Medical Association, 271,* 79-83.

DiMatteo, M.R. (1994b). The physician-patient relationship: Effects on the quality of health care. *Clinical Obstetrics and Gynecology, 37 (1),* 149-161.

DiMatteo, M.R., & Hays, R. (1980). The significance of patients' perceptions of physician conduct: A study of patient satisfaction in a family practice center. *Journal of Community Health, 6(1),* 18-34.

DiMatteo, M.R., Prince, L.M., & Taranta, A. (1979). Patients' perceptions of physicians' behavior: Determinants of patient commitment to the therapeutic relationship. *Journal of Community Health, 4(4),* 280-290.

DiMatteo, M.R., Sherbourne, C.D., Hays, R.D., Ordway, L., Kravitz, R.L., McGlynn, E.A., Kaplan, S., & Rogers, W.H. (1993). Physicians' characteristics influence patients' adherence to medical treatment: Results from the medical outcomes study. *Health Psychology, 12 (2),* 93-102.

DiMatteo, M.R., Taranta, A., Friedman, H.S., & Prince, L.M. (1980). Predicting patient satisfaction from physicians' nonverbal communication skills. *Medical Care, 18,* 376-387.

Doyle, B.J., & Ware, J.E. (1977). Physician conduct and other factors that affect consumer satisfaction with medical care. *Journal of Medical Education, 52,* 793-801.

Earley, P.C., & Lind, E.A. (1987). Procedural justice and participation in task selection: The role of control in mediating justice judgments. *Journal of Personality and Social Psychology, 52,* 1148-1160.

Eisenthal, S., & Lazare, A. (1976). Evaluation of the initial interview in a walk-in clinic: The patient's perspective on a "customer approach." *Journal of Nervous and Mental Disease, 162,* 169-176.

Eisenthal, S., Emery, R., Lazare, A., & Udin, H. (1979). "Adherence" and the negotiated approach to patienthood. *Archives of General Psychiatry, 36,* 393-398.

Ende, J., Kazis, L., Ash, A., & Moskowitz, M. A. (1989). Measuring patients' desire for autonomy: Decision making and information-seeking preferences among medical patients. *Journal of General Internal Medicine, 4,* 23-30.

Epstein, L.H., & Cluss, P.A. (1982). A behavioral medicine perspective on adherence to long-term medical regimens. *Journal of Consulting and Clinical Psychology, 50,* 950-971.

Folger, R. (1977). Distributive and procedural justice: Combined impact of "voice" and improvement on experienced inequity. *Journal of Personality and Social Psychology, 35,* 108-119.

Folger, R., & Cropanzano, R. (1998), *Organizational justice and human resource management.* Thousand Oaks, CA: Sage.

Freemon, B., Negrette, V.F., Davis, M., & Korsch, B.M. (1971). Gaps in doctor-patient communication: Doctor-patient interaction analysis. *Pediatric Research, 5,* 298-311.

Given, B., Given, C. W., & Simoni, L.E. (1979). Relationships of processes of care to patient outcomes. *Nursing Research, 28 (2),* 85-93.

Greenberg, J. (1990). Organizational justice: Yesterday, today, and tomorrow. *Journal of Management, 16,* 401-495.

Greenberg, J. (1991). Using explanations to manage impressions of performance appraisal fairness. *Employee Responsibilities and Rights Journal, 4,* 51-60.

Greenberg, J. (1993). The social side of fairness: Interpersonal and informational classes of organizational justice. In R. Cropanzano (Ed.), *Justice in the workplace: Approaching fairness in human resource management* (pp. 79-103). Hillsdale, NJ: Erlbaum.

Greenfield, S., Kaplan, S.H., & Ware, J.E. (1985). Expanding patient involvement in care: Effects on patient outcomes. *Annals of Internal Medicine, 102,* 520-528.

Greenfield, S., Kaplan, S.H., Ware, J.E., Yano, E.M., & Frank, H.J.L. (1988). Patients' participation in medical care. *Journal of General Internal Medicine, 3,* 448-457.

Greene, M.G., Adelman, R.D., Friedmann, E., & Charon, R. (1994). Older patient satisfaction with communication during an initial medical encounter. *Social Science & Medicine, 38,* 1279-1288.

Greenley, J.R., Young, T.B., & Schoenherr, R.A. (1982). Psychological distress and patient satisfaction. *Medical Care, 20,* 373-385.

Hall, J.A., Feldstein, M., Fretwell, M.D., Rowe, J.W., & Epstein, A.M. (1990). Older patients' health status and satisfaction with medical care in an HMO population. *Medical Care, 28,* 261-270.

Hall, J.A., Roter, D.L., & Katz, N.R. (1988). Meta-analysis of correlates of provider behavior in medical encounters. *Medical Care, 26,* 657-675.

Hall, J.A., Roter, D.L., & Rand, C.S. (1981). Communication of affect between patient and physician. *Journal of Health and Social Behavior, 22,* 18-30.

Hickson, G.B., Clayton, E.W., Githens, P.B., & Sloan, F.A. (1992). Factors that prompted families to file medical malpractice claims following prenatal injuries. *Journal of the American Medical Association, 267,* 1359-1363.

Hughes, T.E., & Larson, L.N. (1991). Patient involvement in health care: A procedural justice viewpoint. *Medical Care, 29,* 297-303.

Hulka, B.S., Cassel, J.C., Kupper, L.L., & Burdette, J.A. (1976). Communication, compliance, and concordance between physicians and patients with prescribed medications. *American Journal of Public Health, 66,* 847-853.

Johnson, C.G., Levenkron, J.C., Suchman, A.L., & Manchester, R. (1988). Does physician uncertainty affect patient satisfaction. *Journal of General Internal Medicine, 3,* 144-149.

Kao, A.C., Green, D.C., Davis, N.A., Koplan, J.P., & Cleary, P.D. (1998). Patients' trust in their physicians: Effects of choice, continuity, and payment method. *Journal of General Internal Medicine, 13,* 681-686.

Kaplan, S.H., Greenfield, S., Gandek, B., & Rogers, W.H. (1996). Characteristics of physicians with participatory decision-making styles. *Annals of Internal Medicine, 124,* 497-504.

Kasteller, J., Kane, R.L., Olsen, D.M., & Thetford, C. (1976). Issues underlying prevalence of doctor-shopping behavior. *Journal of Health and Social Behavior, 77,* 328-339.

Kim, W.C., & Mauborgne, R. (1993). Procedural justice, attitudes, and subsidiary top management compliance with multinationals' corporate strategic decisions. *Academy of Management Journal, 36,* 502-526.

Kincey, J., Bradshaw, P., & Ley, P. (1975). Patients' satisfaction and reported acceptance of advice in general practice: A preliminary study. *Journal of the Royal College of General Practitioners, 25,* 558-566.

Koehler, W.F., Fottler, M.D., & Swan, J.E. (1992). Physician-patient satisfaction: Equity in the health services encounter. *Medical Care Review, 49,* 455-484.

Konovsky, M.A., & Folger, R. (1991). The effects of procedures, social accounts, and benefits level on victims' layoff reactions. *Journal of Applied Social Psychology, 21,* 630-650.

Korsgaard, M.A., & Roberson, L. (1995). Procedural justice in performance evaluation: The role of instrumental and non-instrumental voice in performance appraisal decisions. *Journal of Management, 21*, 657-669.

Korsch, B.M., Gozzi, E.D., & Francis, V. (1968). Gaps in doctor patient communication: Doctor-patient interaction and patient satisfaction. *Pediatrics, 12*, 855-871.

Krantz, D.S., Baum, A., & Wideman, M.V. (1980). Assessment of preferences for self-treatment and information in health care. *Journal of Personality and Social Psychology, 39*, 977-990.

Lence, R.L., & Smith, M.C. (1987). Patient satisfaction and intentive to revisit the hospital: A further test of disconfirmation and equity theory. *Journal of Hospital Marketing, 2(1)*, 19-34.

Lerman, C.E., Brody, D.S., Caputo, G.C., Smith, D.G., Lazaro, C.G., & Wolfson, H.G. (1990). Patients' perceived involvement in care scale. *Journal of General Internal Medicine, 5*, 29-33.

Levinson, W. (1994). Physician-patient communication: A key to malpractice prevention. *Journal of the American Medical Association, 272*, 1619-1620.

Levinson, W., Roter, D.L., Mullooly, J.P., Dull, V.T., & Frankel, R.M. (1997). Physician-patient communication: The relationship with malpractice claims among primary care physicians and surgeons. *Journal of the American Medical Association, 277*, 553-559.

Ley, P., Bradshaw, P.W., Kincey, J.A., & Atherton, S.T. (1976). Increasing patients' satisfaction with communications. *British Journal of Social and Clinical Psychology, 15*, 403-413.

Lind, E.A. (1990, August). Corporate justice: Testing the limits of justice concerns in interorganizational disputes. Paper presented at meetings of the Academy of Management, Chicago.

Lind, E.A., & Tyler T.R. (1988). *The social psychology of procedural justice.* New York: Plenum Press.

Lind, E.A., Kanfer, R., & Earley, P.C. (1990). Voice, control, and procedural justice: Instrumental and noninstrumental concerns in fairness judgments. *Journal of Personality and Social Psychology, 59*, 952-959.

Lind, E.A., Kulik, C.T., Ambrose, M.L., & de Vera Park, M.V. (1993). Individual and corporate dispute resolution: Using procedural fairness as a decision heuristic. *Administrative Science Quarterly, 38*, 224-251.

Linn, L.S., Yager, J., Cope, D., & Leake, B. (1985). Health status, job satisfaction, job stress, and life satisfaction among academic and clinical faculty. *Journal of the American Medical Association, 254*, 2775-2782.

Linn, M.W., Linn, B.S., & Stein, S.R. (1982). Satisfaction with ambulatory care and compliance in older patients. *Medical Care, 20*, 606-614.

Lochman, J.E. (1983). Factors related to patients' satisfaction with their medical care. *Journal of Community Health, 9*, 91-109.

Marquis, M.S., Davies, A.R., & Ware, J.E. (1983). Patient satisfaction and change in medical care provider: A longitudinal study. *Medical Care, 21*, 821-829.

Miles, J.A., & Dansky, K.H. (1998, April). Improving patient satisfaction with triage procedures through fairness perceptions. Paper presented at annual meetings of the Society for Industrial and Organizational Psychology, Dallas.

Nazario, S.L. (1992, March 17). Medical science seeks a cure for doctors suffering from boorish bedside manner. *Wall Street Journal*, p. B1, B8.

Pendelton, L., & House, W.C. (1984). Preferences for treatment approaches in medical care: College students versus diabetic outpatients. *Medical Care, 22,* 644-646.

Putnam, S.M., Stiles, W.B., Jacob, M.C., & James, S.A. (1985). Patient exposition and physician explanation in initial medical interviews and outcomes of clinic visits. *Medical Care, 23,* 74-83.

Rashid, A., Forman, W., Jagger, C., & Mann, R. (1989). Consultations in general practice: A comparison of patients' and doctors' satisfaction. *British Medical Journal, 299,* 1015-1016.

Robbins, J.A., Bertakis, K.D., Helms, J., Azari, R., Callahan, E. J., & Creten, D.A. (1993). The influence of physician practice behaviors on patient satisfaction. *Family Medicine, 25,* 17-20.

Ross, C.E., & Duff, R.S. (1982). Returning to the doctor: The effect of client characteristics, type of practice, and experiences with care. *Journal of Health and Social Behavior, 23,* 119-131.

Roter, D.L. (1977). Patient participation in the patient-provider interaction: The effects of patient question asking on the quality of interaction, satisfaction and compliance. *Health Education Monographs, 5(4),* 281-315.

Sackett, D.L., & Snow, J.C. (1979). The magnitude of compliance and noncompliance. In R.B. Haynes, D.W. Taylor, & D.L. Sackett (Eds.), *Compliance in health care* (pp. 11-22). Baltimore: Johns Hopkins University Press.

Schaubroeck, J., May, D.R., & Brown, F.W. (1994). Procedural justice explanations and employee reactions to economic hardship: A field experiment. *Journal of Applied Psychology, 79,* 455-460.

Schmittdiel, J., Selby, J.V., Grumbach, K., & Quesenberry, C.P. (1997). Choice of a personal physician and patient satisfaction in a health maintenance organization. *Journal of the American Medical Association, 278,* 1596-1599.

Shapiro, R.S., Simpson, D.E., Lawrence, S.L., Talsky, A.M., Sobocinski, K.A., & Schiedermayer, D.L. (1989). A survey of sued and nonsued physicians and suing patients. *Archives of Internal Medicine, 149,* 2190-2196.

Stalans, L., & Lind, E.A. (1997). The meaning of procedural justice: A comparison of taxpayers' and representatives' views of their tax audits. *Social Justice Research, 10,* 311-331.

Stewart, M.A., & Wanklin, J. (1978). Direct and indirect measures of patient satisfaction with physicians' services. *Journal of Community Health, 3,* 195-204.

Stimson, G.V. (1974). Obeying doctor's orders: A view from the other side. *Social Science and Medicine, 8,* 97-104.

Swan, J.E., Sawyer, J.C., Van Matre, J.G., & McGee, G.W. (1985). Deepening the understanding of hospital patient satisfaction: Fulfillment and equity effects. *Journal of Health Care Marketing, 5(3),* 7-18.

Tanouye, E. (1992, March 25). Drug firms start "compliance" programs reminding patients to take their pills. *Wall Street Journal,* p. B1, B5.

Thom, D.H., & Campbell, B. (1997). Patient-physician trust: An exploratory study. *Journal of Family Practice, 44 (2),* 169-176.

Tyler, T.R. (1987). Conditions leading to value expressive effects in judgments of procedural justice: A test of four models. *Journal of Personality and Social Psychology, 52,* 333-344.

Tyler, T.R. (1990). *Why people obey the law.* New Haven, CT: Yale University Press.

Tyler, T.R. (1994). Psychological models of the justice motive: Antecedents of distributive and procedural justice. *Journal of Personality and Social Psychology, 67,* 850-863.

Tyler, T.R., & Caine, A. (1981). The influence of outcomes and procedures on satisfaction with formal leaders. *Journal of Personality and Social Psychology, 41,* 642-655.

Tyler, T.R., Degoey, P., & Smith, H. (1996). Understanding why the justice of group procedure matters: A test of the psychological dynamics of the group-value model. *Journal of Personality and Social Psychology, 70,* 913-930.

Tyler, T.R., & Folger, R. (1980). Distributional and procedural aspects of satisfaction with citizen-police encounters. *Basic and Applied Social Psychology, 1,* 281-292.

Tyler, T.R., & Lind, E.A. (1992). A relational model of authority in groups. In M. Zanna (Ed.), *Advances in experimental social psychology* (Vol. 25, pp. 115-191). New York: Academic Press.

Tyler, T.R., Rasinski, K.A., & Spodick, N. (1985). Influence of voice on satisfaction with leaders: Exploring the meaning of process control. *Journal of Personality and Social Psychology, 48,* 72-81.

Vaccarino, J.M. (1977). Malpractice: The problem in perspective. *The Journal of the American Medical Association, 238,* 861-863.

Van den Bos, K., & Lind, E.A. (In press). Uncertainty management by means of fairness judgments. In M.P. Zanna (Ed.), *Advances in experimental social psychology* (Vol. 34). San Diego, CA: Academic Press.

Van den Bos, K., Lind, E.A., Vermunt, R., & Wilke, H.A.M. (1997). How do I judge my outcome when I do not know the outcome of others? The psychology of the fair process effect. *Journal of Personality and Social Psychology, 72,* 1034-1046.

Van den Bos, K., & Miedema, J. (2000). Toward understanding why fairness matters: The influence of mortality salience on reactions to procedural fairness. *Journal of Personality and Social Psychology, 79,* 355-366.

Van den Bos, K., Vermunt, R., & Wilke, H.A.M. (1997). Procedural and distributive justice: What is fair depends more on what comes first than on what comes next. *Journal of Personality and Social Psychology, 72,* 95-104.

Van den Bos, K., Wilke, H.A.M., & Lind, E.A. (1998). When do we need procedural fairness? The role of trust in authority. *Journal of Personality and Social Psychology, 75,* 1449-1458.

Van den Bos, K., Wilke, H.A.M., Lind, E.A., & Vermunt, R. (1998). Evaluating outcomes by means of the fair process effect: Evidence for different processes in fairness and satisfaction judgments. *Journal of Personality and Social Psychology, 74,* 1493-1503.

Ware, J.E., Davies-Avery, A., & Stewart, A.L. (1978). The measurement and meaning of patient satisfaction. *Health and Medical Care Services Review, 1,* 1-10.

Ware, J.E., Wright, W.R., Snyder, M.K., & Chu, G.C. (1975). Consumer perceptions of health care services: Implications for academic medicine. *Journal of Medical Education, 50,* 839-848.

Weyrauch, K. (1996). Does continuity of care increase HMO patients' satisfaction with physician performance? *Journal of American Board Family Practice, 9,* 31-36.

Willson, P., & McNamara, J.R. (1982). How perceptions of a simulated physician-patient interaction influence intended satisfaction and compliance. *Social Science Medicine, 16,* 1699-1704.

CHAPTER 4

A SOCIAL INFORMATION PROCESSING VIEW OF ORGANIZATIONAL JUSTICE

Barry M. Goldman and Sherry M. B. Thatcher

ABSTRACT

This chapter examines the extension of social information processing (SIP) theory to organizational justice. There has been little justice research to date that has investigated the impact of social influences, generally, or SIP, in particular, on organizational justice. The chapter explains the mechanism by which social information affects justice judgments and behaviors. Propositions are developed and a model presented that specifies the particular linkages. The chapter also discusses the implications of SIP as applied to Fairness Theory and Fairness Heuristic Theory and proposes different consequences to the attitudes formed pursuant to each. Further, a research agenda is proposed relating to theoretical, substantive, and methodological issues.

Theories of organizational justice have proved themselves robust and capable of replication in empirical studies. As a result, they have proliferated both in terms of the number of theories of organizational justice and also in terms of their studied antecedents and consequences. A number of scholars have called for organizational justice researchers to include more measures of social influence in their studies (e.g., Goldman, 2001; Greenberg, 1997; Lind & Tyler, 1988; Tyler & Bies, 1990; Weiss & Cropanzano, 1996). However, organizational justice researchers continue to place relatively little emphasis on social influences in empirical research (for some examples of exceptions, see Goldman, 2001; Umphress, Labianca, Scholten, Kass, & Brass, 2000). The purpose of the present chapter is to investigate the role of social influences on organizational justice. To do this, we address three issues: (1) that social influence theories are an important component of organizational justice; (2) how social information processing (SIP) theory can be applied to organizational justice; and (3) how the SIP model can be adapted for two process theories of organizational justice (we use the terms "fairness" and "justice" interchangeably).

SIP theory, in particular, lends itself to the study of social influences on organizational justice. SIP theory proposes that attitudes and needs are cognitive products that result from the processing of information about the attitude object and past behaviors in a social context (Salancik & Pfeffer, 1978). SIP theory differs from other theories in that it suggests that social information affects perception, attitudes, and behaviors (e.g., Asch, 1952; Festinger, 1954; Hackman, 1976) by its explicit linkage between the social environment and the processing of information in the development of job attitudes and needs. SIP has been primarily shown to be related to task or job satisfaction and performance (Zalesny & Ford, 1990) but has also been related to intentions to quit (Pfeffer, 1980), role perceptions (Schnake & Dumler, 1987), and perceived anxiety about an organizational change (Miller & Monge, 1985).

THE ROLE OF SOCIAL INFLUENCE ON ORGANIZATIONAL JUSTICE

Cognitive psychology has focused on the individual, seeking to delineate the processes by which individual minds perceive and interpret information. Initially, studies in cognitive psychology concentrated on relatively simple tasks. More recently, these studies have looked at more complex tasks. However, even so, there has been little investigation of the problem-solving context with the result that little attention has been devoted to cognitive functioning in the presence of other people (Levine, Resnick, & Higgins, 1993).

The traditional approach to cognition emphasizes the role of symbolic processing by the individual. This approach asserts the importance of individual traits and perceptions (e.g., Alderfer, 1972, 1977) on cognitive functioning. However, a more recent approach emphasizes the role of the environment, and the contextual and social setting (e.g., Salancik & Pfeffer, 1978; Thompson & Fine, 1999). Relatively little of this debate has affected the literature on organizational justice, with the result that there have been relatively few attempts to explore social influences as an alternative explanation for perceptions of organizational justice.

Sussman and Vecchio (1991) defined social influence as "a social occasion wherein one individual exhibits behaviors, emits verbal utterances, and so on, with the intent of altering the behavior of another or others to a desired end" (p. 208). It is now well established that social influences can exert a strong force on individuals' perceptions, attitudes, and behaviors (Asch, 1951; Milgram, 1974; Sherif, 1936) whether or not they are intentional. Festinger's (1954) social comparison theory suggests that individuals compare themselves to others and that one's attitudes can be strongly influenced by seemingly insignificant information. Bandura's work on social learning (Bandura, 1962; Bandura & Walters, 1963) found that people learn vicariously from observing a model's behavior and the consequences of the behavior for the model. Social influence should be particularly interesting to organizational researchers as workers within an organization are constantly trying to influence others for motivational reasons, to achieve an outcome, or for political ends.

Tajfel and Turner (1979) showed how individuals immediately created in-groups and out-groups based on minimal information. When identified with groups, people are thought to stereotype themselves and others. Related to this, Cosmides and Tooby (1995) argued that the goal of cognitive psychology is to uncover the information-processing mechanisms that have evolved to adapt to the problems that organisms must be able to solve in order to survive. From this perspective, evolution has provided humans with the ability to behave adaptively even in the face of incomplete information. Further, Cosmides and Tooby (1995) proposed that survival has provided mankind with "Darwinian algorithms" associated with certain important activities such as: aggressive threat, resource accrual, resource distribution, predator avoidance, and social exchange, to name a few. These "Darwinian algorithms" suggest that human reasoning is the product of a "collection of functionally specialized, evolved mechanism, most of which are content-dependent and content-imparting" (Cosmides & Tooby, 1992, p. 220). One of these "Darwinian algorithms," they argued, is a "cheater detector," which enables humans to detect when someone is not playing by the rules by illicitly taking or withholding benefits. It can be argued that, if true, the quest for justice is part of a Darwinian algorithm, ingrained in all of us, to help ensure survival of the group. It is the inherent ambiguity (or uncertainty) in social interactions that require that social influence theories be viewed when trying to understand organizational justice.

Both social-impact theory (Latané, 1981) and SIP theory (Salancik & Pfeffer, 1978) integrated evidence from these earlier social influence studies. Social-impact theory suggests that, "the degree of social impact (pressure to change) on any given target person in a given situation is a multiplicative function of the *strength, immediacy,* and *number* of other persons who are potential sources of influence in the situation" (McGrath, 1984). SIP theory is similar to social-impact theory but differs in two important ways: (1) SIP theory incorporated the idea of ambiguity; and (2) SIP theory was developed specifically for organizational contexts. Many of the issues involved with organizational justice concern events that are ambiguous in nature and thus can have multiple interpretations for participants. Therefore, SIP theory will be used to illustrate the linkage between social influence theories and organizational justice. Before describing SIP theory, it is necessary to talk about the crucial role of ambiguity.

THE ROLE OF AMBIGUITY

It has been suggested that individuals tend to rely more on social influences when confronted with situations that are novel or ambiguous and when the source of information is perceived as credible (Salancik & Pfeffer, 1978; Zalesny & Ford, 1990). As Salancik and Pfeffer stated: "The worker does not require an elaborate social comparison process to tell him or her that when the plant is 100 degrees, it is hot. The worker is, however, likely to use social information in developing his or her perceptions of the meaningfulness, importance, and variety of the job" (p. 228). Salancik and Pfeffer (1978) argued that perception is a retrospective process and, therefore, even though a worker may experience an immediate event, the interpretation of that event is derived from prior recall and reconstruction.

Recently, Van den Bos and Lind (in press) argued that fairness and uncertainty are closely intertwined. They suggested that fairness matters because people need to assess whether authority figures are abusing the power they have been granted. In particular, workers need some way to assess the outcome they receive from these authority figures. Further, this assessment is particularly important when information as to the trustworthiness of the authority figure is lacking. Therefore, when trust is lacking, fairness, particularly procedural justice, serves as a "heuristic substitute" (Van den Bos & Lind, in press) to aid in judging the outcome received.

Uncertainty (what we refer to as "ambiguity") is a crucial reason that social influence plays such a strong role in the workplace. Furthermore, the need to reduce ambiguity is related to perceptions of fairness in the workplace. The need to reduce ambiguity can lead workers to seek out or be more receptive to the opinions and advice of other people to help resolve these issues (although these opinions and advice may in fact have the opposite effect). As previous research has shown, when faced with uncertainty we seek to reduce it (Van den Bos & Lind, in press). There are few methods that are more helpful in allowing individuals to reduce uncertainty than by seeking the opinions of salient others. After all, at its core, "justice is about social relationships. It is about how people treat one another" (Cropanzano, Weiss, Suckow, & Grandey, 2000, p. 58). For example, social influence has been demonstrated to play an important role in the reduction of stress in the work environment (e.g., Locke & Taylor, 1990). In turn, these social influences act as antecedents or moderators of fairness judgments.

SOCIAL INFORMATION PROCESSING THEORY

SIP theory is a model of work motivation that asserts that work attitudes and behaviors are, to a large degree, the result of the processing of information from the social environment rather than individual predisposition. This theory states that needs, attitudes, and behaviors of an individual are based on socially-derived information and the individual's own behavior. SIP assumes that individuals are adaptive organisms who change their attitudes, behaviors, and beliefs to their "social context and to the reality of their own past and present behavior and situation" (Salancik & Pfeffer, 1978, p. 226). As a result, Salancik and Pfeffer argued that individual behavior can best be understood by studying the "informational and social environment within which that behavior occurs and to which it adapts" (p. 226).

SIP has been used primarily to assess task or job satisfaction, but has been expanded to investigate performance (Zalesny & Ford, 1990), anxiety about organizational change (Miller & Monge, 1985), role perceptions (Schnake & Dumler, 1987), perceptions of the work environment (Zalesny & Farace, 1986), and intentions to quit (Pfeffer, 1980). It has received very little attention by the justice literature to date (for exceptions, see Brockner, Wiesenfeld, Stephan, Hurley, Grover, Reed, DeWitt, & Martin, 1997; Umphress et al., 2000). However, there are compelling reasons why SIP theory is appropriate to the study of the organizational justice.

Salancik and Pfeffer (1978) argued that when important aspects of the work environment are ambiguous, workers are likely to use social information in developing their perceptions of the work environment. Events in the workplace are often ambiguous, mostly because of attributional, emotional, perceptual, or legal issues (Blumrosen, Blumrosen, Carmignani, & Daly, 1999; Lind, Greenberg, Scott, & Welchans, 2000; Youngblood, Trevino, & Favia, 1992). This is, perhaps, more so when employees are deciding whether an event was unfair.

The reasoning of Salancik and Pfeffer (1978) contained two general implications for the impact of the social environment on individuals: (1) there may be direct construction of meaning through exposure to the expressed attitudes of others (e.g., Festinger, 1954); and (2) the context may make certain information or aspects of the situation salient, thereby influencing perception and interpretation (e.g., Taylor & Fiske, 1978). With respect to the first implication, direct construction of meaning, this would include social influence in the form of advice or information from salient others. As a consequence, the advice and information of friends, family, and co-workers (as salient others to most people) may also play a role in the individual's decision to perceive (in)justice. The offering of information, advice, or guidance has been defined as a type of social support known as "social guidance" (Vaux, Riedel, & Stewart, 1987; Williams, 1995) that has been reported as important in discrimination claiming (Goldman, 1998). For example, in a work context, co-workers may tell a recently terminated worker that the "organization always terminates women first."

With respect to the second implication, that context influences perception and interpretation, membership in salient groups could suggest to individuals appropriate attitudes or behaviors by focusing an individual's attention on certain information thereby making that information more salient. Within these groups, there may emerge a consensus about important features of a significant work event, such as a termination, especially if the event is negative and viewed as a potential threat to members of that group (Huo, Smith, Tyler, & Lind, 1996). Thus, groups may develop a normative framework for interpreting and responding to elements of the work environment that result in a stable construction of reality that may vary across work groups faced with objectively similar circumstances. Agreement may suggest to group members that there is verification of an external, objective set of facts, rather than mere group preference or bias. When people think of themselves as group members, they are likely to pay greater attention to group concerns and outcomes, thereby allowing group membership to influence their individual perspectives and experiences (Kramer, 1991; Turner, Hogg, Oakes, Reicher, & Wetherell, 1987). In part, this occurs because the individual wants his or her opinions to conform to that of the group (Festinger, 1954).

Unlike the cognitive judgment approach to the formation of job attitudes, SIP theory proposed that these attitudes evolve (are constructed) based on the context and circumstances. Each construction of attitude integrates stored information relevant to the attitude object as well as unrelated contextual information (Weiss & Cropanzano, 1996). Salancik and Pfeffer (1978) identified four types of "social information." First, the most direct type, are the effects that stated opinions offered by a co-worker have on the worker. For example, if co-workers argue that a certain supervisor's treatment of a worker is unfair, it may have a powerful effect on perceptions of fairness. We expand this aspect of Salancik and Pfeffer's (1978) model to include family and friends since measures of social influence typically include their influence (e.g., Vaux et al., 1987). These opinions may influence a worker in two ways. Firstly, since workplaces frequently contain ambiguous cues and situations, these opinions may suggest how certain events should be interpreted. Secondly, the desire to conform his or her opinion with that of co-workers may exert pressure on the worker to follow the advice implicit in the opinion. This second aspect of peer influence may exert a very powerful effect (Folger, Rosenfield, Grove, & Corkan, 1979).

A second type of social influence is subtler in that other people's statements may cue an individual as to what to consider in the work environment. For example, calling attention to the rumors surrounding imminent layoffs in an organization may serve to make workers even more attuned to issues of procedural fairness as a signal of impending outcome fairness (Van den Bos & Lind, in press). However, this type of social influence differs from the first in that there is no effort by the source of social information to exert influence over the actor. Without this coercive element, this type of social influence is less likely to be a powerful predictor of justice perceptions than the first.

A third type of social influence involves the role that other people play in setting an individual's needs and values which, in turn, affects how ambiguous events are interpreted. Salancik and Pfeffer (1978) provided an example of a supervisor who disciplined a worker who was not doing an adequate job, which may reasonably be interpreted as lacking concern for the worker or, alternatively, as concerned with the success of the firm. The interpretation can be affected by social information (usually comments from others as to values and needs) which, in turn, affects one's frame for interpreting ambiguous events (Tannen, 1999). If, for example, a new employee is told by senior employees that management does not care for workers, this may increase the likelihood that the managers' actions will be viewed as unconcerned with workers. Related to this third type of social information is the subjective concept of deservingness, which is examined elsewhere in this volume.

A final type of social influence involves the interpretation of events. This involves the social construction of events by others. For example, a supervisor's harsh review of a marginal employee may be viewed by other workers as insensitive or, alternatively, honest. The more ambiguous the situation, the more prone it is to multiple interpretations. This type of social influence differs from the previous one mainly in terms of timing: Social construction of events is typically *post hoc* (cf. Ellard and Skarlicki, this volume).

HOW DOES SIP AFFECT WORKERS JUSTICE JUDGMENTS?

Zalesney and Ford (1990) refined Salancik and Pfeffer's (1978) conceptualization of SIP theory based on a review of ten years of research. Their refinement focused on three areas: (1) attention to the mediating processes by which social information affects perceptions, attitudes, and behaviors; (2) incorporation of research since Salancik's and Pfeffer's

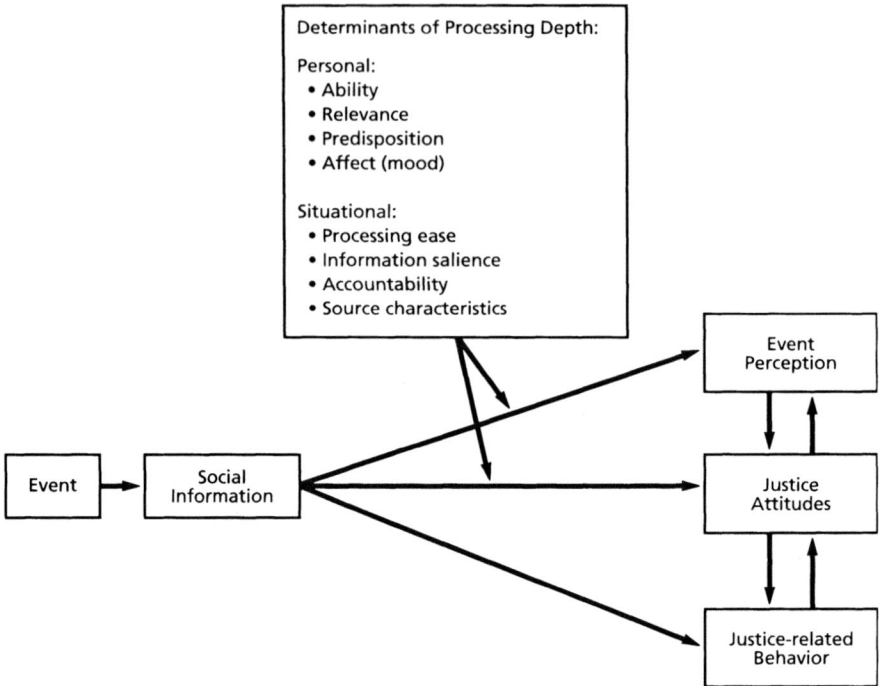

Figure 1. Model of social information processing and organizational justice.

(1978) original article involving attitude development and change; and (3) modification to include attitude change over time. Although the revised model is focused on explaining perceptions, attitudes, and behaviors as they apply to a job or task, the model can also be used to explain perceptions of work-related events, justice attitudes and behaviors associated with organizational justice. The Zalesny and Ford (1990) SIP model, as it applies to understanding organizational justice, is illustrated in Figure 1. The remainder of this section will discuss the model indicated in Figure 1, which focuses on the antecedents of event perceptions, justice attitudes and justice-related behavior.

We will begin by discussing the determinants of processing depth and their implications for justice. In subsequent sections, we will refer back to these determinants as they moderate key relationships.

Determinants of Processing Depth

Zalesny and Ford (1990) proposed a series of mediators between social information and worker perceptions and attitudes. The mediators are labeled as determinants of processing depth, which involve a series of personal or situational factors. Depth of processing is proposed to affect the strength of perceptions and attitudes which, in turn, affect subsequent behavior. The reasons for the increased strength associated with depth of processing is its relationship with conviction (i.e., position "possessed" by an individual as a "true belief," Abelson, 1988), centrality (degree of interconnectedness between the individual and the attitude object, Krosnick, 1986), or accessibility (number of cognitive associations between the object and its evaluation, Fazio, 1986).

Although Zalesny and Ford (1990) referred to the depth of processing variables as "mediators," they are, in fact, moderators as shown in Figure 1. As Baron and Kenny (1986) observed, mediator variables speak to *how or why* certain effects occur, whereas moderators specify *when* these effects occur. One of the tests to determine if a variable is a mediator is whether "variations in levels of the independent variable significantly account for variations in the presumed mediator" (Baron & Kenny , 1986, p. 1176). The depth of processing variables (as delineated below) are not affected by the independent variable of social information. Instead, these variables affect the strength of the relation between social information and justice-related attitudes. Hence, they should be considered moderators.

Zalesny and Ford (1990) proposed two categories of depth of processing: individual and situational determinants. As they suggested, individual differences consist of personal relevance, ability to process information, and predispositions toward effortful thinking. These three are derived from Petty and Cacioppo's (1986) Elaboration Likelihood Model. There is a fourth individual difference that should be considered: moods.

Personal Relevance

Personal relevance refers to the "ego-involvement" of the individual to the attitude object (Sherif, Sherif, & Nebergall, 1965). In a justice context, personal relevance moderates the link from social information to an individual's perception of justice such that high personal relevance increases the conviction with which an employee may seek or accept social information. As personal relevance increases, workers should become more motivated to focus on issues salient to them. This is because individuals perceive important negative consequences to not paying attention to these issues. For example, a termination should be more personally relevant to most workers than a shift of position on the company softball team. Therefore, social information relating to the fairness of the termination should involve more depth of processing than social information relating to the shift of position. If personal relevance is high, this will cause the individual to access previously stored information (e.g., information, attitudes, beliefs, values, and affect) related to the job. Therefore, any resulting justice perceptions "should show temporal persistence, resistance to change, and be predictive of behavior. When personal relevance is low, the resulting job attitude will reflect peripheral (i.e., noncontent) cues in the information source (e.g., expertise), message (e.g., length), or context (e.g., on or off company time), should be susceptible to change, and should not predict job behavior" (Zalesny & Ford, 1990, p. 229).

As a consequence, when workers care deeply about something they are more likely to seek or accept social information related to that issue. When they do not care deeply about something they are less likely to seek or accept social information related to that issue. Perceptions of fairness that result from high personal relevance are likely to be more enduring than those formed from low personal relevance.

Ability to Process Information

The ability to process information refers to the "extent to which a person possesses the skills or resources required for cognitive processing" (Zalesny & Ford, 1990, p. 229). This can include processing factors such as prior knowledge or message comprehensibility. When an event occurs in the workplace, individuals draw on their cognitive resources for understanding the event; without the appropriate skills, individuals may be more likely to turn to social influences for an appropriate response (Petty & Cacioppo, 1986). For example, a person who is denied a promotion for the first time may have little ability to process the event; he or she would be more likely to look to others for an interpretation of the denial. If an individual's ability to process information is low, he or she is more likely to look toward social information to aid in forming justice attitudes. Therefore, social information affects justice perceptions depending upon the worker's ability to process information: the less the worker is able to process information on their own, the more they will seek out or accept social information relating to perceptions of fairness. Differences in levels of processing are also discussed in Ellard and Skarlicki (this volume).

Predisposition

The third personal determinant of processing depth described by Zalesny and Ford (1990) is that of individual predisposition toward effortful thinking. Individuals with a strong predisposition to effortful thinking actively engage in the process of trying to understand the actual "message" conveyed in an event rather than relying on peripheral information (Zalesny & Ford, 1990). For example, an individual who is predisposed toward effortful thinking may seek out reliable information when hearing of an impending merger. Those who are not so predisposed may perpetuate the rumor by talking about the imagined effects of the merger with coworkers. In both cases, social information is involved in the outcome but it is the type of knowledge incorporated into an individual's event perception that informs others of the individual's predisposition toward effortful thinking.

Individuals who are relatively high in the predisposition toward effortful thinking enjoy effortful cognitive activity (Cacioppo & Petty, 1982).

These individuals should enjoy collecting as much information as possible in order to better process the merits of an argument. As such, workers high in the predisposition toward effortful thinking should be more likely to use social information when forming perceptions of justice than workers low in the predisposition toward effortful thinking. However, there could be a counterargument as well. That is, workers low in the predisposition toward effortful thinking could use social information as a substitute for their own cognitive effort resulting in justice perceptions mirroring those of the social information sources.

Moods

An additional personal determinant that was not discussed by Zalesny and Ford (1990) but which has been addressed in other information processing research is moods. Weiss and Cropanzano (1996), in their description of affective events theory, stated that both emotions and moods are affective states. However, an emotion is characterized as a "reaction to an event" (p. 18) while moods, in comparison to emotions, are "less intense, of longer duration, and lack specificity with regard to a particular object or behavioral response" (p. 18). This distinction is crucial in our discussion because in this section we focus on antecedents of event perceptions, not reactions to events. An interesting study by Ingram (1984) found that individuals who were primed by a negative mood experience deeply processed negative feedback whereas individuals who were primed by a positive mood experience did *not* deeply process positive feedback. These results, along with others (Moore, Underwood, Heberlein, Doyle, & Litzie, 1979), suggest that positive and negative moods do not have symmetrical effects on individuals. Watson and Clark (1992) provided more evidence of this relationship when they found that positive and negative affect are not negatively correlated with the five-factor classification for personality traits. Individuals who are in a negative mood when hearing an event may be more likely to retain and process negative social information (Nelson & Craighead, 1977). For example, an individual who is in a negative mood and hears about upcoming organizational changes will be more likely to perceive the event negatively rather than as a positive opportunity. As a result, workers in a negative mood are more likely to seek out or accept negative social information. Furthermore, this negative social information is more likely to lead to perceptions of injustice than justice.

In addition to personal determinants, Zalesny and Ford (1990) discuss four *situational determinants* that are relevant to social information processing at work: the ease of information processing, information salience, the individual's accountability in the situation, and the characteristics of the information source.

Ease of Information Processing

The ease with which one is able to process information is partly dependent on the content of the information and the context in which social communication occurs. Petty and Cacioppo (1986) summarized a number of studies that show that distraction is a key variable that affects an individual's ability to process a message. However, distraction has a differential effect on processing depending on the strength of an argument. As Petty and Cacioppo (1986, p.141) suggested, "distraction should be especially important as a thought disrupter when people are highly motivated and able to process the message. If motivation and/or ability to process the message are low, distraction should have little effect." Distraction is not the only variable that affects ease of processing. For example, repetition may also affect the ability of workers to process social information. Therefore, the ease with which a worker receives social information may make it more or less likely that social information may lead to perceptions of justice. Specifically, situations where there exists increased ease of information processing are more likely to lead to social information affecting justice perceptions than situations where information processing is difficult. For example, advice provided by a group of friends or co-workers in a noisy, crowded bar, may be less likely to be heeded than the same advice provided one-on-one in a quiet, private setting.

Information Salience

The degree of information salience is another situational determinant that will influence how social information is integrated into a worker's perceptions of justice. High degrees of salience may trigger automatic information processing that is not completely accurate (cf. Petty & Cacioppo, 1986). Information salience may also affect social information because of priming cues which, in turn, may affect perceptions of justice. For example, one coworker may inform another worker that project assignment is determined by how much the manager likes an individual. When the worker is trying to make sense of the manager's assignments, this comment may be triggered, leading to a perception of injustice.

Individual Accountability

When an individual is accountable for the result of a particular task or situation, he or she is more likely to partake in systematic information processing as is reflected in models of decision-making strategies (Petty & Cacioppo, 1986). Such systematic information processing would include social information about a task. Individuals engaging in group tasks may pay less attention to relevant information as they may be less accountable for the outcome. This is especially true when rewards are shared equally among group members as may be the case when a legal team is asked to settle a discrimination claim. Each individual within the group may not seek out necessary information; however, if one individual were assigned to the case, it is more likely that he or she will find relevant information. This process is often referred to as social loafing or free-riding (Albanese & Van Fleet, 1985). For example, one party to a mediated dispute settlement typically has high accountability for the success of a negotiated agreement between the parties. As such, the high accountability should result in systematically incorporating social information into an assessment of the justice of the results of the mediation. Thus, high individual accountability should lead to a greater likelihood that social information should lead to perceptions of justice than low individual accountability.

Information Source Characteristics

The final factor that may influence the depth to which one processes social information is reflected in the characteristics of the information source (Petty & Cacioppo, 1986). Information sources believed to be credible have greater influence than those deemed to be less credible (Fisher, Ilgen, & Hoyer, 1979). In addition to credibility, a number of other factors influence the degree to which one values the information provided by a source. Some of these factors are perceived expertise, status, attractiveness, and trustworthiness. In addition, the similarity attraction paradigm (Byrne, 1971) suggests that individuals are influenced more by those that they perceive to be similar to themselves than those who are seen as different. The extent to which status characteristics influence the depth of information processing is extremely relevant to organizational justice. An individual may be more inclined to believe the information provided by a coworker who has held onto his job through a number of layoffs than a newly-hired coworker. In sum, a worker's perception that the source of the social information has more highly-valued characteristics (e.g., high credibility) is more likely to lead to the social information affecting justice perceptions than if the source of the social information is less highly-valued. What is interesting about this determinant however is that information sources with greater credibility, similarity, status, trustworthiness, etc. will have more influence but may cause the information seeker to do less systematic processing.

Antecedents to Event Perceptions

As shown in Figure 1, event perceptions are particularly important in understanding how SIP influences organizational justice since it is this perception that can influence attitudes and ultimately, justice-related behavior. Event perceptions are influenced through two mediators: social information and justice attitudes. As we discussed earlier, the relationship between social information and event perceptions is moderated by processing depth determinants.

Social Information

One way that social information affects event perceptions is by making certain aspects of the environment more or less salient. Social influences may cause a worker to focus on some aspects of an event more than others. For example, after receiving a brief (e.g., 10-minute) performance appraisal in which an employee was told he or she was doing "everything fine," an employee may be miffed to hear co-workers say that most appraisals are at least 30 minutes and involve extensive career development. Although the worker may not have been initially unhappy with his or her brief appraisal, these subsequent co-worker statements may cause some unease and eventually resentment in the worker. The individual may feel as if he or she was not given sufficient "voice" (Bies & Shapiro, 1988).

Perceptions about an event can also be affected by the questioning process, particularly if the questioning process causes a worker to recall certain aspects of an event more frequently than others (Salancik, 1976). After a meeting with the supervisor about a sensitive subject, an employee may be asked a series of questions by workers asking, "How did it go?" or "What did he say about X?" or "How did he react to Y?" Each of these questions, especially when they come shortly after the meeting and before the worker has fully formed his or her own perceptions, may affect worker perceptions of the event by causing certain aspects of the meeting to become salient to the worker. Therefore,

Proposition 1. Social information directly affects a worker's perception of a work-related-event.

However, as noted earlier, we propose that the relationship between social information and a worker's perception of an event is moderated by a series of determinants of processing depth. Therefore, we propose the following propositions:

P1a. The ability to process information moderates the relationship between social information and one's perception of a work-related event.

P1b. The personal relevance of the information moderates the relationship between social information and one's perception of a work-related event.

P1c. The predisposition to effortful thinking moderates the relationship between social information and one's perception of a work-related event.

P1d. An individual's mood at the time of information receipt will moderate the relationship between social information and one's perception of a work-related event.

P1e. The degree of ease with which an individual is able to process information will moderate the relationship between social information and one's perception of a work-related event.

P1f. The degree to which information is salient to an individual will moderate the relationship between social information and one's perception of a work-related event.

P1g. The degree to which an individual perceives him- or herself to be accountable for an outcome will moderate the relationship between social information and one's perception of a work-related event.

P1h. The characteristics of the information source will moderate the relationship between social information and one's perception of a work-related event.

Justice Attitudes

Perceptions of events are also influenced by one's attitudes with regard to justice. This can occur in two ways. First, an individual's attitude with regard to justice can influence how one interprets an event. For example, an individual who does not believe that his organization treats him fairly is likely to perceive an organizational change as a negative event. Another way that attitudes can influence perceptions is through "on-line attitude formation" (Zalesny & Ford, 1990). Zalesny and Ford (1990) suggested that "in a novel situation, the available information may be simultaneously encoded and evaluated. As the initial judgment or attitude is formed, it acts as a filter through which other information is screened" (p. 232). Thus, a worker who witnesses a coworker termination may form an initial impression that the organization is unjust. As other workers are also terminated, the perception of the event is increasingly negative even if the terminations were based on seniority levels.

Proposition 2. Justice attitudes directly affect perceptions of work-related events.

Antecedents to Justice Attitudes

The next box in Figure 1 refers to justice attitudes (which includes perceptions). Justice attitudes result from three causes: (1) the worker's perception and judgment of the event; (2) the information that social information provides as to what attitudes are appropriate, moderated by determinants of depth of processing; and (3) the worker's self-perception of his or her reasons for past behavior. We will discuss each of these below.

Event Perception

A number of theories of justice focus on various types of key events from which workers infer just or unjust conditions. For example, Fairness Heuristic Theory focuses on the unusual uncertainty in events or relationships that cause the worker to question the trustworthiness of the authority. It is the perception and judgment of uncertainty, combined with various conclusions reached as a result of various cognitive shortcuts, that drives this assessment of justice (Van den Bos & Lind, in press). Similarly, it is the perception of an appropriate "referent other" and the results of a self-comparison to that other that drives the assessment of distributive justice (Cropanzano, Byrne, Bobocel, & Rupp, 2001).

Proposition 3. Perceptions of work-related events directly affect justice attitudes.

Social Information and Determinants of Processing Depth

In addition to the direct effects discussed earlier, social information may also affect justice attitudes as moderated by various determinants of processing depth. As noted, these may relate to either personal or situational factors. For example, a worker with a low "ability to process information" may attend less to content and more to process issues in forming justice attitudes because he or she may not have the cognitive resources to fully understand the issue. Therefore, such a worker may be more sensitive to issues of interactional justice (if these are the least difficult to understand in the particular context) and less sensitive to issues of distributive justice (if these are the most difficult to understand in the context). To take another, and more specific, example, a union steward in an organization who has an extensive knowledge of procedural safeguards afforded by the union contract may be more likely to form attitudes relating to procedural justice than an employee who may not be as informed of the union procedures. Therefore:

Proposition 4. Social information directly affects justice attitudes.

However, for similar reasons that we propose a series of moderators for proposition 1, we also propose that the relationship between social information and a worker's justice attitudes is moderated by a series of determinants of processing depth. Therefore, we propose the following propositions:

P4a. The ability to process information moderates the relationship between social information and justice attitudes.

P4b. The personal relevance of the information moderates the relationship between social information and justice attitudes.

P4c. The predisposition to effortful thinking moderates the relationship between social information and justice attitudes.

P4d. An individual's mood at the time of information receipt will moderate the relationship between social information and justice attitudes.

P4e. The degree of ease with which an individual is able to process information will moderate the relationship between social information and justice attitudes.

P4f. The degree to which information is salient will moderate the relationship between social information and justice attitudes.

P4g. The degree to which an individual is accountable for an outcome will moderate the relationship between social information and justice attitudes

P4h. The characteristics of the information source will moderate the relationship between social information and justice attitudes.

Justice Related Behaviors

Past experiences and behaviors may also affect general attitudes (Bandura, 1977) and justice attitudes. This is related to the concept of "latent conflict" in the conflict literature. This concept states that no conflict can be completely understood without an appreciation of the history of conflict between the parties (Nord & Doherty, 1994). In this sense, past behaviors and experiences between the parties should influence the attitudes toward justice. For example, a history of bad relations between a worker and a supervisor may cause the worker to have a belief that fair treatment is unattainable from this supervisor.

Proposition 5. Justice-related behaviors directly affect justice attitudes.

Antecedents to Justice-Related Behavior

Following our discussion of justice attitudes, we will now discuss the antecedents to justice-related behavior.

Justice Attitudes

The relationship between attitudes and behaviors has long been noted in psychological and organizational behavior literature. General attitudes have been found to best predict general behaviors and specific attitudes best predict specific behaviors (Ajzen & Fishbein, 1980). Certainly, there is abundant evidence that justice attitudes lead to various justice-related behaviors (Lind & Tyler, 1988). For example, Lind et al. (2000), in a longitudinal study, reported that the filing of wrongful termination claims by workers were predicted by perceived fairness on the job and perceived fairness during termination. Further, Moorman (1991) reported justice attitudes to be related to organizational citizenship behaviors.

Proposition 6. Justice attitudes directly affect justice-related behaviors.

Social Information

As noted earlier, Salancik and Pfeffer (1978) state that one way in which social information may influence workers is that there may be direct construction of meaning through exposure to the expressed attitudes of others (e.g., Festinger, 1954). This would include social influence in the form of advice or information from salient others. As a consequence, the advice and information of friends, family, and co-workers (as salient others to most people) may also play a role in an individual's decision to engage in certain justice-related behavior. For example, Goldman (2001) reported that social information was a predictor of an employee's decision to claim for discrimination. Further, Bies, Tripp, and Kramer (1997) reported social factors as an important component in bolstering a worker's will toward revenge against his or her organization.

Proposition 7. Social information directly affects justice-related behaviors.

USING SYSTEMATIC AND AUTOMATIC INFORMATION PROCESSING TO EXPLAIN TWO PROCESS THEORIES OF JUSTICE

Zalesny and Ford (1990) identified two broad categories of information processing models. One category encompasses controlled, deep, systematic, or effortful analysis of stimuli. Petty and Cacioppo's (1986) Elaboration Likelihood Model, with its emphasis on a central route to persuasive communication, is an example of this. However, it is not always adaptive to engage in complex cognitive evaluations on all matters. Therefore, there exists a second category, which requires much less cognitive effort for a worker to develop and express attitudes and judgments. The labels used to describe these models are automatic, shallow, mindless, effortless, peripheral, and "heuristic" (Zalesny & Ford, p. 227).

These two categories of information processing models correspond to two process theories (how people make justice judgments) of organizational justice (distributive, procedural, and interactional justice): Fairness Theory (Folger & Cropanzano, 2001) and Fairness Heuristic Theory (Lind, 2001). At the outset, it should be noted that both of these theories implicitly incorporate social elements.

Fairness Theory, which is focused on unfairness (or injustice), proposes that an individual must find three situational factors to be present before he or she concludes that a situation is unjust. Folger and Cropanzano (2001) labeled these situations (in order of increasing cognitive complexity) as *would*, *could*, and *should* factors. Firstly, an unfavorable condition must exist. This can be either materially or psychologically unfavorable. The individual then assesses how an alternative situation *would* have felt:

the greater discrepancy between the actual unfavorable condition and the imagined one, the greater distress. Secondly, the individual assesses if the person responsible for the injustice *could* have acted differently. This step is a cognitively complex step, taking into account factors such as the social account (e.g., apology), if any, and situational constraints provided by or imposed upon the responsible person. Thirdly, the individual assesses whether the treatment received is consistent with prevailing ethical and moral codes of conduct. How *should* people interact and treat each other? This final step, the *should* step, is a very complex step because it involves evaluations of appropriate codes of conduct for various types of people in various situations. Further, it suggests strong elements of social influence as inputs to a determination of normative standards of conduct (see also Ellard & Skarlicki, this volume).

Fairness Heuristic Theory focuses on situations when people feel vulnerable to an authority or a group. In turn, an individual will use information from a number of cognitive shortcuts to assess whether he or she is being treated fairly and whether he or she should obey the authority or group. In short, Fairness Heuristic Theory describes a more-or-less automatic processing of justice judgments. This is particularly helpful in explaining how individuals make decisions when faced with incomplete or ambiguous information. For example, this theory may be useful in explaining how workers may evaluate and react to a new supervisor (Lind, Kray, & Thompson, in press). This theory also has strong suggestions of social influence since one of its key elements centers around the question of whether one is valued by one's group (Lind, 2001).

The Fairness Theory corresponds to the more deliberate type of information processing model in that it assumes that people "expend cognitive effort to evaluate information and to integrate it with prior information in forming an attitude" (Zalesny & Ford, p. 227). Fairness Heuristic Theory corresponds to the second type of information processing model where information is more-or-less automatic. This has implications for the consequences of attitudes formed pursuant to each type of theory. Attitudes formed pursuant to Fairness Theory should have greater depth of processing than those formed pursuant to Fairness Heuristic Theory. As a result, individuals who form attitudes by a Fairness Theory approach should have stronger attitudes resulting in behavioral consistency (Fazio, 1986). As mentioned earlier, attitude strength also influences future information processing and event perception. The respective models to illustrate the differences in depth of processing for Fairness Theory and Fairness Heuristic Theory are presented in Figure 2. Dotted lines indicate weaker relationships proposed for Fairness Heuristic Theory as opposed to Fairness Theory.

The model proposed in Figure 2 has the potential to integrate Fairness Theory and Fairness Heuristic Theory. Although both theories suggest roles for social information, different types of social information lead to

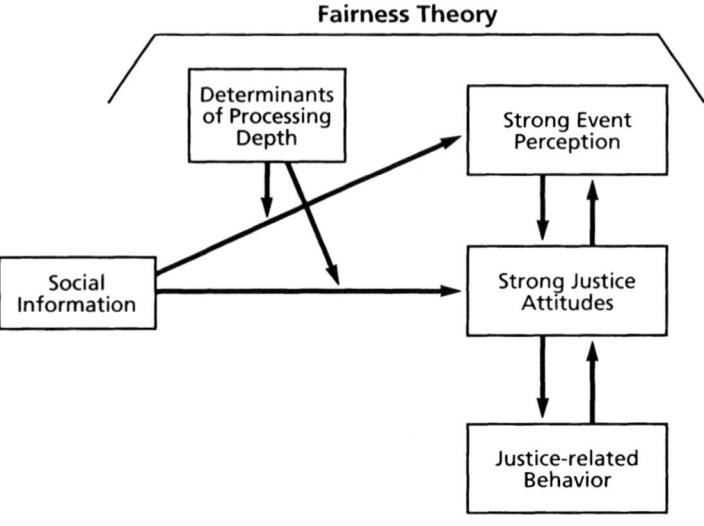

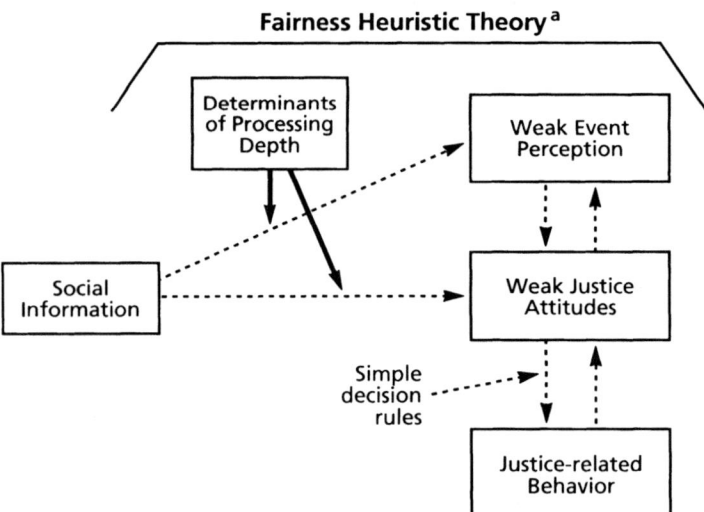

Note: [a] Dotted lines indicate weaker relationships proposed for Fairness Heuristic Theory as opposed to Fairness Theory

Figure 2. Model of social information processing as it applies to Fairness Theory and Fairness Heuristic Theory.

differences in the *strength* of the relationships between perceptions, attitudes, and behavior for each of them. Typically, the strength or effect size of relationships is not something that receives a tremendous amount of attention in the literature. However, this may be one overlooked area where these theories may be useful to detect differences among types of social information. For example, we previously identified four types of social information: opinions, cues, comments affecting needs and values, and interpretation of events. Social cues are more likely to result in automatic processing because they are by nature "automatic," "mindless," or "peripheral" (Zalesny & Ford, 1990, p. 227). However, comments affecting needs and values are more likely to result in "controlled," "deep," or "effortful" analysis because they tend to involve complex cognitive evaluations (Zalesny & Ford, 1990, p. 227). The other two types of social information could, depending on the circumstances and degree of cognition involved, result in either type of processing depth.

RESEARCH AGENDA

The implications of a social information processing approach to justice issues presents a number of possibilities for future research. Generally speaking, these possibilities can be reduced to theoretical, substantive, and methodological issues.

Theoretical Issues

Theoretically, there are possible new avenues of research in the areas of SIP theory and organizational justice. We will discuss each of these below.

SIP Theory
In addition to each of the paths indicated in Figures 1 and 2, this chapter has other implications for SIP theory. SIP theory had been used primarily to explain job satisfaction or performance (Zalesny & Ford, 1990). This chapter extends the theory to include an entirely new construct, organizational justice. In turn, SIP theory can be used to investigate any number of phenomenon that have been found to be related to justice, e.g, pay satisfaction (Greenberg, 1987), reactions to downsizing (Brockner, Konovsky, Cooper-Schneider, Folger, Martin, & Bies, 1994), or legal-claiming (Goldman, 2001; Lind et al., 2000). SIP may be useful in exploring other related phenomenon, such as fairness perception in doctor-patient relationships (Kulik & Holbrook, this volume). Further, the nature of the social information needs greater investigation. As noted, Salancik and Pfeffer (1978) emphasized four types of social influence. However, it is likely that there remain other unexplored types of social influences at work. For example, Goldman (2001) found that advice and information from friends, family, and coworkers predicted the filing of discrimination

claims. Further, he called for additional investigation to parse the differential effects of each source of social information.

Organizational Justice

This chapter proposed different consequences with respect to attitudes formed via Fairness Theory or Fairness Heuristic Theory. It suggests that attitudes formed by Fairness Theory may be stronger and more enduring, capable of being sustained over time, and more predictive of behavior. As noted, the reason for this is the differences in depth of processing proposed for each of the theories. If true, this may have implications in terms of assigning each of these justice process theories their own unique role in explaining justice-related behaviors. For example, Fairness Heuristic Theory may be more useful in understanding why and how individuals form justice judgments when information is incomplete. By contrast, Fairness Theory may be better to explain complex and more enduring attitudes. Longitudinal studies are needed to assess these differences.

Further, the models proposed in Figures 1 and 2 do not differentiate among types of justice. Some of the predictions implicit in the models may vary depending on what type of justice is involved. For example, social information, either directly or as moderated by the determinants of processing depth, may be differentially related to distributive, procedural, or interactional justice. Suppose, for example, that issues of distributive injustice are made more salient because of comparative information provided by friends, family, or co-workers. This, then, suggests that issues of distributive justice may be affected by social information in a way that procedural types of justice are not.

Furthermore, distributive, procedural, and interactional justice may be differentially affected by various determinants of processing depth. For example, Weiss, Suckow, and Cropanzano (1999, p. 791) have observed that certain types of justice may be "more emotional than others." As such, workers experiencing different moods (whether positive or negative) may experience different levels of depth processing which, in turn, may lead to different types of justice as well as to different strengths associated with the justice attitudes.

Substantive Questions

Recognition of the importance of social information to issues of organizational justice should serve to broaden study of the antecedents of justice. For example, the issue of gossip in organizations rarely—if ever—receives serious academic consideration. However, a social information approach encourages consideration of broader contextual issues, such as gossip.[1] In terms of the model proposed in Figure 1, gossip (defined as "trifling, often groundless rumor, usually of a personal, sensational, or intimate nature;

idle talk", Morris, 2000) may be viewed as another type of social information that can affect perceptions, justice attitudes, or justice-related behavior, and is affected by a number of determinants of processing depth, including relevance, predisposition, mood, information salience, or source characteristics - to name only a few. Further, the effects of gossip may vary depending on whether the gossip was later determined to be accurate or not.

A second example of an issue that may be ripe for examination by justice researchers with a social information perspective is the issue of the role of attorneys in affecting justice attitudes and related behavior. The role of attorneys in disputes has received much speculation (e.g., Edelman, Erlanger, & Lande, 1991) but little empirical investigation. An exception is Goldman (1998), who reported that attorney directiveness (attorneys advising aggrieved worker-clients how to proceed with an employment-related claim) and social guidance (advice and information from friends, family, and co-workers) seemed to substitute for each other in predicting employee-related litigation. Goldman (1998) further reported that attorney directiveness was indirectly related to procedural and distributive justice.

These are only a few examples of substantive issues that can benefit from a SIP theory approach to justice issues. Greenberg (1997) has also proposed that issues related to employee theft may benefit from a SIP theory approach.

Methodological Issues

The effects of social information on justice and the models proposed in this chapter suggest certain particular types of methodological issues that are particularly appropriate. For example, standard laboratory experiments with subjects in limited contact with social networks raise questions as to the validity of results with respect to depth of processing issues as well as the larger social and contextual issues. Social cognition research has become more social and contextual in recent years (e.g., Higgins & Sorrentino, 1990; Levine et al., 1993; Wyer & Gruenfeld, 1995).

A social network approach, in particular, seems to offer promise for this area. Social network theory has been deemed as one approach for "elucidating key SIP mechanisms" (Ibarra & Andrews, 1993). Recent advances in the field of network analysis (Wasserman & Faust, 1994) found that networks are important for access to jobs, promotions, and job-related perceptions (Granovetter, 1995; Ibarra & Andrews, 1993; Lai, Lin & Leung, 1998). This suggests that network theory provides a methodological opportunity to study the relationship between SIP theory and organization justice (e.g., Krackhardt, 1990; Shah, 1998; Umphress et al., 2000).

CONCLUSION

In a larger sense, the purpose of this chapter is to encourage justice-related research that includes situational factors such as social influence in the workplace. Specifically, we have argued for a SIP theory approach to justice issues. SIP differs from other theories emphasizing social information because of its explicit emphasis on the usefulness of social information processing in addressing issues of ambiguity (such as those that frequently affect the workplace and issues of fairness). Furthermore, we have also briefly outlined a number of research issues that a SIP theory agenda may examine. Naturally, there exist many other issues in the area of organizational justice that could benefit from inclusion of a SIP theory approach.

NOTES

1. We thank Ilana Haas for this suggestion.

REFERENCES

Abelson, R.P. (1988). Conviction. *American Psychologist, 43*, 267-275.
Albanese, R., & Van Fleet, D.D. (1985). Rational behavior in groups: The free-riding tendency. *Academy of Management Review, 10*, 256-268.
Alderfer, C. (1972). *Human needs in organizational settings.* New York: Free Press of Glencoe.
Alderfer, C. (1977). A critique of Salancik and Pfeffer's examination of need-satisfaction theories. *Administrative Sciences Quarterly, 22*, 658-669.
Ajzen, I., & Fishbein, M. (1980). *Understanding attitudes and predicting social behavior.* Englewood Cliffs, NJ: Prentice-Hall.
Asch, S.E. (1951). Effects of group pressure upon the modification and distortion of judgment. In H. Guetzkow (Ed.), *Groups, leadership, and men.* Pittsburgh: Carnegie Press.
Bandura, A. (1962). Social learning through imitation. In M. R. Jones (Ed.), *Nebraska symposium on motivation* (Vol. 10, pp. 211-274). Lincoln, NB: University of Nebraska Press.
Bandura, A. (1977). *Social learning theory.* New York: Prentice-Hall.
Bandura, A., & Walters, R. (1963). *Social learning and personality development.* New York: Holt, Rinehart & Winston.
Baron, R.M., & Kenny, D.A. (1986). The moderator-mediator variable distinction in social psychological research: Conceptual, strategic, and statistical considerations. *Journal of Personality and Social Psychology, 51*, 1173-1182.
Bies, R., Tripp, T., & Kramer, R. (1997). At the breaking point: Cognitive and social dynamics of revenge in organizations. In R.A. Giacalone & J. Greenberg (Eds.), *Antisocial behavior in organizations* (pp. 18-36). Thousand Oaks, CA: Sage.

Bies, R., & Shapiro, D. (1988). Voice and justification: Their influence on procedural fairness judgments. *Academy of Management Journal, 31*, 676-685.

Blumrosen, A.W., Blumrosen, R.G., Carmignani, M., & Daly, T. (1999). Rosenblum's uncertain defense of employer downsizing. *Employee Rights and Employment Policy Journal, 3*, 167-182.

Brockner, J., Konovsky, M., Cooper-Schneider, R., Folger, R., Martin, C., & Bies, R. J. (1994). Interactive effects of procedural justice and outcome negativity on victims and survivors of job loss. *Academy of Management Journal, 37*, 397-409.

Brockner, J., Wiesenfeld, B., Stephan, J., Hurley, R., Grover, S., Reed, T., DeWitt, R., & Martin, C. (1997). The effects on layoff survivors of their fello survivors' reactions. *Journal of Applied Social Psychology, 27*, 835-863.

Byrne, D. (1971). *The attraction paradigm.* New York: Academic Press.

Cacioppo, J.T., & Petty, R.E. (1982). The need for cognition. *The Journal of Personality and Social Psychology, 42*, 116-131.

Cosmides, L., & Tooby, J. (1992). Cognitive adaptations for social exchange. In J. Barkow, L. Cosmides, & J. Tooby (Eds.), *The adapted mind: Evolutionary psychology and the generation of culture* (pp. 163-228). New York: Oxford University Press.

Cosmides, L., & Tooby, J. (1995). From evolution to adaptions to behavior: Toward an integrated evolutionary psychology. In R. Wong (Ed.), *Biological perspectives on motivated activities* (pp. 11-74). Norwood, NJ: Ablex Publishing.

Cropanzano, R., Byrne, Z., Bobocel, D.R., & Rupp, D. (2001). Moral virtues, fairness heuristics, social entities, and other denizens of organizational justice. *Journal of Vocational Behavior, 58*, 164-209.

Cropanzano, R., Weiss, H., Suckow, K., & Grandey, A. (2000). Doing justice to workplace emotion. In N.M. Ashkanasy, C.E.J. Hartel, & W.J. Zerbe (Eds.), *Emotions in the workplace: Research, theory, and practice* (pp. 49-62). Westport, CT: Quorum Books.

Edelman, L.B., Erlanger, H.S., & Lande, J. (1991). Employers' handling of discrimination complaints: the transformation of rights in the workplace. Working Paper. *Institute for Legal Studies.*

Fazio, R. H. (1986). How do attitudes guide behavior? In R.M. Sorrentino & E.T. Higgins (Eds.), *Handbook of motivation and cognition* (pp. 204-243). New York: Guilford.

Festinger, L. (1954). A theory of social comparison processes. *Human Relations, 7*, 117-140.

Fisher, C., Ilgen, D., & Hoyer, W. (1979). Source credibility, information favorability, and job offer acceptance. *Academy of Management Journal, 22*, 94-103.

Folger, R., & Cropanzano, R. (2001). Fairness theory: Justice as accountability. In J. Greenberg & R. Cropanzano (Eds.), *Advances in organizational justice* (pp. 1-55). Stanford, CA: Stanford University Press.

Folger, R., Rosenfield, D., Grove, J., & Corkan, L. (1979). Effects of "voice" and peer opinions on responses to inequity. *Journal of Personality and Social Psychology, 12*, 2253-2261.

Goldman, B.M. (2001). Toward an understanding of employment discrimination claiming: An integration of organizational justice and social information processing theories. *Personnel Psychology, 54*, 361-386.

Goldman, B.M. (1998). *Employment discrimination-claiming behavior: Test of a model of organizational justice.* Unpublished doctoral dissertation. University of Maryland.

Granovetter, M.S. (1995). *Getting a job: A study of contacts and careers* (2nd ed.). Chicago: University of Chicago Press.

Greenberg, J. (1987). Reactions to procedural injustice in payment distributions: Do the ends justify the means? *Journal of Applied Psychology, 72*, 55-61.

Greenberg, J. (1997). A social influence model of employee theft: Beyond the fraud triangle. *Research on Negotiation in Organizations, 6*, 29-51.

Hackman, J.R. (1976). Group influences on individuals. In M.D. Dunnette (Ed.), *Handbook of industrial and organizational psychology* (pp. 1455-1525). Chicago: Rand McNally.

Higgins, E. T., & Sorrentino, R. M. (1990). *Handbook of motivation and cognition: Foundations of social behavior* (Vol. 2). New York: Guilford.

Huo, Y., Smith, H.J., Tyler, T.R., & Lind, E.A. (1996). Superordinate identification, subgroup identification, and justice concerns: Is separatism the problem; assimilation the answer? *Psychological Science, 7*, 40-45.

Ibarra, H., & Andrews, S.B. (1993). Power, social influence, and sense making: Effects of network centrality and proximity on employee perceptions. *Administrative Science Quarterly, 38*, 277-303.

Ingram, R.E. (1984). Information processing and feedback: Effects of mood and information favorability on the congnitive processing of personally relevant information. *Cognitive Therapy & Research, 8*(4), 371-386.

Krackhardt, D. (1990). Assessing the political landscape: Structure, cognition and power in organizations. *Administrative Science Quarterly, 35*, 342-369.

Kramer, R.M. (1991). Intergroup relations and organizational dilemmas: The role of categorization processes. In L.L. Cummings & B. M. Staw (Eds.), *Research in Organizational Behavior* (Vol. 13, pp. 191-228). Greenwich, CT: JAI Press.

Krosnick, J.A. (1986). *Policy voting in American presidential elections: An application of psychology theory to American politics.* Unpublished doctoral dissertation, University of Michigan.

Lai, G., Lin, N., & Leung, S. (1998). Network resources, contact resources, and status attainment. *Social Networks, 20*, 159-178.

Latané, B. (1981). Psychology of social impact. *American Psychologist, 36*, 343-356.

Levine, J., Resnick, L., & Higgins, E. (1993). Social foundations of cognition. *Annual Review of Psychology, 44*, 585-612.

Lind, E.A. (2001). Fairness heuristic theory: Justice judgments as pivotal cognitions in organizational relations. In J. Greenberg & R. Cropanzano (Eds.), *Advances in organizational justice* (pp. 56-88). Stanford, CA: Stanford University Press.

Lind, E.A., Greenberg, J., Scott, K., & Welchans, T.D. (2000). The winding road from employee to complainant: Situational and psychological determinants of wrongful-termination claims. *Administrative Science Quarterly, 45*, 557-590.

Lind, E.A., Kray, L., & Thompson, L. (in press). Primacy effects in justice judgments: Testing predictions from fairness heuristic theory. *Organizational Behavior and Human Decision Processes.*

Lind, E.A., & Tyler, T. R. (1988). *The social psychology of procedural justice.* New York: Plenum.

Locke, E.A., & Taylor, M.S. (1990). Stress, coping and the meaning of work. In A. P. Brief & W.R. Nord (Eds.), *Meanings of occupational work: A collection of essays* (pp. 135-170). Lexington, MA: Lexington Books.

McGrath, J.E. (1984). *Groups: Interaction and performance.* Englewood Cliffs, NJ: Prentice-Hall, Inc.

Milgram, S. (1974). *Obedience to authority.* London, England: Tavistock Institute.

Miller, K.I., & Monge, P.R. (1985). Social information and employee anxiety about organizational change. *Human Communication Research, 11*, 365-386.

Moore, B., Underwood, B., Heberlein, P., Doyle, L., & Litzie, K. (1979). Generalization of feedback about performance. *Cognitive Therapy and Research, 3*, 371-380.

Moorman, R.H. (1991). Relationship between organizational justice and organizational citizenship behaviors: Do fairness perceptions influence employee citizenship?" *Journal of Applied Psychology, 76*, 845-855.

Morris, W. (2000), *The American heritage dictionary of the English language.* Boston, MA: Houghton Mifflin Company.

Nelson, R. E., & Craighead, W. E. (1977). Perception of reinforcement, self-reinforcement, and depression. *Journal of Abnormal Psychology, 86*, 379-388.

Nord, W.R., & Doherty, E.M. (1995). Toward an improved framework for conceptualizing the conflict process. *Research on Negotiations in Organizations, 4*, 173-240.

Petty, R.E., & Cacioppo, J.T. (1986). The elaboration likelihood model of persuasion. In L. Berkowitz (Ed.), *Advances in Experimental Social Psychology* (Vol.19, pp.123-205). Orlando, FL: Academic Press.

Pfeffer, J. (1980). A partial test of the social information processing model of job attitudes. *Human Relations, 33*, 457-476.

Salancik, G.R. (1976). Extrinsic attribution and the use of behavioral information to infer attitudes. *Journal of Personality and Social Psychology, 34*, 1302-1312.

Salancik, G.R., & Pfeffer, J. (1978). A social information processing approach to job attitudes and task design. *Administrative Science Quarterly, 23*, 224-253.

Schnake, M.E., & Dumler, M.P. (1987). The social information processing model of task design. *Group and Organization Studies, 12*, 221-240.

Shah, P. (1998). Who are employees' social referents? Using a network perspective to determine referent others. *Academy of Management Journal, 41*, 249-268.

Sherif, M. (1936). *The psychology of social norms.* New York: Harper.

Sherif, C.W., Sherif, M., & Nebergall, R.E. (1965). *Attitude and attitude change: The social judgment-involvement approach.* Philadelphia, PA: Saunders.

Sussman, M., & Vecchio, R.P. (1991). A social influence interpretation of worker motivation. In R.M. Steers and L.W. Porter (Eds.), *Motivation and work behavior* (5th ed., pp. 208-219). New York: McGraw-Hill, Inc.

Tajfel, H., & Turner, J.C. (1979). An integrative theory of intergroup conflict. In W.G. Austin & S. Worchel (Eds.), *The social psychology of intergroup relations* (pp. 34-47). Monterey, CA: Brooks/Cole.

Tannen, D. (1999). Framing and reframing. In R. Lewicki, D. Saunders, & J. Minton (Eds.), *Negotiation: Readings, exercises, and cases* (3rd ed., pp. 68-78). Boston: Irwin/McGraw-Hill.

Taylor, S., & Fiske, S. (1978). Salience, attention and attribution: Top of the head phenomena. In L. Berkowitz (Ed.), *Advances in experimental social psychology* (Vol. 11, pp. 249-288). New York: Academic Press.

Thompson, L., & Fine, G.A. (1999). Socially shared cognition, affect, and behavior: A review and integration. *Personality and Social Psychology Review, 3*(4), 278-302.

Turner, J.C., Hogg, M.A., Oakes, P.J., Reicher, S.D., & Wetherell, M.S. (1987). *Rediscovering the social group: A self-categorization theory.* New York: Basil Blackwell.

Tyler, T.R., & Bies, R. (1990). Beyond formal procedures: The interpersonal context of procedural justice. In J.S. Carroll (Ed.), *Applied Social Psychology & Organizational Settings.* (pp. 77-98). Hillsdale, NJ: Lawrence Erlbaum Associates.

Umphress, E., Labianca, G., Scholten, L., Kass, E., Brass, D. (2000). The social construction of organizational justice perceptions: A social networks approach. *Proceedings of the Academy of Management, Toronto, Canada.*

Van den Bos, K., & Lind, E.A. (in press). Uncertainty management by means of fairness judgments. In M.P. Zanna (Ed.), *Advances in experimental social psychology* (Vol. 34). San Diego, CA: Academic Press.

Vaux, A., Riedel, S., & Stewart, D. (1987). Modes of social support: The social support behaviors. *American Journal of Community Psychology, 15,* 209-237.

Wasserman, S., & Faust, K. (1994). *Social network analysis: Methods and applications.* Cambridge: Cambridge University Press.

Watson, D. & Clark, L. (1992). On traits and temperament: General and specific factors of emotional experience and their relation to the five-factor model. *Journal of Personality, 60,* 441-476.

Weiss, H.M., & Cropanzano, R. (1996). Affective events theory: A theoretical discussion of the structure, causes and consequences of affective experiences at work. *Research in Organizational Behavior, 18,* 1-74.

Weiss, H.M., Suckow, K., & Cropanzano, R. (1999). Effects of justice conditions on discrete emotions. *Journal of Applied Psychology, 84,* 786-794.

Williams, H.A. (1995). There are no free gifts! Social support and the need for reciprocity. *Human Organization, 54,* 401-409.

Wyer, R.S., & Gruenfeld, D.H. (1995). Information processing in interpersonal communication. In D.E. Hewes (Ed.), *The cognitive bases of interpersonal communication* (pp. 7–47). Hillsdale, NJ: Lawrence Erlbaum Associates.

Youngblood, S., Trevino, L., & Favia, M. (1992). Reactions to unjust dismissal and third-party dispute resolution: A justice framework. *Employee Responsibilities and Rights Journal, 5,* 283-307.

Zalesny, M.D., & Farace, R.V. (1986). A field study of social information processing: Mean differences and variance differences. *Human Communication Research, 13,* 268-290.

Zalesny, M.D., & Ford, K. (1990). Extending the social information processing perspective: New links to attitudes, behaviors, and perceptions. *Organizational Behavior and Human Decision Processes, 47,* 205-246.

PART II

EXPANDING THE DOMAIN OF UNFAIRNESS

CHAPTER 5

A THIRD-PARTY OBSERVER'S REACTIONS TO EMPLOYEE MISTREATMENT:

Motivational and Cognitive Processes in Deservingness Assessments

John H. Ellard and Daniel P. Skarlicki

ABSTRACT

We discuss how deservingness can be a useful construct for understanding third-party reactions to employee mistreatment. Deservingness reflects observers' sense that the employee is more or less deserving of his or her fate by virtue of the employee's actions or who the employee is, which in turn affects fairness judgments. Studies of deservingness indicate that judgments can be a function of whether the relevant information is processed implicitly and in the service of motivational concerns or processed explicitly and rationally. In the context of employee mistreatment, implicit, motivated processing can give rise to reactions such as victim blaming or psychological distancing from the victim. Under conditions that favor more rational and explicit processing, observers more thoroughly consider antecedents of mistreatment and arrive at judgments that are consistent with more rational models of blame assignment and deservingness. The implications of a deservingness analysis of observer reactions for both theory and practice are considered.

A report by Ernst and Young on the sporting goods giant Nike's employment practices in third world countries found numerous occasions of employee physical and sexual abuse. In one incident, a manager taped a woman's mouth shut for talking during working hours. On another occasion, a supervisor hit a worker on the back of the head with a Nike shoe. Subsequent to the report's release, Nike's sales decreased and its stock experienced a significant drop in price. Executives at Nike credit part of the company's significant loss in 1998 third quarter sales to its negative image (Saporito, 1998).

A majority of research on organizational justice has tended to focus on mistreatment from the victim's perspective. The Nike story illustrates, however, that third-party observers (in this case investors and customers) can also react to mistreatment. It is precisely this possibility that gives rise to our focus on how observers are affected by the justice implications of employees' experiences. The story suggests that observers' perceptions of employee mistreatment have the potential to erode a company's reputation, goodwill, and competitive advantage. This incident also highlights the importance of understanding third-party reactions to employee treatment.

Third-party observers are defined as individuals who might not be the target of an injustice, but who make fairness judgments nonetheless. Examples of observers include customers, potential employees, investors, judges, and other members of the general public. These observers might not necessarily directly observe the mistreatment or the victim's behavior, but their awareness must be sufficient to instigate a cognitive appraisal of the mistreatment.

Organizational justice theories would locate Nike's investors' and customers' decisions to either abandon or withdraw support from the firm in the "mistreatment" of the employees. Employee mistreatment is defined as the perception that a *transgressor*—a responsible agent or agency—neglected or violated the entitlements of an employee, who becomes the *victim* (Montada, 1992). Entitlements can include aspects of distributive (i.e., outcomes), procedural (i.e., procedures used to derive one's outcomes), or interactional justice (i.e., interpersonal treatment by one's supervisor). This definition also acknowledges that events not seen as unfair by the victim can be seen as unfair by the observer.

From a justice perspective, investors and/or customers in the Nike scenario may have made a moral decision to withdrawal their support from a company that treats its employees unfairly. Yet, other, equally plausible, possibilities readily come to mind that do not require assumptions about concerns for employees. For example, investors, quite reasonably, may have decided that the mistreatment was symptomatic of a company in trouble, or at the very least, people of questionable judgment were running the company.

Our focus on justice leads us to consider some basic issues, such as why observers would be at all concerned about fair treatment of employees in situations such as this. We consider critical factors involved in arousing fairness concerns in observers along with analysis of the different forms those concerns can take in observer reactions. For instance, our analysis leads us to consider that there were also those Nike investors who were made aware of the report, but chose *not* to sell their stock. Some investors, for example, may have deemed the Nike treatment to be suitable for correcting inappropriate behavior, or perhaps their justice concerns were superseded by the opportunity for financial gain (i.e., holding on to the stock). Similarly, not all customers who learned of the Nike report decided to withdraw their support from Nike; some customers rationalized reasons to purchase Nike products.

The analysis we develop to understand such variability in observer reactions builds on recent justice theory and research and focuses on observer judgments of deservingness as a key component of justice-based observer reactions to mistreatment. Following consideration of the role of deservingness in distributive, procedural, and interactional justice, we examine the nature of deservingness, noting in particular that observer deservingness assessments are significantly affected by whether the relevant information is processed explicitly and rationally or implicitly and in the service of motivational concerns including justice motivation. Understanding the observer's information processing mode is crucial for determining, for instance, whether the observer will react to mistreatment by blaming the victim, or by deeming that the treatment was undeserved and hence unfair. Drawing on research that has approached deservingness from a justice motive perspective, we consider in detail how motivated deservingness cognitions give rise to a number of different possible reactions to employee mistreatment. The analysis then turns to studies of deservingness that have emphasized the capacity people have, under certain circumstances, to consider deservingness rationally and explicitly. Finally, we consider factors that may govern implicitly- versus explicitly-based deservingness judgments.

A THIRD-PARTY OBSERVER'S VIEW OF UNFAIRNESS

Organizational scientists seeking to understand the implications of employee mistreatment have found organizational justice theories to have considerable explanatory power. By conceptualizing mistreatment as injustice, researchers have been able to shed considerable light on the antecedents of a variety of potentially problematic employee behaviors including theft (e.g., Greenberg, 1990), absenteeism (e.g., Cropanzano & Folger, 1991), litigation against employers (e.g., Bies & Tyler, 1993), retaliation (Skarlicki & Folger, 1998), voluntary turnover (e.g., Aquino, Griffeth,

Allen, & Hom, 1997), and withdrawal of citizenship behavior (Jermier, Knights, & Nord, 1994). The relatively few empirical studies on third-party observers suggest that observers' perceptions of fairness are indeed affected by how employees are treated, including the views of co-workers (Brockner, 1990; Brockner, Davy, & Carter, 1985; Brockner, Grover, Reed, DeWitt, & O'Malley, 1987), potential employees, customers, and investors (Skarlicki, Ellard, & Kelln, 1998), friends (Crosby, 1982; Goldman, 1999) and members of the public (Leung, Chiu, & Au, 1993). A conclusion of these studies is that reactions to injustice do not depend on one's personal experiences–they can be initiated vicariously.

It is interesting to note that current organizational justice theories, to the extent that they have addressed third-party reactions, have assumed that perceptions of injustice for observers parallel those of the directly affected but are less intense (e.g., Lind, Kray, & Thompson, 1998; Tyler & Smith, 1998; Walster, Walster, & Berscheid, 1978). From the growing body of justice research, however, we know that this is not always so. Observers and victims can respond in significantly different ways. Studies have found that, for example, although a layoff victim can feel mistreated, observers can view the situation as fair, even to the point of derogating the victim (Skarlicki et al., 1998). Other studies have shown that observers' concerns for fairness can be more intense than those of the victim. Crosby (1984) reported that despite objective data showing wage discrimination, working women tended not to report feelings of personal injustice. Thus, knowing that an employee has been mistreated, and knowing how he or she has responded is not sufficient to predict how an observer will respond to the event. A complex set of processes operate for observers in the context of employee mistreatment that can differ from those of a victim. In order to understand observers' responses to unfair treatment more clearly, there is a need to identify the motivational, cognitive, and social processes that determine them. We propose that analysis of observers' deservingness judgments can shed light on their reactions to mistreatment.

INJUSTICE AND DESERVINGNESS

Recent justice research has highlighted the extent to which reactions to injustice for both victims and observers hinge critically on judgments of deservingness (e.g., Feather 1999a & b; Heuer, Blumenthal, Douglas, & Weinblatt, 1999; Lerner, 1987; Lupfer & Gingrich, 1999; Major, 1994; Miller, 2001). Deservingness refers to the judgment, determined implicitly or explicitly, that peoples' circumstances are the ones they are entitled to by virtue of their actions or who they are. Thus, deservingness judgments rest on an observer's evaluative assessments of persons and their outcomes, and the alignment of the two (Feather, 1999a; Lerner, 1980). Individuals are furthermore evaluated in terms of their character and their behavior. Thus, individuals are deemed to be "good" or "bad" by virtue of the things they have done or their moral character. A "good" person is deserving of "good" outcomes and undeserving of "bad" outcomes. The outcomes an individual receives will be perceived as deserved if the valence and magnitude of the outcome corresponds with the observer's evaluation of the person.

The link between deservingness judgments and fairness arises from the sense of requiredness and "ought" that govern expectations about the relation between people and their outcomes (Lerner, 1987). It is not merely that we recognize outcomes as deserved when their valence matches the valence for the person, but that we expect and assume that good and bad outcomes *should* align themselves with good and bad people accordingly. Moreover, the moral imperative associated with deservingness judgments is a proximal psychological determinant of an observer's sense that what has happened to the victim is "fair" or "unfair."

We propose that an observer's fairness assessments of employee mistreatment are most immediately and proximally determined by the observer's deservingness judgments of the employee's fate. In the Nike episode, observers are likely to have imagined the treatment as undeserved, which has important implications for their reactions.

Deservingness constitutes a useful point of departure for understanding third-party reactions to mistreatment for a number of reasons. First, there is an increasing recognition that the distributive, procedural, and interactional aspects of justice have their effects on fairness judgments through their impact on people's sense of deservingness (Heuer et al., 1999; Miller, 2001). Although relational approaches to procedural justice (Lind & Tyler, 1988) emphasize the importance of standing and respect in a social organization for perceptions of fairness, the actual experience of such treatment as fair requires considering whether it was deserved in the first place. For instance, Heuer and colleagues (1999, Study 1) found that deservingness significantly moderated the effect of a manager's treatment of a hypothetical coworker on observers' perceptions of procedural justice. In this study, the manager either showed respect or disrespect for the employee. Deservingness was manipulated in terms of the quality of the employee's performance and his responsibility for it. The moderating effects of deservingness were apparent in the finding that the highest ratings of procedural fairness were assigned when respectful treatment followed good performance for which the employee was responsible. When the employee was not responsible (good performance due to luck) but was treated with respect, observers' fairness ratings were relatively lower. The expected mirror image pattern was also observed when managers responded to good behavior with disrespect. Particularly low ratings occurred when the employee was responsible for good performance, but these ratings were less negative than when the employee's performance was due to luck.

Of particular interest was the finding that when the employee was viewed as responsible for poor performance, disrespectful treatment from management was viewed as significantly *more fair* than respectful treatment. This finding highlights an important distinction between normatively derived deservingness prescriptions such as "everyone deserves respect" or "everyone deserves their day in court" and psychologically based experiences of deservingness reflecting basic processes of cognitive development. Thus psychologically based rules of entitlement can differ from normative expectations and can dominate an observer's reactions to mistreatment. The psychologically based deservingness expectations are largely preconscious constructions of "who is entitled to what" based on evaluations of the actor and his or her outcomes.

Whereas Heuer and colleagues (1999) focused on deservingness as a critical mediating variable for procedural justice, similar arguments have been made for distributive (Lerner, 1987; Major, 1994; Skitka & Tetlock, 1992; Wenzel, 2000) and interactional justice (Miller, 2001). Thus, a deservingness approach to justice is consistent with writings proposing that fairness judgments might not require distinctions between distributive, procedural, and interactional justice (see Cropanzano & Ambrose, 1996 for a general discussion of this issue). Specifically, observers would be expected to view procedures, outcome distributions, and interpersonal treatment as fair to the degree that they believe the consequences for the target person are deserved, and unfair to the degree that the consequences are not deserved.

A second reason for focusing on a deservingness framework for understanding observer fairness judgments is that much is known about motivational and cognitive determinants of deservingness assessments (Feather, 1999b; Lerner & Miller, 1978; Lerner, 1980, 1998; Lerner & Goldberg, 1999; Lupfer & Gingrich, 1999). For instance, the broad distinction between sympathetic and unsympathetic reactions to victims (Brockner & Greenberg, 1990) can be meaningfully approached through consideration of the extent to which observers view the victim's fate as deserved (cf. Skarlicki et al, 1998). In the context of employee mistreatment, factors contributing to observers' sense that the employee's fate is undeserved will increase observer judgments of unfairness while factors suggesting the mistreatment is "deserved" will serve to diminish observer concerns' about unfairness.

Third, deservingness offers an explanation for why an observer's and victim's perspective may differ. Although both victims' and observers' are likely to consider deservingness in their fairness judgments, there is an important distinction: the observer is more likely than the victim to deem the mistreatment as deserving. A victim's sense of deservingness will be influenced by its threat to his or her self-esteem, whereas these processes may be less critical to an observer (e.g., Jones, 1976). For example, Heuer and colleagues (1999) in a follow-up study to the research described above, found that when participants were asked to consider the fairness implications of respectful treatment directed at *themselves* as a function of the quality of their own behavior and how responsible they were, the deservingness manipulations continued to moderate fair process effects, but participants no longer rated disrespect as more fair than respect for negative behavior (i.e., there was a stronger main effect for the respect manipulation that resulted in an ordinal rather than a cross-over interaction for the deservingness variable). Presumably, the sense of entitlement for self is stronger than for others.

Finally, a deservingness approach to examining observer reactions provides a strong theoretical and empirical basis for understanding observer reactions to employee mistreatment beyond fairness judgments, including retributive justice and social protest. Feather (1998), for instance, developed a social–cognitive process model of observer retributive reactions to transgressions that incorporates deservingness as a central mediating variable.

Given that deservingness can play a significant role in third-party observers' perceptions of fairness, it is relevant to consider how deservingness judgments form. We now turn to a discussion of how deservingness views can emerge via two different modes of information processing.

Modes of Observer Information Processing and Deservingness

Recent investigations of different modes of information processing have important implications for observer deservingness assessments. For instance, dual-processing theories distinguish between implicit, automatic, and motivated information processing and explicit or rational[1] processing (cf. Chaiken & Trope, 1999). On the automatic, implicit side, information processing is characterized by motivated inferences, reliance on heuristics, speed, associative rather than logical connections, and little or no cognitive elaboration. Alternatively, the explicit, rational mode of information processing is associated with relatively greater cognitive elaboration, logical or "psycho-logical" connections, and slower and intentional processing. In a variety of contexts including attitude change (Chaiken, 1987; Petty & Cacciopo, 1986), person perception (Uleman, 1999), probability assessments (Epstein, 1994), and moral judgment (Shweder & Haidt, 1993), researchers have found that the mode of processing has important implications for the information processing outcome. For example, under conditions conducive of cognitive elaboration and rational processing (e.g., judges and arbitrators), observers are more inclined to consider situational factors in forming impressions of others than when they are required to make their judgments under time pressure (Gilbert & Malone, 1995).

Distinguishing between implicit and explicit modes of processing is useful in the domain of deservingness judgments because the distinction has implications for predicting observers' reactions to employee mistreatment. The usefulness of understanding the dual modes of information processing has also been raised by other writers (e.g., Goldman, this volume). Lerner and Goldberg (1999) argued that the implicit nature of just world beliefs and phenomena associated with them (i.e., victim blaming) represent how deservingness judgments take form when the observer's mode of processing is characterized by motivated cognition (e.g., the need to believe in a just world), automaticity, and preconscious implicit judgment. Deservingness judgments made in this mode can depart from normatively rational deservingness judgments. Feather's (1999) model of deservingness, in contrast, highlights observers' capacities for making complexly derived deservingness assessments that incorporate not only information about the valences associated with people and their outcomes and actions but also elements of responsibility judgments such as forseeability and controllability.

How might these modes of processing affect observers' reactions to mistreatment? Beginning with implicit pre-conscious processing, we consider first how reactions to employee mistreatment would be expected to take form when observers' deservingness concerns result in "motivated judgments". We then consider another subset of implicit preconscious processes that are more purely cognitive, such as information processing heuristics, that have implications for deservingness. Finally, we discuss how observers' deservingness assessments of employee mistreatment take form when their mode of information processing is more explicit and rational.

Motivated Cognition and Deservingness

To speak of employee "mistreatment" is to assume that by some generally accepted criterion of fairness, an employee has been unfairly treated or somehow victimized. As noted earlier, an extensive body of literature has demonstrated that observers of mistreatment may or may not react with concern depending on whether or not they decide that the employee's fate was deserved (cf. Lerner, 1980; Lerner & Miller, 1978). This literature also highlights the extent to which learning of mistreatment can motivate observers to view it as deserved to reduce their justice-based distress. According to just world theory (Lerner, 1980), this occurs because the injustice of mistreatment is threatening to the idea of a just world. The resulting negative drive to restore one's sense of the world as a just place can be accommodated through any of a number of behavioral and psychological mechanisms, all designed to restore the observer's sense that people do in fact get what they deserve. Just world theory therefore reminds us that observers can be disinclined to acknowledge mistreatment as unfair because to do so is threatening to our sense of a just world.

In some instances observers may be moved to take action to redress the injustice themselves, but usually only when they have reason to believe that their efforts will succeed in fully ameliorating what has happened. Lerner and Simmons (1966) found that when given a behavioral option to compensate someone participants had just observed suffering innocently, 92% exercised that option and as a result were significantly less likely to derogate the victim than participants who did not have the option to intervene. Of course, observers of employee mistreatment are rarely in a position to compensate employees through their own actions, but they may well be willing to support employees' own efforts at seeking compensation or the efforts of other third parties in doing so, particularly if they believe that their expressions of support are likely to fully address the injustice (Walster, Berscheid, & Walster, 1976). Public support for the Nike employees in the above story, for instance would, in this analysis, hinge significantly on the perception that the status quo is effectively undeserved treatment for which the employees are entitled compensation. At the same time, support will be fragile if it is hard for observers to sense that anything they might do in support of employees will effectively redress the injustice. When observers doubt the effectiveness of their actions, they may be motivated to implement other less rational and more psychological tactics to reduce their injustice distress (Lerner & Simmons, 1966).

There are a number of psychological reactions that people can have to the mistreatment of others to help them reduce injustice distress. Perhaps the most common and powerful but least studied directly, is simply to deny the injustice or to withdraw psychologically (Lerner, 1980). For example, Pancer (1988) found that participants maintained more physical distance from a public display soliciting assistance for child victims when the display included a vivid picture of a child than when it did not. Moreover, on a subsequent cued recall measure, participants scoring high on a measure of just world beliefs recalled significantly fewer details from the vivid victim display than did low scorers. Thus, individuals with a high (versus low) belief that the world is a place where people get what they deserve were less able to recall information that threatened the belief. In the same way, to the extent that employee mistreatment is upsetting, observers in many instances may literally or psychologically "move on" and think about something else.

In our Nike example, this effect might cause some investors to "tune out" information regarding employee mistreatment when buying Nike stock. On the other hand, "moving on" can be problematic for organizations if the observer is a potential customer or investor in an environment where establishing and maintaining people's attention is vital for business success. Writers have argued that in the current global environment, with its vast array of consumer and investor choices, attracting and maintaining stakeholders' attention is the key variable for success in the new millennium (Friedman, 2000). Thus the notion of "moving on" that can arise from motivated cognition has important implications for organizations.

Observers can alternatively ameliorate their concerns by deeming that the outcomes are deserved. This can be done by attributing the outcome to the victim's behavior (i.e., victim blame, Walster, 1966) or by derogating the victim (Lerner & Simmons, 1966). In the context of an organizational layoff, for example, Skarlicki and colleagues (1998) found that by derogating the laid-off employees, participants' tendency to see procedural unfairness in the layoff was diminished. Presumably, by seeing the employees as deserving of their fate, participants were able to see what happened as fair.

In circumstances where observers are unable or unwilling to blame or derogate the victim, they may alternatively choose to reevaluate the outcome instead by minimizing its negativity ("those laid-off employees won't have trouble finding work again") or imagining compensation for the victim ("laid-off people often find that it forces them to become more self-reliant and entrepreneurial").

Thus, to the extent that observers' justice concerns are aroused by employee mistreatment, a variety of deservingness reactions are possible, all of which are guided not only by a concern for the victim, but also by a desire to minimize the observer's justice distress. The variety of mechanisms that serve this end, combined with their apparent frequent use, suggests that observers are often motivated to make the unfairness associated with mistreatment disappear through redress, psychological disengagement, or distortion. These efforts can have nontrivial implications for the employer, employees, or both, including the desire to avoid the organization psychologically, actively support compensation initiatives for employees, or alternatively, blame or derogate the victim. In the latter instance, opportunities for double victimization arise if customers, for instance, treat employees poorly because the employer's unfair treatment has led the employee to be derogated.

Of course, observers at times can also be engaged by the unfairness of the victims' fate and become immersed in the injustice of it all rather than strive to make it go away. This reaction, however, comes at a psychological price in two ways. First, active engagement in the distress of others usually involves experiencing increased levels of distress and negative affect oneself, particularly feelings of anger (Keltner, Ellsworth, & Edwards, 1993; Smith & Ellsworth, 1985). Second, it is difficult to involve oneself in the unjust fates of others without, at the same time, jeopardizing one's own personal deservingness (Miller, 1977). Nonetheless, observers may be unavoidably caught up in the unjust fates of others if they strongly identify with the victim (Aderman, Brehm, & Katz, 1974; Chaikin & Darley, 1973; Stokols & Schopler, 1973) or see their own fate linked to the victim's fate (Lerner & Matthews, 1967). The research on the effects of psychological links between observer and victim demonstrates the power of these processes in the opposite direction. When observers identify with the harmdoer, they are inclined to blame anything but the harmdoer and are more given to victim derogation (Chaikin & Darley, 1973). Thus, in circumstances where employee mistreatment is personally relevant to the observer, reactions will hinge significantly on whether or not the observer identifies primarily with the victim or the transgressor. For example, layoff survivors, by virtue of their status as employees in the same organization that laid off other employees, have cause, on the basis of their own immediate experience, to be concerned about their own fates. In this case, the more observers of mistreatment are concerned for their own fates, the less they will deem the victim as deserving.

The implications of identification with either the victim or the source of the injustice was made apparent in a series of studies reported by Brockner and Greenberg (1990). They found that whether layoff survivors respond sympathetically or unsympathetically toward the layoff victim depended on the survivor's relationship with both the victims of the layoff and/or the organization. The findings showed that the closer the relationship between the survivors and the organization (rather than the victim), the more likely that survivors would respond unsympathetically toward the victims, and sympathetically toward the organization. Presumably, the experience of common fate resulting in identification with the victim reduces deservingness-restoring mechanisms such as victim derogation or blame, leaving the observer more likely to focus their attention on the source of the injustice (Lerner & Miller, 1978).

Perceived personal similarity between observer and victim may also forge psychological links that serve to moderate observer reactions. Similar attributes to the victim can arouse self-concern, particularly where the similar attributes are thought to have played a role in the mistreatment. Women, for instance, might become highly focused on an injustice if they believe that women were at particular risk for the mistreatment (e.g., glass ceiling effects) (Mollica, Gray, Trevino, & DeWitt, 1999). Brockner, Davy, and Carter (1985) found that when participants perceived that someone like themselves had been laid off unfairly, they took out their strong feelings of injustice on the organization. The more that observers saw themselves as similar to the victim, the greater their sympathetic response to the mistreatment. Conversely, the less that observers saw similarities between themselves and the victim, the less sympathetic their response to the mistreatment.

The effects of personal similarity for observer reactions do not always follow this pattern however. Novak and Lerner (1968) found that a person with very similar background, attitudes, and aspirations elicited more avoidance from observers than a dissimilar person when they learned that the person had experienced a "nervous breakdown." Thus, when personal similarity is threatening to personal deservingness ("if this has happened to someone so much like me then I must be vulnerable too"), observers may be inclined to distance themselves psychologically and physically.

Motivated Cognition and Heuristic Processing

Motivated cognition can also affect an observer's deservingness perceptions through heuristic processing (Lerner & Goldberg, 1999). Stroessner and Heuer (1996) provide an illustration of heuristic processing in procedural justice judgments. They examined the effects of illusory correlations--that people often misjudge the covariation between two distinctive or unusual events–on observers' responses to perceived unfairness. In this study, participants read a set of sentences, each describing members of one of two groups (A or B) as having either fair or unfair interactions with the police. The sentence set included twice as many descriptions of Group A as of Group B. Despite an identical ratio of fair and unfair exchanges within groups, the participants reported that the police had demonstrated an unfair bias against the smaller group (Group B). The participants were then asked to adjudicate a case involving infractions purportedly committed by members of Group A or B. Results showed that if they perceived that the group had received relatively unfavorable treatment from the police (Group B), then they were less likely to find the members of the group guilty. Conversely, if participants believed that a group received relatively favorable treatment (Group A), harsher judgements followed.

These findings are significant to the study of observers' justice judgments for at least two reasons. First, they illustrate that cognitive bias alone can make observers "see" unfair treatment even when it does not exist. Second, it shows a paradoxical effect of cognitive bias on behavioral responses to mistreatment: In addition to making erroneous procedural justice judgements, observers in this study attempted to restore justice and by doing so, created inequity among the experimental groups.

Deservingness assessments can also be affected by correspondence bias. Attribution researchers have extensively documented a common tendency for observers to attribute more causal significance to the actor for his or her behavior than is warranted given the presence of other, usually situational influences (Gilbert & Malone, 1995; Ross, 1977). This attributional bias of course invites a parallel bias toward seeing victims as deserving of their fate by making it more likely for observers to see the victim's fate as the result of his or her actions.

A similar automatic heuristic affecting reactions to the fate of others has been described as "hindsight bias" (Fischoff, 1975). This "I knew it all along" bias leads observers, given knowledge of an outcome, to feel that the outcome that actually occurred was more inevitable and likely than other possible outcomes. The phenomenon constitutes an alternative, cognitive explanation, for observers blaming the victim. For instance, Janoff-Bulman, Timko, and Carli (1985) demonstrated in a study of observer reactions to a rape victim that participants with knowledge of the outcome prior to reading about activities involving the victim and her date rated her behavior as more foolhardy and irresponsible than participants rating the same behavior without prior knowledge of the outcome. Observers with the benefit of hindsight appear to assume that the victim should have been able to foresee the outcome and thus have taken steps to avoid it.

Although our discussion of biases and heuristics is not meant to be exhaustive, the correspondence and hindsight biases illustrate some of the automatic cognitive heuristics that can implicitly inform observer reactions to employee mistreatment through the effects on deservingness. Because the organizational context contains numerous dynamics of power, control, and identity, extrapolations from nonorganizational research need to be studied in the context of employee mistreatment.

EXPLICIT AND RATIONAL PROCESSES OF OBSERVER DESERVINGNESS JUDGMENTS

Feather (e.g., 1992, 1994, 1999a) proposed an alternative model for deservingness judgments that emphasizes systematic and explicit consideration of information. Whereas other models focus on how deservingness concerns can motivate observers to alter their perceptions of the target person's moral responsibility for an outcome or alter perceptions of his or her character, Feather focused on attributions of responsibility and character judgments as *antecedents* of deservingness judgments. His analysis of deservingness provides insight into how people decide whether or not an outcome such as employee mistreatment is deserved or not when they have the willingness and ability to process the relevant information.

In Feather's analysis, deservingness assessments are guided by at least four factors: (1) the nature of the relationship between observer and observed; (2) evaluation associated with the outcome; (3) the evaluation of the action that gave rise to the outcome; and (4) the culpability of the actor for his or her action. These elements can be combined using Heider's (1958) balance principles to generate predictions about deservingness. In the context of employee mistreatment, the mistreatment would be perceived as undeserved if the employee's actions prior to the mistreatment were evaluated positively. If, on the other hand the mistreatment were to happen to an employee whose antecedent behavior was viewed negatively, then the requirements of balance have been met and the outcome would be viewed as deserved.

These basic deservingness relationships are moderated by the observer's considerations of responsibility and the relationship between the target and observer. Feather drew on the sizeable extant literature on attributions of responsibility to determine the role of responsibility in his model and in particular the work of Heider (1958), Shaver (1985), and Weiner (1995, 1996). He showed that observers will be reluctant to see outcomes sharing the same valence as the antecedent actions as deserved if there is reason to believe that the target was not responsible for their actions, perhaps because they lacked control or did not foresee the outcome.

In the earlier described study of observers' perceptions of manager treatment of an employee, Heuer and colleagues (1999, Study 1), incorporated elements of Feathers' deservingness model through consideration of observers' evaluations of the employee's behavior and his responsibility for same. In support of Feather's model, the results showed that disrespectful treatment of an employee will be perceived as most unfair when the disrespect was deemed to be undeserved, that is, when the employee was responsible (hard-work, punctuality, cooperativeness, and helpfulness) for positive behavior (always gets work done on time) prior to the mistreatment or not responsible (flare-up of a serious genetic illness) for negative behavior (almost never gets work done on time). As noted above, the same disrespectful treatment was perceived as fair when the criteria for deservingness were met: the employee was judged to be responsible (laziness, lack of punctuality, and uncooperativeness) for negative behavior or not responsible (because of nothing other than sheer luck) for positive behavior. As Feather's analysis would suggest, these effects were strongest under conditions of high responsibility, such that disrespectful treatment was actually viewed as more fair than respectful treatment, when the employee was responsible for negative behavior. Thus, Heuer and colleagues demonstrated that deservingness is a significant moderator of observers' fairness judgments.

Turning to the second moderator, Feather (1999b) also showed that the nature of the relation between observer and target is also an important moderator of deservingness judgments. Extrapolating from this work to employee mistreatment, an observer belonging to the same group (e.g., union, gender, racial, or ethnic group) as a mistreated employee may be more inclined to see the mistreatment as undeserved than an out-group observer, either because the in-group observer views the employee's behavior more positively and/or sees the employee as less responsible for negative behavior.

An important contribution of Feather's analysis of deservingness is the central role given to perceiver values for determining the valences in his model (Feather, 1992, 1999b). Values will not only determine whether a valence will be positive or negative, but also its magnitude. Consider our Nike example. While some observers would assign a negative valence to such treatment of employees, others may place a positive value on the use of coercive power in organizations. Indeed, in a different context, Feather (1998) has found right-wing authoritarianism to be an important determinant not only of the valence observers assigned to an authority figure's (police officer) misdeeds, but also of their assessments of deservingness for those actions.

Finally, Feather's model has considerable explanatory potential for understanding observer reactions to employee mistreatment as a result of what it has to say about the consequences of deservingness judgments. In studies exploring his social-cognitive process model of retributive justice, he found deservingness to be an important determinant of not only reactions to retributive responses of different magnitudes of harshness, but also affective reactions. The perceived harshness of retribution depends on the degree to which it is perceived as deserved as a function of the seriousness of the offense. The match between offense and penalty also affects affective reactions. When the penalty is perceived as deserved, observers will report positive affect, reminding us that another person's distress can be a source of pleasure, if we think they deserve it. Conversely, undeserved penalties make observers angry and arouse sympathy for the offender.

The relevance of Feather's retributive justice research for employee mistreatment is unclear however, because his work to date has been limited to assessing observer reactions to the application of different penalties within a prescribed legal framework, rather than assessing observer motivation for retributive action themselves or in support of the actions of others. His predictions need testing in organizational settings in which power relationships and organizational culture can play an important role in behavioral norms.

Taken together, Feather's explorations of deservingness and their consequences provide a potentially powerful conceptual framework for understanding observer reactions to employee mistreatment when the psychological state of the observer is most compatible with the assumptions of the model. Most importantly, the observer must be both willing and able to process information relevant to the various components of the model.

In summary, the analysis of modes of information processing suggests the possibility for two somewhat different types of deservingness judgments that observers of employee mistreatment might make. Deservingness is a judgment that observers are capable of arriving at through implicit, automatic or explicit rational processes or some combination thereof.[2] In the implicit, automatic, and nonrational scenario, deservingness judgments will be rapid, preconscious and conditioned more by a perceiver's need to believe in a just world than balanced consideration of potentially mitigating considerations. Alternatively, as more or less well-intentioned "lay jurists," observers may determine an employee's deservingness for his or her fate only after explicit and deliberate consideration of relevant factors.

Although the two approaches are indeed not mutually exclusive and likely operate in tandem, the two approaches have different implications for observers' deservingness judgements. For example, in Feather's model, affect appears primarily as a consequence of deservingness judgments, whereas Lerner has recently explored ways in which affect may have determining effects on deservingness (Lerner & Goldberg, 1999). Conversely, perceptions of moral character appear as antecedents of deservingness judgments in Feather's model, whereas just world theory commonly treats character perceptions as derivative of motivated deservingness based processes. In the next section we discuss the implications of automatic versus explicit information processing for deservingness judgements.

EXPLORING THE INTERPLAY BETWEEN MODES OF DESERVINGNESS JUDGMENTS

Our analysis of deservingness argues for the usefulness of knowing whether observer deservingness judgments are based in either implicit or explicit processing. A study by J. S. Lerner, Goldberg, and Tetlock (1998) highlights the significance of processing information either implicitly and automatically or explicitly and rationally for observer reactions to mistreatment. Their study also demonstrates how factors such as observer accountability can induce explicit rational processing even when circumstances favor implicit processing. Some participants were first exposed to a video portraying a victim being severely mistreated designed to elicit feelings of anger (Gross & Levenson, 1995). The remaining participants viewed a video of abstract shapes and colors that had previously been shown to elicit little or no emotion. Participants then began a second, ostensibly unrelated study requiring them to make judgments about culpability and compensation for harm caused by employees in four different work settings (construction worker, parking attendant, used car salesman, and assembly line foreman). The blame and punishment recommendations for each scenario constituted the major dependent variables. The researchers also included a manipulation of accountability that in the accountability conditions led them to believe that they would be interviewed by a "postdoctoral researcher" about either their perceptions of the video or their responsibility judgments for the harm scenarios. In the unaccountable condition, participants were merely reminded that their responses would remain private.

Consistent with the notion that anger simplifies thought and activates in heuristic fashion, blame cognitions, angered participants made more punitive attributions in the four scenarios than nonangered participants. Thus, judgments in a context different than the one eliciting the anger were nonetheless implicitly affected by it. However, accountable participants were also less vulnerable to the carryover effects of anger and as a result made less punitive attributions. Of particular interest here was the finding that the attenuation of punitive attributions occurred because accountability had the effect of inducing more consideration of mitigating information in the vignettes. Thus, these researchers combined in a single study variables capable of significantly enhancing both implicit and explicit processing with parallel augmenting and attenuating effects on culpability and punishment reactions in observers.

SUMMARY, PROPOSITIONS, AND PRACTICAL CONSIDERATIONS

Our analysis has endeavored to establish the usefulness of focusing on deservingness as a useful organizing theme for understanding observers' reactions to employee mistreatment. Central to the analysis is the observation that deservingness functions as the proximal psychological experience to observers' reactions whether those reactions are denial, outrage, victim blame, or retribution. Given the strong theoretical and empirical links between deservingness and fairness, we propose that deservingness provides a common psychological denominator for other dimensions of justice (i.e., distributive, procedural, and interactional justice) because from an observer perspective, these aspects of justice are very likely largely mediated in their effects on observers by their implications for perceived deservingness.

Proposition 1. Deservingness moderates observer reactions to employee mistreatment through its effects on perceived fairness. Undeserved mistreatment will be perceived as unfair and deserved mistreatment as fair.

Our review of research relevant to deservingness also highlights the importance of understanding *how* observers process information relevant to employee mistreatment. Lerner's just world research emphasizes observers' capacity for motivated behavior and cognition based in the fundamental need to believe that people, including mistreated employees, get what they deserve. While this may lead observers in some instance to blame employees for their fate, this is far from being the only reaction observers can have. Moreover, a number of yet to be explored factors, such as identification with the employee and sense of common fate are potentially important moderating factors on the basis of the just world literature.

Proposition 2. When employee mistreatment threatens just world beliefs, observers' reactions will be in the service of maintaining their belief that they live in a world were people get what they deserve. As a result it is unlikely the mistreatment will be perceived as undeserved.

In broad terms, and following Lerner's (1980) analysis of the justice motive, motivated judgments are most likely to occur in emotionally charged situations where the seriousness of the outcome is great. Under such conditions, observers' reactions will reflect their own need to see deservingness more than a need to properly understand whether or not the observed outcome is in fact deserved according to the normative matching criteria described in Feather's (1999a, 1999b) model. Stated another way, emotionally-charged observers are more motivated to look for blame than to understand the context in which the mistreatment occurred. Such motivated judgments also impede efforts on the part of organizations to successfully provide rational accounts and justifications for how employees were treated. While much of the available research has focused on victim blame as a typical response in such situations, the available research indicates that observers are more motivated to blame and punish transgressors than compensate victims (Hogan & Emler, 1981; Miller & McCann, 1979; Miller & Vidmar, 1981), suggesting that organizations have potentially much to lose in situations where observers are emotionally affected by learning about employee mistreatment. The observations here are nonetheless speculative and extrapolated from literature not explicitly concerned with employee mistreatment so that much remains to be learned about how particular observer perspectives affect their reactions.

Proposition 2a. Just world threat will be greatest when the victims are innocent and their suffering is vivid and emotionally impactful.

Under conditions that favor the observer being both able and willing to consider relevant information explicitly and rationally, judgments are more likely to conform to normatively rational models of deservingness such as Feather's (1999a, 1999b). Importantly, because observers just world motivational concerns are assumed to be less dominant in such situations, observers are able to consider the possibility that the employee mistreatment is either deserved or undeserved.

Proposition 3. Explicit, rational deservingness judgments depend on the observer's ability and willingness to process the relevant antecedent information. Under such conditions, the observer may decide that employee mistreatment is deserved or underserved.

A number of factors will govern observer willingness and ability to process relevant information. Most obviously, observers will only be able to process the information they have and the more limited the information, the greater difficulty they will have making normatively rational judgments. Thus, the more information that a company can reasonably provide regarding a perceived mistreatment (versus stonewalling the public) the more observers will be able to understand the variables associated with the mistreatment.

The emotional status of the observer will also moderate their ability and willingness to process deservingness relevant information. Bobocel, Mcline, and Folger (1997) have argued that the relationship between negative emotion and observer information processing may be curvilinear (i.e., inverted-U shaped). Specifically, at low levels of negative emotion, the "disengaged" observer is not motivated to process information regarding employee mistreatment, resulting in ambivalence or if information is processed at all, contains shortcuts and a high degree of heuristics and biases (e.g., the victim deserved the mistreatment) in observer deservingness judgments. If the observer's negative emotion is relatively greater, the observer will be motivated to process information so as to understand the situational factors associated with the mistreatment, and thus engage in relatively greater cognitive elaboration when making deservingness judgments. At some point, however, if negative emotion becomes extremely high, the observer's information processing may be simplified and is once again highly vulnerable to heuristics and biases.

On the facilitation side, accountability looks to be an important variable as shown in the earlier described S. J. Lerner and colleagues (1998) study. What is particularly impressive about accountability is that it appears to facilitate systematic processing even when participants were experiencing anger, suggesting that the two modes of processing information can operate in parallel.

Proposition 3a. Explicit, rational deservingness judgments will be most likely to occur when relevant information is available and the observer is accountable and experiencing moderate rather than very low or high levels of negative affect.

When unable or unwilling to make explicit rational deservingness judgments, observers may make judgments nonetheless through reliance on heuristics. For example, Van den Bos (2001) showed that fairness perceptions are determined by heuristics and whatever information is available, particularly when the facts surrounding treatment are highly ambiguous. Fairness heuristic theory proposes that individual processing is highly automatic, and that individuals take a number of cognitive shortcuts to make fairness judgments and to determine how to react to mistreatment. This theory is helpful in explaining how individuals make decisions when faced with incomplete or ambiguous information, which often reflects reality. Other types of heuristic processing such as hindsight bias, illusory correlations, and correspondence bias may also contribute to deservingness judgments as noted above.

Proposition 3b. When the observer is unable or unwilling to process relevant antecedent information, deservingness judgments will reflect reliance on heuristic processing.

Understanding heuristic-based deservingness judgments may be important in light of recent explorations of automaticity (Bargh, 1996) and the notions of "cognitive miser" (Fiske & Taylor, 1991) and "mindlessness" (Langer, 1989) which suggest that individuals process information in less than systematic ways. However, such default arguments need to be considered cautiously in the context of employee mistreatment insofar as awareness of such events may capture attention and induce more processing than many other daily experiences. From a practical perspective, observers who have been asked to consider the deservingness of a mistreatment (e.g., judges, arbitrators) should be less vulnerable to heuristics and biases than members of the general public. Nonetheless, other variables examined in dual-process models, such as cognitive load and motivation to process information, would be important to consider in predicting how observers will process information about employee mistreatment.

While some researchers have argued that implicit, preconscious processing tends to dominate most human information processing (Epstein & Pacini, 1999), it would be practically useful to know whether different observers favor different processes. For instance, given that investors can have a financial stake in understanding why the mistreatment occurred, would they be more motivated to consider such information explicitly than customers or potential employees? Thus, the mode of information processing might be an important dimension on which to build a taxonomy of third-party observers.

CONCLUSIONS

While the distinction between the modes of processing has considerable heuristic value, much work needs to done to explore the factors that direct and govern information processing modality. Researchers examining different modes of information processing in other content areas have also discovered that in many instances there is interplay between the implicit and explicit (e.g., Epstein, 1991, 1999). Examining the implications of how implicit and explicit processing combine will be important to pursue in the context of reactions to employee mistreatment, particularly in situations where, because of the decision-making power of some observers, rational, explicit processing would be desired.

Indeed, not all observers are the same with respect to their deservingness assessments associated with employee mistreatment. The mode of information processing might be an important dimension on which to distinguish among observers. Thus a judge is likely to react differently to mistreatment (e.g., consider more situational variables) than the victim's significant other. An investor can react differently than a co-worker. Information processing as a factor might be instrumental in developing a taxonomy of third-party observers.

As noted earlier, it is also important to acknowledge that observers' reactions to employee mistreatment can undoubtedly be informed by considerations other than deservingness. For instance, Batson, Klein, Highberger, and Shaw (1995) found that observers whose dominant motivational concern to a victim is altruism will react very differently than observers preoccupied with justice. Finally, our prologue example reminds us that in the context of employee mistreatment, observers may only be concerned about the mistreatment as a marker for other dynamics that are of greater concern such as their own profitability or the profitability of the organization. In such instances, it goes without saying that the deservingness of employees for what has happened to them will be of no consequence for observers. Sometimes self-interest easily trumps justice-based concern for others.

ACKNOWLEDGMENT

The authors would like to thank David Jones and an anonymous reviewer for their comments on an earlier version of this paper.

NOTES

1. Rational as used here does not mean compliance with formal rules of logic but rather cognition that reflects systematic normatively rational processing of information. That is to say, what sensible people would be likely to do with the information if they have the capacity and inclination to consider it.

2. Most dual process theories allow for parallel or sequential processing of information in both systems.

REFERENCES

Aderman, D., Brehm, S.S., & Katz, L. B. (1974). Empathic observation of an innocent victim: The just world revisited. *Journal of Personality and Social Psychology, 29,* 342-347.

Aquino, K., Griffeth, R.W., Allen, D.G., & Hom, P.W. (1997). Integrating justice constructs into the turnover process: A test of a referent cognitions model. *Academy of Management Journal, 40,* 1208-1227.

Bargh, J.A. (1996). Automaticity in social psychology. In E. T. Higgins & A.W. Kruglanski (Eds.), *Social psychology: Handbook of basic principles* (pp. 169-183). New York: Guilford Press.

Batson, C.D., Klein, T.R., Highberger, L., & Shaw, L.L. (1995). Immorality from empathy-induced altruism: When compassion and justice conflict. *Journal of Personality and Social Psychology, 68,* 1042-1054.

Bies, R.J., & Tyler, T.R. (1993). The "litigation mentality" in organizations. *Organizational Science, 4,* 352-366.

Bobocel, D., McCline, R., & Folger, R. (1997). Letting them down gently: Conceptual advances in explaining controversial organizational policies. In C.L. Cooper & D.M. Rousseau (Eds.), *Trends in organizational behavior* (Vol. 4, pp. 73-88). Chichester, Sussex: John Wiley & Sons.

Brockner, J. (1990). Scope of justice in the workplace: How survivors react to co-worker layoffs. *Journal of Social Issues, 40,* 95-106.

Brockner, J., Davy, J., & Carter, C. (1985). Layoffs, self-esteem, and survivor guilt: Motivational, affective, and attitudinal consequences. *Organizational Behavior and Human Decision Processes, 36,* 229-224.

Brockner, J., & Greenberg, J. (1990). The impact of layoffs on survivors: An organizational justice perspective. In J.S. Carroll (Ed.), *Applied social psychology and organizational settings* (pp. 45-75). Hillsdale, NJ: Erlbaum.

Brockner, J., Grover, S., Reed, T., DeWitt, R., & O'Malley, M. (1987). Survivors reactions to layoffs: We get by with a little help from our friends. *Administrative Science Quarterly, 32,* 526-541.

Chaiken, S. (1987). The heuristic model of persuasion. In M.P. Zanna, J.M. Olson, & C.P. Herman (Eds.), *Social influence: The Ontario Symposium* (Vol. 5, pp. 3-39). Hillsdale, NJ: Erlbaum.

Chaiken, S., & Trope, Y. (Eds.). (1999). *Dual-process theories in social psychology.* New York: The Guilford Press.

Chaikin, A.L., & Darley, J.M. (1973). Victim or perpetrator: Defensive attribution of responsibility and the need for order and justice. *Journal of Personality and Social Psychology, 25,* 268-275.

Cropanzano, R., & Ambrose, M.L. (1996, April). *Procedural and distributive justice are more similar than you think: A monistic perspective and research agenda.* Paper presented at the 11th Annual Conference of the Society for Industrial and Organizational Psychology, San Diego, CA.

Cropanzano, R., & Folger, R. (1991). Procedural justice and worker motivation. In R.M. Steers & L.W. Porter (Eds.), *Motivation and work behavior* (Vol. 5, pp. 131-143). New York: McGraw-Hill.

Crosby, F.J. (1982). *Relative deprivation and working women.* New York: Oxford.

Crosby, F.J. (1984). Relative deprivation in organizational settings. *Research in Organizational Behavior, 6,* 51-93.

Epstein, S. (1994). Integration of the cognitive and the psychodynamic unconscious. *American Psychologist, 49,* 709-724.

Epstein, S., & Pacini, R. (1999). Some basic issues regarding dual-process theories from the perspective of cognitive-experiential self-theory. In S. Chaiken &

Y. Trope (Eds.), *Dual-process theories in social psychology* (pp. 462-482). New York: Guilford.

Epstein, S., Lipson, A., Holstein, C., & Huh, E. (1992). Irrational reactions to negative outcomes: Evidence for two conceptual systems. *Journal of Personality and Social Psychology, 62,* 328-339.

Feather, N.T. (1992). An attributional and value analysis of deservingness in success and failure situations. *British Journal of Social Psychology, 31,* 125-145.

Feather, N.T. (1994). Attitudes toward high achievers and reactions to their fall: Theory and research concerning tall poppies. In M.P. Zanna (Ed.), *Advances in experimental social psychology* (pp. 1-73). San Diego: Academic Press.

Feather, N.T. (1998). Reactions to penalties for offenses committed by the police and public citizens: Testing a social-cognitive process model of retributive justice. *Journal of Personality and Social Psychology, 75,* 528-544.

Feather, N.T. (1999a). Judgments of deservingness: Studies in the psychology of justice and achievement. *Personality and Social Psychology Review, 3,* 86-107.

Feather, N.T. (1999b). *Values, achievement, and justice: Studies in the psychology of deservingness.* New York: Kluwer Academic/Plenum.

Fischhoff, B. (1975). Hindsight (does not equal) foresight: The effects of outcome knowledge on judgments under uncertainty. *Journal of Experimental Psychology: Human Perception and Performance, 1,* 288-299.

Fiske, S. & Taylor, S.E. (1991). *Social cognition* (2nd ed.). New York: McGraw-Hill.

Friedman, T.L. (2000). *The lexus and the olive tree.* New York: Anchor Books.

Gilbert, D.T., & Malone, S.P. (1995). The correspondence bias. *Psychological Bulletin, 117,* 21-38.

Goldman, B.M. (1999, August). *Employment discrimination-claiming behavior: The effects of organizational justice, social guidance, and perceived discrimination.* Paper presented at 1999 Academy of Management meetings, Chicago, IL.

Greenberg, J. (1990). Employee theft as a reaction to underpayment inequality: The hidden costs of pay cuts. *Journal of Personality and Social Psychology, 75,* 561-568.

Gross, J., & Levenson, R. (1995). Emotion elicitation using films. *Cognition and Emotion, 9*(1), 87-108.

Heider, F. (1958). *The psychology of interpersonal relations.* New York: Wiley.

Hogan, R., & Emler, N.P. (1981). Retributive justice. In M.J. Lerner & S.C. Lerner (Eds.), *The justice motive in social behavior: Adapting to times of scarcity and change* (pp. 125–143). New York: Plenum Press.

Heuer, L., Blumenthal, E., Douglas, A., & Weinblatt, T. (1999). A deservingness approach to respect as a relationally based fairness judgment. *Personality and Social Psychology Bulletin, 25,* 1279-1292.

Janoff-Bulman, R., Timko, C., & Carli, L.L. (1985). Cognitive biases in blaming the victim. *Journal of Experimental Social Psychology, 21,* 161-177.

Jermier, J. M., Knights, D., & Nord, W. (1994), *Resistance and power in organizations,* London: Routledge.

Jones, E.E. (1976). How do people perceive the causes of behaviour? *American Scientist, 64,* 300-305.

Keltner, D., Ellsworth, P.C., & Edwards, K. (1993). Beyond simple pessimism: Effects of sadness and anger on social perception. *Journal of Personality and Social Psychology, 64,* 740-752.

Langer, E.J. (1989). Minding matters. In L. Berkowitz (Ed.), *Advances in experimental social psychology* (Vol. 22, 137-173). New York: Academic Press.

Lerner, M.J. (1980). *The belief in a just world: A fundamental delusion.* New York: Plenum Press.

Lerner, M.J. (1987). Integrating societal and psychological rules of entitlement: The basic task of each social actor and fundamental problem for the social sciences. *Social Justice Research, 1,* 107-125.

Lerner, M.J. (1998). The two forms of belief in a just world: Some thoughts on why and how people care about justice. In L. Montada & M. J. Lerner (Eds.), *Responses to vicitmization and belief in a just world* (pp. 247-269). New York: Plenum

Lerner, M.J., & Goldberg, J.H. (1999). When do decent people blame victims? The differing effects of the explicit/rational and implicit/experiential cognitive systems. In S. Chaiken & Y. Trope (Eds.), *Dual-process theories in social psychology* (pp. 627-640). New York: Guilford.

Lerner, M.J., & Matthews, P. (1967). Reactions to suffering of others under conditions of indirect responsibility. *Journal of Personality and Social Psychology, 5,* 319-325.

Lerner, M.J., & Miller, D.T. (1978). Just world research and the attribution process: Looking back and ahead. *Psychological Bulletin, 85,* 1030-1051.

Lerner, M.J., & Simmons, C.H. (1966). The observer's reaction to the "innocent victim": Compassion or rejection? *Journal of Personality and Social Psychology, 4,* 203-210.

Lerner, S.J., Goldberg, J.H., & Tetlock, P.E. (1998). Sober second thought: The effects of accountability, anger, and authoritarianism on attributions of responsibility. *Personality and Social Psychology Bulletin, 24,* 563-574.

Leung, K., Chiu, W., & Au, Y. (1993). Sympathy and support for industrial actions: A justice analysis. *Journal of Applied Psychology, 78,* 781-787.

Lupfer, M.B., & Gingrich, B.E. (1999). When bad (good) things happen to good (bad) people: The impact of character appraisal and perceived controllability on judgments of deservingness. *Social Justice Research, 12,* 165-188.

Lind, E.A., Kray, L., & Thompson, L. (1998). The social construction of injustice: Fairness judgments in response to own and other's unfair treatment by authorities. *Organizational Behavior and Human Decision Processes, 75,* 1-22.

Lind, E.A., & Tyler, T.R. (1988). *The social psychology of procedural justice.* New York: Plenum.

Major, B. (1994). From social inequality to personal entitlement: The role of social comparison, legitimacy appraisals, and group membership. In M.P. Zanna (Ed.), *Advances in Experimental Social Psychology* (Vol. 26, pp. 293-355). New York: Academic Press.

Miller, D.T. (1977). Personal deserving versus justice for others: An exploration of the justice motive. *Journal of Experimental Social Psychology, 13,* 1-13.

Miller, D.T. (2001). Disrespect and the experience of injustice. *Annual Review of Psychology, 52,* 527-553.

Miller, D.T., & McCann, D. C. (1979). Children's reactions to the victims and perpetrators of injustices. *Child Development, 50,* 861-868.

Miller, D.T., & Vidmar, N.. (1981). The social psychology of punishment reactions. In M.J. Lerner & S.C. Lerner (Eds.), *The justice motive in social behavior: Adapting to times of scarcity and change* (pp. 145-172). New York: Plenum Press.

Mollica, K.A. Gray, B., Trevino, L.K., & DeWitt, R. (1999, August). *A social identity perspective on organizational justice among layoff survivors.* Paper presented at the Academy of Management meetings, Chicago, IL.

Montada, L. (1992). Attribution of responsibility for losses and perceived injustice. In L. Montada, S. Filipp, & M. J. Lerner (Eds.), *Life crises and experiences of lost in adulthood* (pp. 133-161). Hillsdale, New Jersey: Erlbaum.

Novak, D.W., & Lerner, M.J. (1968). Rejection as a consequence of perceived similarity. *Journal of Personality and Social Psychology, 9,* 147-152.

Pancer, S.M. (1988). Salience of appeal and avoidance of helping situations. *Canadian Journal of Behavioural Science, 20,* 133-139.

Petty, R.E., & Cacioppo, J.T. (1986). The elaboration likelihood model of persuasion. In L. Berkowitz (Ed.), *Advances in experimental social psychology* (Vol. 19, pp. 123-205). New York: Academic Press.

Ross, L. (1977). The intuitive psychologist and his shortcomings: Distortions in the attribution process. In L. Berkowitz (Ed.), *Advances in experimental social psychology, 10.* New York: Academic Press.

Saporito, B. (1998, March 30). Taking a look into Nike's factories. *Time, 151,* 12.

Shaver, K.G. (1985). *The attribution of blame: Causality, responsibility, and blameworthiness.* New York: Springer.

Shweder, R.A., & Haidt, J. (1993). The future of moral psychology: Truth, intuition, and the pluralist way. *Psychological Science, 4,* 360-365.

Skarlicki, D.P., Ellard, J.H., & Kelln, B.R.C. (1998). Third-party perceptions of a layoff: Procedural, derogation, and retributive aspects of justice. *Journal of Applied Psychology, 83,* 119-127.

Skarlicki, D. P., & Folger, R. (1997). Retaliation in the workplace: The roles of distributive, procedural, and interactional justice. *Journal of Applied Psychology, 82,* 434-443.

Skitka, L.J., & Tetlock, P.E. (1992). Allocating scarce resources: A contingency model of distributive justice. *Journal of Experimental Social Psychology, 28,* 491-522.

Smith, C.A., & Ellsworth, P.C. (1985). Patterns of cognitive appraisal in emotion. *Journal of Personality and Social Psychology, 48,* 813-838.

Stokols, D., & Schopler, J. (1973). Reactions to victims under conditions of situational detachment: The effects of responsibility, severity, and expected future interaction. *Journal of Personality and Social Psychology, 25,* 199-209.

Stroessner, S.J., & Heuer, L.B. (1996). Cognitive bias in procedural justice: Formation and implications of illusory correlations in perceived intergroup fairness. *Journal of Personality and Social Psychology, 71,* 717-728.

Tyler, T.R., & Smith, H.J. (1998). Social justice and social movements. In G. Gilbert, S. Fiske, and G. Lindzey (Eds.), *Handbook of social psychology* (Vol. 2, pp. 595-629). Boston, MA: McGraw-Hill.

Uleman, J.S. (1999). Spontaneous versus intentional inferences in impression formation. In S. Chaiken & Y. Trope (Eds.), *Dual-process theories in social psychology* (pp. 141-160). New York: Guilford.

van den Bos, K. (2001). Fairness heuristic theory: Assessing the information to which people are reacting has a pivotal role in understanding organizational justice. In S. Gilliland, D. Steiner, & D. Skarlicki (Eds.), *Theoretical and cultural perspective on organizational justice* (pp. 63-84). Greenwich CT: Information Age Publishing.

Walster, E., (1966). Assignment of responsibility for an accident. *Journal of Personality and Social Psychology, 3,* 73-79.

Walster, E., Berscheid, E., & Walster, G.W. (1976). New directions in equity research. In L. Berkowitz & E. Walster (Eds.), *Advances in experimental social psychology,* Vol. 9. New York: Academic.

Walster, E., Walster, G.N., & Berscheid, E. (1978). *Equity: Theory and research.* Boston: Allyn & Bacon.

Weiner, B. (1995). *Judgments of responsibility: A foundation for a theory of social conduct.* New York: Guilford.

Weiner, B. (1996). Searching for order in social motivation. *Psychological Inquiry, 7,* 199-216.

Wenzel, M. (2000). Justice and identity: The significance of inclusion for perceptions of entitlement and the justice motive. *Personality and Social Psychology Bulletin, 26,* 157-176.

CHAPTER 6

EMPLOYEE STRESS, INJUSTICE, AND THE DUAL POSITION OF THE BOSS

Riel Vermunt

ABSTRACT

According to recent census data, 25 percent of Dutch employees who enter into the disablement program have reported having problems with their bosses. Vermunt and Steensma (1996, 2001) have developed the Injustice-Stress Theory (IST) to explain stress phenomena and subsequent absenteeism resulting from supervisors' unjust behavior. In the present chapter, I provide some preliminary data that support our previous ideas. Moreover, the chapter describes the dual position of the boss as an important factor for why bosses may maintain their unjust behavior. An underlying assumption is that the boss is confronted with two forms of fairness, one form has to do with allocating resources to subordinates (proactive justice; Greenberg. 1996), and the other is reactive justice and has to do with the evaluation of allocation behavior of the boss' superior. It is argued further that because of the dual position of the boss, appearing fair towards his/her subordinates may be preferred to actually being fair, given the potential for negative consequences in terms of subordinates' behavior. The paper concludes with some suggestions for improvement.

In most countries, especially in North America and Western Europe, profound changes are taking place. The average level of income is relatively high, and higher than it has ever been. Life in these countries has a high standard and the prospects for the near future are good. Increases in economic activity, values of stocks in the stock market are rising, and the average income is high. However, despite these apparent good fortunes, a coin always has two sides. The positive side of the coin is formed by the positive economic and objective prospects that are visible in the long run. The negative side of the coin is demonstrated in at least two forms. First, there is an increasing number of people in these countries who are unable to work because of illness, stress symptoms, and burnout. Second, lower levels of commitment to family, organizations, and society are being observed. The discrepancy between high economic welfare and low psychological well-being forms one of the core issues of modern life. It is not so much a conflict between groups of individuals, but a conflict within the individual: The relatively high economic prospects versus the psychological strains that are laid upon the individual. This conflict can best be observed in the work situation.

Work is still a very important area in most people's lives. Work provides an individual with a good living, forms one's personality, can increase one's competence and skill, and can fulfill one's needs for social relationships and group belongingness. In the Netherlands, for instance, workers in general are satisfied with their salaries (de Beer, 2001). Negotiations between worker unions and federations of entrepreneurs are hard but workers are still prepared to compromise and refrain from making overly excessive demands. For several years now, workers fully agree with the policy to set aside a salary increase in favor of employment for others. Entrepreneur organizations and unions negotiate contracts in which a limited salary rise for employees is compensated by better opportunities for formal education and by other regulations.

Additionally, workers demand better working conditions. This may not surprise us: workers' education and training have improved; the individualistic tendency in our society has increased people's self-confidence and workers have more opportunities for work than in the past. Workers and employees are focused on attaining good social and physical working conditions. If individuals do not receive these in a given job, they have a marked tendency to search for other employment. If the conditions repeatedly do not meet certain standards, workers may get sick, or show signs of stress, burnout and/or other symptoms. In the Netherlands, for instance, the high number of 100,000 (NRC-Handelsblad, June 8, 2001) working people entered into the disablement regulations in 2000. And this figure is rising. Of these individuals, 25 percent claimed disablement because of problems related to their bosses. This percentage is high indeed, and one may wonder why the influence of the supervisor on stress and other symptoms is so strong.

In this chapter, I will briefly present the Injustice-Stress Theory (Vermunt & Steensma, 2001) that will shed some light on the importance of the supervisor's role in the sickness process. Data demonstrating that the supervisors' fair behavior has enormous positive effects on subordinates'

accepted interpretation of stress. Another interpretation is possible as well. The other interpretation emphasizes the active role of the supervisor as allocator of resources in the development of stress. From the perspective of allocation decision processes, and the related feelings of justice and injustice, one might argue that subordinates are workers who have not been allocated sufficient resources by their supervisors in order to perform their tasks properly. For example, a supervisor's allocated time (or control) to complete a given task is insufficient to carry out the task adequately. Conceived in this way, stress reflects an important aspect of the supervisor-subordinate relationship that is exemplified by the distribution (the insufficient amount of time) and the procedure (supervisors' inaccurate estimations of the capacities of the subordinates) of an allocation decision process. The contribution of the justice literature to the phenomenon of stress is not only that the perceived discrepancy is crucial for experiencing stress, but the fact that the discrepancy is caused by a decision of the supervisor. In other words, the elements of the social environment that are experienced as unreasonable by the subordinate are attributed to the decisions of the supervisor, and the way that the supervisor treats the subordinate. Therefore, one may state that distributive and/or procedural unfairness adds an independent influence to the stress that subordinates already experience because of the overload of work, for instance. The prediction is that unfair treatment will result in more experienced stress than will fair treatment.

The work situation can best be characterized as an exchange relationship where an employer hires a person (the employee, who has more or less specific abilities) to perform tasks that are structured according to a more or less explicit plan. The employee is rewarded for his/her contribution according to a payment scheme. One could say that an employer allocates jobs, tasks, salaries and other "things" to employees. The employer applies certain procedures to allocate jobs and salaries. For instance, in many companies and institutions, employers use a set of procedures to hire personnel - the employer recruits qualified candidates for a vacant job, composes a committee, sets up criteria for selection, and so on. In other words, many facets of the work situation can be conceived as intricate resource allocation processes, in which an authority allocates resources (Foa & Foa, 1974) by applying a procedure. The authority may be a supervisor as well, although the supervisor has less power then an employer.

Employees evaluate the end result of the resource allocation process, the procedure used to arrive at the end result, as well as the overall allocation process. Foa and Foa (1974) distinguish six types of resources: money, goods, information, status, services, and love. Although all six resources may be present in an exchange relationship between employer and employee, in practice some resources are more salient than others. We assume that in the work situation money and status will be quite promi-

behavior and well-being will be presented as a first test of the theory. Given the apparent consequences of fair behavior, these results lead one to question why more supervisors do not engage in fair behaviors. It is assumed that the dual position of the supervisor, that is, being a superior but also a subordinate, greatly hinders supervisors from behaving fairly towards their subordinates. In the last section some solutions to these issues are presented. But first, we start with an introduction to the social justice approach to stress: The Injustice-Stress Theory. For a detailed description of the theory, the reader is referred to Vermunt and Steensma (2001).

INJUSTICE-STRESS THEORY

In short, Injustice-Stress Theory postulates that individuals are adverse to experiencing a discrepancy between what they think they are capable of and the requirements of the environment. The theory suggests that individuals may experience a discrepancy between two types of information: the perception of their own capacities, and the perception of the demands of both social and physical environments. Many theories, such as Michalos' Multiple Discrepancy Theory (Michalos, 1986), and Folger's Reference Cognition Theory (Folger, 1987), start from the assertion that people may experience discrepancies between two types of information. The central issue of the Injustice-Stress Theory is that the perceived physical and psychological demands of the environment are attributed to the allocation behavior of the decision maker, authority or supervisor. In other words, at least part of the discrepancy is not something that comes from the working situation or something that comes from "out of the blue." On the contrary, subordinates attribute the discrepancy to the supervisor's allocation decisions.

The Injustice-Stress Theory further postulates that individuals are motivated to decrease or eliminate the discrepancy. In the original stress theory, individuals reduce stress predominantly by leaving the situation, by seeking social support, or by learning effective coping behaviors. The Injustice-Stress Theory suggests that reduction of stress or, even better, the prevention of stress, can be achieved simply by having superiors who engage in fair behavior. These postulates and assumptions are delineated in the next sections.

A common characteristic of stress, which is frequently referred to in the literature, is that stress occurs mainly when individuals sense a difference between their own capacities and the demands of the social and physical environment (Lazarus & Folkman, 1984). For example, workers having to do too many tasks in a time period which is short, or perceived as too short, may feel stressed. Emphasizing the mismatch between one's response capacity and demands from the environment has long been an

nent. Money may take the form of salary and financial bonuses. Status is a resource in which the relationship between employer and employee is most relevant in the daily routine. Most employees are very sensitive to status and possible changes in their status. Status has to do with allocation of: (1) positions (Bruins & Wilke, 1996), for instance, whether one will be promoted or not, (2) tasks, for instance, whether one is allocated new and challenging tasks or not, and (3) the quality of the relationship, for instance, the relationship with the employer may be good or may be bad (Bales, 1980). Because of the salience of status (Tyler & Lind, 1992), employees will feel strongly affected by changes in their work situation that affect their status position.

People evaluate allocation of resources predominantly in terms of fairness. Fairness is an important part of people's lives (Lerner, 1980, 1991). According to Lerner, justice or fairness is such an important element that people will go to great lengths to maintain the belief that the world in which they live is a just place. For instance, people will blame innocent victims of crime in order to maintain their belief in a just world (Lerner, 1980). People vary in the strength of their belief in a just world. The just world belief affects people's attitudes, cognitions and behavior. Moreover, Tyler and Lind (1992) have stated that people who cede power to an authority feel uncertain and uneasy about their relationship with the authority. Subordinates will look for signs indicating whether the authority can be trusted, will show respect, and is neutral. According to Lind and Tyler (1988), the fairness of an authority's allocation decision provides subordinates information which they can use to ascertain the trustworthiness and neutrality of the superior, as well as the degree of respect that the superior holds for them. Thus, from a normative point of view (Lerner, 1980), as well as from a social relationship point of view (Lind & Tyler, 1988; Tyler & Lind, 1992; Vermunt, Blaauw, & Lind, 1998) one may infer that employees will look sharply at the fairness of the superior's allocation behavior.

Evaluation Standards

How do employees determine the fairness of the allocation decision of their boss? One avenue is social comparison (Crosby, 1976; Folger, 1987; Vermunt, Wit, Van den Bos, & Lind, 1996; Van den Bos, Vermunt, & Wilke, 1997). This theory suggested that employees compare the resources they have received with the resources allocated to others (social comparison), the resources they have received in the past (temporal comparison), and/ or with an internalized norm. Employees may conclude from the comparison process that the received resource fits with the comparison standard. According to most justice researchers, when the received outcome is not in agreement with what one expected, people will evaluate the outcome as unfair. Further, the more the received outcome deviates from the comparison standard, the more the outcome will be perceived as unfair.

Authors do not agree about the impact of each of the comparison standards on fairness evaluations. Adams (1965) developed the concept of own equity (comparing the actual input/outcome ratio with one experienced before) and comparison equity (comparing own input/outcome ratio with that of a comparison other). Lerner (1980) emphasized the importance of the internalized norm, as this norm is the result of a personal contract of the growing child with itself. The personal contract suggests that people will get what they deserve. This internalized norm is a strong motivational force for the evaluation of one's own behavior as well as for the evaluation of others. It can explain, for instance, why people blame innocent victims (Lerner, 1980). Folger (1987) applied the simulation heuristic (Kahneman & Tversky, 1982) to social justice phenomenon. According to Folger, when people are confronted with an outcome and are motivated to evaluate the fairness of that outcome, they will simulate other potential outcomes that could have been achieved. Folger labels the simulated outcomes referent outcomes. These outcomes may be evaluated by comparison with others, comparison with a standard, or comparison with one's own situation earlier in time. Lind and Tyler (1988) seem to emphasize an absolute norm that people apply when they evaluate the fairness of procedures. Lind and Tyler argued that procedures can be interpreted more easily than outcomes because one can directly evaluate the fairness of authorities' behavior without the use of simulation or comparison processes. Vermunt (Vermunt & Shulman, 1996; Vermunt, Wit, Van den Bos, & Lind, 1996; Van den Bos, Vermunt, & Wilke, 1997) states that procedures, just as outcomes, are evaluated by comparing the actual procedure with a simulated procedure. Empirical evidence supports these different theoretical positions, although at the present it is not clear which of the standards is most effective in affecting fairness evaluations. The way individuals apply evaluation standards is an integral part of the Injustice-Stress Theory and therefore essential to explain individuals' justice evaluations.

By presenting two small-scale studies, I will indirectly address the issue of evaluation standards. The studies are based on the Injustice-Stress Theory, and are intended to demonstrate that a supervisor's behavior contributes to the stress of his/her subordinates.

Some Empirical Evidence

Study 1

The aim of this study (see Oskam, 1998) was to find out what kinds of supervisory behavior contribute to stress. We therefore interviewed 10 respondents who were recruited via an advertisement in the local newspaper. Participants did not hold management positions and evaluated themselves as victims of stress caused by their (former) supervisors. The sample is small, but fairly representative with respect to age, training, and type of job. Six respondents were female. The mean age was 42.5 years, the youngest respondent was 22 years, and the oldest was 58 years. The respondents' jobs varied from car-park attendant, systems analyst, executive secretary, to financial controller. Five respondents worked in the public administration, five worked in private companies.

The interviews lasted about one hour. The main part of the interview consisted of the description of stressful events in the work situation. The respondent could freely mention all relevant events. The technique used was the STAR- method, which involves asking the respondent to identify a stressful event. The interviewer follows-up the response by asking for information pertaining to: (a) the task (i.e., the role of the respondent), (b) the actions taken by the respondent, and (c) the results of these actions. After the respondent spontaneously mentioned stressful events, the respondent was asked whether he/she recognized certain behaviors of the supervisor, such as rude behavior, withholding relevant information, lack of consideration with opinion of the subordinate, and/or emphasizing status difference between him/herself and subordinate. If the respondent recognized one or more of these behaviors, he/she was asked to give concrete examples of the behavior, as well as the frequency of the behavior.

More than three respondents spontaneously mentioned each of the following five stress behaviors. First, a lack of trust; one of the respondents mentioned that her supervisor was not willing to delegate responsibilities. "Endlessly, the supervisor revised the letter I was working on. I am convinced that the supervisor most likely did the job himself." Second, an emphasis on hierarchical relations; respondents were irritated by the sick jokes of the supervisor that were intended to assess his/her authority. "As if he has to strengthen his power." Third, a lack of consideration; a male worker who could not do evening shifts, but offered to work on the weekends instead, was told that his wife had to look for another job so that she could care for the children. Fourth, failure to reward good performance; workers complained that they did not receive a pat on the back after a good performance. Fifth, an incorrect reprimand; respondents stated that when supervisors reprimanded them, they did it in an inappropriate way. These behaviors corresponded fairly well with respondents' recognition of the list of stress-causing behaviors, especially with respect to the lack of consideration of subordinate's opinions and well-being, and the emphasis on hierarchical relations. Many respondents recognized inadequate communication of information as well.

Respondents' reactions to the stressful events included less effort in carrying out the job and decreased tendencies to seek personal contact with the supervisor. Several respondents mentioned dissatisfaction, fatigue, problems with relaxing, uncertainty, feelings of being powerless, and illness. Van Meer (1997), a Dutch psychiatrist and expert in treating supervisor-related stress, describes many examples of the negative consequences for the subordinate which occur as a result of supervisors' behaviors. The reactions of our respondents correspond well with Van Meer's description of symptoms. We may conclude that respondents' reactions were highly similar to Van Meers's descriptions.

Reflecting on supervisors' behaviors, one may conclude that most of the behaviors can be subsumed under criteria of distributive and procedural justice that several authors (Bies & Moag, 1986; Leventhal, 1980; Tyler & Lind, 1992) have mentioned. Lack of recognition and incorrect reprimand may be subsumed under criteria of distributive justice, while lack of trust, lack of consideration, inadequate communication of information can be related to procedural justice criteria. At first sight some of the behaviors may be difficult to subsume under existing justice criteria, such as emphasizing hierarchical relations. But if one considers emphasizing hierarchical relations as a type of humiliation, one can subsume this behavior as a lack of respect for the subordinate.

From the analysis of the participants' responses, who were under strain as a consequence of their relationship with their supervisor, we may conclude that supervisors' behaviors can be viewed in justice terms, i.e., supervisors' behaviors have to do with the allocation of material and immaterial resources. From this interview study we may conclude that unfair behavior of the supervisor and stress reactions are related in a rather direct way.

Study 2

A second modest study was conducted to find out how respondents would evaluate a fictitious situation in a controlled scenario study. The aim of the study was to show that in addition to high workload, unfair treatment is an important stressor. Participants were presented a short story in which a supervisor in a small firm allocated to a subordinate a sufficient amount of time to finish a task or an insufficient amount of time to finish the task. The supervisor treated the subordinate in a fair way or in an unfair way. In this 2 (Workload: High versus Medium) X 2 (Treatment: Fair versus Unfair) design, the dependent variable was the amount of stress that will be experienced by the subordinate. It was predicted that participants in the high workload condition would perceive more stress than in the medium workload condition. It was further predicted that participants in the unfair treatment condition would perceive more stress than in the fair treatment condition. The prediction that workload would affect stress reactions was based on traditional theory of stress, which states that the experience of stress is a function of the discrepancy between the capacities of a person and requirements of the environment. The prediction that treatment would affect stress reactions was based on the Injustice-Stress Theory.

Eighty participants, who were employed, older than eighteen years, and from the social network of students from Leiden University who were acting as experimenters, were asked to fill out a questionnaire about experiences at work. Participants were assigned to one of the four conditions, resulting in 20 participants in each condition. Participants were asked to read the story and to answer the questions.

Each scenario started with a description: "Imagine that you find yourself in the following situation: You have been working for nine years at a small commercial advertising company with fifteen employees. You are a fine and dedicated designer." In the following block, the workload was manipulated: "Because of the large amount of work, you are constantly unable to finish your work in time. You are aware that you cannot cope with the amount of work" (High Workload); or "Despite the large amount of work, you are able to finish your work in time. You are aware that you can cope with the amount of work" (Medium Workload).

Next, procedural fairness was introduced: "Your boss, who has worked for four years at the company, continually urges you to work hard. He shows no consideration for your speed of work and never informs himself about your work" (lack of "due consideration"; Lind & Tyler, 1988; Unfair Treatment); or "Your boss, who has worked for four years at the company, continually urges you to work hard. He shows consideration with your speed of work and informs himself from time to time about your work" ("due consideration"; Fair Treatment).

To test whether the manipulations of Workload and Treatment were perceived as intended, two control questions were planned: "What is your opinion of the amount of work?" (1 = too little, 5 = too much), "Do you judge the treatment by the boss as proper or improper?" (1 = proper, 5 = improper). The dependent variable, imagined subjective stress, was measured with one item: "Would you, in such a situation, experience stress?" (1 = no stress, 5 = very much stress).

The manipulations of workload and treatment were successful. A t-test with workload as the independent variable and imagined workload as the dependent variable showed a significant effect of workload ($t(78) = 8.75$; $p < .001$). In the high workload condition participants evaluated the workload as higher ($M = 4.5$) than in the medium workload condition ($M = 3.17$). In the unfair treatment condition participants evaluated the treatment as less fair ($M = 4.05$) than in the fair treatment condition ($M = 3.07$; $t(78) = 5.45$; $p < .001$). We conclude that the manipulations were successful.

The results of a 2-way ANOVA, with workload and treatment as independent variables and stress as the dependent variable, indicate a main effect of workload ($F(1,71) = 16.53$; $p < .001$) and of treatment ($F(1,71) = 3.59$; $p < .05$). In the high workload condition stress was perceived as higher ($M =$

TABLE 1
Mean Stress Scores for the Two Levels of Workload and Treatment

	Workload		
Treatment	Medium	High	Total
Fair	2.2	2.5	2.3
Unfair	2.4	2.9	2.6
Total	2.1	2.8	

Note: A high score indicates high stress

2.8) than in the medium workload condition ($M = 2.1$). In the unfair treatment condition the stress was perceived as higher ($M = 2.6$) than in the fair treatment condition ($M = 2.3$). As shown in Table 1, Treatment and Workload have an additive effect on perceived stress.

We may conclude from these findings that participants are able to recognize stressful situations, and that both workload and treatment influence their perceptions, not necessarily the direct experience of stress. We assume that because participants did not personally experience the stress, the effects of treatment are less than expected. In situations where participants personally experience stress, the effects of treatment will probably be stronger.

The Dual Position of the Supervisor

From both studies, we may conclude that unfairness had an effect on stress. Of course, more rigorous testing is necessary, but both studies are a promising start for investigating the relationship between unfairness and stress. If these findings are corroborated by other research, an interesting question arises: When unfairness caused by the boss has such impact on stress reactions of subordinates, one may wonder why supervisors do so little to reduce or to prevent stress of subordinates. If a simple gesture of fair treatment seems to have such an effect on subordinates' stress reactions, why do supervisors not perform these simple acts? One answer to this question is that managers may be under pressure of the situation to act less fairly. For example, Folger and Skarlicki (1998) found that managers tended to distance themselves from layoff victims more so than managers who were not to blame (i.e., external market forces were to blame) for the layoff. These findings suggest that organizations wishing to decrease managerial distancing might, where appropriate, also take extra steps to reassure their managers that a layoff was not their fault and that it was a result of external conditions over which they had no control. These findings point to the direction of the difficult position of many middle managers. I will focus on the dual position most managers or supervisors occupy in the organization and the consequences this dual position has on the behaviors and decisions supervisors make in relation to their subordinates. The issue of the dual position of middle managers is not a new one. In the literature (e.g., Yukl, 1989), the dual position of the supervisor is subsumed under the heading of the situational determinants of leadership behavior, in which leadership behavior is directed toward subordinates and the relationship with the superior is conceived as a situational determinant. The dual position of the supervisor may then be described and explained in terms of incompatible demands from different people, the superior and the subordinate. Cook and Emler (1999) illustrated the effects of incompatible demands. Middle managers were asked to play the role of the subordinate, middle-manager, or superior. From these perspectives they rated the suitability of six candidates for a position vacancy. The results showed that superiors preferred candidates high in technical competence and social skill and moderate in moral integrity, while subordinates preferred candidates low in skill and high in moral integrity. The conclusion from this study might be that supervisors can be confronted with incompatible demands from superiors and subordinates. I adopt the view of the incompatible demands on supervisors, but add two comments. First, the relation with the superior is not a determinant of leadership behavior, but instead may be an integral part of it. Second, incompatibility is related to allocation of scarce resources. In questionnaires completed by the supervisors at middle levels of an organization, respondents tend to be asked how many subordinates they have. It is seldom asked how many superiors or bosses they have. Asking how many bosses they have would probably confuse the respondents, because it is not the standard way they perceive an organization. Most people see an organization as a pyramid, in which a small number of people supervise a larger number of people. However, from a bottom-up perspective, one can see that a boss is supervised by many bosses as well. Clearly, we have a preference to look top-down rather than bottom-up.

This preference for looking top-down is also reflected in leadership theories. Whether one considers personality theories of leadership, situational theories of leadership, or contingency theories of leadership (Yukl, 1989), they all stress the downward vertical linkage with subordinates. An upward vertical linkage with the bosses of the supervisor is not included in models of leadership. In most theories, the relationship of the supervisor with his/her boss is conceived as a situational factor affecting leadership behavior, but it is not seen as an integral part of leadership behavior and effectiveness.

In most theories and in most studies on leadership behavior the person who performs leadership behavior is conceived as a kind of highest authority who has no higher superior above him/her. But as common practice shows, there are few bosses that can be defined as absolute leaders. Supervisors performing leadership behavior are most often situated at middle ranges of the organization. In other words, leadership behavior should not only be defined in terms of behavior towards subordinates, but in terms of behavior towards superiors as well: the dual position of the boss.

The dual position of the supervisor becomes all the more pressing when one considers allocation of resources as an important part of the supervisor's behavior (see Yukl, 1989). In many leadership theories, but especially Yukl's integrative model of effective leadership, an important component of the behavior of leaders is the service the leader can offer in providing resources. This includes the extent to which the group has budgetary funds, tools, equipment, supplies, personnel, and facilities needed to do the work, and necessary information or assistance from other units. In terms of Foa and Foa (1974), a supervisor may be successful if he/she provides the group with sufficient goods, services, and information. In fact a supervisor is an allocator who allocates resources to the group and group members. But most resources are scarce and cost money. Allocation of resources is therefore dependent on company policy and the boss's superior who emphasize production at the lowest cost. The boss has to maneuver between the demands of her/his superior and the demands brought forward by group members. The supervisor will evaluate the resources he/she receives from his/her superior in terms of justice. And because these justice evaluations are a reaction to what the superior is allocating, this type of justice will be called *reactive* justice (Greenberg, 1996). The other type of justice is aimed at allocating resources to others and this type of justice is termed *proactive* justice by Greenberg. The question I would like to answer here is how both types of justice are incorporated in the behavior and decisions of supervisors in the middle ranges of an organization. To answer this question, I will review the literature that investigates the behavior of participants in economic games (Van Dijk & Vermunt, 2000), and specifically I will focus on participants' behavior in an Ultimatum Bargaining game (UBG) and a Dictator game (DG). In both games an allocator distributes money (mostly coupons) to a recipient. In a DG the recipient has to accept the offer, whether the recipient agrees with it or not. An UBG differs from a DG in that the recipient can refuse the offer. If so, both players get nothing.

According to game theoretical predictions, individuals are profit maximizers who make their decisions based solely on rational arguments. Applying economic rationality to the behavior of recipients in an UBG, would result in recipient's acceptance of the smallest amount offered because otherwise the recipient receives nothing. The allocator, in this instance, can keep virtually all coupons for him/herself. Everyday laboratory reality is different. In an UBG most recipients do not accept an offer that is less than 30% of the total amount of coupons. Allocators mostly offer a division of coupons of 50% for him/herself and 50% for the recipient. DG allocators offer less to recipients than UBG allocators. This disconfirmation of game-theoretical predictions has led to the conclusions that some allocations are ruled by norms of fairness. Equity theory predicts that individuals prefer outcomes that are in proportion to their inputs. In the case of equal inputs—the standard situation in research on games—individuals are expected to prefer an equal distribution of the outcomes.

Fairness seems to be an important factor of the decision behavior of allocators in UBGs. More recently, Weg and Zwick (1994) have argued that allocators in bargaining situations make fair offers out of fear that lower offers will be rejected. An equal division, in this view, is not motivated by fairness considerations but reflects a motivation to maximize one's own outcomes. This behavior suggests that allocators in an UBG are motivated by strategic considerations rather than fairness considerations. To test this hypothesis, Weg and Zwick conducted an UBG and manipulated the type of information about the worth of the coupons to be divided. The allocator was informed that the coupons were worth ten dollars for him/her and five dollars for the receiver. In the asymmetric information condition, the allocator was told that receiver did not know this. In the symmetric information condition, the allocator was told that the coupons were worth ten dollars for him/her and five for the receiver and that receiver did know this. If the allocator was acting fairly, he/she should offer the recipient 67% of coupons and should keep for him/herself 33% of the coupons. This was what most allocators did in the symmetric information condition, where recipients knew the difference in the value of the coupons. In the asymmetric information condition, however, in which recipients were unaware of the difference in value of the coupons, the allocator divided the coupons 50-50. This may seem fair for an uninformed recipient, but it was not fair at all. A 50-50 division means that the allocator kept $5.00 for him/herself and gave $2.50 to the recipient. Weg and Zweick (1994) concluded from these findings that allocators act in order to seem fair rather than to be fair. It is plausible that supervisors, in allocating scarce resources to the group, want to look fair rather than to be genuinely fair. It is quite disturbing for subordinates that supervisors are not motivated to be fair but only want to look fair. According to fairness heuristic theory, supervisor's fair behavior is seen as a passport to stable and reliable social relationships.

A supervisor has a relationship not only with his/her subordinates but also with his/her higher-up superior. In a sense, a supervisor is also a subordinate. Supervisors are seen as enablers who enable the production workers to do their job, which is to produce. The main difference between "production subordinates" and "superior subordinates" is that the latter are expected to be loyal to the organization and have less discretion in their behavior towards the organization. For the "superior subordinate," it counts more that an order is an order than for the "production subordinate." In other words, a "superior-subordinate" may be characterized as an employee who is more dependent on his/her superior than the "production subordinate." A "superior-subordinate" is similar to a recipient in a

Dictator Game who only can accept the offer, whether he/she likes the offer or not. From the scarce literature that is focused on recipients' reactions to an offer (Handgraaf, Van Dijk, Wilke, & Vermunt, 1999; Hsee, Blount, Loewenstein, & Bazerman, 1999) it can be shown that the framing of an offer is of great importance for the acceptance of it. If the allocator presents the unfair offer as a choice between alternatives (in a UBG: 70-30 or 0-0 for allocator and recipient), the recipient is more inclined to accept the offer than when it is presented as a judgment (accepting or rejecting the 70-30 offer with the added stipulation that rejection results in both individuals receiving nothing). A smart superior (supervisor) will present his/her offer as a choice in which the consequences for the supervisor (subordinate) are made clear, and to increase the chances that the supervisor will accept the unfair offer. But it is an unfair offer and the presentation does not change that.

Because the "superior subordinate" is a *recipient* in a Dictator Game as well as an *allocator* in an Ultimate Bargaining Game, he/she is in a dual and difficult position. It has been abundantly shown that recipients of a resource in an allocation process evaluate the resource in terms of fairness (Adams, 1965; Folger, 1987; Tyler & Lind, 1992; Törnblom & Vermunt, 1999). As a recipient, the "superior subordinate" will evaluate the allocation of his/her superior in terms of fairness. But the "superior subordinate" is expected to be committed to the organization, and will consequently not complain when the allocation is evaluated as unfair. Research shows that "superior subordinates" show more satisfaction than rank and file members (Bruins & Wilke, 1992). In the position of allocator, the "superior subordinate" can not exhibit the same behavior as his/her superior has done. Being unfair will have repercussions on the performance of the "production subordinate" on which the "superior subordinate" is dependent. S/he has to be fair in allocation decisions directed towards his/her subordinates. Being fair brings the "superior subordinate" into a potentially conflicting situation with his/her superior, because by giving subordinates a greater say in the decisions, the "superior subordinate" may be accused of not being capable of doing his/her job as leader properly.

One may conclude from the literature on economic games that because of the difficult position, the supervisor will be tempted to appear fair instead of being fair. By appearing fair, the supervisor will satisfy both the subordinates who will evaluate his/her behavior in terms of fairness as well as the superior to which the supervisor can show that he/she has settled the issue according to the prevailing organizational standards. However, it is likely that the happiness of all parties involved will be short-lived. In the long run, this kind of leadership behavior might be detrimental for all involved. If subordinates discover the incorrect behavior of the supervisor, this will deteriorate the trust relation among all parties, with negative consequences for both the performance and the well-being of subordinates. In the long run, all parties will be worse off with this leadership behavior. It is therefore advisable to supervisors to be fair, although they are caught between incompatible demands. If an injustice cannot be prevented, supervisors may be able to repair justice in a different way.

Repairing Justice

The reduction of stress in an organizational context is accomplished predominantly by making it the responsibility of the individual employee. To reduce stress, the individual employee is urged to adopt coping strategies and to seek social support (for an overview see Thoits, 1995): Van Meer (1997) treats employees who experience stress from the boss by finding ways to help them cope. Heaney, Israel, Schurman, Baker, House, and Hugentobler (1993) define social support as a resource that people call upon when they cope with stress. In other words, coping as well as social support are strategies that are initiated by and focused on the stressed employee.

Another way to reduce and to prevent stress is by directly involving the supervisor. As we have discussed, a supervisor is an authority who allocates resources (tasks, time, bonuses, equipment) to subordinates by applying rules and procedures. Resources, as well as the application of the rules and procedures to arrive at the distribution, can be allocated unjustly. We assume that the unjust allocation of a resource, and the unfair application of a procedure, are seen by subordinates as a threat to their relationship with the supervisor. The threat may increase the already existing stress due to negative appraisal of the difference between environmental demands and the person's capacities. A subordinate may judge the allotted time for performing the task as unjust and as a severe demand to which s/he can not respond properly. However, the main factor that causes stress is the subordinate's threat that the allocation is seen as unjust and that the injustice can be viewed as an indication of a negative relationship with the supervisor. Based on these arguments, the following basic propositions can be stated:

Proposition 1. Stress will be increased by the subordinate's insight that the supervisor evidently did not do justice to the ability and capacity of the subordinate, as well as by showing little consideration for the subordinate.

Proposition 2. By engaging in fair behaviors and by compensating for eventual injustices, supervisors may reduce or even prevent stress of their subordinates.

These propositions are fundamental in that they offer both explanations for specific stress reactions and opportunities for reducing stress.

Underlying the propositions is the conception that (in)justice is an independent cause of stress in addition to other causes. There is scarce empirical evidence that justice works as an independent cause of stress. Zohar (1995) asked hospital nurses to indicate how fairly or unfairly role senders reacted to possible sources of stress (role justice). Next, Zohar measured other potential stressors as well, including role conflict, role ambiguity, role overload, and decision latitude (control). Role strain was measured by the General Health Questionnaire and by the Intentions to Leave index, and formed the dependent variables. It was found that role justice acts as an independent contributor of stress.

We may conclude that by repairing justice, stress may be reduced. One of the ways to overcome an initial unfairness is through behaviors seen as fair. It is in this respect that Folger, Rosenfield, Grove and Corkran (1979) introduced the term "fair process effect": the beneficial effects of a fair procedure on an unfair outcome. The fair process effect, however, is just one way to overcome the unfairness of a previous decision. A distribution as well as a procedure may be judged as unfair. An unfair distribution may be followed by a fair distribution as well as by a fair procedure. An unfair procedure may be followed by a fair distribution or by a fair procedure. That results in three additional ways (besides the fair process effect) of handling unfairness: compensation (an initially unfair distribution is followed by another but fair distribution); appraisal (an initially unfair procedure is followed by a fair distribution); and mitigation, (an initially unfair procedure is softened by another but fair procedure). For a more detailed description of the four modes of reducing unfairness, we refer to Vermunt and Steensma (2001).

In addition, researchers have not only found additive effects of injustice on stress, but also moderator effects. After a stressful task, participants who strongly believe that the world is a just place, where everyone gets what he/she deserves reported less strain, had better performance, and experienced the task as more challenging than participants who had weak just world beliefs (Tomaka & Blascovich, 1994). Based on Tomaka and Blascovich's experimental paradigm, experiments can be designed in which participants are treated fairly after a stressful task. We predict that stress will be reduced after a fair treatment as compared to a control condition. In conducting these types of experiments we hope to get more information about the injustice-stress relationship as well as to offer dual-position supervisors the tools to reduce or even prevent the stress of their subordinates effectively.

REFERENCES

Adams, J. S. (1965). Inequity in social exchange. In L. Berkowitz (Ed.), *Advances in experimental social psychology* (Vol. 2, pp. 267-299). New York: Academic Press.

Bales, R. (1980). *SYMLOG*. New York: Free Press.

Beer, P. T. de (2001). *Work in the postindustrial society.* Den Haag: SCP.
Bies, R.J., & Moag, J.S. (1986). Interactional justice: Communication criteria of fairness. In R. Lewicki, B. Sheppard, & M. Bazerman (Eds.), *Research on negotiations in organizations* (pp. 43-55). Greenwich, CT: JAI Press.
Bruins, J., & Wilke, H. (1996). Feelings of injustice after violation of succession rules in simulated organizations. *European Journal of Social Psychology, 26,* 149-155.
Cook, T., & Emler, N. (1999). Bottom-up versus top-down evaluations of candidates' managerial potential: An experimental study. *Journal of Occupational and Organizational Psychology, 72,* 423-439.
Crosby, F. (1976). A model of egoistical relative deprivation. *Psychological Review, 83,* 85-113.
Foa, U.G., & Foa, E.B. (1974). *Societal structures of the mind.* Springfied, IL: Charles C. Thomas Publishers.
Folger, R. (1987). Reformulating the preconditions of resentment: A referent cognitions model. In J. Masters & W. Smith (Eds.), *Social comparison, social justice, and relative deprivation: Theoretical, empirical, and policy perspectives* (pp. 183-215). Hillsdale, NJ: Erlbaum.
Folger, R., Rosenfield, D., Grove, J., & Corkran, L. (1979). Effects of "voice" and peer opinions on responses to inequity. *Journal of Personality and Social Psychology, 37,* 2253-2261.
Folger, R., & Skarlicki, D. P. (1998). When tough times make tough bosses: Managerial distancing as a function of layoff blame. *Academy of Management Journal, 41,* 79-87
Greenberg, J. (1996). *The quest for justice on the job.* Thousand Oaks, CA: Sage.
Handgraaf, J., Van Dijk, E., Wilke, H., & Vermunt, R. (1999). De saillantie van alternatieven binnen ultimatum spellen (The salience of alternatives in ultimatum games). In C. Rutte, D. van Knippenberg, C. Martijn, & D. Stapel (Ed.). *Fundamentele Sociale Psychologie, 13,* 196-208.
Heaney, C.A., Israel, B.A., Schurman, S.J., Baker, E.A., House, J.S., & Hugentobler, M. (1993). Industrial relations, work-site stress reduction, and employee well-being: A participatory action reserach investigation. *Journal of Organizational Behavior, 14,* 495-510.
Hsee, C.K., Blount, S., Loewenstein, G.F., & Bazerman, M.H. (1999). Preference reversals between joint and separate evaluations of options: A review and theoretical analysis. *Psychological Bulletin, 125,* 576-590.
Kahneman, D., & Tversky, A. (1982). Availibility and the simulation heuristic. In D. Kahneman, P. Slovic, & A. Tversky (Eds.), *Judgment under uncertainty: Heuristic and biases* (pp. 201-208). New York: Cambridge University Press.
Lazarus, R.S., & Folkman, S. (1984). *Stress, appraisal and coping.* New York: Springer.
Lerner, M.J. (1980). *The belief in a just world: A fundamental delusion.* New York: Plenum Press.
Lerner, M.J. (1991). Integrating societal and psychological rules. The basic task of each social actor and a fundamental problem for the social sciences. In R. Vermunt & H. Steensma (Eds.), *Social justice in human relations, Part 1* (pp. 13-32). New York: Plenum Press.
Leventhal, G.S. (1980). What should be done with equity theory? New approaches to the fairness in social relationships. In K. Gergen, M. Greenberg, & R. Willis (Eds.), *Social exchange theory* (pp. 27-55). New York: Plenum Press.

Lind, E.A., & Tyler, T. R. (1988). *The social psychology of procedural justice.* New York: Plenum Press.

Michalos, A.C. (1985). Multiple discrepancies theory (MDT). *Social Indicators Research, 16,* 347-413.

Oskam, M. (1998). *The boss's behavior as cause of stress.* Leiden: Doctoral thesis. NRC-Handelsblad, June 8, 2001.

Thoits, P. A. (1995). Stress, coping, and social support: Where are we? What next? *Journal of Health and Social Behavior, 36,* 53-79.

Tomaka, J., & Blascovich, J. (1994). Effects of justice beliefs on cognitive appraisal of and subjective, physiological, and behavioral responses to potential stress. *Journal of Personality and Social Psychology, 67,* 732-740.

Törnblom, K.Y., & Vermunt, R. (1999). A theoretical framework for the integration of distributive and procedural fairness in positive and negative resource allocations. *Social Justice Research, 12,* 39-64.

Tyler, T.R., & Lind, E.A. (1992). A relational model of authoriy in groups. In M. Zanna (Ed.), *Advances in experimental social psychology* (Vol. 25, pp. 115-191). San Diego: Academic Press.

Van den Bos, K., Vermunt, R., & Wilke, H.A.M. (1997). The relationship between procedural and distributive justice: What is fair depends more on what comes first than on what comes next. *Journal of Personality and Social Psychology, 72,* 95-104.

Van Dijk, E., & Vermunt, R. (2000). Strategy and fairness in social decision making: Sometimes it pays to be powerless. *Journal of Experimental Social Psychology, 36,* 1-25.

Van Meer, R. (1997). *Stress through the boss; sick making stress and what to do about it.* Utrecht/Antwerpen: Kosmos Uitgevers

Vermunt, R., Blaauw, E., & Lind, E.A. (1998). Fairness evaluations of encounters with police officers and correctional officers. *Journal of Applied Social Psychology 28,* 12, 1107-1124.

Vermunt, R., & Shulman, S. (1996). Responding to an unfair procedure. *Nederlands Tijdschrift voor de Psychologie, 51,* 35-46.

Vermunt, R., & Steensma, H. (1996). Leadership and Justice. In R. Van der Vlist & H. Steensma (Eds.), *Leadership in organizations* (pp. 157-174). Heerlen: Open Universiteit.

Vermunt, R., & Steensma, H. (2001). Stress and justice in organizations: An exploration into justice processes with the aim to find mechanisms to reduce stress. In R. Cropanzano (Ed.), *Justice in the workplace, from theory to practice,* Vol. 2 (pp. 27-48). Mahwah, NJ: Erlbaum.

Vermunt, R., Wit, A., Van den Bos, K., & Lind, E.A. (1996). The effects of unfair procedure on negative affect and protest. *Social Justice Research, 9,* 109-120.

Weg, E., & Zwick, R. (1994) Toward the settlement of the fairness issues in ultimatum games. *Journal of Economic behavior and Organization, 24,* 19-34

Yukl, G.A. (1989). *Leadership in organisations.* Englewood Cliffs NJ: Prentice-Hall, Inc.

Zohar, D. (1995). The justice perspective of job stress. *Journal of Organizational Behavior, 16,* 487-495.

CHAPTER 7

DISTRIBUTION OF TASKS:

A View from the Social Psychology of Justice

Gerold Mikula

ABSTRACT

This chapter presents a framework for the study of the distribution of tasks in social systems. The approach builds on social psychological theory and research on distributive justice. The framework considers three sets of variables: Arrangements and rules which can be used in the distribution of tasks, the nature of tasks to be distributed and the nature of social systems. Based upon these variables and their interrelations, research questions and hypotheses are derived. The empirical studies which are reported in the chapter serve to illustrate how one can proceed in the empirical study of the distribution of tasks and provide some preliminary findings. The concluding discussion points to limitations of the presented framework and research, addresses some neglected topics, and suggests research questions which need to be studied in the future.

The present chapter deals with the distribution of tasks or, more generally speaking, the organization of work in social systems. The distribution of tasks is important because social systems must handle the requirements which emerge from internal and external conditions in order to be effective and survive. Successful handling in turn presupposes regulations which coordinate members' activities, distribute tasks and responsibilities, and the assignment of the members to different tasks (cf. Kelley & Thibaut, 1978; Rusbult & van Lange, 1996). For instance, work teams typically have to accomplish a variety of different tasks. These tasks can be assigned to certain members based upon characteristics like seniority, skills etc., they can rotate among the members, can be done by all members together, or can go unregulated. Family members or students sharing flats have to decide who performs the various tasks which have to be done in a household (e.g., washing dishes, cleaning the bathroom, taking out the rubbish etc.). The members of a department of psychology who agreed to organize the next annual conference of a certain scientific association have to decide who shall be in charge of doing the various tasks which come along with the organization of a conference (e.g., negotiation and booking of accommodations, sending out the call for papers, collecting fees, setting up the program, etc.). Interestingly, in spite of its importance, the distribution of tasks has received little attention as a research topic thus far.

This chapter describes a framework for the study of the distribution of tasks and its consequences, and reports on preliminary empirical findings. The approach builds upon social psychological theory and research on distributive justice (Deutsch, 1975, 1985; Leventhal, 1976; Mikula, 1980a; Törnblom, 1992). Obviously, justice is not the only or main criterion according to which distributions of tasks can be organized and evaluated. For instance, the effectiveness and efficiency of task accomplishment, that is, the quality with which a given task is carried out and the economic use of time and resources, may represent other important criteria of evaluation for task distributions. But the present discussion proceeds from the assumption that justice is important with the distribution of tasks, as it is with distributions of positively valued goods and conditions. Decision making about the distribution of tasks can take justice into account as a criterion. In addition, distributions of tasks can become subjects of justice evaluations. Perceived injustice can affect satisfaction with and the efficiency of the organization of work (Adams, 1965; Cropanzano & Greenberg, 1997; Greenberg, 1982; Miles & Klein, 1998; Walster, Walster & Berscheid, 1978). For instance, members of work teams who regard given task distributions as unfair may become dissatisfied, less motivated to perform well, and prone to absenteeism and turnover. Similarly, perceived injustice of the division of household labor among people who share a flat may cause conflicts in the flat sharing group and bring people to leave the group. Thus, it seems appropriate to deal with the distribution of tasks from a justice point of view.

It is not only the understanding of the distribution of group tasks and its consequences which can profit from a justice-based approach. Social psychological theory and research on justice can also profit from the study of task distribution. Aside from a few exceptions (see below), justice researchers have not yet paid attention to the distribution of tasks, either in the context of organizational justice or in any other research area.[1] The majority of empirical research on distributive justice has focused on the distribution of positively valued or desired goods, outcomes, and conditions. The few available studies on distributions of negatively valued objects, and possible asymmetries between distributions of positive and negative resources, have mostly dealt with negative outcomes such as financial losses and money cuts (e.g., Griffith, 1989; Northcraft, Neale, Tenbrunsel & Thomas, 1996; Törnblom, 1988, 1992). Thus, we do not know to what extent the theories and evidence of distributive justice research apply to the distribution of tasks. Relevant studies have been conducted by Goodnow and colleagues (see Goodnow, 1998, for a review), Mikula, Freudenthaler, Brennacher-Kröll, and Schiller-Brandl (1997b), and Miles and Klein (1998). These studies and their findings will be described later in this chapter.

The present chapter describes a framework for the study of distribution of tasks, provides samples of predictions for different parts of the framework, and describes some preliminary studies and their findings. The final part of the chapter provides a critical assessment of the framework, addresses some applied issues and makes suggestions for future research. The framework should be equally suitable for the study of proactive and reactive types of questions, that is, how actors distribute tasks within social systems as well as how members of social systems will react to different kinds of task distributions.

A final introductory remark: Our interest in the topic of task distribution has been instigated by our research on issues of justice in relation to the division of household labor in different kinds of household systems such as families and groups of people sharing flats (cf. Freudenthaler & Mikula, 1998; Kluwer & Mikula, 2002; Mikula, 1998; Mikula et al., 1997a,b). This information may be important because some of the propositions and assumptions in the following discussion presumably are colored by our preoccupation with this particular kind of tasks and social systems. We will come back to this issue in the discussion section.

A FRAMEWORK FOR THE STUDY OF THE DISTRIBUTION OF TASKS

The present framework considers three sets of variables and their interrelations: *distributive regulations*, that is, the arrangements and rules which can be used in the distribution of tasks, the *nature of tasks* to be distributed, and the *nature of social systems*.[2] The latter two variables are assumed to operate as moderators of the choice and evaluation of the distributive regulations. The framework and the predictions which will be presented build upon the following basic propositions. We assume that people have ideas about kinds of arrangements and rules that "fit" certain kinds of tasks and certain kinds of relationships (cf. Fiske & Haslam, 1996; Goodnow, 1998). The ideas are based upon personal experiences and socially transmitted knowledge and are at least partly socially shared. They refer to such diverse aspects as practicability, effectiveness, efficiency, and justice. This means that people have ideas about which regulations are suitable for the distribution of certain tasks. They have ideas about how well certain tasks are typically carried out when the task distribution is made according to certain arrangements and rules. They have ideas that given tasks can be more efficiently accomplished with certain regulations than with others. And they have ideas about which tasks distributions are just or fair with given tasks and social relationships. We further assume that the ideas which people hold shape the use and evaluation of distributional regulations. People will choose and prefer rules and arrangements that fit given tasks and social systems. Dissatisfaction and feelings of injustice will arise when given distributions of tasks do not agree with the regulations which are regarded as appropriate in the given circumstances.

Regulations for the Distribution of Tasks

There is no systematization of regulations of task distribution available at present. Which rules and arrangements are used, and regarded as appropriate, is an empirical question. Distributive justice research has studied a variety of distribution rules (cf. Törnblom, 1992), the most prominent being the equality principle, the equity (or contribution) principle, and the need principle (cf. Deutsch, 1975, 1985; Leventhal, 1976; Mikula, 1980b; Schwinger, 1980). However, as the focus of distributive justice research was on the distribution of positive outcomes, it is not clear to what extent these rules also apply to the distribution of tasks. Given the lack of knowledge, it seems appropriate to start from more general features of distributive regulations and proceed to concrete instances of arrangements and rules only in a second step. We regard two features as particularly relevant to our purposes: the *balance of work load* and the *amount of regularization* which follow from the application of a given regulation. Balance of work load refers to the degree to which a regulation leads to an equal workload of the individual members of a social system. Regularization refers to the degree to which the distribution of tasks (i.e. the question of who is doing what) is fixed or left unregulated by a given arrangement or rule.

We regard the balance of work load as relevant because it is immediately related to the notion of equality which represents the most basic rule of distributive justice (cf. Buchanan & Mathieu, 1986). We maintain that distributions which balance the work load among group members generally will be regarded more just than regulations which lead to an unequal work load of group members. Consequently, when people are concerned about justice, distributions which balance the work load among group members generally will be preferred over regulations which do not balance the load. For instance, the concern with justice, and, in a next step, the desire for equal work loads, may increase in a given group when there is a high conflict potential with respect to the distribution of tasks.

Regularization is seen as relevant with respect to the two moderators of the choice and evaluation of distributive regulation which we consider in our approach, i.e. task characteristics and characteristic of the social system. We maintain that certain tasks and certain systems call for more regulated forms of task distribution than other tasks and other systems. For instance, we expect that more regulated forms of task distributions will be preferred over less regulated forms when a task is perceived as important, or when there is a risk that the task may not be carried out properly without strict regulations (e.g., when the task is disliked), or there is a risk that some members of the team will free-ride at the expense of others by not contributing to the accomplishment of the task.

Examples of Distributive Rules and Arrangements

Balance of work load among the members of a social system can be achieved either with respect to individual tasks or across different tasks. Prominent regulations which balance the workload with respect to individual tasks are collaboration (i.e., the members of the group do the task together) and taking turns in the case of recurring tasks (i.e., the task is done by each of the members in turn). Balance of the work load across different tasks can be achieved by regulations of specialization with reciprocation (i.e., one person does one particular task and others do other tasks in exchange). Regulations of specialization imply task assignment of individual members according to individual attributes. Different attributes or person characteristics can be used for that purpose such as roles, skills, personal preferences, threshold of necessity, availability, and so on (see below). Obviously, regulations of specialization do not always balance the work load among group members.

Arrangements and rules of tasks distribution also differ in the degree of regularization. More regulated forms include collaboration, taking turns, various kinds of specialization, and individual responsibility (e.g. "people should do "their own work," see below). Arrangements according to availability, personal importance or threshold of necessity, personal preferences, and random arrangements (see below) represent examples of less regulated forms of task distributions.

The different distributive rules and arrangements which have been mentioned above as examples have been taken from our research on the distribution of household labor (Mikula et al., 1997b). Thus, it seems appropriate to illustrate the regulations in more detail by means of examples from this particular area. Consider a group of four students who share a flat. They have to deal with various household tasks such as cleaning (bathroom, floor, etc.), cooking, washing dishes, doing laundry, taking out rubbish, household shopping, household repairs, and calculating the phone bill. Let us take cleaning bathroom as an example. The students may do it together (collaboration) or they may take turns. The may also decide that one of them will always do this job while the other members do other jobs (e.g., cooking, washing dishes, etc.) in exchange. This kind of specialization may be based upon the fact that one of them particularly likes to clean the bathroom, or because he or she is doing it so well. They may also come to the agreement that everybody should clean the bathroom after having used it (personal responsibility), or that cleaning of the bathroom should be done by the person who has most time for it (availability), or by the person who feels it to be of highest importance (personal importance or threshold of necessity). Finally, they may leave the task unregulated. In this latter case, personal liking of cleaning bathrooms or the threshold of necessity will take effect, or the bathroom will not been cleaned at all.

Moderators of the Application and Evaluation of Distributive Regulations

Previous distributive justice research has shown that different distribution rules are used, and regarded as just, depending on various situational factors (Deutsch, 1975, 1985; Leventhal, 1976; Mikula, 1980b, 1981; Törnblom, 1992). This should equally hold for the distribution of tasks. The present framework considers two variables as moderators of the choice and evaluation of the distributive arrangements and rules: the nature of the tasks to be distributed and the nature of the social system.

The Nature of Tasks

The assertion that the kind of tasks makes a difference is not new. It has been made by numerous authors and numerous task classification systems have been published in the social, industrial and organizational psychology literature (e.g., Fleishman, 1967, 1975; Hackman, 1968; Shaw, 1973, 1976; Steiner, 1972). However, to our best knowledge, there is no systematization of tasks which is immediately suitable for the focal topic of the present discussion, that is, the distribution of different kinds of tasks in social systems. Given the lack of a more general task classification system which is directly relevant to our purpose, we focus on two classificatory approaches which have been developed in recent research on the distribution of tasks and responsibilities in families and other kinds of households. Obviously, the task characteristics which have been established as relevant with this particular kind of tasks may not be relevant to other kinds of group tasks and social systems. Future studies will have to find out whether the task characteristics are relevant to the distribution of group tasks in general.

Mikula and colleagues (1997b) distinguished between periodically recurring vs. not recurring tasks, time-consuming vs. not time-consuming tasks, tasks which require vs. do not require special skills or training, tasks where causal agents can or cannot be easily identified, and tasks that benefit all as opposed to only some of the participants. The authors proposed that different kinds of arrangements and rules will be used in the distribution of tasks, differing with respect to one or several of these characteristics (see below for further details).

Goodnow and colleagues (cf. Goodnow, 1998, for a review) introduced the concept of "ownership" of tasks. The ownership of tasks can be defined in different ways. Ownership can be based on having caused a problem or generated the need for work to be done. Ownership can also be perceived when the task is to the benefit of a particular person only. Possible other bases of ownership include that the task arose in a person's own space, that the task was assigned to a particular person in the first place, or that the task is "owned" by virtue of gender, status, or other personal attributes. According to Goodnow (1998), an important effect of work being "one's own" is that it is typically regarded as not easily movable to other persons. Particular circumstances or justifications are required so that it not be regarded as unfair when someone takes over a job owned by another person. Obviously, there is some overlap between Goodnow's notion of task ownership and two of the task categories which have been discussed by Mikula and colleagues (1997b), that is, tasks where causal agents can be easily identified, and tasks that are to the benefit of some participants only.

Some Predictions

Based on these task classifications and our framework, the following predictions can be made.

Proposition 1. Regulations which balance the workload of the members (e.g., cooperation, taking turns), will be preferred and regarded as just for recurring and time consuming tasks.

Proposition 2. More regulated modes of task distribution (and rules of specialization in particular) will be applied and regarded as just for tasks which require particular training or skills, tasks where the causal agent can be easily identified, tasks which are to the benefit of some participants only, or, in Goodnow's terms, tasks which are "owned" by a person for some reason.

The nature of the social system

How tasks are distributed probably also depends on particular characteristics of the social system. For instance, work very likely will be differently organized in systems with formalized role structures and in systems without such role structures. Systems with formalized role structures generally will have more regularized forms of task distribution. The size and the complexity of social systems can also influence the distribution of tasks. The larger and the more complex social systems are, the more regulated forms of task distribution they will need and develop. In addition, and particularly in systems without formalized role structures, the degree of interdependence and the quality of intermember relationships (e.g., mutual liking and trust, and the prevailing interpersonal orientations) will have an impact on the distribution of tasks. Finally, the duration and time perspective of the system can make a difference. Further, more theory-based predictions as to how the distribution of tasks will be related to the relationship types can be derived from Clark and Mills' theory of communal and exchange relationships (1979, 1993; Mills & Clark, 1982) and Fiske's relational models theory (Fiske, 1991, 1992; Fiske & Haslam, 1996).

Clark and Mills' distinction between communal and exchange relationships is based on the norms that govern the giving and receiving of benefits. Communal relationships are often exemplified by relationships with close friends, family members, and romantic partners. Relationships between strangers, acquaintances, and people who do business with one another are examples of exchange relations. In exchange relationships, benefits are given with the expectation of receiving a comparable benefit in return or as repayment for a benefit received previously. In contrast, the norm in communal relationships is to give benefits in response to needs and to demonstrate a general concern for the other person. Keeping track of individual inputs into joint tasks is important in exchange relationships, but not in communal relations. This is because in the former, but not in the latter, benefits should be allocated in proportion to inputs.

Fiske (1991, 1992; Fiske & Haslam, 1996) distinguished four elementary forms of social relations: communal sharing, authority ranking, equality matching, and market pricing. These basic social modes are assumed to govern the motivation, planning, production, comprehension, and coordination in, and the evaluation of all domains of social life. In communal sharing relations, people have a sense of equivalence. They attend to what they have in common and disregard differences between them. They are responsive to each other's needs and contribute what they can. They regard work as a joint responsibility and work collectively, without assessing individual inputs and without necessarily assigning distinct responsibilities to individuals. Authority ranking relations are characterized by strongly attending to people's ranks or positions in a hierarchical ordering. Privileges and responsibilities reflect the standing of the individual members. Higher ranking persons manage, direct, and control the labor of those in subordinate positions. In equality matching relations, people keep track of the differences among them using even balance as the reference point. People actively seek equality per se, for example, by taking turns or by applying equal contributions, egalitarian distributions, or balanced exchanges in which people get back just what they gave. Market pricing relations are most common in large-scale, complex social systems. They are governed by a model of proportionality and operate with reference to socially significant ratios or proportions such as prices or wages. Activities are organized in terms of cost-benefit ratios and rational calculations of efficiency or expected utility. Contractual work arrangements in which payment is a rate per unit of time, task, or output typically prevail in this kind of relations.

Obviously, the two kinds of relationships distinguished by Clark and Mills (1979) and the four forms of social relations distinguished by Fiske (1992) have much in common. Clark and Mills' communal relationship is equivalent with Fiske's communal sharing mode.[3] The exchange relationship conflates the modes of equality matching and market pricing. Only Fiske's authority ranking has no equivalent in Clark and Mills' theory.

Some Predictions

A sample of predictions which can be derived from the classifications of social relations by Clark and Mills (1979) and Fiske (1992) and our framework of distribution of tasks is summarized in the following:

Proposition 3. The distribution of tasks will be generally less regulated in communal relationships than in the remaining three forms of social relations.

Proposition 4. More regulated modes of task distribution, and rules of specialization in particular, will be more likely in authority ranking and market pricing relations than in equality matching and communal relations.

Proposition 5. Exchange relationships, as well as equality matching and market pricing relations, call for regulations which allow to keep track of each member's contributions. Thus, taking turns and various rules of specialization will be applied more frequently and evaluated more positively than collaboration and various unregulated forms of task distribution in this kind of relationships.

Proposition 6. Members of communal relationships generally will be less concerned about the balance of work load and about justice than members of the remaining three forms of social relations.

Proposition 7. The regulation of the distribution of tasks follow different criteria in authority ranking, equality matching, and the market pricing type relations. Accordingly, different versions of a generic specialization rule will be preferred and considered as just. In authority ranking systems, the individual members will be responsible for distinct tasks which reflect their standing in the hierarchy. In equality matching systems, people actively seek a balance of work load within a given task. Collaboration and taking turns are possible means towards this end. In market pricing relations, wage labor is the predominant mode of work organization. Balance is important here too. But, different to equality matching, it is the equality of some outcome/input ratios which matters. This kind of equality can also be achieved by compensation across different tasks. Thus, market pricing relations will be characterized by differentiated and specialized task responsibilities.

Proposition 8. Violations of the ownership rule, "to each one's own," are more likely, and regarded less unjust, in communal sharing than in other kinds of relationships. Here, people care about the well-being of their partner and the quality of their relationship and thus respond to a request or even volunteer to do the other's self-care jobs.

EMPIRICAL STUDIES AND FINDINGS

This section reports on a few studies which analyzed the distribution of tasks from a distributive justice point of view. All studies deal with the distribution of household tasks. As has been mentioned above, this raises questions about the generalizability of the findings. But the setting also has advantages for the present purposes. Since there are no strict and formalized regulations of the distribution of tasks in many households, one can expect to observe a great variety of distributive regulations and considerable variation in their use and evaluation.

The aim of the first two studies (Mikula et al., 1997b; Studies 1 and 2) was to set up a list of arrangements and rules which are used in the distribution of tasks, and to analyze their frequencies or preferences of use, and their justice evaluation with different kinds of tasks. The studies dealt with two different types of household systems: groups of students sharing flats (Study 1) and adolescent children living together with their families (Study 2). The participants reported the regulations which they used with different tasks in their household and rated how just they perceived each regulation in general (Study 1) or with respect to each individual task (Study 2). The wording of the ratings is given in the Appendix. The following household tasks were considered in the study with flat sharing students: cleaning bathroom, cleaning toilet, cleaning kitchen, cleaning floor in shared rooms, cleaning household appliances, washing dishes, taking out rubbish, household shopping, household repairs, and calculating the phone bill. In the family study, the list of tasks contained preparing meals, ironing, vacuuming, washing dishes, household shopping, taking out rubbish, household repairs, and car washing.

Study 3 (Mikula & Schilde, unpublished) was designed to replicate parts of Study 1 and to provide a first experimental test of the moderating role of characteristics of the social system. The study used a scenario methodology. The participants received one of two different descriptions of a group of four students sharing a flat and were asked to imagine themselves as being members of the group. The scenario methodology was used to manipulate experimentally the nature of the relationships within the group. One scenario described the students living together as close friends. The other scenario described students who did not know each other before sharing the flat and did not like each other very much. Thus, the first scenario resembled a communal relationship and the second one an exchange or equality matching relationship.[4] The list of household tasks was set up to contain two time-consuming tasks (cleaning floor and cleaning bathroom), two not time-consuming tasks (storing away purchased common goods, separating rubbish), two tasks which require special skills (calculating the phone bill, doing repairs) and two tasks where causal agents can be easily identified (washing dishes, doing laundry). The study considered six different arrangements and rules of task distribution (see below). The participants rated the six distributional regulations for all eight tasks with respect to how much they would prefer the regulations to be used, and perceived justice (cf. Appendix).

Use and Preference of Different Arrangements and Rules

Studies 1 and 2 identified eight different arrangements and rules which covered 95% of the regulations mentioned: collaboration, turn taking, individual responsibility, specialization with reciprocation, nonreciprocated specialization, threshold of necessity, availability, and unregulated (cf. left part of Table 1 for descriptions of the eight arrangements and rules). The frequencies of use of the individual regulations (Studies 1 and 2) and the preference ratings obtained in Study 3 covaried with the nature of household tasks in a meaningful way, reflecting the differential practicability, usefulness, and efficiency of the regulations for different tasks (cf. Table 1, right part). Arrangements which balance the burdens of all household members, such as collaboration or taking turns, were particularly frequent (or preferred) with tasks that are time consuming and have to be done periodically (e.g., cleaning common rooms). Distribution of tasks according to individual responsibility prevailed for tasks where causal agents were easily identified or which benefited only some participants (e.g., washing dishes, car washing, cleaning own room). Tasks which require particular training or skills (e.g. calculating the phone bill, preparing meals, ironing, repairs) were predominantly allocated according to

TABLE 1
Arrangements and Rules for the Distribution of Tasks and Their Covariation with Task Characteristics

Arrangements and Rules	Task Characteristics
COLLABORATION "Several or all people do it together most of the time"	Task which are time-consuming and have to be done periodically
TURNTAKING "Everyone in the group has to do it from time to time, we take turns"	Task which are time-consuming and have to be done periodically
INDIVIDUAL RESPONSIBILITY "The casual agent, that is, the person who has generated the tasks, does it"	Tasks were causal agents can be easily defined, or tasks which are to the benefit of some participants only
SPECIALIZATION WITH RECIPROCATION "One person does it always/most of the time and others do other chores in exchange"	Tasks requiring particular training or skills
NONRECIPROCATED SPECIALIZATION "One person does it always/most of the time without others doing anything in exchange"	Tasks requiring particular training or skills
THRESHOLD OF NECESSITY "The one who feels it to be necessary first does it"	Tasks which are not urgent, not time-consuming, and do not require any particular training or skills
AVAILABILITY "The one who has most time for it does it"	Tasks which are not urgent, not time-consuming, and do not require any particular training or skills
UNREGULATED "One time one person and the next time somebody else"	Tasks which are not urgent, not time-consuming, and do not require any particular training or skills

rules of specialization (with or without reciprocation). Tasks which are not urgent, not time-consuming and do not require any particular skills (e.g. taking out rubbish, household shopping) were less regulated and allocated predominantly according to individual availability, threshold of necessity, or went unregulated.

Justice Ratings of Different Arrangements and Rules

The justice ratings of the regulations (cf. Table 2) by students sharing flats (Study 1 and 3) and adolescents in families (Study 2) provided a consistent picture apart from a few exceptions. Collaboration, taking turns, and specialization with reciprocation were consistently perceived as just. Threshold of necessity and nonreciprocated specialization were consistently perceived as unjust. Individual responsibility was regarded as fair by

TABLE 2
Justice Ratings of Arrangements and Rules

	Study 1 Students (N=98)	Study 2 Families (N=208)	Study 3 Students (N=120)
Collaboration	5.96 [a]	5.31 [a]	6.16 [b]
Turntaking	6.51	4.96	6.37
Individual Responsibility	5.77	3.65	6.02
Specialization With Reciprocation	5.89	4.95	N.C.
Nonreciprocated Specialization	N.C.	3.56	3.51
Threshold of Necessity	3.13	3.93	3.54
Availability	2.89	4.82	N.C.
Unregulated	3.61	4.68	3.10

Notes: N.C.= not considered
[a] 8-point rating scale (1=very unjust, 8= very just)
[b] 7-point rating scale (1= very unjust, 7= very just)

students sharing flats but slightly unfair by adolescents in families. Availability and random assignment were considered unjust by students but just by adolescents living with their families. Generally speaking, more regulated modes of task distribution and regulations which balance the work load were regarded as more just than arrangements which leave the distribution unregulated or lead to uneven work load. Possible interpretations of the differences between students' households and family households will be discussed below in connection with the effects of system characteristics.

Regulation X Task Interaction

Significant regulation by task interactions in Studies 2 and 3 indicated that the justice ratings of the distributive regulations differed with respect to individual tasks.[5] Since the pattern of results was rather complicated, the nature of the interactions will be illustrated here by a few examples only. In the students scenario study, the rule of individual responsibility was regarded as particularly just for tasks for which causal agents can be easily identified (washing dishes, doing laundry) and as unjust for calculating the phone bill. Specialization was regarded as just for the calculation of the phone bill but not for the remaining tasks. Taking turns was considered most just for time consuming and demanding tasks (cleaning bathroom, cleaning floor, separating rubbish). Adolescents in families generally regarded the individual responsibility rule unjust except for tasks which are mostly to the benefit of a particular person only, and tasks for which the causal agent generating the task can be easily identified (e.g., car washing). Specialization without reciprocation, which was generally perceived as unjust, was regarded as least unjust for preparing meals, ironing, and repairs, that is, for tasks which require skills. Collaboration, which was generally appreciated, was regarded as less just for tasks where collaboration is practically impossible, for example, ironing or vacuuming. Finally, specialization with reciprocation received higher justice ratings, and availability and taking turns received lower justice ratings, for tasks requiring skills (e.g., ironing, preparing meals) as compared to tasks requiring no skills. Taken together, the significant regulation by task interactions reflect that different kinds of regulations are regarded as just with different kinds of tasks. The pattern of the justice ratings suggests that justice evaluations were partly shaped by the applicability and usefulness of the regulations for different tasks.

The Moderating Role of System Characteristics

The first three studies did not provide strong evidence in support of the proposition that the nature of the social system moderates the use, preference, and justice evaluation of distributive regulations. Indirect support comes from informal comparisons of the households of students sharing flats (Study 1) and adolescents living with their families (Study 2). Traditional arrangements according to which mothers do the majority of the housework (and nonreciprocated specialization in particular) prevailed in the households of families. Contrary to this, households of students were characterized by arrangements and rules which ensure that all members contribute equally to household tasks. These differences correspond to the different role structures of the two kinds of household systems.

The justice ratings were partly similar and partly different with households of students and families (cf. Table 2). Collaboration, turn taking, and specialization with reciprocation were regarded as just, and nonreciprocated specialization and threshold of necessity were considered unjust in both household systems. Availability, random assignment, and individual responsibility received different ratings in the two social systems. Availability and random assignment were rated slightly positively within families but regarded as unjust by students. Possibly, this indicates that flat-sharing students disapprove of regulated task distributions (i.e., availability and random) which can be misused for exploitation by free-riding cohabitants, while adolescents in families are less concerned about this possibility. No compelling interpretation can be offered for the finding that individual responsibility was regarded unjust by adolescents in families but rated as fairly just among students.

More direct, albeit weak, evidence for the moderator effect of system characteristics comes from the scenario study (Study 3) in which, by experimental manipulation, the relationship among the group members was either described as a communal or as an exchange/equal matching relationship. Some of the findings of the study suggest that participants of communal relationships are less strict in rejecting task distributions that do not fit the general ideas of what is an appropriate arrangement or rule. For instance, nonreciprocated specialization, which was generally perceived as unjust, was regarded as less unjust in communal as compared to exchange relationships. Interestingly, the difference was most pronounced with time consuming tasks such as cleaning the floor and the bathroom.

Two additional scenario studies of the distribution of household tasks in flat sharing groups which were conducted for partly different purposes (Study 4: Mikula, Habsa & Sprung, unpublished; Study 5: Mikula, unpublished) provide further support for the moderating function of social system characteristics. Both studies were conducted with students samples (Study 4: $N = 120$; Study 5: $N = 370$). Similar to Study 3, two different scenarios were used to manipulate experimentally the kind of relationship among the members of the flat sharing group. One scenario described a communal relationship and the second one an exchange or equality matching relationship. Study 4 considered six different tasks (cleaning bath, doing laundry, washing dishes, weekly household shopping, taking out rubbish, and getting the mail) and five distributive regulations (collaboration, taking turns, individual responsibility, threshold of necessity, and unregulated). Study 5 considered three tasks (cleaning bathroom, washing dishes, and taking out rubbish) and four regulations (taking turns, individual responsibility, availability, and threshold of necessity). The participants in both studies rated their preference, perceived justice, and perceived effectiveness of each regulation for each of the individual tasks (cf. Appendix).

Significant regulation by relationship interactions in Study 4 supported the predicted moderator effect of system characteristics. The participants who got the exchange/equal matching relationship scenario discriminated more strongly in their ratings of the four regulations than the participants who got the communal relationship scenario. In addition, cooperation was rated less positively, and unregulated arrangements more negatively, with exchange/equal matching relationships. A significant regulation by relationship interaction was also obtained with the preference ratings in Study 5. Arrangements according to availability were rated more negatively, and individual responsibility was rated more positively, in exchange/equal matching than in communal relationships. Taken together, these findings suggest that the kind of regulation which is used in the distribution of tasks makes more difference with exchange/equal matching relationships as compared to communal relationships. In addition, less regulated task distributions are more negatively evaluated in exchange/equal matching than in communal relations.

Further analyses tested the prediction that justice will be of less concern in communal relationships than in exchange/equality matching relations.

Based upon this proposition, we expected that perceived justice will have more impact upon the preference of given regulations of task distribution in exchange/equality matching relations as compared to communal relationships. We tested the hypothesis with the data of the Studies 4 and 5 by a series of multiple stepwise regression analyses (one for each regulation X task combination) in which the ratings of effectiveness and justice served as predictors and the ratings of preference as the criterion variable. The results of Study 4 lend support to our prediction. Justice turned out to be a better predictor of preference than effectiveness in groups with exchange/equal matching relations in 14 of 23 cases. In communal relationship groups, justice was the better predictor than effectiveness only in 5 of 22 cases. The results of Study 5 show a similar picture. Justice was a better predictor than effectiveness in 10 out of 12 cases with exchange/equal matching relations and in 7 out of 12 cases with communal relations. But the difference did not reach significance.

The Ownership of Tasks

A series of studies by Jacqueline Goodnow and colleagues explored adults' and children's perceptions of fairness associated with the assignment or redistribution of household tasks to particular people based upon the notion of "ownership" of tasks (cf. Goodnow, 1998, for a review). According to this view, task performance should respect the ownership of tasks and work that is "one's own" will be regarded as not easily transferable to other persons. Consequently, perceptions of injustice or unfairness will result if work which is owned by a particular person is left to somebody else without sufficient justification.

Goodnow (1998) summarizes a number of findings which lend support to these propositions. For instance, mothers avoid, and regard it as not "right," to shift a self-care job to another child (e.g., making another's bed or putting away the toys the other child has used) while they see no problem asking a child to take over an other-care job (e.g., setting or clearing the table) from another child (Goodnow & Delaney, 1989). Similarly, children regard it as unjust to be asked to put away all the pieces of a game which they played together with a child, when the other child left without cleaning up its share of the joint game (Warton & Goodnow, 1991). Children are also sensitive to different justifications of requests to take over an other-care job. Justifications in terms of need, reciprocity, or the special status of being a family are judged as fair while references to one's authority or to particular characteristics of the child are not regarded as fair. Finally, adult couples endorse the rule "to each their own" for "direct causation tasks" such as ironing and taking care of cars but not for cooking or vacuuming (Goodnow & Bowes, 1994).

DISCUSSION

The present chapter began with the proposition that the distribution of tasks is an important element in the functioning of social systems of any kind and size. Effective functioning of social systems presupposes coordination of the activities of the members and task distributions which ensure that important tasks are carried out orderly and the available resources are optimally used. The present focus on justice aspects of task distributions seems warranted as previous research has shown that perceptions of injustice can lead to a variety of negative consequences at the individual and group level, such as loss of motivation, poor job performance, high rates of withdrawal behavior, social conflict, and so on (cf. Cropanzano & Greenberg, 1997; Greenberg, 1982; Mikula, 1993; Miller, 2001; Tyler, Boeckmann, Smith, & Huo, 1997; Walster et al., 1978).

Our framework for the study of the distribution of tasks considered the regulations which can be used in the distribution of tasks, the nature of tasks, and the nature of social systems as relevant variables. Based upon these three sets of variables and their interrelations, a number of research questions and hypotheses have been formulated. The studies which have been reported are preliminary in many respects but provide examples of how one can proceed in empirical research. The findings of the studies permit the following conclusions. First, a limited number of arrangements and rules cover the majority of regulations which are used within given conditions. These rules agree only partly with the "classical" principles of distributive justice. Second, people seem to have rather clear and socially shared ideas about appropriate ways of distributing tasks within their social system. Third, the use and evaluation of different regulations depend on the particular characteristics of the task at hand and characteristics of the social system. The empirical evidence of the moderating function of social system characteristics was less strong than expected. This may be explained by the scenario character of the studies. Presumably, differences in the kind and quality of social relations matter more in real life settings.

Our preoccupation with the distribution of household tasks has probably influenced our framework in multiple respects. This holds especially with respect to our systematization of distributive regulations and the systematization of tasks. The systematization of social relations builds upon more elaborated theoretical models, the usefulness of which has already been established in other fields of research. In addition, the exclusive focus of our studies on one particular kind of task within one particular kind of social system precludes any generalization of the findings. Thus, future studies will have to establish the usefulness of the present approach for other social settings.

Given the somewhat narrow focus of our approach, it may be worthwhile to point out briefly the relevance of task distribution to work teams and team performance (Jackson & Ruderman, 1995; Swezey & Salas, 1992; Williams, 1996). Work teams need clear task schedules and assignments of members to different tasks in order to be effective. The distribution of tasks may be decided upon by some authority or, in the case of autonomous or self-managing work teams, by the team members themselves (cf. Cummings, 1978; Manz & Sims, 1987). Actually, self-managing work teams have much in common with household systems, and households of flat sharing people in particular, which have been the focus of our empirical studies. In both cases, the members of the group or team themselves decide about methods of work, tasks schedules and assignment of members to tasks. Independent of who decides, distribution of tasks in work teams will become subject to justice evaluations by the team members. Perceived injustice of task distribution may be one of the key obstacles to team effectiveness and additionally bring about various other negative consequences. Organizational justice literature shows impressively that perceptions of justice and injustice affect a variety of work outcomes, such as performance, commitment, turnover intentions, and organizational citizenship behaviors (cf. Cropanzano & Greenberg, 1997; Folger & Cropanzano, 1999; Gilliland, Steiner, & Skarlicki, 2001). Social loafing in teams may represent a particularly good example of the interplay between task distribution, perception of injustice and performance. Social loafing of individual members of self-managing work teams may contribute to the perception of injustice on the part of the other team members. Simultaneously, perceptions of injustice with respect to the distribution of tasks may induce team members to social loafing. Thus, it is important for work teams to regulate the distribution of tasks in a way which is perceived as just and prevents social loafing.

Household tasks do not only provide a useful example for the discussion of distribution of tasks but also represent a relevant research topic in their own right. Due to the increased participation of women in the paid labor force and the parallel changes in traditional gender roles, the division of household labor and the problems of coordinating professional and family work have become important topics both in research (e.g., Goodnow, 1994; Hertz, 1986; Lewis, Izraeli & Hootsmans, 1992; Sekaran, 1986; Shelton & John, 1996) and presumably even more so in family life. While research on this topic is increasing, relatively less attention has been devoted to the question of how the tasks are distributed, and how balance of the load with professional and family work is achieved. The latter aspects of task distribution seems particularly interesting to study with dual-career couples.

The remaining part of the concluding discussion will be used to point to limitations of our framework and research, address topics which have been neglected in our treatment of the distribution of tasks, and suggest some research questions which need to be studied in the future. The above reference to self-managing work teams made evident that our discussion neglected the important question of who decides about the distribution of tasks. As mentioned above, the distribution can be decided upon by the group members who have to carry out the tasks or by some authority. In the cases of household systems and self-managing work teams the decision will be made by the members themselves, and often be made implicitly rather than explicitly. In other cases, managers or external authorities decide about the distribution of tasks and formally assign certain group members to certain tasks. Future studies should consider both possibilities and explore possible differences with respect to the regulations which are chosen and their acceptance, evaluation and consequences. In the case of group decisions, the degree to which group members agree about how to distribute the group tasks and their commitment to such an agreement provide additional interesting topics of research.

The empirical studies which have been conducted thus far and reported above concentrated on the choice or preference and the evaluation of task distributions. Other consequences which may result from given task distributions and their evaluation have been mentioned in the framework but were not considered in the studies. Thus, the effects of different task distributions and the evaluation of them on the functioning of social systems, the intermember relations, and the satisfaction, well-being, and behavior of the individual members would be interesting topics for future empirical studies. Research evidence from early distributive justice research (e.g., Greenberg, 1982; Walster et al., 1978) and the organizational justice literature (e.g., Cropanzano & Greenberg, 1997; Folger & Cropanzano, 1999; Gilliland, Steiner & Skarlicki, 2001) provide valuable suggestions as to which consequences one can expect to follow from perceived justice and injustice of task distributions.

Another question which deserves to be considered relates to the particular aspects of task distributions to which judgments of justice refer. Obviously, feelings of injustice do not necessarily arise whenever people feel that a distributive regulation in use does not fit the respective task and/or system. It needs additional preconditions in order to elicit feelings of injustice. Two likely candidates which come to mind, and which have been addressed in our framework, are the imbalance of workloads of different people and the violation of the ownership of tasks. (Further possibilities which refer to procedural aspects will be mentioned below.)

A major limitation of our approach may be seen in the exclusive focus on distributive justice and the apparent neglect of procedural justice. Recent reviews of justice research, both with respect to organizational settings (e.g., Cropanzano & Greenberg, 1997) and more general reviews (e.g., Lind & Tyler, 1988; Miller, 2001; Tyler et al., 1997; Tyler & Smith, 1998), show impressively that procedural justice is at least as important as distributive justice. Thus, one can assume that procedural justice also matters with the distribution of tasks. Actually, there is some overlap with what we have discussed in the chapter and procedural justice. For instance, what has been said about regularization may be regarded as an issue of procedural rather than distributive justice, as one of the reviewers of an earlier version of this chapter correctly pointed out. This suggests that the distinction between the two facets of justice sometimes may be less clear than some writings in the field maintain.

The main reason why the present discussion did not deal with procedural justice is that we believe that procedural elements very likely affect the perceptions of justice and injustice independent of the particular topic of decision making. Thus, the knowledge that has been acquired in previous research about procedural elements that contribute to the perceptions of procedural justice and injustice, and the consequences of these perceptions, should be immediately applicable to the distribution of tasks. For instance, the perceptions that one had a voice in the decision of how tasks are distributed within one's group and feelings of being accepted and treated with dignity and respect should contribute to perceived procedural justice. Similarly, the way in which decisions about distributions of tasks are made and communicated to the members of social systems, the procedures that accompany the assignment of people to tasks, such as giving reasons or justifications for the assignment, and procedures of surveillance of the performance of assigned tasks very likely affect the perceptions of procedural fairness of the distribution of tasks in the same way as in other distributional settings. Empirical research that considered procedural justice with respect to the distribution of tasks is rare. We are only aware of the following studies. Miles and Klein (1998) studied group members' fairness perceptions of four different methods or procedures of assigning some of the members of a group to an extra task: assignment based upon a random procedure, assignment based upon individual ability, assignment by an arbitrary personal decision without any justification, or assignment based upon an arbitrary personal decision plus justification of the assignment with an explanation. The authors report that the random assignment procedure was perceived as most fair.[6] Part of the research of Goodnow and colleagues which has been briefly described earlier in this chapter (cf. Goodnow, 1998, for a review) provides further examples of procedural aspects which contribute to the perception of justice and injustice. The authors conducted interviews with children to get their views and evaluations of procedures related to everyday occasions of making requests for carrying out a task for somebody else, declining work, responding to a declined request, and monitoring delegated work. Goodnow's finding, which has been mentioned earlier, that the justification which is given for the request to carry out an "other-care task" influences the reaction to the request provides an additional example of the importance of procedural justice in the distribution of tasks.

CONCLUDING REMARKS

It was the aim of the present chapter to draw attention to the distribution of tasks in social systems and to provide some suggestions for its study from a distributive justice point of view. The length of our discussion of limitations, neglected topics, and promising research questions indicates the preliminary nature of the present approach. Hopefully, the present chapter has nevertheless convinced readers that the distribution of tasks is an important topic that has not received enough attention in the research literature.

ACKNOWLEDGMENT

I thank Allan Fiske, Harry Freudenthaler, Stephen Gilliland, Jacqueline Goodnow, Michael Wenzel and an anonymous reviewer for their comments on an early version of this chapter.

APPENDIX

Rating Questions Used in Different Studies

Study 1
Justice: "How just do you regard each of the following arrangements of distribution of household labor in shared flats in general, that is, without considering any particular tasks?" (1= very unjust, 8 = very just).

Study 2
Justice: "How just do you regard each of the following arrangements of distribution of household labor in shared flats for the task XXX?" (1= very unjust, 8 = very just).

Study 3
Preference: "To what extent should the following regulations be used for the distribution of the task XXX?" (1 = on no account, 7 = by all means)
Justice: "How just do you regard the individual regulations for the distribution of the task XXX?" (1 = very unjust, 7 = very just)

Study 4
Preference: "How much do you believe that the following regulations should be used for the distribution of the different tasks?" (1 = should not be used by no means, 6 = should be used by all means")

Justice: "How just do you regard the individual regulations for the distribution of the different tasks?" (1 = very unjust, 7 = very just)

Effectiveness: "How suitable are the following regulations to accomplish the following tasks orderly?" (1 = not at all suitable, 6 = very suitable)

Study 5

Preference: "To what extent should the following regulations be used for the distribution of the different tasks?" (1 = should not be used on any account, 7 = should be used by all means)

Justice: "How just do you regard the individual regulations for the distribution of the different tasks?" (1 = very unjust, 7 = very just)

Effectiveness: "How well (i.e. with what quality) will the different tasks be carried out when the individual regulations are used with the different tasks?" (1 = carried out very badly, 7 = carried out very well)

NOTES

1. Interestingly, Homans (1961), one of the founders of distributive justice research, used task assignment (more concretely, the ledger clerks' temporary assignment to cash posting) as an example to illustrate some of the preconditions of the sense of injustice.
2. The phrasing "arrangements and rules" is used to indicate that the distribution of tasks can be accomplished by informal regulations, which are referred to as arrangements, and by more formalized regulations which are called rules in the present discussion.
3. To simplify matters, we will use the term "communal relationships" for both Clark and Mills' communal relationships and Fiske's communal sharing relations.
4. The descriptions of the two relationships and the differences between them do by no means capture the full richness of Fiske's distinction between communal sharing and equality matching relations and Clark and Mills' conceptualization of exchange versus communal relationships. But they may be regarded as a approximation, which is sufficient for the present purposes.
5. No justice ratings were obtained for the individual tasks in Study 1.
6. Miles and Klein (1998) also considered distributive justice in their study. But, due to the way in which it was manipulated, distributive justice did not refer to the distribution of the task but to the distribution of the compensation for doing the task.

REFERENCES

Adams, S.J. (1965). Inequity in social exchange. In L. Berkowitz (Ed.), *Advances in Experimental Social Psychology* (Vol. 2, pp. 267-299). New York: Academic Press.

Buchanan, A., & Mathieu, D. (1986). Philosophy and Justice. In R. L. Cohen (Ed.), *Justice: Views from the Social Sciences* (pp. 11-45). New York: Plenum.

Clark, M.S., & Mills, J. (1979). Interpersonal attraction in exchange and communal relationships. *Journal of Personality and Social Psychology, 37,* 12-24.

Clark, M.S., & Mills, J. (1993). The difference between communal and exchange relationships: What it is and is not. *Personality and Social Psychology Bulletin, 19*, 684-691.

Cropanzano, R., & Greenberg, J. (1997). Progress in Organizational Justice: Tunneling through the maze. In C.L. Cooper & I.T. Robertson (Eds.), *International Review of Industrial and Organizational Psychology* (Vol. 12, pp. 317-372). Chichester: Wiley.

Cummings, T. (1978). Self-regulated work groups: A socio-technical synthesis. *Academy of Management Review, 3*, 625-634.

Deutsch, M. (1975). Equity, equality, and need: What determines which value will be used as the basis of distributive justice? *Journal of Social Issues, 31*, 137-149.

Deutsch, M. (1985). *Distributive justice: A social psychological perspective*. New Haven, CT: Yale Univ. Press.

Fiske, A.P. (1991). *Structures of social life: The four elementary forms of social relationships*. New York: Free Press.

Fiske, A.P. (1992). The four elementary forms of sociality: Framework for a unified theory of social relations. *Psychological Review, 99*, 689-783.

Fiske, A.P., & Haslam, N. (1996). Social cognition is thinking about relationships. *Current Directions in Psychological Science, 5*, 143-148.

Folger, R., & Cropanzano, R. (1999). *Organizational justice and human resource management*. Thousand Oaks, CA. Sage.

Freudenthaler, H.H., & Mikula, G. (1998). From unfilled wants to the experience of injustice: Women's sense of injustice regarding the lopsided division of household labor. *Social Justice Research, 11*, 289-312.

Gilliland, S., Steiner, D., & Skarlicki, D. (2001). *Theoretical and cultural perspectives on organizational justice*. Greenwich, CT: Information Age Publishing.

Goodnow, J.J. (1998). Beyond the overall balance: The significance of particular tasks and procedures for perceptions of fairness in distributions of household work. *Social Justice Research, 11*, 359-376.

Goodnow, J. J. & Bowes, J. M. (1994). *Men, women, and household work*. New York/Sydney: Oxford University Press.

Goodnow, J. J., & Delaney, S. (1989). Children's household work: Task differences, styles of assignment, and links to family relationships. *Journal of Applied Developmental Psychology, 10*, 209-226.

Greenberg, J. (1982). Approaching equity and avoiding inequity in groups and organizations. In J. Greenberg & R.L. Cohen (Eds.), *Equity and Justice in Social Behavior* (pp. 389-435). San Diego, CA: Academic Press.

Griffith, W. I. (1989). The allocation of negative outcomes: Examining the issues. *Advances in Group Processes, 6*, 1-51.

Hertz, R. (1986). *More equal than others: Women and men in dual-career marriage*. Berkeley, CA: University of California Press.

Homans, G. (1961). *Social behavior: Its elementary forms*. New York: Harcourt, Brace.

Jackson, E. & Ruderman, M.N. (1995). *Diversity in work teams*. Washington, DC: APA.

Kelley, H.H., & Thibaut, J.W. (1978). *Interpersonal Relationships: A Theory of Interdependence*. New York: Wiley.

Kluwer, E.S., & Mikula, G. (2002). Gender-related inequalities in the division of family work in close relationships: A social psychological perspective. In

W. Stroebe & M. Hewstone (Eds.), *European Review of Social Psychology* (Vol. 13, in press). Chichester, UK: Wiley.

Leventhal, G.S. (1976). The distribution of rewards and resources in groups and organizations. In L. Berkowitz & E. Walster (Eds.), *Advances in Experimental Social Psychology* (Vol. 9, pp. 91-131). New York: Academic Press.

Lewis, S., Izraeli, D.N., & Hootsmans, H. (Eds.) (1992). *Dual-earner families. International perspectives*. London: Sage.

Lind, E.A., & Tyler T. R. (1988). *The social psychology of procedural justice*. New York: Plenum.

Manz, C.C., & Sims, H.P. (1987). Leading workers to lead themselves: The external leadership of self-managing work teams. *Administration Science Quarterly, 32*, 106-120.

Mikula, G. (Ed.). (1980a). *Justice and social interaction*. New York: Springer.

Mikula, G. (1980b). On the role of justice in allocation decisions. In G. Mikula (Ed.), *Justice and social interaction* (pp. 127-166). New York: Springer.

Mikula, G. (1981). Concepts of distributive justice in allocation decisions. A review of research in German-speaking countries. *The German Journal of Psychology, 5*, 222-236.

Mikula, G. (1993). On the experience of injustice. In W. Stroebe & M. Hewstone (Eds.), *European Review of Social Psychology* (Vol. 4, pp. 223-244). Chichester, UK: Wiley.

Mikula, G. (1998). Division of household labor and perceived justice: A growing field of research. *Social Justice Research, 11*, 215-241.

Mikula, G., Freudenthaler, H.H., Brennacher-Kröll, S., & Brunschko, B. (1997a). Division of household labor, perceived justice, and satisfaction in student-households. *Basic and Applied Social Psychology, 19*, 275-289.

Mikula, G., Freudenthaler, H.H., Brennacher-Kröll, S., & Schiller-Brandl, R. (1997b). Arrangements and rules of distribution of burdens and duties: The case of household chores. *European Journal of Social Psychology, 27*, 189-208.

Miles, J.A., & Klein, H.J. (1998). The fairness of assigning group members to tasks. *Group and Organizational Management, 23*, 71-96.

Miller, D.T. (2001). Disrespect and the experience of injustice. *Annual Review of Psychology, 52*, 527-553.

Mills, J., & Clark, M.S. (1982). Exchange and communal relationships. In L. Wheeler (Ed.), *Review of Personality and Social Psychology* (Vol. 3, pp. 121-144). Beverly Hills, CA: Sage.

Northcraft, G.B., Neale, M.A., Tenbrunsel, A., & Thomas, M. (1996). Benefits and burdens: Does it really matter what we allocate? *Social Justice Research, 9*, 27-45.

Rusbult, C.E., & Van Lange, P.A.M. (1996). Interdependence processes. In E.T. Higgins & A. Kruglanski (Eds.), *Social Psychology: Handbook of basic mechanisms and processes* (pp. 564-596). New York: Guilford.

Schwinger, T. (1980). Just allocations of goods: Decisions among three principles. In G. Mikula (Ed.), *Justice and social interaction* (pp. 95-125). New York: Springer.

Sekaran, U. (1986). *Dual-career families*. San Francisco: Jossey-Bass Publishers.

Shelton, B.A., & John, D. (1996). The division of household labor. *Annual Review of Sociology, 22*, 299-322.

Steiner, I. D. (1972). *Group process and productivity*. New York: Academic Press.

Shaw, M.E. (1973). Scaling group tasks: A method for dimensional analysis. *JSAS Catalog of Selected Documents in Psychology, 3,* 8.
Shaw, M.E. (1976). *Group dynamics. The psychology of small group behavior.* New York: McGraw-Hill.
Swezey R.W., & Salas, E. (1992). *Teams: Their training and performance.* Norwood, NJ: Ablex.
Törnblom, K.Y. (1988). Positive and negative allocations: A typology and a model for conflicting justice principles. *Advances in Group Processes, 5,* 141-148.
Törnblom, K.Y. (1992). The social psychology of distributive justice. In K. R. Scherer (Ed.), *Justice: Interdisciplinary perspectives* (pp. 177-236). Cambridge: Cambridge University Press.
Tyler, T.R. Boeckmann, R.J., Smith, H.J., & Huo, Y.J. (1997). *Social justice in a diverse society.* Boulder, CO: Westview.
Tyler, T. R., & Smith, H.J. (1998). Social justice and social movement. In D. Gilbert, S.T. Fiske, & G. Lindzey (Eds.), *Handbook of social psychology* (Vol. 2, pp. 595-662). New York: McGraw-Hill.
Walster, E., Walster, G, & Berscheid, E. (1978). *Equity: Theory and research.* Boston: Allyn & Bacon.
Warton, P.M., & Goodnow, J.J. (1991). The nature of responsibility: Children's understanding of "your job". *Child Development, 62,* 156-165.
Williams, H. (1996). *The essence of managing groups and teams.* London: Prentice Hall.

CHAPTER 8

"HOT FLASHES, OPEN WOUNDS":

Injustice and the Tyranny of Its Emotions

Robert J. Bies and Thomas M. Tripp

ABSTRACT

Whereas experiencing the sense of injustice is so much a part of the fabric of organizational life, justice scholars have given relatively little attention to the emotions of injustice and how people experience them. In this chapter, we begin our analysis by identifying events that can arouse the emotions of injustice. That analysis is based on the premise that to better understand justice, we need to focus on the experience and emotions of injustice. We argue that the assignment of blame is a "triggering" judgment that arouses the emotions of injustice. After exploring the emotions of injustice, and some of their facets, we explore social-cognitive factors that can amplify the emotions of injustice. We conclude the chapter with an analysis of why the emotions of injustice have been "missing in action" in relation to justice research.

> *There are days I don't think about it, think about what he did to me. In fact, I consciously try to focus on "happy thoughts." But then someone will remind me of what happened and my anger and bitterness will just break through, overwhelming me like a "hot flash." Despite my efforts to control my feelings, they just overtake me.*
> —Manager, consumer products company

> *I am letting it "eat" at me. I hate him for what he did to me, I really do. The mere thought of him causes me heartburn, and I am constantly thinking about him. Sometimes my colleagues find me mumbling to myself, and this causes them to worry about me. Each day, I live with knots in my stomach, resenting his very being.*
> *I want him to suffer....forever!*
> —Manager, telecommunications company

The sense of injustice ... the anger, the bitterness, the fears, the helplessness. These are emotions that all people have experienced on the job, some more frequently than others and some more intensely than others. While experiencing the sense of injustice is so much a part of the fabric of organizational life, justice scholars have yet to fully explore what we call "the psychological geography" of injustice. It is true that there have been some efforts to map that emotional terrain, which we will acknowledge below; however, it is also true that organizational researchers have focused more on the cognitive "high ground" of justice (and on identifying the criteria that people use to assess it) than they have on the emotional "valley of darkness" of pain and anger of those who have experienced injustice in the workplace. But we are not the first to raise these conceptual and empirical concerns about the lack of attention given to the emotions of injustice. For, a quarter of a century ago, Adams and Freedman (1976), in assessing the state of research inspired by equity theory, observed: "The concept of (inequity) distress has been typically endowed with existential characteristics and surplus meaning. For example, it is stated to have the characteristics of anger and guilt in inequitable situations. Yet, research on the phenomenological quality of distress is not to be found" (p.45). For the most part, that observation still rings true today, with some notable exceptions (e.g. Bies & Tripp, 1996; Mikula, 1986; Mikula, Petri, & Tanzer, 1990; Miller, 2001).

In this chapter, we begin our analysis with the premise that to better understand justice, we need to focus on the experience and emotions of injustice. We identify events that can arouse the emotions or "sense of injustice." We then argue that the assignment of blame is a "triggering" judgment that arouses the emotions of injustice. After exploring the emotions of injustice, and some of their facets, we explore social-cognitive factors that can amplify the emotions of injustice. We conclude the chapter with an analysis of why the emotions of injustice have been "missing in action" in relation to justice research.

IT'S INJUSTICE, NOT JUSTICE: SHIFTING THE FOCUS OF ANALYSIS

Our analysis begins with the premise that, to understand justice in organizations, one must understand the events that arouse the sense of injustice—the emotions of injustice (Bies, 1987, 2001; Solomon, 1990). Choosing the sense of injustice as the starting point for analyzing justice dynamics has its intellectual roots in the seminal legal theory of Edmond Cahn. In his book, *The Sense of Injustice* (1949), Cahn asks "Why do we speak of the 'sense of injustice' rather than the 'sense of justice'?" Cahn answers: "Because 'justice' has been so beclouded by natural-law writings that it almost inevitably brings to mind some ideal relation or static condition or set of perceptual standards, while we are concerned, on the contrary, with what is active, vital, and experiential in the reactions of human beings" (p. 13).

For Cahn, justice is "not a state, but a process; not a condition, but an action. 'Justice,' as we shall use the term, means the *active process* of remedying or preventing that which would arouse the sense of injustice" (p. 13). He defines the sense of injustice as "the sympathetic reaction of outrage, horror, shock, resentment, and anger, those affections of the viscera and abnormal secretions of the adrenals that prepare the human animal to resist attack. Nature has thus equipped all men to regard injustice to another as personal aggression" (p. 24).

The Cahnian perspective has guided the theory-building and empirical research of Bies and colleagues. For example, Bies (1987) focused on the emotions of injustice as the creator of a "predicament" for the harmdoer, thus stimulating research on the use of social accounts as a strategy to manage the moral outrage associated with the sense of injustice (Bies & Sitkin, 1992; Sitkin & Bies, 1993). Similarly, Bies (2001) and Bies and Tripp (1996, 1998a; Tripp & Bies, 1997) have taken an inductive approach, "grounding" their theory-building in the empirical study of the events and actions that arouse the sense of injustice and the cognitions and emotions that accompany the experience of injustice.

This is not to suggest that we have the "right answer," but we are suggesting that, in taking our perspective, we add to the completeness of understanding of justice dynamics in organizations. To elaborate further, we argue that organizational justice researchers, with their focus on identifying different justice concerns, have inadvertently and ironically led us further away from a more complete understanding of justice dynamics in organizations. As the two introductory quotations so vividly illustrate, when people are asked to talk about justice, their responses are narratives of the *in*justices they have experienced (Shreve & Shreve, 1997). In these stories, injustice is described in very vivid emotional terms and often as a "hot and burning" experience (Mikula, 1986). The intense and personal pain associated with the experience of injustice is a profound harm to one's psyche and identity (Bies & Tripp, 1996)—that is, one's sense of self. Indeed, the experience and emotions of injustice are underemphasized and under-appreciated in organizational justice theory.

As evidence in support of this line of reasoning, a search of the *Social Sciences Index* and *PsycINFO* suggest a strong asymmetry in the popularity of the two topics, justice and injustice. From 1991 to 2001, an analysis of journal articles cited in *Social Sciences Index* found that "justice" beat out "injustice" in the titles of those articles by a count of 1995 to 69. (In a similar comparison, "fairness" conquered "unfairness" 190 to 8). From 1991 to 2001, a similar analysis of journal articles cited in another database, *PsycINFO,* found that "justice" beat out "injustice" in the titles of those articles by a count of 659 to 47. In a similar comparison, "fairness" conquered "unfairness" 206 to 9).

One could argue that the titles of journal articles may be intentional misnomers—that is, that the researchers theorize about injustice but label their theories in terms of justice and fairness. Perhaps the most notable example is Adams, who, as we describe above, was primarily interested in *in*equity, but entitled his theory, "equity theory."[1] Even so, we argue that, when the vast majority of researchers apparently believe that it is best to entitle all research on justice and injustice as "justice," it actually reveals a bias toward studying the positive to the relative neglect of the negative. Perhaps this bias is a result of conformity or even groupthink among (in)justice scholars, or perhaps it reveals a deeper concern that one can't get tenure by focusing on injustice, as it is too "negative" and aligns one too closely with workers, rather than managers, in organizations. Still, all of these interpretations lead to us the same conclusion: injustice is underemphasized and underappreciated in the literature.

But again, this is not to suggest that we are the only researchers focusing on injustice. In addition to the previously cited work of Mikula and Miller, another notable exception to the current emphasis on justice is the work of Gilliland and colleagues. For example, Gilliland, Benson, and Schepers (1998) demonstrate that reactions to unjust acts are more intense than reactions to just acts. In fact, Gilliland et al. (1998) found a threshold of which no amount of just acts can compensate for unjust acts. Moreover, Gilliland, Goldman, Tripp, and Beach (2001) argue that justice and injustice are separate constructs that provoke qualitatively different reactions. That is, "justice" and "injustice" are two different, albeit related, constructs.

A similar epiphany moment has occurred among researchers who study phenomena related to justice and injustice. For example, Lewicki, McAlister, and Bies (1998) demonstrate that trust is not the opposite of distrust, that they are not two ends of the same construct, because it is possible for a person to simultaneously trust and distrust another party. Similarly, in the study of affectivity, Watson and Clark (Watson & Clark, 1984; Watson, Clark, & Tellegen, 1988) find that negative affectivity is not the opposite of positive affectivity because each consists of, not different quantities of the same emotions, but of different emotions.

In sum, injustice and justice are distinct. Moreover, more attention needs to be paid to injustice than to justice because it is injustice to which employees react most strongly. Next, we offer suggestions as to how scholars might study injustice.

AROUSING THE SENSE OF INJUSTICE: VIOLATIONS OF COMPARATIVE AND NONCOMPARATIVE PRINCIPLES

What justice fundamentally means is to give a person *his or her due* (Feinberg, 1974). Thus, it follows that when one does not receive his or her due, it should arouse the sense of injustice. Following Feinberg (1974), "in some cases one's due is determined independently of that of other people, while in other cases, a person's due is determinable *only* by reference to his relations to other persons . . . the contexts, criteria, and principles of the former kind (are referred to) as *noncomparative*, and those of the latter sort as *comparative*" (p. 297).

Principles of comparative justice underlie the research on distributive justice. For example, research inspired by equity theory (e.g., Adams, 1965; Walster, Walster, & Berscheid, 1978) and relative deprivation theory (e.g., Crosby, 1976; Martin, 1981) explicitly assumes that justice is determined through comparison with others. Comparative principles also underlie our models of procedural justice. Whether it be the opportunity for voice or process control (Thibaut & Walker, 1975) or the consistent application of different procedural rules (Leventhal, 1980), or the neutrality of the decision maker (Lind & Tyler, 1988), any deviation from equality of opportunity or the equality of administration of the rules forms the basis for claims of procedural injustice.

But, as Feinberg (1974) demonstrates, there is another class of principles, those that are noncomparative in nature, that can form and shape perceptions of justice and injustice. As Feinberg (1974) notes:

> When our problem is to make assignments, ascriptions, or awards in accordance with noncomparative justice, what is "due" the other person is not a share or portion of some divisible benefit or burden; hence it is not necessary for us to know what is due in order to know what is due the person with whom we are dealing. *His* rights-or-deserts alone determine what is due him; and once we have come to a judgment of *his* due, that judgment cannot be logically affected by subsequent knowledge of the condition of other parties.... When our task is to do noncomparative justice to each of a large number of individuals, we do not compare them with each other, but rather we compare each in turn with an objective standard and judge each (as we say) "on his merits" (p. 282).

Examples of such objective and absolute standards might include truth, freedom, and human dignity, concerns that are clearly central to people's assessments of justice and injustice (Bies, 2001; Lind & Tyler, 1988; Tyler & Lind, 1992).

To further illustrate the difference between comparative and noncomparative principles, consider the following example taken from Bies (1987). Let us assume there is a "rude and abusive" journal reviewer who makes caustic and derogatory remarks about five different manuscripts reviewed. Let us further assume that each of the manuscripts was of equal quality. Given that the manuscript "inputs" were the same and the outcomes were the same, applying principles of comparative justice would suggest there should no sense of injustice aroused as the result of this process.

Yet, for most of us, there would be some residual resentment or anger as the target of such treatment. The principles that would explain our sense of injustice would be noncomparative in nature. For example, we might have some conception that we have a *right* to be treated with respect, and that no one deserves to be the target of such mean-spirited comments or insults. Further, if the reviewer made derogatory and false accusations about the work, one would feel unjustly treated because they had not been "done justice." Regardless of the fact that everyone else was treated in the same manner, it would not totally mitigate the sense of injustice aroused by the violation of noncomparative principles.

In addition to this example, other research highlights the importance of distinguishing between comparative and noncomparative principles of justice in analyzing the emotions of injustice. For example, Bies and Tripp (1996, 1998a) have found in their empirical research that, relative to violations of comparative principles, violations of noncomparative principles like truth, as in the case of lies and defamatory statements, or like human dignity, as in the case of public beratement or harassment, are often associated with the most negative, intense, and enduring emotions. Also, if we build on the research of Gilliland and colleagues (Gilliland et al., 1998), it may be that when violations of noncomparative principles of justice occur, as in the case of the betrayal of trust caused by the unwarranted disclosure of confidential information (Bies & Tripp, 1996), there is no compensation that can restore justice in the relationship. That is, relative to violations of comparative principles, the consequences of violations of noncomparative principles may be "irreversible."

"ALL INJUSTICE IS PERSONAL": EXPLORING THE COGNITIONS AND EMOTIONS OF INJUSTICE

Thus far, we have argued in our analysis that, relative to cognitions, emotions should become more figural elements in an analysis of justice dynamics (Bies, 1987, 2001). But, with that said, what frequently triggers the emotions is a cognitive appraisal of the action or the consequences (Lazarus & Lazarus, 1994). In particular, in perceiving an injustice, the assignment of blame is critical (Folger & Cropanzano, 2001). Moreover, in perceiving an injustice, one usually construes the action as a personal attack (Bies, 2001). Following Cahn (1949), the attack is viewed as an act of aggression that will trigger emotions that are often described vividly— and not in terms that are frequently found in justice research (e.g., furious, enraged, hate).

It Begins with Blame

Whether an action or outcome triggers the sense of injustice depends on how one makes sense of, or cognitively processes, the harm or wrongdoing (Bies, Tripp, & Kramer, 1997). Taking a sense-making perspective (Weick, 1995), a provoking incident is one which violates social or normative expectations, and such a violation triggers a search for causal explanation as to "why" the event occurred (Wong & Weiner, 1981). In this causal analysis, people will search for factors that might "discount" the perpetrator's responsibility for the action (Kelley, 1972). If there are any mitigating circumstances to create "reasonable doubt" in people's minds, then the emotions are less likely to intensify (Bies, 1987; Bies & Tripp, 1996). However, given the evidence of a "negativity bias" in evaluation (Kanouse & Hanson, 1972) and the "actor-observer" effect (Jones & Nisbett, 1972), people will likely focus on the perpetrator as the causal agent responsible for the harm and wrongdoing. Indeed, whether the provoking incident arouses intense emotional reactions will depend on the outcome of a causal analysis (Bies, 1987; Utne & Kidd, 1980).

What aspects of the sense-making process can amplify the blame assigned to others? Our research on revenge has identified several such cognitive processes that can bias the blame assignment process (Bies et al., 1997). First, there is the *overly personalistic attribution* (Bies & Tripp, 1996). For example, when individuals over-attribute sinister and malevolent motives to others' actions (e.g., "she wasn't just being careless or even just selfish; she was mean-spirited;" and "she was out to get *me*; it wasn't just business, it was *personal*"), they may perceive harmful intent or believe they are being belittled even in their otherwise seemingly benign social encounters. Kramer (1994) refers to this general process as the "sinister attribution error."

A second important cognitive process contributing to individuals' perceptions that they are being intentionally harmed or singled out unfairly is the *biased punctuation of conflict* (Bies et al., 1997). Biased punctuation of conflict refers to a tendency for individuals to construe the history of conflict with others in a self-serving and provocative fashion. For example, in a tit-for-tat feud, each party perceives itself as the avenging victim and perceives its opponent as the aggressor against whom one must defend.

A third important cognitive process is *rumination and obsession* (Bies et al., 1997). Rumination and obsession are associated with more extreme emotions. Indeed, rumination and obsession can be reinforced in social gatherings and when people vent their emotions (Bies & Tripp, 1996), or what Morrill (1992) refers to as "bitch sessions."

Finally, a fourth cognitive process that may intensify blame is *ego-defensiveness*. That is, when an unfavorable outcome occurs, one may "search" for someone else to blame for the outcome so that one feels better about oneself. Indeed, there may be a bias toward believing procedures are not fair when one receives an unfavorable or an unfair outcome. For example, Shah and Schroth (2000) found that it is better for recipients of unfavorable outcomes to believe that they got "screwed" by an unfair procedure (see also Brockner, 2001). Otherwise, if they believe the procedure was fair, then they are more likely to conclude that they *deserved* the unfavorable outcome due to some negative behavior or trait such as incompetence or laziness. Thus, people are biased to believe that the procedures are unfair every time they get hurt, particularly if no procedural information exists that says otherwise (Daly & Tripp, 1996; Lind, 2001). Consequently, they may be more likely to see an injustice where perhaps none exists, and further blame the decision-maker for the outcome.

From Cognitive Appraisal to Experienced Emotions

Drawing on findings from our own research (Bies & Tripp, 1996, 1998a), along with findings from studies of other researchers (Hornstein, 1996; Mikula, 1986; Mikula et al., 1990), the emotions of injustice can be characterized in terms of a variety of facets. These facets include: *intensity, sense of violation, feelings of helplessness, feelings of terror,* and *obsession*.

Intensity

In almost existential terms, people often focus on the intensity of the emotions they experience in injustice, often belying a strong visceral response of physiological and psychological pain. For example, the initial emotions of injustice are often described as quite hot and volatile, characterized by expressions of pain, anger, and rage (Bies & Tripp, 1996). In describing these emotions, people use such words as "furious," and "bitter," and describe how they felt engulfed in "white-hot" emotions. One person described herself as "inflamed" and "enraged," and "consumed" by thoughts of revenge, while another person needed to satisfy the "burning desire of revenge."

Sense of violation

When describing the experience of injustice, people's descriptions of the emotions often reflect a sense of violation that was more than mere "unmet expectations." Indeed, the violation was much deeper, reflecting a violated psyche or sense of sacred self (Bies, 2001). For example, in Bies and Tripp (1996), one individual described a betrayed confidence as causing her world to be "shattered," as that what she assumed to be "sacred and true—the trust of a friend" was violated, if not destroyed forever.

Feelings of Helplessness

At least initially, the emotions of injustice can be associated with feelings of helplessness. For example, Bies and Tripp (1998b) found that people described initially being "confused" or "stunned" by the harm. A typical comment by people was found in the words of one person: "I couldn't believe what had just happened. I trusted him. When he attacked me in front of my co-workers, I was paralyzed and speechless" (p. 210). In addition, several respondents reported a variety of physiological symptoms including uncontrollable crying, "knots in the stomach," and physical exhaustion.

Feelings of Terror

Related to feelings of helplessness, several respondents in Bies and Tripp (1998b) reported feeling "paranoid," while others reported being "fearful for their well-being," after being victimized by their bosses. One person reported that "I would stay at my desk and not even go to the bathroom, for the fear, if I was away from my desk, my boss would 'hammer' me in public" (p. 210). Not surprisingly, such people reported feeling vulnerable and powerless, for the boss's tyranny had "broken the spirit and willingness to fight back," as described by one respondent.

Obsession

Further, the emotions of injustice can create a psychological and physiological stranglehold over the individual. The emotions of injustice can endure over time, sometimes for days, even weeks and months, if not longer. Indeed, the emotions of injustice can be like a "social toxin" (Hornstein, 1996), "poisoning" their professional and personal lives over time, as was illustrated in the second introductory quotation. As another example, Matthews (1988) recounts an example of an individual who describes his obsession as letting the harmdoer "live inside his head rent free" for years. Finally, as Morrill (1992) found, often the emotions endure due to the social support of co-workers who continually "vent" about the injustice.

Summary and Punctuation

In sum, several empirical studies provide converging evidence that points to this conclusion: injustice is not just a judgment; it also is an emotional and physiological experience. Further, the preceding analysis suggests physiological, psychological, and performance correlates that should broaden the scope of justice theory and research (see Hornstein, 1996, for a more comprehensive analysis). Finally, the data also suggest that people "cope" with the emotions of injustice. Future research on the emotions of injustice should be guided by the Lazarus and Lazarus (1994) framework of "problem-focused" and "emotion-centered" coping strategies.

Which Comes First—Cognition or Emotion?

In the analysis thus far, it has been assumed that the cognitions of injustice precede the emotions of injustice. That is, first one thinks about the injustice, and then one reacts emotionally. However, that assumption may be limited. For, we are reminded of the famous debate between Lazarus and Zajonc in the 1980's over which came first, cognitions or emotions. In response to the claim by Lazarus (1984) that cognition precedes emotion, Zajonc (1984) argued that emotion often precedes cognition, that individuals may feel an emotion before knowing what caused it. As such, it should also be assumed that, sometimes, the emotions of injustice may precede the cognitions about injustice.

Schacter and Singer (1962) provide perhaps the most famous evidence that emotion can precede cognition about that emotion, and that evidence carries implications for justice researchers. In a laboratory experiment, Schacter and Singer injected subjects with the drug epinephrine, which causes physiological arousal. The aroused subjects were then placed in a waiting room with a confederate of the experimenters. In one condition, the confederate acted angry, complaining about the experiment; in the other condition, the confederate acted happy as he shot wadded-up paper basketballs into the waste basket. Even though in both conditions the subjects experienced the same physiological arousal, how they thought about and labeled the emotional arousal differed significantly across conditions: in the first condition they reported feeling angry, and in the second condition they reported feeling happy.

Two aspects of their experiment interest us here. First, the emotion occurred without being triggered by any cognition – the epinephrine was injected, not triggered by their brains. Thus, because the emotions occurred without cognition, this experiment provides evidence that emotions can precede cognition, or at least that cognitions are not required to create emotions. Second, the only difference between the conditions was the social context. Thus, how an emotion gets labeled after the fact can be dramatically influenced by social context. This is a tenet of Social Information Processing Theory: in ambiguous circumstances, people will look to other people for interpretive information (Salancik & Pfeffer, 1978).

Next, we extend this line of reasoning to the context of injustice. For example, Felstiner, Abel, and Sarat (1980-81) theorize how the emotional experience of injury precedes the cognitive process of determining the cause of the injury and assigning blame. They propose that the emotions associated with injury come first, followed by the "naming" or labeling of the injury, followed by "blaming" where the victim determines cause and whether injustice was involved, and finally by "claiming" where the victim decides how to seek justice.

When emotion precedes cognition, when one is wounded or frustrated by another, he or she can feel shocked, outraged, and angry without immediately articulating why, and certainly without knowing the causes of the harm or if any injustice occurred. In such situations, Bies (1987) argued that the social environment was a source of information that shapes the "labeling" process, and in particular, he focused on the influence of social accounts given by the harmdoer.

More evidence of the social environment shaping the emotions of injustice can be found in a study by Folger, Rosenfield, Grove, and Corkran (1979). In a laboratory experiment, these researchers found that peer opinions on inequity—where peers either confirmed or disconfirmed to an individual that an inequity had occurred to him or her—influenced the individual's perception of whether the process was fair. Moreover, the social context influences not only the assignment of blame, but also what response an individual should take. For instance, Morrill (1992) found that executives who engage in revenge first discuss their feelings and attributions in social, "bitch sessions." Also, consider Goldman (2001) who studied people at EEOC offices who filed discrimination claims against former employers. He found that social guidance had a large influence on whether terminated employees filed claims. Similarly, Bies and Tripp (1996) found that group "venting" sessions either encouraged or discourage acts of revenge.

In sum, it is clear that sometimes cognition precedes emotion where one determines what is wrong and then decides how to respond. This is the rational model of injustice. Other times, emotion precedes cognition where one is first frustrated or angry, and then looks for something to explain the frustration and justify the anger. This is the rationalization model of injustice. In extreme cases, this is where the emotions "hijack" the mind and interfere with one's ability to reason.

THE EMOTIONS OF INJUSTICE: EXPLAINING WHY THEY HAVE BEEN "MISSING IN ACTION"

Despite the calls for the study of the emotions of injustice (e.g., Adams & Freedman, 1976), very little research has been conducted on the phenomena. Perhaps it is because such phenomena are not easily captured by the positivist research paradigm (Treviño & Bies, 1997). Yet, social psychologists study emotions, even the messy ones. We have thought about this question for a long time, and each time we keep coming back to the ideological underpinnings of our field, one that is decidedly "pro-management" in its orientation and analysis of issues. We refer to this as the "Managerial-Centered Perspective." By contrast, to deal with the ideological and conceptual limitations of that perspective, we propose a new perspective: the "Employee-Centered Perspective."

The Managerial-Centered Perspective

The dominant perspective for understanding the emotions of injustice is what we refer to as the managerial perspective. This perspective views conflict primarily through the "eyes" and interests of the organization and its managers (Scott & Hart, 1979). The managerial perspective begins with the premise that anger and rage in the workplace are dysfunctional and wrong. Anger and rage are viewed in such pejorative terms because they can disrupt workplace relationships, which will undermine, if not impede, workplace efficiency and productivity.

A second premise of the managerial perspective is that the emotions of injustice are rooted solely in the personalities of malcontent employees. While certain managerial actions and coworker behaviors may trigger or provoke an employee's rage, it is expected that the employee, if he or she is a professional," will squelch, swallow, suppress, eliminate or otherwise control that rage. That is, if employees can't keep their anger to themselves, then there is something *wrong* with *them*.

These two premises shape managerial responses to anger and discontent. Specifically, following from these premises, managers focus on developing strategies and "solutions" to seriously control, if not eliminate, anger and discontent in the workplace. Such strategies can range from implementing different employee selection procedures to increased surveillance of employees to employee termination. While these managerial strategies and solutions may somewhat reduce anger and rage, they certainly won't eliminate it.

Indeed, the managerial perspective portrays an incomplete and skewed picture of emotions (Bies, 1987; Cahn, 1949; Solomon, 1990). While it is true that the emotions of injustice can lead to *destructive* and *anti-social* acts, as in the cases of employee theft (Greenberg, 1990a), workplace violence (Swisher, 1994), and other forms of social deviance in organizations (Robinson & Bennett, 1995), it is also true that such emotions can lead to *constructive* and *pro-social* outcomes. For example, the emotions of injustice can motivate the threat of revenge, which can be a powerful deterrent against power abuse by authority figures and organizational decision-makers (Tripp & Bies, 1997). To address the limitations of the managerial perspective, we outline an alternative framework below.

The Employee-Centered Perspective

I do not try to justify [Fletcher Christian's] crime, his mutiny, but I condemn the tyranny that drove him to it.
—Roger Byam, Mutiny on the Bounty

As an alternative to the managerial perspective, we propose *the employee-centered perspective*. This perspective begins with the premise that feelings of discontent, such as anger and rage, are inevitable in the workplace, part of the social fabric of organizational life. While the expression of discontent can be dysfunctional and costly to the organization, they can also be viewed as "signals" that something may be profoundly wrong in and with the organization. These signals, if viewed as useful feedback, may act as catalysts for constructive organizational change.

A second premise of the employee-centered perspective is that, to understand discontent in the workplace, one must also focus on the situational events and the social context that trigger the emotions of injustice. Moreover, we argue that, what is important to understand is that the harmed individuals interpret the situational triggers of anger and rage as acts of injustice. This construal is important as it provides the moral justification for acts of discontent. Indeed, for these people, their acts of discontent are viewed in righteous terms as "doing the right thing," or "doing justice."

This type of justification is not too surprising, once one remembers that few people in the world see their own acts of incivility, deviance, disobedience, and even violence, as indicators of an evil being. That is, "evil" people rarely see themselves as evil. At the time they make choices that are unacceptable to the majority, they do not believe they are doing the "wrong thing." As is often said, the road to hell is paved with good intentions.

Consider the following example from Bies and Tripp (1998a). In an organization with a culture of delegation and chain-of-command, there was a manager who could not resist micromanaging. No matter how small the detail, he demanded that his direct reports seek his approval before making a decision. Worse, he often went around his direct reports without informing them, violating the chain-of-command, telling their subordinates what to do. Three of his direct reports had had enough and plotted to teach him a lesson so that they could regain their autonomy. These employees supervised the same department, but each covered a different eight-hour shift; collectively, they supervised 24 hours a day. Their strategy was to give their boss exactly what he wanted, sort of: they called him in on every minor emergency, no matter what time of day. As their vengeance progressed, they deprived their boss of sleep. Soon after, unforeseen to them, their boss suffered a nervous breakdown, which effectively ended his career.

These employees did not believe they were doing the wrong thing when they hatched their plot. On the contrary, they believed they were not only restoring justice, but also improving workplace productivity by discouraging the boss's unproductive micromanaging. Given that the consequences were tragic, in hindsight, their plot is unnecessarily hurtful, and one that gives revenge a bad name. But our points are this: at the time, they thought the revenge would make everybody better off, and one must also focus on the petty tyranny of the manager as a triggering cause of the events that unfolded.

Sometimes the emotions of injustice lead not only to good intentions, but also to great outcomes. Take the case of the Eclipse team at Data General in the early 1980's, made famous by Tracy Kidder's Pulitzer-prize winning book, *Soul of a New Machine*. A group of engineers were passed over to work on Data General's newest, and most exciting and challenging computer project—a project that upper management deemed necessary to save the company. A senior manager named Tom West took the demoralized, bitter engineers and challenged them on a different project. In fact, he played off their feelings of resentment, encouraging them to be angry with upper management. He channeled their anger into proving wrong the CEO and other engineers about who were the best engineers in the firm. To prove the others wrong, they built a better computer much faster, and their computer ended up being the one Data General ended up producing and marketing.

The avenging engineers at Data General did not have the most benign, company-oriented motivations. They didn't work so hard and brilliantly just for the company; rather, their primary motivation to work so hard was to regain their reputations. But two points are important here. First, while the avenging engineers may not have judged their own intentions as noble, they believed they were justified. They believed they were, in every sense of the word, good people. Second, regardless of their intentions, their approach benefited the company tremendously.

CONCLUDING THOUGHTS: FROM THE EMOTIONS OF INJUSTICE TO THE RHETORIC OF INJUSTICE

Throughout our analysis, we have focused on the emotions of injustice as a "dependent variable" in and of itself, or as a possible "mediating variable" between cognitions and behavior. Yet, that view of the emotions of injustice, while advancing the domain of justice theory, we feel is still limited. And, thus, we wish to conclude this chapter with some additional thoughts on the emotions of injustice that takes us beyond the arguments we have advanced in this chapter.

To wit, it is assumed by most, if not all justice researchers, that the emotions of injustice can motivate people to action as there is energy waiting to be expended (see Adams, 1965). But the emotions of injustice can motivate action in a different manner as well. Specifically, the emotions of injustice can serve as a *moral justification* for action. For example, people who seek revenge often consider their actions as acts of doing justice, of getting even (Tripp & Bies, 1997). Their anger and indignation propels them to right wrongs and deter future injustices.

But even more interesting, the moral justification provided by the emotions of injustice can also be transformed into the rhetoric of injustice used by activists and leaders to rally or mobilize people to action (Martin, Scully, & Levitt, 1990). For, when an individual or group cries "injustice," such an act can be a threat to the social identity of the target of such a claim (Bies, 1987; Greenberg, 1990b), as it was clearly in the case of the Nike controversy (Bies & Greenberg, 2002). In other words, the emotions of injustice may not only empower individuals to action, but they may also be used in the rhetoric of those who seek empowerment through political means. And that opens the door to another world of theory and research for justice scholars.

NOTE

1. We thank Dirk Steiner for this interpretation of the above data.

REFERENCES

Adams, J.S. (1965). Inequity in social exchange. In L. Berkowitz (Ed.), *Advances in experimental social psychology* (Vol. 2, pp. 267-299). New York: Academic Press.

Adams, J.S., & Freedman, S. (1976). Equity theory revisited: Comments and annotated bibliography. In L. Berkowitz (Ed.), *Advances in experimental social psychology* (Vol. 9, pp. 43-90). New York: Academic Press.

Bies, R.J. (1987). The predicament of injustice: The management of moral outrage. In L.L. Cummings and B.M. Staw (Eds.), *Research in organizational behavior, 9,* 289-319. Greenwich, CT: JAI Press.

Bies, R.J. (2001). Interactional (in)justice: The sacred and the profane. In J. Greenberg & R. Cropanzano (Eds.), *Advances in organizational behavior* (pp. 89-118). Palo Alto, CA: Stanford University Press.

Bies, R.J., & Greenberg, J. (2002). Justice, culture, and corporate image: The swoosh, the sweatshops, and the sway of public opinion. In M.J. Gannon & K.L. Newman (Eds.), *Handbook of cross-cultural management* (pp. 320-334). Oxford, England: Blackwell.

Bies, R.J., & Sitkin, S.B. (1992). Explanation as legitimation: Excuse-making in organizations. In M.L. McLaughlin, M.J. Cody, & S.J. Read (Eds.), *Explaining one's self to others: Reason-giving in a social context* (pp. 183-198). Hillsdale, NJ: Lawrence Erlbaum Associates.

Bies, R.J., & Tripp, T.M. (1996). Beyond distrust: "Getting even" and the need for revenge. In R.M. Kramer & T. Tyler (Eds.), *Trust in organizations* (pp. 246-260). Newbury Park: Sage Publications.

Bies, R.J., & Tripp, T.M. (1998a). Revenge in organizations: The good, the bad, and the ugly. In R.W. Griffin, A. O'Leary-Kelly, & J. Collins (Eds.), *Dysfunctional behavior in organizations, Vol. 1: Violent behaviors in organizations* (pp. 49–67). Greenwich, CT: JAI Press.

Bies, R.J., & Tripp, T.M. (1998b). Two faces of the powerless: Coping with tyranny. In R.M. Kramer & M.A. Neale (Eds.), *Power and influence in organizations* (pp. 203–219). Thousand Oaks, CA: Sage Publications.

Bies, R.J., Tripp, T.M., & Kramer, R.M. (1997). At the breaking point: Cognitive and social dynamics of revenge in organizations. In R.A. Giacalone & J. Greenberg (Eds.), *Antisocial behavior in organizations* (pp. 18-36). Thousand Oaks, CA: Sage Publications.

Brockner, J. 2001. The pleasure and pain of high procedural justice. In J. Greenberg (Chair), *Controversial Issues in Organizational Justice*. Symposium conducted at the annual meeting of the Academy of Management, Washington, D.C.

Cahn, E. (1949). *The sense of injustice*. New York: New York University Press.

Crosby, F. (1976). A model of egoistic relative deprivation. *Psychological Review, 83*, 85-113.

Daly, J.P., & Tripp, T.M. (1996). Is outcome fairness used to make procedural fairness judgments when procedural information is inaccessible? *Social Justice Research, 9*(4), 327-349.

Feinberg, J. (1974). Noncomparative justice. *The Philosophical Review, 83*, 297-338.

Felstiner, W.L.F., Abel, R.L., & Sarat, A. (1980-81). The emergence and transformation of disputes. *Law and Society Review, 15*, 631-654.

Folger, R., & Cropanzano, R. (2001). Fairness theory: Justice as accountability. In J. Greenberg & R. Cropanzano (Eds.), *Advances in organizational behavior* (pp. 1-55). Palo Alto, CA: Stanford University Press.

Folger, R., Rosenfield, D., Grove, J., & Corkran, L. (1979). Effects of "voice" and peer opinions on responses to inequity. *Journal of Personality and Social Psychology, 37*, 2243-2261.

Gilliland, S.W., Benson, L. III., & Schepers, D.H. (1998). A rejection threshold in justice evaluations: Effects on judgment and decision making. *Organizational Behavior and Human Decision Processes, 76*, 113-131.

Gilliland, S.W., Goldman, B.M., Tripp, T.M., & Beach, L.R. (2001). Which Matters More, Justice or Injustice? Asymmetric Reactions to Just and Unjust Treatment by Terminated Employees Who File Filing Legal Claims with the EEOC. Working paper, University of Arizona.

Goldman, B.M. (2001). Toward an understanding of employment discrimination claiming: An integration of organizational justice and social information processing. *Personnel Psychology, 54*, 361-386.

Greenberg, J. (1990a). Employee theft as a reaction to underpayment inequity: The hidden costs of pay cuts. *Journal of Applied Psychology, 75*, 561-568.

Greenberg, J. (1990b). Looking fair vs. being fair: Managing impressions of organizational justice. In L.L. Cummings & B.M. Staw (Eds.), *Research in organizational behavior* (Vol. 12, pp. 111-157). Greenwich, CT: JAI Press.

Greenberg, J. (1996). *The quest for justice on the job: Essays and experiments.* Thousand Oaks, CA: Sage.

Greenberg, J. (1997). A social influence model of employee theft: Beyond the fraud triangle. In R.J. Lewicki, R.J. Bies, and B.H. Sheppard (Eds.), *Research on negotiation in organizations* (Vol. 6, pp. 29-51). Greenwich, CT: JAI Press.

Hornstein, H. A. (1996). *Brutal bosses and their prey.* New York: Riverhead Books.

Jacoby, S. (1983). *Wild justice: The evolution of revenge.* New York: Harper & Row.

Jones, E.E., & Nisbett, R.E. (1972). The actor and the observer: Divergent perceptions of the causes of behavior. In E.E. Jones, D.E. Kanouse, H.H. Kelley, R.E. Nisbett, S. Valins, & B. Weiner (Eds.), *Attribution: Perceiving the causes of behavior* (pp. 79-94). Morristown, NJ: General Learning Press.

Kanouse, D.E., & Hanson, L.R. (1972). Negativity in evaluations. In E.E. Jones, D.E. Kanouse, H.H. Kelley, R.E. Nisbett, S. Valins, & B. Weiner (Eds.), *Attribution: Perceiving the causes of behavior* (pp. 47-62). Morristown, NJ: General Learning Press.

Kelley, H.H. (1972). Attribution in social interaction. In E.E. Jones, D.E. Kanouse, H.H. Kelley, R.E. Nisbett, S. Valins, & B. Weiner (Eds.), *Attribution: Perceiving the causes of behavior* (pp. 1-26). Morristown, NJ: General Learning Press.

Kramer, R.M. (1994). The sinister attribution error. *Motivation and Emotion, 18,* 199-231.

Lazarus, R.S. (1984). On the primacy of cognition. *American Psychologist, 39,* 124-129.

Leventhal, G.S. (1980). What should be done with equity theory? New approaches to the study of fairness in social relationships. In K. Gergen, M. Greenberg, & R. Willis (Eds.), *Social exchange: New advances in theory and research* (pp. 27-55). New York: Plenum Press.

Lewicki, R.J., McAllister, D., & Bies, R.J. (1998). Trust and distrust: New relationships and realities. *Academy of Management Review, 23,* 438-458.

Lind, E.A. 2001. When and how are heuristics used in making judgments? In J. Greenberg (Chair), *Controversial Issues in Organizational Justice.* Symposium conducted at the annual meeting of the Academy of Management, Washington, D.C.

Lind, E.A., & Tyler, T.R. (1988). *The social psychology of procedural justice.* New York: Plenum.

Martin, J. (1981). Relative deprivation: A theory of distributive injustice for an era of shrinking resources. In L.L. Cummings and B.M. Staw (Eds.), *Research in organizational behavior* (Vol. 3, pp. 53-107). Greenwich, CT: JAI Press.

Martin, J. Scully, M., & Levitt. B. (1990). Injustice and the legitimation of revolution: Damning the past, excusing the present, and neglecting the future. *Journal of Personality and Social Psychology, 59,* 281-290.

Matthews, C. (1988). *Hardball: How politics is played—told by one who knows the game.* New York: Summit Books.

Mikula, G. (1986). The experience of injustice: Toward a better understanding of its phenomenology. In H. W. Bierhoff, R. L. Cohen, & J. Greenberg (Eds.), *Justice in interpersonal relations* (pp. 103-123). New York: Plenum Press.

Mikula, G., Petri, B., & Tanzer, N. (1990). What people regard as just and unjust: Types and structures of everyday experiences of injustice. *European Journal of Social Psychology, 20,* 133-149.

Miller, D.T. (2001). Disrespect and the experience of injustice. *Annual Review of Psychology*, 52, 527-553.

Morrill, C. (1992). Vengeance among executives. *Virginia Review of Sociology*, 1, 51-76.

Robinson, S.L., & Bennett, R.J. (1995). A typology of deviant workplace behaviors: A multidimensional scaling study. *Academy of Management Journal*, 38, 555-572.

Salancik, G.R., & Pfeffer, J. (1978). A social information processing approach to job attitudes and task design. *Administrative Science Quarterly*, 23, 224-253.

Schacter, S. & Singer, J.E. (1962). Cognitive, social, and physiological determinants of emotional state. *Psychological Review*, 69, 379-399.

Scott, W.G., & Hart, D.K. (1979). *Organizational America: Can individual freedom survive within the security it promises?* Boston: Houghton Mifflin.

Shah, P.P., & Schroth, H.A. (2000). Procedures, do we really want to know them? The effects of procedural justice on performance self-esteem. *Journal of Applied Psychology*, 85, 462-471.

Shreve, S.R., & Shreve, P. (1997). *Outside the law: Narratives on justice in America*. Boston: Beacon Press.

Sitkin, S.B., & Bies, R.J. (1993). Social accounts in conflict situations: On using explanations to manage conflict. *Human Relations*, 46, 349-370.

Solomon, R.C. (1990). *A passion for justice: Emotions and the origins of the social contract*. Reading, MA: Addison-Wesley.

Thibaut, J., & Walker, L. (1975). *Procedural justice: A psychological analysis*. Hillsdale, NJ: Lawrence Erlbaum Associates.

Tjosvold, D., & Chia, L.C. (1989). Conflict between managers and workers: The role of cooperation and competition. *The Journal of Social Psychology*, 129, 235-247.

Trevino, L.K., & Bies, R.J. (1997). Through the looking glass: A normative manifesto for organizational behavior. In C.L. Cooper and S.E. Jackson (Eds.), *Creating tomorrow's organizations: A handbook for future research in organizational behavior* (pp. 439-452). London: John Wiley & Sons Ltd.

Tripp, T.M., & Bies, R.J. (1997). What's good about revenge? The avenger's perspective. In R.J. Lewicki, R.J. Bies, and B.H. Sheppard (Eds.), *Research on negotiation in organizations* (Vol. 6, pp. 145-160). Greenwich, CT: JAI Press.

Tyler, T.R., & Lind, E.A. (1992). A relational model of authority in groups. In M.P. Zanna (Ed.), *Advances in experimental social psychology* (Vol. 25, pp. 115-191). New York: Academic Press.

Utne, M.K., & Kidd, R.F. (1980). Equity and attribution. In G. Mikula (Ed.), *Justice and social interaction* (pp. 63-93). New York: Springer-Verlag.

Walster, E., Walster, G., & Berscheid, E. (1978). *Equity: Theory and research*. Boston: Allyn & Bacon.

Watson, D., & Clark, L.A. (1984). Negative affectivity: The disposition to experience aversive emotional states. *Psychological Bulletin*, 96, 465-490.

Watson, D., Clark, L.A. & Tellegen, A. (1988). Development and validation of brief measures of positive and negative affect: The PANAS scales. *Journal of Personality and Social Psychology*, 54, 1063-1070.

Weick, K.E. (1995). *Sensemaking in organizations*. Thousand Oaks, CA: Sage.

Wong, P.T., & Weiner, B. (1981). When people ask "why" questions, and the heuristics of attributional search. *Journal of Personality and Social Psychology, 40,* 650-663.

Zajonc, R.B. (1984). On the primacy of affect. *American Psychologist, 39,* 117-123.

PART III

COMMENTARY

CHAPTER 9

SOME REFLECTIONS ON THE MORALITY OF ORGANIZATIONAL JUSTICE

Russell Cropanzano and Deborah E. Rupp

ABSTRACT

The goal of this chapter is to provide an integrative commentary on the contributions contained in this volume. We present this analysis within the context of the existing literature on organizational justice. Toward this end, we first examine why fairness is important to people in work organizations. Based on previous work, we suggest that justice can provide at least three things—economic benefits, validation of close interpersonal relationships, and the sense that moral principles are being upheld. Paying special attention to the importance of moral principles, we explore how a sense of fairness is translated into action. In this regard, we draw heavily from Rest's (1979, 1984) Four Component Model of organizational behavior. Using these ideas as a lens, we then turn our attention to each chapter, providing a specific analysis as well as suggestions for future research.

Georges Seurat's (1859-1891) masterpiece *Un dimanche à la Grande Jatte* now hangs in the Chicago Art Institute. It is an extraordinary composition, difficult to put into words. In the center a mother holds her child's hand, while in the park around them are a circle of characters. In the dark foreground, a man in a sleeveless shirt reclines with a pipe. Behind him stands a couple, the man with a black tophat and cane, the woman holding an umbrella in her right hand and a monkey on a leash in her left. Further back, a woman fishes, a man plays a horn, and a little girls skips. On the river are boats with smokestacks or sails, and one quaint rowboat with four men rowing a woman in a blue dress. More wonders are visible as the viewer steps closer—a French tricolor, a white dog with a brown face and spot, a solitary man in a topcoat looking out over the water. But as you get closer still, you begin to see more of the substance behind Seurat's style. We leave our description in abler hands, those of the symbolist writer Félix Fénéon:

> If, in M. Seurat's *Grande Jatte,* you take a small patch of uniform tone, you will find that it is made up of a whirling host of tiny dots, and those dots spell out the constituent elements of the tone.... Isolated on the canvas, these colours re-compose on the retina: what we have is not, therefore, a mingling of colours conceived in terms of pigment. It is a mingling of colours conceived in terms of light (Cited in Russell, 1965, p. 181)

This same Fénéon, who coined the term "neo-impressionism" (Herbert, 1991), was describing "Seurat's *fracture"* (Smith, 1997, p. 47, italics in original). The image on the canvas is composed of many small marks or dots that blend together as one moves away from the painting. In fact, the art critic Charles Blanc suggested moving as much as nine meters away from the *Grande Jatte.* Even at this distance, the constituent parts are not lost to the naked eye.

Un dimanche à la Grande Jatte makes a fitting metaphor for our humbling position. Having read through each of these chapters, we are then asked to pull them together with our commentary. But there are so many good things here! Taking our inspiration from *Grande Jatte,* we will step away from each composition with the goal of discerning an overarching unity. But not forgetting Seurat's fracture, we will remain mindful of each unique contribution. In the pages that follow we shall discuss organizational justice from the perspective of ethical choices. We use the chapters and other important research to argue that human beings can be moral actors. In this approach, we utilize the literature on moral decisions to help inform our thinking about workplace justice. Let us begin with a historical overview.

THREE PERSPECTIVES ON ORGANIZATIONAL JUSTICE

Recently, we have argued for a three-fold approach to justice (see Cropanzano, Rupp, Mohler, & Schminke, 2001). Historically speaking, the first to be proposed was the instrumental model. This framework maintains that justice is important because it serves individuals' self-interests. The second approach was the noninstrumental or interpersonal model. This perspective asserts that justice is important because it is indicative of one's standing within a social group. The third and most recent approach is the deontological or moral virtues model. This framework maintains that justice is important because people often want to behave morally and may actively seek to do so. As a consequence, justice can serve as an end in itself. In the pages that follow, we shall use this three-part taxonomy to frame our review, paying special attention to the contrast between deontological and self-interested justice motives.

Instrumental Approaches to Organizational Justice

Much of the social science literature works from an implicit or explicit assumption of material self-interest (Bazerman, 1998; Miller, 1999), and this was no less true for nascent research on organizational justice (Cropanzano, Byrne, Bobocel, & Rupp, 2001a). For example, some early equity theory researchers presumed that people obeyed a rule of equity because it offered the most advantageous long-term payoffs (e.g., Hatfield, Walster, & Piliavin, 1978; Walster, Walster, & Berscheid, 1978) rather than because such a rule was viewed as morally correct. Since justice, in this view, works as an enlightened means to an end, the self-interested perspective has sometimes been termed the "instrumental model" of justice (e.g., by Konovsky, 2000; Korsgaard & Sapienza, this volume). Theorists taking the instrumental view have generally drawn from two theoretical frameworks: economic rationality and some venerable versions of social exchange theory.

A theory of economic rationality presupposes that human beings attempt to maximize self-interest, usually by logically weighting costs and benefits in order to obtain an estimate of value (though these theories certainly allow for decision biases, see Bazerman & Neale, 1992; Plous, 1993, especially his Chapter 9). Many models posit that individuals weight these value functions by their likelihood of success (Bazerman, 1998). Subjective expected utility theory (Schoemaker, 1982) is a model of economic rationality, as is expectancy-valence theory (Wanous, Keon, & Latack, 1983).

Another instrumental approach to justice involves some older versions of social exchange theory (Tyler & Blader, 2000). We shall see later that newer approaches to social exchange are less likely to emphasize material self-interest and more likely to emphasize relationships (Cropanzano, Rupp et al., 2001). Though there are numerous approaches to social exchange, all tend to assume that material (and other) resource transactions are guided by a set of rules, such as reciprocity or equity. These rules guarantee favorable long-term advantages. Hence, early theories proposed that social exchange was largely a self-interested matter (e.g., Gergen, 1969), though this was not necessarily true for all human behavior (e.g., Blau, 1986).

Models of economic rationality and (classical) models of social exchange have some different features and emphases. Most notably, social exchange theories are more likely to emphasize the norms or rules that govern resource transactions. Thus, these frameworks stress obedience to normative rules, such as reciprocity, equity, or equality, among others. Theories of economical rationality emphasize the maximization of benefits and the minimization of costs. Consequently, they tend to view individuals as attempting to get the most possible in their interactions with others. Despite these differences, classic social exchange and economic rationality are compatible frameworks in that they share a common assumption that self-interest is the ultimate driver of human behavior (Dawes, 1994).

Though this may be disquieting to some, as Ellard and Skarlicki (this volume) remind us, self-interest often trumps other concerns (for empirical evidence, see Wade-Benzoni, Tenbrunsel, & Bazerman, 1996). Given these considerations, a self-interested account of organizational justice can make a valuable contribution to our understanding. An amusing demonstration of this can be found in a study presented by Damon (1977). Damon interviewed a group of children as to their preferred distributions of ten hypothetical candy bars. When asked how these candy bars ought to be divided, the participants provided a variety of different schemes. Damon then provided the children with ten *actual* candy bars and told them to divide them among a group. What happened? When faced with an actual decision task, the children were more self-interested than when they were describing a hypothetical allocation.

Other evidence suggests that adults can behave like Damon's (1977) children (e.g., Ordóñez, Connolly, & Coughlan, 2000). Vermunt's contribution (this volume) takes up this possibility is his review. In his chapter Vermunt compares findings from the Ultimate Bargaining Game to those from the Dictator Game. In the Ultimate Bargaining Game, one player makes an offer and the other player retains veto power. Thus, it behooves the offering player to maintain at least the appearance of justice. Otherwise, her or his offer may be refused, depriving the player of any profit whatsoever. In the Dictator Game, on the other hand, there is no veto power. The allocation decision lies entirely with a single player. In these circumstances, allocations are less fair than they are in the Ultimate Bargaining Game. As Vermunt points out, this suggests that selfish concerns may drive some efforts at fairness. By extension, individuals manage impressions, attempting to appear as just as possible in order to maximize their benefits (Greenberg, 1990). Clearly, there is much self-interest in our social worlds.

But there is also much else. Evidence does not support a perspective that attempts to account for all human actions exclusively in terms of material self-interest (Etzioni, 1988; Kohn, 1990; Mansbridge, 1990). Miller and Ratner (1998) go so far as to remark: "Much of the most interesting social science research of the last 20 years points to inadequacy of self-interest models of behavior" (p. 53). For example, in a thorough review Sears and Funk (1991) found that self-interest was only a partial determinant of many social and political attitudes (for similar evidence, see Miller & Ratner, 1996). A similar case can be made for prosocial behaviors. As Batson (1991, 1995) discusses, individuals often act out of altruistic, rather than self-interested, motives. The organizational justice literature is consistent with research on attitudes and altruism. Many studies have found that justice remains an important concern, even after accounting for material gain (Lind & Tyler, 1988; Tyler & Lind, 1992; Tyler & Smith, 1998). Resource acquisition remains an important human concern, but there are others.

Interpersonal Approaches to Organizational Justice

Overview

In addressing the limitations of the instrumental model, many organizational justice researchers used the classical social exchange theories as a point of departure. There were two immediate responses, and both of these emphasized the importance of interpersonal relationships. The first response, as Korsgaard and Sapienza (this volume) point out, was to integrate social identity theory into organizational justice (Lind & Tyler, 1998; Tyler & Blader, 2000; Tyler & Lind, 1992; Tyler & Smith, 1998). According to this group-value or relational model, individuals are interested in their standing and inclusion within important social groups (such as work organizations). Injustice signals that individuals have a poor relationship with the group and/or with a decision-maker. Consequently, injustice is hurtful to people, and this is especially true when the group is important (Brockner, Tyler, & Cooper-Schneider, 1992; Holbrook & Kulik, 1996; Tyler & Degoey, 1995).

While the relational model involved integrating a new conceptual (social identity theory) perspective into organizational justice, a more recent response has involved re-tooling the early theories of social exchange. Contemporary models of social exchange are no longer limited to economic self-interest. They now incorporate the role of interpersonal associations. In particular, justice is helpful in building close relationships among coworkers. These relationships, in turn, engender constructive work activities, such as organizational citizenship behavior and job performance (e.g., Cropanzano, Prehar, & Chen, in press; Konovsky & Pugh, 1994; Masterson, Lewis, Goldman, & Taylor, 2000; Rupp & Cropanzano, in press). Like the relational model, contemporary social exchange suggests that justice is important because it conveys information about how we are viewed by others. Of course, there are some differences. The relational model emphasizes reactions to injustice in on-going relationships, whereas contemporary social exchange tends to emphasize the development of interpersonal associations (Cropanzano, Prehar, et al., in press). Nevertheless, these two perspectives share the idea that justice is important because it conveys information about what others think of us.

Though a detailed review of the evidence is beyond the scope of this chapter, it will suffice to say that most interpersonal models are consistent with research data (for more details see Cropanzano, Rupp, et al., 2001). For our purposes here we need only illustrate the importance of group membership in a general way. An especially informative series of experiments was reviewed by Dawes (1994), Dawes, van den Kragt, and Orbell (1990), and Tyler and Dawes (1993). Research in this paradigm invites seven research participants into the lab. Each is given a piece of paper with two options. They can check "keep" or "give." If they check "keep," the participant is guaranteed six dollars. If they check "give," the money reverts back to the experimenter. The experimenter, in turn, doubles the amount (to $12) and gives two dollars to each of the *other* participants. That is, the person who checks "give" loses everything, but he or she allows each coworker to earn an additional $2.

From the point of view of material self-interest, the best option is to keep your own six dollars, and then hope that the other six individuals will give away their money. If this occurs, the participant earns $18 (the original six, plus two dollars from each of the other six subjects). A cooperative response, whereby each of the seven participants simultaneously vote to "give" their money back to the experimenter, yields an advantageous $12 to each subject (two dollars from each of the other six subjects). Thus, participants are involved in a social dilemma—should they compete and keep a certain six dollars (maybe more) or cooperate and try for $12? When groups can talk through the situation, about 80% of subjects elect to cooperate. When they cannot talk things out, only about 30% cooperate (Dawes, 1994). Consequently, there is always some cooperation, but less when the individuals have not formed agreements among themselves.

Even more important here is the case of when another group is present. When there are two groups of 14 individuals (seven apiece), participants are much less likely to select a cooperative response. Additionally, this tendency for groups to compete is maintained even when discussion is allowed (cf., Kollock, 1998). From this we can see that cooperation is most likely when (a) groups can discuss their mutual problems and (b) it involves members of an in-group. These findings attest to the importance of interpersonal relationships.

But is There Anything Else?

An interesting finding in the Dawes (1994) experiments is that about 30% of the subjects checked "give," even when they could not discuss the problem and even when the money went to outgroup members. This suggests that there was something driving their allocation decisions other than (exclusively) self-interested or even relational concerns. That "something" could be a commitment to internalized moral values, but we cannot be sure from the evidence presented by Dawes. Fortunately, three of the chapters in this volume shed some light on this important issue.

Let us first consider the work of Stone and Stone-Romero (this volume). According to these authors, individuals' sense of what is fair is derived partially from religious beliefs. It is certainly true that individuals worry about their standing in religious organizations. For example, devote Catholics would fear excommunication. However, the act of social ostracism is only one part of maintaining religious obedience. Over time, many religious or spiritual people may come to internalize the teachings of their faith. That is, they maintain adherence because they truly believe what they have been taught, not (only) because they fear exclusion.

We can illustrate this using Stone and Stone-Romero's example of Buddhists. Like other faiths, Buddhists believe strongly in compassion toward other human beings. As a consequence, many Buddhists *really are* compassionate people. These individuals do not simply affect a compassionate air in order to maintain their social standing in the community. Certainly, there may exist some hypocrites whose behavior is driven by material self-interest, but the point is that there are more than a few sincere believers. This can be said of all faiths. By extension, Stone and Stone-Romero's chapter suggests that there is more to justice than material self-interest and a concern with group inclusion. If religious and other belief systems can be internalized, then these beliefs can become direct motivators of just behavior. In other words, many people attempt to live in accordance with a set of moral principles.

From a different route, Ellard and Skarlicki's (this volume) chapter can bring us to the same place. While these authors consider a variety of things that could impact third-party reactions to injustice, one elegant construct is the notion of "deservingness." Deservingness implies a certain worthiness to receive an outcome or type of treatment. If fact, the term "deserve" can be understood as "a claim or right to; be worthy of." Likewise, "deservedly" can be defined as "justly" (Barnhart, 1958, p. 229). These definitions connote a sense of moral "oughtness" or a concern with what another person *should* receive. In Ellard and Skarlicki's model, therefore, the third-party observer is attempting to make an ethical or principled judgment about some event. While the individual remains concerned with self-interest or group standing, she or he is also trying to divine what is "right" or "moral" in a particular situation.

Bies and Tripp (this volume) share a similar perspective. They define justice as getting one's due. That is, receiving the treatment or outcomes to which one is entitled. Of course getting what one *deserves* is conceptually distinct from getting what one *wants*. The former concerns elements of entitlement and/or morality while the latter is more focused on favorability. Significantly, Bies and Tripp emphasize that getting one's due may be determined in comparison to other people (as in equity theory), but it may also be determined in relation to noncomparative principles of justice. For instance, one is not entitled to treat someone disrespectfully, just because he or she treats others the same way.

These three chapters break new theoretical ground. One need not endorse every particular to recognize at least one important implication: human beings can be moral actors. It is easy to picture Ellard and Skarlicki's third-party observers looking out at a potential injustice and attempting to make sense of it by using their religious values. But this takes us well past instrumental and interpersonal models and into the terrain of the deontological.

The Deontological Model of Justice

The limitations of traditional justice models have lead to the development of a third major approach to organizational justice. This model has been termed the moral virtues (Folger, 1994) or deontological model (Folger, 1998, 2001). The deontological model purports that people are not only concerned about fairness to protect their own self-interests, but they also may hold a collective concern that all people be treated fairly. In this sense, fairness may be an internalized virtue rather than a selfish motive. Consequently, justice is an end to itself, rather than a means to an instrumental or relational end, and people care about fairness because acting fairly is "the right thing to do."

In introducing the deontological model of justice, Folger (2001) explains that organizational justice research has focused so heavily on self-interested motives for fair and unfair behavior that it has circumvented necessary attention away from the moral motives that influence justice. Where instrumental and relational factors might explain a portion of the variance in justice effects, what Folger refers to as the "ought" forces of just behavior have largely been ignored despite arguments made by the broader research community (Miller, 1999; Montada, 1998). In other words, we have lost sight of how justice relates to morality. According to the deonance model of justice, observing or experiencing an act of injustice triggers a deonic state. Deonance is a motivational state that arises within a person when an observed individual violates (willingly or not) a moral norm of interpersonal conduct held by the perceiver. This state creates a desire to see that people are held accountable for their moral injunctions.

At the same time that Folger (1994, 1998, 2001) was laying the groundwork for the deontological model, Bies (1993) and Treviño and Bies (1997) were making similar observations. Indeed, Bies (2001, p. 110) has explicitly called for a "moral discourse" as a remedy to the pro-management bias which Bies views as existing within some organizational research. Bies (2001) raises the concern that "the instrumental orientation ... has put ... justice scholars in the role of apologists and excuse-makers for management" (p. 111). Consistent with Folger, Bies and his colleagues share a concern that all workers are not treated with the dignity and respect to which they are entitled. In their current chapter, Bies and Tripp (this volume) further develop these vital ideas. These authors argue that some standards are "noncomparative." Violation of these noncomparative standards can provoke a sense of outrage, regardless of whether others are treated in a similar fashion. Treating everyone equally badly does not excuse immoral behavior!

Thus, the work of Folger (1994, 1998, 2001) and Bies (1993, 2001) reaffirms the importance of interpersonal conduct and universal ethical standards (e.g., truth, freedom) that are vital to an understanding of justice. It is important to note that neither Bies nor Folger is arguing that individuals are never self-interested. Rather, they are proposing a pluralistic framework whereby individuals can be motivated by instrumental and interpersonal factors, as well as by morally-motivated noncomparative standards of interpersonal conduct.

Evidence for the Deonance Model

Kahneman and colleague's findings. Kahneman, Knetsch, and Thaler (1986) conducted several studies providing the earliest evidence that instrumental and interpersonal models cannot always account for justice reactions. In their earlier studies, experiments consisted of a "first round" where participants chose how a $20 resource pool would be split between themselves and a hypothetical partner. Subjects chose *Even* ($10 to self, $10 to partner) or *Uneven* ($18 to self, $2 to partner) allocations. Then in a second round (the true experimental condition), participants were matched with two partners: one who was fair (chose Even) in the previous round and one who was unfair (chose Uneven) in the previous round. In this round, participants were also given two allocation choices. They could either split a $12 pool with the *unfair* partner ($6 to self, $6 to unfair partner) or sacrifice a dollar to instead split a $10 pool with the *fair* partner ($5 to self, $5 to fair partner).

Although the Kahneman and colleagues studies each took a slightly different approach (e.g., earlier studies actually conducted the first round where later studies only described it), results generally showed that a significant majority of participants picked the sacrificial choice so as not to allocate resources to the unfair partner. This evidence is in clear opposition to both instrumental and relational models of justice. Participants did not act out of economic rationality, but instead chose the option that paid the least possible to themselves. Likewise, participants were not acting out of future concern for their relationships with their partners, in that there was to be no subsequent rounds and participants never even met their "partners" in the first place. The experimental design removed the possibility for material or relational motives, thereby leaving the explanation that participants must have chosen to reward fairness/punish unfairness because it was the right thing to do, deeming justice more as an end-in-itself than a means-to-a material or relational-end.

Although these results provided promising evidence that their must be additional reasons for justice concerns beyond instrumental and relational explanations, Turillo and colleagues (in press) identified a possible confound in the Kahneman and colleagues (1986) studies that somewhat limit conclusions. Participants allocated *either* $6 to the unfair partner *or* $5 to the fair partner. Thus, the act of rewarding fairness and punishing unfairness occurred simultaneously. Therefore, conclusions cannot be drawn about the unique motivation to punish individuals for moral transgressions.

Turillo and Colleague's Findings: Publicity of Decisions Does Not Matter. To avoid this problem, Turillo, Folger, Lavelle, Umpress, and Gee (in press) designed additional experiments continuing this line of research. As mentioned above, within the Kahneman and colleagues (in press) paradigm, participants may have varied in their understanding of the degree to which partners were to be made aware of their allocation decisions. To avoid this ambiguity, Turillo and colleagues (in press), in their first study, used "partner information" as an independent variable. That is, participants were either told that: a) only the unfair partner would learn of the decision, b) only the fair partner would learn of the decision, c) both partners would receive information about the decision, d) no one would receive information about the decision unless they were among the 10% to get paid, or e) the participant's choice would remain completely confidential.

Results showed no effect for partner information. That is, participants' allocation decisions were the same regardless of the anonymity of their decisions and regardless of actual punishment or reward of the partners for unfairness/fairness. This finding further validated the notion that individuals can act out against unfairness for fairness' sake, rather than only in situations where their group identity or relationships might be enhanced.

Turillo and Colleague's Findings: Two Wrongs Do Not Make a Right. In this first study, Turillo and colleagues (in press) also addressed the simultaneous reward/punish problem described above. They did this by making "partner" a between-subjects variable rather than a within-subjects variable. The Kahneman and colleagues (in press) studies had one condition where all participants had a fair and unfair partner (a three-person paradigm). Turillo and colleagues modified this design by using a two-person paradigm where participants were paired with *either* a fair *or* an unfair partner.

In other words, participants were matched with a hypothetical partner who had chosen either a $18/$2 split or a $10/$10 split in a previous round (modeled after the Kahneman first round). Participants were also assigned to either a punish or reward payout condition. In the punish condition, participants could split a $12 pool with a partner ($6 for self, $6 for partner) or sacrifice a dollar to allocate $5 to themselves and $0 to their partner. In the reward condition, participants could take $6 for themselves and allocate $0 to their partners, or act sacrificially by taking $5 for themselves and allocating (rewarding) $5 to their partner. Thus, the study was a 2 (partner: fair vs. unfair) x 2 (payout: reward vs. punish) design.

Results from this study indicated that subjects were more likely to act sacrificially (i.e., take $5 instead of $6 for themselves) to reward someone who had been fair than to punish someone who had been unfair. The authors felt this finding was due to the fact that in order to punish the partner who had been unfair (choosing a $5-for-self/$0-for-unfair partner as opposed to an even split), the participants themselves had to act selfishly, because they would be taking all of the money in the resource pool. Thus, the absence of a main effect may have been caused by a moral confound where participants believed that "two wrongs don't make a right." The researchers also felt that a strong egalitarian urge may have overpowered all effects in the direction of the reward choice.

Thus, in a second study, Turillo and colleagues (in press) included conditions where subjects allocated the resource pool between themselves and two partners: a partner who had been unfair in a previous round, and a partner who had either been fair previously or was from a completely different study. In this variation, subjects could choose to allocate $6 for themselves, $6 to the unfair partner, and $6 to the fair or unrelated partner. Alternatively, they could choose to punish unfairness sacrificially by distributing $5 for themselves, $5 for the fair or unrelated partner and $0 for the unfair partner. This way, participants were allowed to take less money for themselves to punish an unfair partner, but still split the slightly smaller pool with another individual (and therefore not have to act selfishly themselves to punish the unfair partner). Likewise, in the reward condition, as in their first study, it did not matter whether the third partner was unknown or had acted fairly. Results indicated that when participants were allowed to split the resource pool with this third person, they were more likely to punish an unfair partner. These findings provided evidence that individuals are more likely to act sacrificially and seek retributive justice when they themselves are not acting unfairly in the process.

Turillo and Colleagues (in press) Findings: There is More to Justice Than Group Identification. Turillo and colleagues conducted a third, scenario-based study, where participants were told about a manager who had been acting interpersonally unfairly toward his employees. Interpersonal or interactional fairness differs from fairness of outcomes (also known as distributive justice) in that it deals with the presence or absence of interpersonal sensitivity toward others (Bies, 1987). In this study, the results from the previous studies were generally replicated in that approximately fifty percent of the subjects chose to sacrifice a dollar so that an unfair individual would receive nothing (and an unknown third person would receive the same amount as the participant). These results were slightly weaker than those of the previous two studies, however, which the researchers attributed to the fact that participants did not identify with the group to which the unfair person belonged (he was presented as a supervisor from a Virginia company whereas participants were Louisiana college students).

Therefore, in a final study, Turillo and colleagues manipulated the level of identification with an unfair actor as well as the perceived level of intent this person had for being unfair. Also, instead of measuring allocation decisions, the researchers this time measured how offended participants were by the unfair person and the extent to which the they were angered by the unfair person's behavior. Identification was manipulated by describing the unfair person as either a university professor (high identification) or an Olympic gymnast (low identification). Intent was manipulated by having participants read the comments of others expressing that the unfair person's actions were either clearly deliberate (high intent) or very uncharacteristic of the person (low intent). Whereas level of identification with the unfair person had no effect on participant reactions, participants took more offense to and were more angered by the offender's actions when it was clear that the offender intended to harm.

Although the authors suspected that group identification would have an effect on participants' reactions to unfairness, this was not found to be the case. Nonetheless, the findings provided further evidence against a purely relational model of justice. Here, individuals were not acting against injustice out of allegiance to group identity. Nor were they acting out of self-interest (as illustrated by their sacrificial behavior). These results allow for the continued plausibility of a morality-based theory of justice.

Summary. The results of these four studies suggest that individuals have strong reactions to distributive and interactional injustice, and that offenders' identities or the publicness of the participants' reactions does not have strong effects on the deonic state elicited by these unfair acts. Furthermore, participants are less likely to take sanctions against an offender if it would mean that they themselves would have to act unfairly. This suggests a code of interpersonal conduct that individuals strive to uphold, not for instrumental reasons, but because of what Folger (2001) refers to as an "ought" force that helps to regulate interpersonal behavior.

Justice and Moral Principles: One More Look Before We Move On

As we have seen, available evidence suggests that individuals are partially motivated by moral principles. Of course, we need to emphasize that there are other consequential motives as well, such as economic self-interest and group standing. That having been said, "doing the right thing" remains important to people. It is important to emphasize, however, that self-interest is an interpretive idea devised by human beings. More specifically, to be consistent with the work of other scholars, this chapter has tended to equate "self-interest" with "economic self-interest." If self-interest were understood in a different way, then perhaps this new version of the construct could accommodate the disconfirmatory findings reviewed thus far.

Batson (1991, 1995) and Greenberg (2001) have reviewed one possibility. Some scholars have suggested that "moral" choices may be driven by the positive feelings one gets from behaving in accordance with moral standards, as well as by the negative feelings that occur when one violates important ethical standards. Since the ultimate goal is a good feeling, then it might be plausible to view all just behaviors as self-interested.[1] Using Batson's (1995) terminology, we refer to this as the "mood enhancement" model. Unfortunately, we were unable to locate any direct evidence for this model in the context of organizational justice. Nevertheless, research strongly supports the view that individuals sometimes consider the affective consequences of their actions and further use these anticipated consequences as a guide to their judgments (e.g., Ordóñez, Benson, & Beach, 1999, Study 3). Hence, the mood enhancement model is quite plausible and worthy of consideration.

Additionally, it is important not to mischaracterize the mood enhancement view. The possibility that affect drives moral behavior does not mean that ethical principles are unimportant. Indeed, even if one accepts that justice is motivated by this sort of self-interest (where self-interest is understood to include the mood enhancement effects that result from behaving morally), ethical principles remain critical for a fuller understanding of workplace justice. This is because the mood enhancement view conceptualizes these principles as one cause of positive affect. Consequently, this broad reformulation of the self-interest construct does not fundamentally threaten Folger's (1994, 1998, 2001) deontological model.

Nevertheless, there are some differences in emphasis that are worth considering. These distinctions center on each model's respective understanding of the term "self-interest." Specially, the mood enhancement model holds that something could plausibly be viewed as "self-interest" to the extent that it engenders a positive feeling state or favorable self-evaluation. The deontological model, on the other hand, holds that something can engender a good feeling, while not being self-interested as such. Consequently, for the mood enhancement model the term "self-interest" subsumes a broad class of mood-relevant events. On the other hand, in the deontological model these are not included (or at least not necessarily included) under the rubric "self-interest." Given this, we might say that the mood enhancement model takes a broad view of self-interest, while the deontological model takes a narrower view.

Seen in this light, the question we face here is whether a broader definition is the most useful conceptual tool for advancing our knowledge. With these thoughts in mind, a few issues are in need of resolution. In the pages that follow we will discuss three lingering philosophical concerns (for a more thorough review, see Holley, 1999).

Treating Justice as a Class of Motivated Behavior

Overview. One philosophical problem appears when one considers justice as a specific case of motivated behavior. By "motivated," we mean only that one attempts to pursue some objective (in this case, the objective is to be fair), and that one attempts to monitor progress toward that objective. At least in this loose sense, proactive attempts at justice can be viewed as motivated. This is because the pursuit of justice requires that we sometimes possess (at least implicitly) a goal to behave in a fair manner (e.g., Feese & Sabini, 1985). Likewise, and as we have observed elsewhere (cf., Cropanzano, Byrne, Bobocel, & Rupp, 2001b; Cropanzano, James, & Citera, 1993), a motivated actor recognizes that her or his goal has been achieved by means of a feedback signal. The key here is that fair behavior is our goal or standard, and the feedback signal indicates how much progress one is making toward behaving fairly. When one is meeting one's moral principles, then the signal will likely be positively toned affect (e.g., the pride of living up to one's ethical standards) or, at the very least, a favorable evaluation of one's efforts. When one is falling short of one's own standards, then the signal will likely be negatively toned affect (e.g., the guilt of hypocrisy), or at least a negative self-evaluation.

From this, one could term all motivated behavior (including just behavior) "self-interested." This would be true in the very broad sense that one feels good when a goal is achieved and bad when one falls short of the goal. It should also be clear that the affective state that results from goal progress can plausibly be called a *cause* of moral behavior. This is because motivated behavior (ethical or otherwise) could not occur without a feedback signal (such as positive affect) to indicate success. Therefore, just behavior is self-interested in the sense that the individual *wants* to be fair (i.e., has accepted a goal to work toward justice) and feels good when she or he has behaved with justice (i.e., experiences the effects of a positive feedback loop). It could be that this sort of reasoning is what some scholars have in mind when they say that all behavior (including just behavior) is self-interested (see Sullivan, 1989, for a general review).

Mechanisms and Goals. The analysis of justice as motivated behavior suggests that fairness, in some measure, is an attempt to maintain a moral standard or goal. Progress toward these goals is regulated by positive and negative feeling states. Thus, affect is a mechanism by which one accomplishes justice. However, a motive is understood to be the goal one is trying to achieve not the means by which it is pursued. The moral standard, therefore, remains the ultimate objective (i.e., the goal of justice). The affective feedback is the means by which this ultimate objective is achieved. Hence, the claim that all behavior is self-interested because it feels good when you live up to your standards, and bad when you do not, confuses the goal (justice) with the mechanism by which we monitor progress toward the goal (positive and negative affect). Perhaps a metaphor might make this point clearer.

Consider a physiological analogy. All human life is sustained by respiration. If one stopped breathing, then moral action (as well as all other actions) would cease within a few minutes. For this reason, we can plausibly assert that oxygen is necessary for just behavior. But of course, no one would assert from this analysis that all fairness is motivated by the need for oxygen. Likewise, positive and negative affect, or at least self-evaluation, is necessary to maintain fair behavior. However, it does not follow that the only motive for justice is a desire to obtain this good feeling. The pursuit of morality is better gauged by one's intentions and objectives, rather than by the feeling states that regulate progress.

Interestingly, a more general variant of this critique has appeared in the work of Turillo and colleagues (in press) and Holley (1999). These scholars distinguish between *self-serving* actions and *self-interested* actions. A self-serving action is one with benefits for the individual. A self-interested action is a course of behavior that was taken with the intent of achieving benefits. Consequently, an action can be self-serving (i.e., have benefits) without being self-interested (i.e., taken to obtain those benefits). Within our treatment of justice as motivated behavior, it appears that some fair actions are self-serving (i.e., they make us feel good) while not necessarily being self-interested (i.e., they are not undertaken with the ultimate objective of obtaining a good feeling). Put differently, just because one feels good from doing the right thing does not mean that mood enhancement was the underlying incentive for the action.

Indeed, such a mechanism would have difficulty explaining the activities of principled people throughout history. As illustrative examples, let us recall that Nelson Mandela was imprisoned for 27 years (Avolio, 1999), and that Joan of Arc allowed herself to be burned at the stake (Gordon, 2001) because they refused to recant the justice of their causes. Making their sacrifices must have been incredibly painful and emotionally costly to these heroes. To say the least, it is not at all clear that their commitment to principle provided a net gain in terms of positive affect. Indeed, it seems more likely that these individuals (and others like them) persisted in spite of such emotional costs as doubt, exhaustion, fear, loneliness, and an occasional sense of futility.

Begging the Fundamental Question

There is another concern that needs to be considered. Our analysis of justice as a motivated behavior might be helpful here. As we have seen, successful progress toward a goal will cause one to experience a positive self-evaluation and/or positive affect (Cropanzano et al., 1993). Likewise, Bies and Tripp (this volume) convincingly argue that a violation of moral standards can provoke a good deal of negative emotion. If this favorable hedonic experience is regarded as self-interest, however, it begs a more basic question: *Why* would adherence to moral standards make us feel good?

At some meta-cognitive level, moral standards must have some value to people or else they would be incapable of producing feeling states. We feel good when we achieve something that is important to us. If fairness is unimportant, then a good feeling will not result. Moreover, according to research on emotion, the *more* we want something the *stronger* will be the affect that is evoked (cf., Weiss & Cropanzano, 1996). Consequently, the fact that virtue has the potential to yield a good feeling presupposes that just behavior is a desirable state-of-affairs, at least for some people at some times.

Parenthetically, we should emphasize that this same analysis can be applied to negative feeling states. Behaving immorally can cause us to feel guilt (Tangney, 1995). By extension, people sometimes feel guilty when they benefit from an injustice (Krehbiel & Cropanzano, 2000). However, individuals are more likely to experience guilt when they violate a nontrivial standard. We should not feel guilty when we have done nothing wrong! Hence, the experience of negative emotion does not explain away the importance of the moral standards. Rather, it demonstrates that moral standards are critical for justice. In the end, the mood enhancement model leads to the conclusion that moral principles are important. Your mood won't change unless you care about the standard in question.

There is a more general way to make this same point. Based on our analysis of justice as a class of motivated behaviors, we might observe that affect (or at least some self-evaluation) is a necessary cause of moral behavior. This is because feelings provide internal performance feedback. Lacking this feedback loop, individuals will find it difficult to assess whether or not they are making progress toward their goals. However, by itself, affect (or a self-evaluation) is not sufficient to explain moral behavior, since motivated action (including the motivation to be fair) also requires some goal, standard, intention, or objective that the individual is trying to pursue. Said differently, these feelings are *about* something. In the case of behavior motivated to pursue a moral standard, your feeling is about the ethical principle that is directing your actions. Consequently, the existence of affect implies the existence of a moral standard.

Three (or More) Distinct Types of Self-Interest

The final concern regarding the broad definition of justice is practical. Conceptual definitions are designed to serve as guides for scholars. Scholars propose conceptual definitions based on their utility in explaining phenomena in the real world. To be useful, a definition needs to enhance our understanding. In our desire to understand, predict, and control behavior, we need to be able to make valid distinctions among constructs. In other words, part of understanding what an event *is* involves understanding what it is *not*. This requires that our definitions be sufficiently precise so as to avoiding lumping many distinct behaviors into a single conceptual category. When behaviors have somewhat distinct antecedents and consequences, it is often suitable to treat them as separate constructs (Cronbach & Meehl, 1955; Schwab, 1980).

If a conceptual definition is too general, then our ability to offer useful explanations is compromised. To illustrate this problem, let us consider six hypothetical cases. While these examples are fictional, they are based on real life events. In reading each, the reader may want to reflect on how she or he would explain these behaviors.

- A junk bond kingpin finances a hostile take-over, brutally destroys a firm, and displaces thousands of workers and their families. Over lunch she laughs about the "losers" she put out of work.
- An impoverished single mother is abandoned by her husband and lives with her children in public housing. Tired and lonely at the end of each day, she still finds time to read to her children and the energy to make sure they are well.
- A serial killer sexually assaults and brutally murders small children.
- An anonymous "Samaritan" gives up her weekends to work among the homeless. She volunteers to supply them hot meals, a friendly face, and decent medical care.
- An intoxicated college student rapes a young woman.
- An off-duty police officer spots a burning apartment building. Heedless of his own safety, he rushes inside to rescue a trapped child.

The protagonists of each story have made moral choices. Each begs for an explanation. How are social scientists to answer the following question: What motivated these six individuals? We could say "self-interest" in every case, but it is not entirely clear how much knowledge is gained by incorporating these exceedingly different behaviors under a single label. We might be better served by motivational theories that allow us to make distinctions among these hypothetical actors. The ability to make such distinctions might allow us to prevent the behaviors we do not want (e.g., sexual assault, socially irresponsible management, mass murder) and encourage those we do (e.g., protection for children, commitment to duty, compassion for the less fortunate). Using a single term to describe the motives for all of these behaviors obfuscates important differences.

This illustrates the dilemma of broad definitions. Words are like sacks that hold ideas. When they are stuffed too full, they burst and lose their usefulness. A theorist who wanted to include all just behaviors under any single motive is likely to have difficulty contending with the rich diversity of human behavior. At the very least one would have to distinguish among different manifestations of that single motive. Based on contemporary justice research organizational scientists would need to describe at least three types of "self-interest." These would include: (a) the kind of self-interest where one desires personal material gains (the instrumental model), (b) the kind of self-interest where one seeks inclusion and full standing in a valued group (the relational model), and (c) the kind of self-interest where one seeks to do the fair thing even though it is sometimes difficult (the deontological model). Thus, rather than collapsing these three theoretically rich areas of inquiry into a single category, it would seem to be of greater scientific value to define self-interest more narrowly. This would allow us to treat these components as separate motives for acting fairly.

Some Concluding Thoughts

While it seems that justice researchers are generally accepting of the notion that moral standards are important (Bies, 1993, 2001; Folger, 1994, 1998, 2001) there is less than complete consensus as to how these should be interpreted. We don't pretend to have all of the necessary answers. However, given the concerns raised in this section, it may be premature to reduce all just behaviors to manifestations of self-interest.

BEHAVING JUSTLY/BEHAVING MORALLY

If, as we maintained, justice is partially derived from moral principles, then we must confront a second question: How does one apply these principles in order to behave justly? For our knowledge to promote fairness within organizations, we need to move from abstract principles to concrete moral decisions in the real world. Many of our current theories tell us how people decide whether or not they have been treated fairly. This is, of course, of critical importance. However, as ethics researchers have long known, people do not always behave in accordance with their espoused values (cf., Blasi, 1980; Thoma, 1994).

A famous study by Corey (1937) provides a classic example. Corey measured students' attitudes toward cheating. He then presented them with a series of five weekly tests. The students were also given a chance to cheat when scoring their own answers. Corey found students' attitudes toward cheating were unrelated to whether or not they actually cheated. (Interestingly, though Corey's study was conducted roughly 65 years ago, his conclusions may not be terribly different than those from more recent research, see McCabe & Treviño, 1996.) Of course, this modest relationship between behavior and beliefs has been widely documented (e.g., Ajzen, 1988; Sherman & Fazio, 1983). Sometimes individuals behave in accordance with their ethical principles, but other times they do not.

Understanding why moral principles do not always predict moral behavior has been a major concern of ethics researchers, and sundry models have been proposed (for reviews see Schminke, 1998; Treviño, 1986). These frameworks have in common the realization that moral judgment (deciding what is right) is only one step on the road to moral action (doing the right thing). There are other considerations involved, such as conceptualizing the situation in ethical terms and abiding by one's principles in the face of adversity.

We approach this issue by using Rest's (1979, 1984) Four Component Model of Moral Behavior as a conceptual framework. We selected the Four Component Model because of its flexibility in providing a straightforward look at the major processes involved in moral behavior. The four major processes are (1) moral sensitivity, (2) moral judgment, (3) moral motivation, and (4) moral action. Following from Rest (1994) we view these four processes as forming a logical sequence, but at the same time acknowledge that there is no single order in which the components occur. The "stages" are not intended to imply an invariant order. Additionally, future researchers may well discover more components (or elect to subdivide the four we will discuss). Indeed, Bredemeier and Shields (1994) have suggested that there could be as many as ten processes involved in moral behavior. For all these caveats, the Four Component Model is at least a good place to start.

We have presented our version of the Four Component Model in Figure 1. The easiest way to understand this framework is to consider it from the perspective of an employee who is in a questionable situation. There are at least four reasons why he or she might not respond fairly:

- *A lack of moral sensitivity.* In particular, the individual may not recognize that a moral issue is involved. For instance, some individuals might rely on the law as their exclusive guide to ethical decision-making (cf., Hosmer, 1996; Chapter 3). If no law is violated, then they might not see a reason for a moral judgment. Hence, they may not even think about events in terms of organizational justice.
- *Poor moral judgment.* As we have remarked elsewhere (Cropanzano, Byrne, et al., 2001a), to decide whether or not an injustice has occurred, one must evaluate an event in terms of some standard.

Some employees, such as those who are moral relativists (cf., Velasquez, 1992), may lack such standards. Thus, even if these individuals decide that fairness is involved, their lack of principles could limit their ability to make sound judgments.

- *A lack of moral motivation.* As we have emphasized throughout this chapter, moral principles are only one consideration when it comes to organizational justice. Individuals also consider their self-interest as well as their interpersonal relationships. These three motives, and perhaps others as well, must be weighed against each other when an individual chooses a course of action. For example, sometimes people will consent to work for an "unfair" organization (e.g., one whose manufacturing processes exploits underprivileged employees and damages the environment) if doing so is profitable (Bazerman, Schroth, Shah, Diekmann, & Tenbrunsel, 1994).
- *Failing to Act on Moral Inclinations.* Behaving fairly is often not easy. It may require offending powerful others in order to remain true to one's moral principles. Many times we fail to follow through even when we believe a course of action is morally correct.

These four components may help us recognize why fair behavior does not always result from compassionate principles. We may not recognize an injustice, we may lack moral judgments, we may defer to self-interest or interpersonal exigencies, and we may not have the character to adhere to our own principles. Any break in this chain will thwart justice. In the pages that follow, we will review these four components in more detail. We caution the reader that we are not attempting a complete review of the literature. Rather, our comments only offer descriptive examples. Since we are most interested in moral judgment and weighting (Stages 1-3), and less interested in moral actions (Stage 4), we will de-emphasize the final stage in favor of its predecessors.

Component 1: Moral Sensitivity

For those of us who are immersed in the organizational justice literature, the first component may be the most difficult to recognize. It is, in a

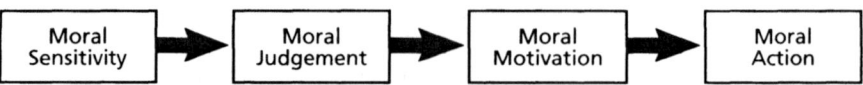

Figure 1. The Four Component Model of Moral Action.

sense, all too obvious. For people to behave justly, they need to recognize that there is a moral issue at stake within a given situation. As Rest (1994) puts it, we need to be morally sensitive to ethical concerns. As an example, consider research on conflict management. Much of the literature encourages managers to use tactics that are participative and respectful of everyone's needs. Of course, managers often do not use such tactics (for a review, see Folger & Cropanzano, 1998, especially Chapter 6). Why this disparity between prescription and description?

To investigate this matter, Sheppard, Blumenfeld-Jones, Minton, and Hyder (1994) interviewed managers as to how they handled recent conflicts among subordinates. Consistent with other literature, these respondents had tended to rely on autocratic approaches. According to Sheppard and his colleagues, this finding had to do with the manner in which the managers understood their roles. In particular, these individuals construed conflicts as calling for a decisive decision—much as other managerial tasks are viewed. Hence, when confronted with a conflict, the respondents simply rendered a decision through the easiest mechanism possible (a pronouncement). Unfortunately from the perspective of workplace justice, these conflict situations were unlikely to be viewed as moral encounters that called for a just resolution. These participants simply did not recognize the ethical parameters of the situation.

Moral insensitivity can strike at times when, at least to an outsider, an injustice seems obvious. For instance, as part of a developmental exercise, McNeel (1994) had male and female college students watch a videotape of a man pressuring a woman to have sexual intercourse with him. The female character had earlier been date raped and had been experiencing depression. Despite these concerns, many of the male students did not recognize this situation as a moral one.[2] Before we can behave morally, we must recognize that a moral response is what's called for. Unfortunately, the moral parameters are not always clear to everyone. Below we will consider some specific personal and situational elements that might impact moral sensitivity.

Personal Factors

Moral sensitivity can be treated as an individual difference factor. Which is to say, some individuals are more sensitive to the moral implications of decisions. The important work of Bebeau and her colleagues (e.g., Bebeau, & Brabeck, 1989; Bebeau, Rest, & Yamoor, 1985; Bebeau & Waithe, 1988) is especially instructive.[3] In this line of inquiry, dental students were exposed to vignettes describing ethical dilemmas. After viewing the vignettes, each participant's sensitivity was assessed. There were individual differences, with some of the respondents showing greater sensitivity and some lesser. Fortunately, an ethical training program especially designed for dental students effectively raised the moral sensitivity of the low scorers (Bebeau, 1994).

Situational Factors

Another way to understand the issue of moral sensitivity is to think of it as a sort of signal detection problem. In this paradigm, an individual must detect an injustice (the signal) from the work environment (the background). The environment may have a good deal of background "noise," which masks the signal. Similarly, the signal itself could be too weak to detect. Of course, we need to consider the strength of the signal with respect to the discord in the background. In a "cleaner" environment, a weaker signal can be located. In a "noisier" environment, the signal must be stronger. The analogous relationship between moral sensitivity and signal detection theory suggests that scholars can examine elements of the environment, elements of the event (i.e., the signal), or both.

Rest (1984, p. 35) provides a list of environmental elements that might make it more difficult to spot an injustice. Among others, Rest includes "ambiguity of people's needs," "familiarity with the situation," "time allowed for interpretation," "sheer number of elements in the situation," and "complexity in tracing out cause-effect paths." Essentially, this list suggests that individuals are most likely to be morally insensitive when the task is cognitively demanding. This could be because the signal itself is difficult to process (e.g., it is complex) or because other demands have been placed on the decision-maker (e.g., the individual must hold multiple things in mind simultaneously).

The strength of the signal would seem to be analogous to the moral intensity of the event. In particular, a morally intense event should be easier to detect than one that is less intense. Jones (1991) lists six determinants of moral intensity:

- The magnitude of harm or benefits that result from the event.
- The degree of social consensus that a behavior is ethical or unethical.
- The probability that the event will take place.
- The probability that the anticipated harm will occur.
- The time duration between the action and its consequences.
- The psychological distance between the observer and the victim or beneficiary of the act (this idea also appears in the Ellard & Skarlicki chapter, this volume).
- The extent to which the effects are diffused among a large number of people or concentrated onto a small group.

All things being equal, an unfair act is most likely to be detected when: it does great harm, there is social consensus that it is wrong, it will almost definitely occur, the ill-effects will certainly result, there is a short period of time between the act and its consequences, the victim is psychologically near the observer, and the effects are concentrated on a very small group. When these conditions go unmet, detection is less likely.

Component 2: Moral Judgment

Component 2 comprises the realm of moral judgment. Organizational justice researchers have devoted considerable attention to understanding how justice decisions are formulated, and at least some of this work has framed fairness in moral terms (for two views of our progress, see Cropanzano, Bryne et al., 2001b; van den Bos, 2001). In this section we will make the following argument: Justice researchers have tended to describe this decision-making process from two complementary perspectives.

Loosely speaking, it is possible to describe a prototypical model of justice with only three steps (Cropanzano, Byrne et al., 2001a; Cropanzano, Rupp et al., 2001). This scheme does not represent a new theory. Rather, our goal is only to distill existing frameworks into a very simple blueprint. Within our illustrative model, an event (process, outcome, or interpersonal treatment) is observed in a person's environment. The individual then compares this event with some standard of justice (e.g., equity, dignity, etc.). If the event does not match the standard, then all things being equal, one is apt to decide that an injustice has occurred. Other than the event itself, this schema contains two key elements. To make a justice judgment, a person requires (a) some standard of comparison and (b) a set of cognitive operations by which this standard is applied in a particular case.

These two elements—standards and operations—describe the two perspectives on just decision-making we alluded to earlier. The first perspective attempts to explicate the rules and principles that are used to gauge whether an outcome, process, or interpersonal encounter is unfair. The second perspective attempts to describe the cognitive steps that are used to make these judgments. As we shall see, some literature has already begun to address the first question. But just as important, the work of Ellard and Skarlicki (this volume) and Goldman and Thatcher (this volume) has begun to address the second.

An Initial Approach to Just Decision-Making: Specifying the Moral Standards that Produce (In)Justice

Like other human evaluations, deciding whether or not something is fair requires a point-of-view or frame of reference. In effect, the individual is answering the question: Fair with respect to what? (Though he or she would probably not put it that way.) While there has been a good deal of work on the different standards people use to answer such a question, two particular standards are especially relevant to moral decision-making: moral mandates (Skitka, in press; Skitka & Houston, in press; Skitka & Mullen, 2001) and ethical orientations (Schminke, Ambrose, & Noel, 1997). Let us review these frameworks in more detail.

Moral Mandates. Skitka and Mullen (2001) have raised an intriguing possibility. Consistent with other work (e.g., Rokeach, 1973), Skitka and Mullen observe that individuals are often deeply committed to certain core values. Given the importance of these values, individuals wish to express them in their day-to-day life and in their social and political beliefs. However, these value-expressions are often selective and incomplete. As an example, Skitka and Mullen consider a person committed to the sanctity of life. An individual might express this commitment by opposing legalized abortion. However, this same individual might also favor capital punishment, overlooking the possibility that it is inconsistent with the value of life. Likewise, a campus activist might be deeply committed to free speech, and express this value through artistic endeavors that challenge injustices within the prevailing social order. However, this same individual might support campus speech codes, which regulate "offensive" speech (cf., Kors & Silvergate, 1998).

As these examples illustrate, many (perhaps most) of us do not have fully consistent (Skitka and Mullen, 2001, use the term "constrained") belief systems. In particular, we pick and choose which attitudinal positions will be used to express our core values. In so doing, we may neglect other positions that would do equally well (at least in terms of value-consistency). The attitudinal positions that are chosen to express our values are called "moral mandates." These moral mandates are strongly held and difficult to change.

Skitka and Mullen's (2001) work has some important implications. While they do not deny the importance of values, they add a new dimension. In particular, Skitka and Mullen argue that moral mandates, the positions taken by individuals as an expression of their values, could be especially efficacious predictors of perceived justice. Evidence supports these ideas. For example, Skitka (in press) examined three attitude areas that sometimes act as moral mandates: abortion, civil rights, and immigration. Using a community sample, Skitka first identified people who either had a moral mandate (on either side of these issues) or who did not. In a second survey, she asked these respondents to imagine a decision about these issues that had been made by either (a) a state referendum or (b) the Supreme Court. When a decision went against a moral mandate, individuals tended to derogate the process (regardless of whether it was an election or a court decision), report low distributive fairness, and were unlikely to accept the decision. Indeed, strength of the moral mandate was a better predictor than were Time 1 judgments of procedural fairness. When the outcome involved a moral issue, it trumped other aspects of the decision-making process. Skitka and Mullen (2001) reported similar results.

Likewise, in two recent experiments Skitka and Houston (in press) examined participants' reactions to simulated verdicts in a murder trial. In both studies there were three levels of guilt: (a) clearly innocent, (b) clearly guilty, and (c) ambiguous. The accused was either treated with procedural fairness (e.g., a just trail) or unfairness (e.g., killed by a vigilante). Skitka and Houston (Study 1) found that individuals often view trial verdicts as moral mandates. Thus, they viewed the accused's treatment as more fair when it convicted a guilty person or acquitted an innocent person, and less fair when it acquitted a guilty person or convicted an innocent one. Thus, when the accused were either clearly innocent or clearly guilty, the outcome impacted fairness perceptions more than did the process. Conversely, when guilt or innocence was ambiguous, the fairness of the process was a stronger predictor of participant reactions.

Ethical Ideologies. Two especially interesting studies were reported by Schminke and colleagues (1997). These authors set out to integrate organizational justice theories with those in moral philosophy. Building on work by Brady (1985, 1990), Schminke and his colleagues identified two perspectives on business ethics. The first of these was utilitarianism, which focuses on the fairness of the outcomes that are received. According to utilitarianism, actions themselves are neither moral or immoral. Rather, morality is defined based on the impact these actions have on others. The second approach considered was formalism. Formalists maintain that certain modes of conduct are inherently immoral (e.g., lying), regardless of the outcomes they produce.

Schminke and colleagues (1997) argued that when an organization took steps to create distributive fairness, utilitarians would be especially likely to see this as justice. Similarly, steps to produce fair procedures should be especially appealing to ethical formalists. These effects were demonstrated in two studies, suggesting that people with different orientations make different judgments about environmental events. In terms of our earlier comments, utilitarians and formalists have different standards for evaluating fairness.

Summary. Both moral mandates and ethical orientations describe certain standards by which moral decisions can be made. In the case of moral standards, endorsement of a certain social or political position is taken as a manifestation of some core value. Violation of this position is a violation of the value and therefore a threat to the self (Skitka & Mullen, 2001). Consequently, individuals can become quite devoted to a moral mandate. The work of Schminke and his colleagues (1997) describes a more general mechanism. According to Schminke et al., ethical orientations influence the weighting given to various environmental events—outcomes receive importance for utilitarians and processes receive importance for formalists. Consequently, peoples' orientations tell them which *class* of events deserves the greater emphasis.

This is an intriguing distinction and merits further attention from scholars. It could be that individuals' normal proclivities are to first select relevant criteria for deciding whether an injustice has been committed. These criteria could further vary based on a person's ethical orientation. In particular, utilitarians might elect to examine the set of outcomes, while formalists might look to the set of processes. Once this first choice has been made, individuals might then look more closely at the event, picking out those notable elements that are most relevant. Thus, a utilitarian would more closely scrutinize a few specific outcomes relevant to a particular incident, while a formalist might do the same for a few particular processes. However, this two-step operation (if it occurs at all) could be short-circuited by a concrete challenge to a specific moral mandate. According to the evidence presented by Skitka (in press), the violation of a moral mandate could override the process by which the violation came about. Of course, we must admit that this is only speculation on our part. What we can say with greater confidence is that individuals evaluate fairness using certain standards, and that these standards are not identical for everyone.

A Second Approach to Just Decision Making: Processing Strategies for Fairness-Relevant Information

Having laid this background, we would like to take a closer look at the ideas presented by Ellard and Skarlicki (this volume) and Goldman and Thatcher (this volume). These authors present frameworks that examine how individuals decide whether an event or course of action is/was fair. The Ellard and Skarlicki chapter approaches the matter from the perspective of a third-party observer, while Goldman and Thatcher focus on the individual in some sort of encounter where justice could be (or could become) an issue. Although slightly different in perspective, these two chapters do an excellent job of describing dual-processing models of workplace fairness (for a similar discussion, see Bobocel, McCline, & Folger, 1997). According to these models, justice-relevant information can be processed in either a controlled/deliberate fashion, or in a manner that is automatic and heuristic.

These two chapters provide thorough reviews of the processing literature. Although there is little to add (at least, there's little that we could add!), what we will do instead is consider systematic and automatic processing in terms of the evaluative standards we discussed above. Put differently, it would be helpful to learn a bit more about the way that cognitive operations impact the use of moral principles. Based on the work of Ellard and Skarlicki (this volume) and Goldman and Thatcher (this volume), we suggest that there are at least two issues worthy of consideration.

Processing May Impact Which Standards Are Used. The first and most obvious possibility is that information processing demands may impact which ethical standards are employed. For instance, some principles may be less cognitively demanding than others. When one labors under a heavy cognitive load, he or she may resort to the simplest strategy available (Bobocel et al., 1997). In fact, if cognitive resources are scarce enough, individuals may yield their ethical judgment altogether. Goldman and Thatcher (this volume) provide an especially compelling argument when they view organizational justice through the lens of social information processing theory. These authors suggest that when an event is ambiguous, then individuals may rely more heavily on social information to decide whether or not an injustice has occurred. Rather than using specific ethical orientations or moral mandates, individuals may simply turn to others for their justice evaluations. In this case, no moral standard is being applied at all! Here the demands of the situation may override our better (ethical) judgment. More specifically, a given standard might not be employed if the situation is demanding. Instead, individuals may utilize various cognitive heuristics (Ellard & Skarlicki, this volume).

Conversely, there may be other times when situational demands make us *more* fair. Roch, Lane, Samuelson, Allison, and Dent (2000) provide an interesting example of this. These authors propose a two-stage model of resource overconsumption (which parallels Ellard & Skarlicki's and Goldman & Thatcher's Heuristic-Systematic Model of cognitive processing). In their model, individuals initially use an equality heuristic to make resource allocation decisions. However, if they are given the opportunity for more controlled/systematic processing, they will more carefully analyze the available information in order to adjust their request from equality in a self-serving direction. Thus, according to this model, individuals will be as self-serving as possible if they have the cognitive resources to do so, all other things being equal. Therefore, Roch and colleagues predicted that individuals under high cognitive load will remain in the first stage, allocating resources equally out of inadequate resources to assess available information that would lead them to act otherwise.

Roch and colleagues (2000) tested these hypotheses via a resource allocation task where individuals requested the amount of a $60 resource pool shared by eight people to be allocated to themselves. Under conditions of either high or low cognitive load, participants requested the amount they desired and verbalized the cognitions that led to their decisions. In support of the two-stage model, results indicated that participants under low cognitive load requested more resources for themselves. Also, the variance in requests of low load subjects was larger than the variance in requests of high load subjects (which closely approximated equality). Low load subjects were also found to make more verbal statements that attempted to justify their decision to give themselves a large percentage of the resource pool and the number of these verbalized cognitions increased as request size increased.

In a second study, Roch and colleagues (2000) explored whether social value orientation would interact with these effects. Roch proposed that the more cooperative people's value orientations, the more likely they would be to remain in the equality stage, even under conditions where they have the cognitive capacity to use more systematic processing to maximize their outcomes. Results confirmed this hypothesis. They found that even under conditions of low cognitive load, individuals with cooperative social value orientations voiced fewer intentions to adjust their decisions in a self-serving direction than individuals with more competitive social value orientations. Thus, those who were high in social value orientation tended not to be self-serving even when they were given sufficient opportunity.

Processing May Impact How Carefully a Given Standard is Applied. A second processing issue comes into play after a particular ethical orientation has been chosen. Given the evidence presented by Ellard and Skarlicki (this volume) and Goldman and Thatcher (this volume), it seems likely that individuals collect evidence more carefully when they are in a systematic as opposed to a heuristic mode. For example, Ellard and Skarlicki suggest that automatic processing may lead individuals to consider situational variables less fully. In this second case, individuals may consider situations in terms of justice, and even adhere to their principles, but they may do so in a less thorough fashion.

This idea might be easiest to illustrate with an example. Consider the case of an ethical utilitarian. Utilitarianism, when properly used, takes into account the interests of everyone impacted by a behavior (Singer, 1979; Velasquez, 1992). Considering justice from a utilitarian perspective could be quite demanding when one has to examine multiple stakeholders. In fact, one criticism of utilitarianism is that it is computationally demanding (Cropanzano & Grandey, 1998). Under demanding circumstances, individuals may consider fewer stakeholders than they do under less demanding circumstances. This is, of course, a matter for future inquiry. The key point is that processing type could impact the completeness with which we consider the ramifications of an event according to our own moral principles.

Component 3: Moral Motivation

An individual who has successfully navigated through components one (moral sensitivity) and two (moral judgement) knows that a moral decision is called for and that an injustice has been committed. If justice were the only consideration of importance, then we could skip this third component. However, as we have seen, individuals also value their self-interest. This sets the stage for conflicts between what we want and what we believe is right.

Self-Interest vs. Principles of Justice

When we ask ourselves about the effect of self-interest relative to the effect of social justice, we need to be very careful of how the question is framed. There is an important distinction here. Perhaps most obviously, an individual could recognize that he or she has been unfairly treated, while not allowing this fact to determine his or her subsequent behavior. For example, research on job choice decisions has found that procedural injustice during the selection process is often a less important consideration than are other factors (Ployhart & Ryan, 1997; Ployhart, Ryan, & Bennett, 1999). In this example, individuals acknowledge that things are not as fair as they could be, but still elect to accept the position. It is as if these individuals have weighed the three motives (economic self-interest vs. interpersonal relationships vs. moral principles) and are willing to accept a dearth of justice for a gain elsewhere. Moreover, as we have seen, there is evidence that individuals sometimes prefer favorable allocations, even when they are not as fair as other alternatives (e.g., Damon, 1977; Ordóñez et al., 2000). People sometimes acknowledge injustice, while doing nothing about it.

There is an additional way to frame the relationship between justice and self-interest. It is also possible for self-interest to impact whether or not an event is viewed as unfair to begin with. In other words, if an outcome is to a person's advantage, then it might come to be construed as just. In this situation, self-interest and justice are not in conflict. Rather, the latter determines the former. There is evidence for this self-interest effect in influencing fairness judgments (e.g., Ambrose, Harland, & Kulik, 1991; Conlon, 1993; Ployhart & Ryan, 1998; Wade-Benzoni et al., 1996). However, considerable research by Tyler and his colleagues (Tyler, 1991, 1994; for reviews see Tyler, 1997; Tyler & Smith, 1998; Tyler & Blader, 2000; Tyler & Lind, 1992) suggest that self-interest provides only a partial cause of justice perceptions.

As illustrated in Figure 2, these two questions are important but distinct from one another. Reading this figure from right to left, we first encounter path a. This path illustrates the impact of self-interest on work behavior. Notice there is also a path from justice to behavior, but the impact of justice works through a different route. The second possibility is illustrated in path b of Figure 2. As shown, path b runs from self-interest to justice perceptions. Tracing the causal path along this route, we see that self-interest continues to impact behavior, but justice mediates its effect.

Obviously, it is methodologically and conceptually important to distinguish between self-interest as a *competitor* with justice versus self-interest as a *cause* of justice. When these two research traditions are considered together, it seems that individuals are able to recognize an injustice (e.g., Tyler, 1997), but they sometimes choose to ignore this recognition in favor of other concerns (Ployhart & Ryan, 1997). It would be interesting for

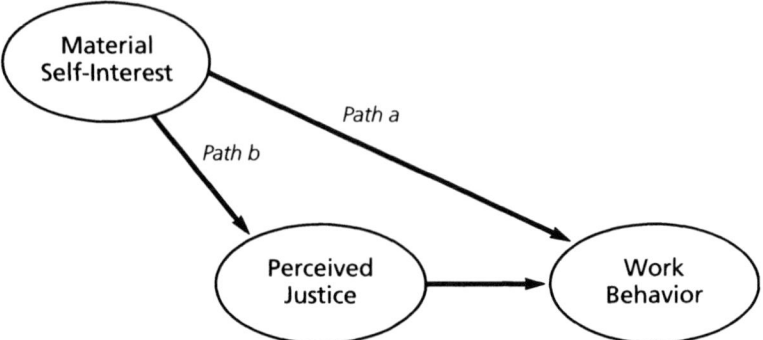

Figure 2. The relationship of self-interest and just principles to work behavior.

future research to distinguish the circumstances under which each effect is most likely.

How Self-interest Can Serve the Cause of Justice. Organizations sometimes pursue economic gains and forgo justice (Cropanzano, Chrobot-Mason, Rupp, & Prehar, in press; Ermann & Lundman, 1987). In his recent book, Schlosser (2001) explores certain injustices within the American fast food industry. For instance, in the pursuit of wider profit margins there are organizations that compromise work safety, discourage unionization, and may violate labor laws. At least for these firms, justice seems to be a secondary consideration.

On the other hand, there are also cases where profit motivates individuals toward constructive social change. Sowell (1995, see his Chapter 5), for example, examines the system of apartheid in South Africa. In the interest of profit, white businesspeople often skirted apartheid laws by hiring more native African workers than were allowed. They also placed them into higher-level management positions than were legally acceptable. When it was to their advantage, South African realtors could be equally dismissive of "whites only" policies. Indeed, in some cases so much land was sold to native Africans that they became the numerical majority in areas nominally reserved for whites. Notice that there is no evidence that these white businesspeople and realtors were any more egalitarian than other South African whites. Perhaps they were, perhaps they weren't. More to the point here: Their actions were motivated, at least in a large measure, by the quest for profit. Nonetheless, these self-interested actions produced positive social consequences.

Though economic gain and ethical justice are often at odds, it is not the case that they *always* are. This suggests that organizations could arrange financial incentives for acting justly. For instance, one could tie managers' compensation to the achievement of equitable diversity goals (Cropanzano, Chrobot-Mason, et al., in press). In a related vein, Bethell (1998) discusses how free market interventions can be used to increase environmental responsibility. There is nothing inherently wrong with individuals' pursing their self-interests, as long as they are also concerned with the needs of the collective (the relational and contemporary social exchange models) and with moral principles (the deontological model). To the extent that these three motives are aligned (e.g., in an ethical culture that rewards organizational members for behaving fairly toward others), then just actions are most likely.

So, Should We Leave Everything to Profit? While incentive systems for just behavior have a place (Cropanzano, Chrobot-Mason, et al., in press), we would not recommend that organizations rely entirely (or even mostly) on financial incentives. There are at least three considerations that are likely to curtail severely the effectiveness of such a strategy.

First, as we have argued throughout this chapter, material self-interest is only one motivator of just behavior, and it may not be the strongest (cf. Tyler & Smith, 1998). Consequently, encouraging moral development, perhaps through education (McNeel, 1994), training (Rest, 1994) and role-taking (Sprinthall, 1994) is likely to be as or more effective in the long run. Likewise, the professionalization of occupations can be valuable, so long as the profession actively promotes ethical considerations (Bebeau, 1994).

Second, relying entirely on incentives to promote ethical justice provides a misleading understanding of what morality is all about. While we like to believe that the world is a fair place (Lerner, 1980; Lerner & Miller, 1978), this is a dubious contention (Sowell, 1999). In fact, if ethics were always economically rational, then moral principles and self-interest would always be in alignment. If this were the case, then there would be fewer ethical dilemmas and probably more justice. The philosopher Joshua Halberstam (1993) states the matter more eloquently:

> When it comes to the important things in life, moral goodness seems to matter even less. Very bad things do happen to very good people, and vice versa. Think of the decent couple with the severely retarded child, or the wonderful woman in the prime of her life brought down by breast cancer, or the industrious, talented worker fired unjustly from his job. And very good things happen to very bad people. Think of the scoundrel enjoying the winter days on his yacht in the Caribbean. The memory of the suffering he has inflicted on others doesn't disturb his peace of mind one bit. (p. 168)

Third, using financial incentives, to the exclusion of other types of growth experiences, equates moral actions with profitable ones. Employees may learn the lesson that "what is right is what pays." To the extent that this occurs, it would clearly undermine moral growth rather than facilitate it. It is inevitable that individuals will encounter opportunities to cheat or bend the rules to their advantage. Thus, organizations should encourage individuals to be responsible moral actors in their own right, even when a supervisor is not looking over their shoulders with a financial bonus. Managers and employees need to internalize responsibility to their peers as well as a commitment to ethical principles.

Given considerations of these kinds, we do not rule out the judicious use of economic incentives as a tool for promoting justice, but we also do counsel caution. If, as we have asserted in this chapter, justice is not only about self-interest but also about moral principles, then an organization that reduces these principles to economic gain—without simultaneously encouraging moral maturity among its workforce—may find itself disappointed in the results. Clearly, more research is necessary for us to specify when financial incentives are best for encouraging just behavior and when they should be avoided altogether.

Component 4: Moral Action

One of the more discouraging aspects about work life is that an individual can recognize an injustice (Component #1), make a principled judgment (Component #2), weigh injustice above self-interest (Component #3), and still *not* take any requisite action. Somehow the intention to do the right thing is never transformed into a coherent sequence of action steps. This is a classic problem of human motivation, and it is especially likely to occur when the necessary action steps are complicated (for a more complete discussion, see Cropanzano et al., 1993). Unfortunately, this topic has not been extensively considered within the literature on organizational justice. Thus, we will offer two speculative suggestions based on research exploring human self-regulation (e.g., Vallacher & Wegner, 1985).

Lack of Skill

The most self-evident problem is a lack of skill. The "right thing" is sometimes difficult to execute. For instance, managers might not know how to provide respectful and socially sensitive behaviors recommended by interactional justice research. Likewise, supervisors may sometimes design unfair processes because they do not know the principles of formal procedural justice. If lack of skill is a problem, and it almost certainly is in some settings, then well-designed training programs could provide an effective remedy. This possibility was explored in two studies conducted by Skarlicki and Latham (1996, 1997). These researchers trained union shop stewards to be more procedurally and interactionally just. As a consequence of this training, workers showed heightened levels of organizational citizenship behaviors.

A related training problem has more to do with processes than with people. Organizations often attempt to promote justice by providing workers with formal policies, precedents, and rules (e.g., Sitkin & Bies, 1993; Sitkin & Roth, 1993). While these procedures can, of course, yield many benefits, they can also become complex and difficult to use (Cropanzano & Byrne, 2001). Given this complexity, managers might simply not know the procedures to, say, dismiss a problem employee or file a sexual harassment complaint. For this reason, organizations often need to teach managers to use their particular policies. (Handing out an employee handbook with dozens of pages of small print is often not enough.) As an illustration of this, consider a quasi-experimental study conducted by Taylor, Tracy, Renard, Harrison, and Carroll (1995). Taylor and her colleagues implemented a new performance appraisal program for a government agency. Among other things, they trained workers and managers to use the system. Though the average performance rating of employees decreased somewhat, worker reactions to the new system were superior to those of the older procedure.

Lack of Power

Individuals often endure injustice because other options are closed to them (Meara, 2001). For example, in the United States, certain manufacturing plants are known to employ undocumented alien workers. Complaints from these workers could lead to retaliation (Schlosser, 2001). Immigrant workers, documented or not, are vulnerable to exploitation. As these individuals are often recent arrivals, they may lack the financial resources to pursue legal action, may not be aware of their rights within the United States, and in some cases cannot speak English well enough to avail themselves of alternative possibilities. As a consequence, these workers often endure low pay and unsafe working conditions. Likewise, many single parents (mostly but not entirely mothers) live in poverty (Bennett, 1994). Under these conditions, young women feel compelled to accept almost any opportunity for paid work. The general decline of unions among the American workforce (Schor, 1991) has further weakened workers' ability to bargain from a position of strength. Conditions such as these can promote a sense of futility. Employees may take no action because they sense that it will do no good.

Conclusions

Implementing justice requires skills and power, among other things. When these ingredients are lacking, individuals may fail to act fairer, despite a clear-headed recognition of the moral issues and good faith intentions to behave morally. To understand why this is the case, it would behoove researchers to consider building a comprehensive theory of just behavior. Such a theory could build on existing models of work motivation (e.g., Cropanzano et al., 1993; Vallacher & Wegner, 1985) and may result in justice-enhancing interventions (such as those recommended by Skarlicki & Latham, 1996, 1997; and Taylor et al., 1995).

THE THREE ROADS IN CONTEMPORARY JUSTICE RESEARCH

Thus far our comments have been oriented around the three roads to organizational justice: self-interested models, interpersonal models, and deontological models that emphasize moral principles. Given their recent development and concomitant importance, we have paid special attention to ethical issues. In particular, we used Rest's (1979, 1984, 1994) four-component model to describe how justice perceptions are (or are not) translated into just actions. Where have these ideas taken us? In this final section we will address this issue in detail. In keeping with the nature of this chapter as a commentary, we will apply our model to chapters in this volume we have yet to discuss and, in particular, chapters that place an emphasis on applied issues.

Mikula and the Three Roads to Task Assignment

We begin with Mikula's chapter (this volume) on the assignment of work tasks. We will start here, because this chapter provides a good illustration of two of the three motives for organizational justice. In his chapter on justice and the organization of work, Mikula presents an interesting thesis regarding the perceived fairness of the process and outcomes of task distribution methods. This is indeed an important topic that has yet to be directly addressed in the justice literature. The distribution of tasks is certainly among the most prominent processes that occur in work organizations. Therefore, findings suggesting that distributive, procedural, and interactional justice of task assignments affect organizational outcomes such as performance on, commitment to, and satisfaction with the tasks would have serious implications for organizational practitioners.

Moreover, there is a profound timeliness about Mikula's work. As the nature of work has evolved, the jobs held by individuals have become dynamic, boundryless, and increasingly hard to define (Anderson, Rupp, & Thornton, 2001; Lees & Cordery, 2000; Sanchez, 1994). Thus, implementing fair task distribution rules (e.g., collaboration, turn-taking, specialization with reciprocation) and avoiding task distribution rules perceived as unfair (e.g., nonreciprocated specialization, threshold of necessity) may be increasingly important (and challenging) in the years ahead.

Task Assignment and Self-Interest

It is perhaps easiest to conceptualize the distribution of tasks from a self-interest or instrumental perspective. This is because reactions to task assignments can be easily thought of in equity terms. This is especially the case when one is studying how household chores are distributed. As Mikula demonstrates, there are certain tasks that some people may just *not* want to do (we both are personally opposed to cleaning both toilets and ovens). Therefore out of self-interest, individuals may actively avoid certain tasks they perceive as unfavorable, or, given the norm that "somebody has to do it," may complete the tasks but ensure that others do extra work or carry out equally unfavorable tasks such that equity is restored. Similar mandatory but stereotypically negative tasks exist in organizations, such as completing paper work.

What is interesting, however, is that there will be other tasks that are more favorable from a self-interest perspective. For example, individuals sometimes seek tasks that are highly visible and offer opportunities for rewards. At other times, certain duties may just be fun. Thus, the jobs we do at work are often bundles of pleasant and not-so-pleasant activities. This observation raises interesting justice considerations. To what extent do individuals attend to the package of assignments? For instance, if one person has to perform two moderately unpleasant tasks, is he or she better or worse off than one who has a very pleasant and a very unpleasant task? Understanding the calculus of these justice judgments could be an interesting area for future research.

Task Assignment and Relational Concerns

In his 1970 book, the influential Social Psychologist Daryl Bem accounts a true story from the 1960s:

> Consider, for example, the first student rebellion at Columbia University, which took place in the spring of 1968. You will recall that students from the radical left took over some administration buildings in the name of equalitarian ideas which they accused the university of flouting.... But no sooner had they occupied the buildings than the male militants blandly turned to their sisters-in-arms and assigned them the task of preparing food, while they—the menfolk—would presumably plan further strategy. (p. 89)

Bem's (1970) account is telling. In large measure, it demonstrates how our stereotypes can overcome our better judgment, and this occurs even among people who should know better. But, more subtly, it also tells us something about task assignments. Some activities are highly valued within a social group. They could be said to convey full standing. Taking a leadership role in strategic planning is one such task. Other tasks are relegated to the less powerful. Acquiring food or coffee would fall into this latter category (at least for many Americans). The lesson here is an important one. The tasks an individual does (or is allowed to do) convey a message about his or her position within a valued group. Furthermore, as suggested by the group-value/relational model (Lind, 1995; Lind & Tyler, 1988; Tyler,

1997; Tyler & Lind, 1992; Tyler & Smith, 1998; Tyler, Degoey, & Smith, 1996), information about group standing is relevant to justice evaluations.

This leads to some interesting hypotheses regarding justice. A task that is indicative of high standing, even if it is difficult, might be highly sought after. Therefore, an employee being assigned the extra (but esteemed) work may recognize this reasoning and perceive the assignment as fair even though the tasks may be unfavorable and inequitable. Indeed, someone may feel unfairly treated because they do not have enough to do!

Conclusions

Mikula's chapter raises some important issues for justice theorists. That having been said, we should not lose sight of its importance for practitioners as well. In the workplace of the future, where loosely defined jobs and floating task assignments become increasingly common, the issues raised by Mikula will become all the more pressing.

Korsgaard and Sapienza on the Ethics of Agency

Korsgaard and Sapienza's chapter (this volume) provides an insightful contrast of agency theory and procedural justice theory in the context of an illustrative case study about the relationship between entrepreneurs and venture capitalists. In keeping with a good deal of the organizational justice literature, these scholars focus on two reasons why fairness is important: it is instrumental to self-interest and it is indicative of standing within a group. We found their analyses to be insightful and valuable.

Interestingly, Korsgaard and Sapienza's approach to justice differed from our own in one significant respect. Whereas these authors focused on two roads to justice (self-interest and interpersonal relationships), we have framed our entire chapter around the three approaches to organizational justice (instrumental, interpersonal, and deontological). In our view, the deontological model in no way compromises the high quality of Korsgaard and Sapienza's work. However, it would be useful to ascertain whether or not a consideration of deontology could extend their work on agency theory. With regard to principal-agent relationships, we can state the question this way: Might parties treat each other fairly, and thereby develop a sense of interpersonal trust, out of a commitment to a code of interpersonal conduct? We think the answer is yes, although we confess that this is somewhat speculation on our part. To explore this notion, let's first look to the moral codes held by two types of "collectives."

Cultural Groups

In their chapter, Stone and Stone-Romero (this volume) review evidence suggesting that religious values can shape standards of justice. James (1993) and McFarlin and Sweeney (2001) make similar points with respect to culture. Taken together, these papers raise the possibility that at least some groups of people are likely to behave fairly and ethically even when they cannot be actively monitored. In other words, a moral code can be internalized and, as such, come to serve as an ethical navigator.

One interesting example of this can be found in the case of Russia's Baltic Germans. According to Sowell (1996) these Germans were prized for government service because they were believed to be scrupulously honest. In a similar vein, Fukuyama (1995) argues that some national cultures, such as those of Japan and Germany, have high zones of trust. That is, individuals are especially likely to trust someone outside of their immediate family. This level of trust, Fukuyama argues, is useful for developing large business organizations. In effect, principles can delegate authority to agents with greater confidence that these agents will fulfill their obligations.

From these cross-cultural examples, it seems likely that groups of individuals are capable of forming collective sets of moral values which provide a rule structure that group members can abide by in an open-ended way. Our point here is not that some cultures are somehow "better" and others "worse." Rather, we wish to convey a more modest idea. From this evidence it seems that at least some agents, at least some of the time, will behave in accordance with ethical principles.

Professional Associations

Even if one accepts the evidence presented thus far, it is primarily relevant for *between* culture comparisons. It is useful to ascertain if there are any differences *within* cultures that might support the deontological view. Evidence suggests that values are spawned by a sense of professional identity resulting from codes of conduct and ethical guidelines that professions collectively impose on themselves. For example, within the United States many Industrial/Organizational Psychologists have internalized a code of behavior set forth by the SIOP Principles (1987), the SHRM Code of Ethics (1999), the Academy of Management Standards (2001), the APA Standards (1999), and the APA Code of Conduct (1992). In the same manner, professionals such as venture capitalists also internalize norms of behavior shared by the profession in which they practice. Notice our use of the term *internalization*. This is to say, professionals may not only attempt to be fair and trustworthy because their group-affiliation is important to them (this would be a social-identity or group-value account for justice). Instead, it seems likely that over time professionals come to internalize the moral code affiliated with their professional identity and consequently act in accordance with it, not only for self-serving reasons, not only to enhance their group standing, but because they truly feel it is *the right thing to do*. Thus, we feel the addition of deontological fairness motives, stemming from notions of professional identity, may be a useful and informative addition to Korsgaard and Sapienza's model.

Conclusions

Korsgaard and Sapienza (this volume) have demonstrated that self-interest, though important, provides an incomplete understanding of why agents fulfill their obligations to principles. Based on the group-value/relational model, they argue that interpersonal trust is also an important element. We concur, but would add that many people fulfill their obligations simply because they view it as the right thing to do. These individuals have internalized some code of business that allows them to monitor their own behavior. These codes are helpful, because they empower individuals to behave as moral actors. Moreover, this sense of normative justice can transcend self-interest, to be sure, but also the bonds of a particular social group.

Vermunt and Knowing What *Really* Hurts

Like the previously discussed chapters, Vermunt (this volume) makes both a theoretical and practical contribution to our knowledge of organizational justice. According to Vermunt's model, stress is caused by an insufficient allocation of resources (i.e., a discrepancy between ones capabilities and the demands placed on him or her). These problems become even greater when an employee is treated interpersonally unfairly. In addition, the role of the supervisor is crucial to fairness' additive effect on stress because it is the supervisor who allocates resources, makes demands, and potentially mistreats the employee.

Viewing Vermunt's (this volume) chapter in the context of the three approaches to organizational fairness raises an interesting issue. What is it that *really* hurts about injustice at work? Our three motives raise the possibility, albeit very tentatively, that workers may be hurt when (a) their instrumental self-interest is unmet, (b) when valuable relationships are disrupted (in Lind's, 2001, terms, when their "standing" is compromised), and (c) when they recognize their treatment violates some moral norm. Vermunt's analysis touches on the first two of these possibilities, but we will argue that it is also consistent with the third. To know what *really* hurts, it's useful to consider all three.

Stress and Self-Interest

Vermunt argues convincingly that our reactions are partially influenced by self-interest. As Vermunt explains, when the demands placed on us exceed our perceived ability to cope, we may begin to experience stress. For example, individuals who experience demands from both work and family are likely to suffer ill-feelings and poor health (Grandey & Cropanzano, 1999; Grzywacz & Marks, 2000). Many of these stressors can be self-interested in the most economic form. For instance, the very poor report lower levels of life satisfaction (though the benefits of money level off quickly, see Myers & Diener, 1995).

Stress and Interpersonal Relationships

Vermunt (this volume) suggests that the relationship a supervisor has with subordinates plays a crucial role in affecting both employee stress and subsequent behavior. We are very sympathetic to this observation (Rupp & Cropanzano, in press). We have recently found that social exchange relationships formed with one's supervisor mediated the relationship between perceived fairness of the supervisor and important organizational outcomes benefiting both the supervisor and the organization. We feel the supervisor-employee relationship is an important avenue of inquiry, especially as it relates to employee stress and its consequences.

Of more direct relevance to Vermunt's thesis is evidence amassed by stress researchers. These scholars have found that interpersonal phenomenon that involve elements of injustice (e.g., discrimination, conflict) tend to produce stress symptoms. To take one noteworthy example, James, Lavato, and Khoo (1994) explored how workers' social identities affected their health. This study showed that minority workers employed by primarily nonminority organizations often perceived themselves to have low social status in the organization. These individuals also felt that they faced obstacles to gaining and maintaining positive work relationships and in-group membership. As a result, the James and colleagues data revealed a connection between such perceptions and both high blood pressure and self-reported health symptoms. This would suggest that the relational components outlined in social identity theory and the group-value model may be important for further understanding workplace stress.

An additional piece of evidence comes from research on stress and mood by Bolger, DeLongis, Kessler, and Schilling (1989). This study found that interpersonal conflicts were by far the most distressing events of all potential stressors studied. As Vermunt's model suggests, interpersonal conflict with regard to employee stress may arise in many forms. Managers and subordinates may find themselves in conflict because of resources allocated (by the supervisor) and expected (by the employee). In addition, supervisors may find themselves in conflict with their authorities who expect them to have their subordinates complete as much work as possible with as few resources as possible. As Vermunt explains, supervisors are often caught in a precarious position of being both an *allocator* and an *allocatee*, which puts them at increased risk of interpersonal conflict, stress, and the severe consequences associated with each.

Lastly, Folkman, Lazarus, Gruen, and DeLongis (1986) found that individuals high on interpersonal trust had better somatic health than individuals low in interpersonal trust. Although trust was used as a personality variable in this study, the construct has been explored a great deal in research on justice and social exchange relationships (Deckop, Mangel, &

Cirka, 1999; Konovsky & Pugh, 1994). It seems that trust may have the ability to reduce stress both directly, via its effects on health, and indirectly, by reducing the potential for perceived injustice. Being that trust is a crucial element to any social exchange relationship, it seems that exploring the fairness-stress relationship from a relational or interpersonal perspective may be quite informative.

While none of these studies is singularly conclusive, taken together they provide support for Vermunt's (this volume) ideas. In particular, it seems that individuals experience stress when they suffer interpersonal ill-treatment (e.g., discrimination and conflict) and feel more comfortable when they are in trusting relationships.

Stress and Deontology

At the outset we note that there is very little evidence suggesting that deontology is related to stress. Nevertheless, we feel that such an inquiry is warranted. In particular, the literature suggests that there are two possibilities. The first is that injustice directly causes stress through the violation of an important moral value. The second possibility is subtler. It suggests that strongly held principles may be psychologically comforting in times of travail. In the following paragraphs, we will discuss both possibilities.

Stress and the Violation of Moral Standards. Skitka and Mullen (2001) recently proposed that a threat to moral values threatens one's self-identity. By extension, these threats could propose psychological and perhaps physical stress. At the present time, the evidence for this thesis is indirect, but generally consistent with Skitka and Mullen's hypotheses. For example, Weiss, Sukow, and Cropanzano (1999) conducted a laboratory study examining negative emotions and stress. These authors found that individuals who lost a desirable outcome due to an injustice felt anger. Conversely, those participants who benefited from injustice reported guilt. Finally, when individuals lost in a fair process, they reported lower levels of anger and guilt. These findings, which were replicated by Krehbiel and Cropanzano (2000), suggest that the same negative event can produce harsher emotional states when it is coupled with injustice. Would such emotions persist over time, then they might gradually produce stress.

Deontology and the Quest for Meaning. Another possibility is that moral principles may provide a buffer or shelter from negative events. When this buffer is lacking, individuals may experience stress. As we have argued elsewhere, internalizing and abiding by moral principles helps provide one's life with a sense of meaning and purpose (Cropanzano, Byrne et al., 2001a). This sense of meaning may have practical benefits, at least under some circumstances (cf. Paloutzian & Kirkpatrick, 1995). In this regard, Tomaka and Blascovich (1994) conducted two noteworthy experiments.

These scholars examined participants' reactions to potentially difficult laboratory tasks. Tomaka and Blascovich discovered that those who believed the world was basically just tended to report less stress and display more modest autonomic responses. Those who were lower in just world beliefs tended to report more stress and displayed more extreme autonomic responses. Apparently, the sense that "in the end everything will work out as it should" offered some comfort.

Conclusions

Vermunt (this volume) has taken organizational justice theory into the domain of occupational health. This is an especially creative area of inquiry. Moreover, this line of research has great promise for promoting more humane work organizations. When we consider Vermunt's work in view of our three motives, and in view of the relevant literature of work stress, we strongly suspect that self-interest and interpersonal motives might be important. Given the dearth of deontological research, we are less certain that the violation of moral standards produces stress. However, a strong circumstantial case can be made (e.g., by Skitka & Mullen, 2001), and we would recommend further research.

Kulik and Holbrook on Medical Practices

Kulik and Holbrook (this volume) present an insightful model explaining how fair treatment from doctors affects patient compliance to prescribed medical regimens. Changes in the health care industry, including the rise of managed care and other third-party payers, have produced a trade-off between patient service and economic rationality. As Kulik and Holbrook put it, there is a need to increase the "cost effectiveness" of medical care. We agree with Kulik and Holbrook's observations about recent and on-going changes in the health care industry. However, we would like to step further back in history in order to describe the problem in a different way. That is, we argue that the historical role of the physician as a professional healer within Western society has shaped *patient* expectations regarding the doctor-patient relationship (May, 1983). However, advances in bioscience and medicine have affected *doctors* expectations away from this traditional model. Consequently, we feel that a possible source of patient noncompliance is the differential relational expectations between these two parties. To outline this thesis, we must first consider medical practices prior to the 1900s.

The Historical Roots of Scientific Medicine

American medical history can be treated positively (i.e., early physicians were close to their patients) or negatively (i.e., early physicians were not especially knowledgeable). These two views, as we shall argue, are not mutually exclusive. Let us first consider the more sanguine view of things. There was a time when the presence of a physician comforting the family at the bedside of a sick child would have surprised no one. The practice of house calls continued well into the twentieth century. When compared to our times, the erstwhile relationship between physicians and their clientele was probably more egalitarian. While doctors were respected members of the community, they enjoyed less social status than did clergy and lawyers (Bettman, 1974) and may have earned as little as a mechanic (Berliner, 1976). Hence, the distinct social status enjoyed by physicians with respect to the rest of society was not yet established.

But there was a less flattering view of the pre-1900 physician, stemming from a general ignorance of much of the medical knowledge we have today. For example, doctors of the 1800s did not even wash their hands between surgeries, as this practice was viewed as "unmanly" (Dawes, 1994). The fact that the hospital infant death rate was over four times that of midwife assisted births did little to dissuade doctors from their unhygienic practices. At the same time, physicians continued to use rusted instruments, and to keep their sutures in their lapels, or, for convenience, their teeth (Bettman, 1974). Prior to 1900, medical diagnosis was based primarily on guesswork and any therapy was largely unreliable. Scientific training for physicians was very limited in the United States (Berliner, 1976). In fact, in the late 1800s, Harvard Medical School had no formal exams because the majority of the medical students had very poor literacy skills (Bettman, 1974).

However, as medical knowledge began to increase, the scientific community began to respond. One response was the formation of the American Medical Association (AMA). Established in 1947, the AMA sought to address concerns regarding "bad practices" by supporting (among other things) a greater emphasis on scientific and technical skills (Starr, 1982).[4] Such efforts gained even more momentum from a 1910 Carnegie Foundation report (for details, see Flexner, 1910). In this document, the foundation issued a scathing critique of medical schools that did not have a scientific curriculum. This report strengthened the AMA's efforts to accredit medical schools (Berliner, 1975). Henceforth, science would become a major component of professional medical training.

As we shall see in the next section, the particular scientific trend adopted by the medical community tended to de-emphasize the close relational models that existed in the pre-scientific era. As a consequence, society bought instrumental benefits at an interpersonal price. Of course, the fact that one becomes more "scientific" does not necessitate that one becomes less relational. However, it is important to recognize that science is not a purely objective undertaking. Individual and social values inform scientific investigation and application. The problem was not with science per se, but rather with the modern medical community's understanding of what it meant to be "scientific" (Starr, 1982). The emphasis on "hard" science, as opposed to "soft" people skills, came about for three reasons.

Three Reasons Why Scientific Professionalization May Compromise Interpersonal Relationships

Modern Medicine's Use of the Machine Metaphor. According to Starr (1982), physicians, like many Western thinkers, have historically been trained in mind-body dualism. That is, they see the two as separate entities. Moreover, the job of a professional healer is to treat the body. In this regard, the body is often likened to a machine that is in need of repair. This analogy, of course, separates human beings from their sociocultural context. Likewise, it affords less room for interpersonal relationships in the context of physical health.

Medical Practices Seen As "Relational" Were No Longer Practical. Prior to 1900, doctors may have proffered more interpersonal support because they had fewer scientific and technical skills to offer instead. To take an obvious example, house calls were more practical in an era when the physician had few tools and no access to modern testing equipment. They are less practical in an era of blood samples, X-Ray machines, and MRI scans. As a consequence, the emphasis on relationships (from the doctor's point of view) began to wane. Nevertheless, the history of medicine established a *relational* norm with regards to patients' expectations of doctors, a norm which continues to frame patient expectations today.

Nonrelational, Science-based Practice Is Viewed by Doctors as Ethical. Professional physicians are very concerned with ethical codes (May, 1983) and ethical training (Self & Baldwin, 1994). The issue at hand is not ethics in general, but rather a particular type of ethics that is rooted in a particular understanding of medical care. If the human body is a machine to be maintained through the application of objective science, then interpersonal relationships are potentially risky. This is because these relationships could produce a conflict of interest that compromises the doctor's objectivity. Consequently, doctors sometimes keep a certain "professional distance" from their clientele. Of course, a different view of science might well have produced a different set of behaviors.

Current Perspectives

To summarize, prior to 1900, medical practitioners were certainly less scientific than their modern counterparts. However, these pre-scientific healers were reputed to be more interpersonally oriented and better acquainted with their patients. With this history in mind, we can revisit the instrumental and interpersonal approaches to justice within the context of medical practice. From the perspective of the physician, a more scientific approach makes medical treatments fair, in the sense that it improves the quality of care (in our present jargon, the instrumentalites are more favorable to the patient this way). However, the interpersonal cost falls largely on the patient. That is, where doctors may view themselves as being more fair than their historical counterparts, patients coming from an interpersonal perspective may view such treatment as less fair.

By extension, we should note that managed care, and its ancillary effects, emerge from this social context. Recall that this understanding of "scientific" medical care views the body as a sort of organic machine that can be meaningfully separated from the rest of the person. Within this sort of conceptual framework, it is relatively easy to treat medical services as a commodity that is provided on the open market and subject to economic considerations (cf. Freund & McGuire, 1991). Thus, managed care may not be the only cause of the concerns identified by Kulik and Holbrook (this volume). Instead, it may be the most recent manifestation of a more systemic problem.

We found Kulik and Holbrooks's contribution a unique and practical approach to applied justice research. In the final analysis, our comments only further underscore the importance of research in this area. Justice might not entirely solve the problem, but it would be a useful start. At the very least, it may offer us a new perspective on the doctor/patient relationship.

Some Closing Thoughts

This chapter has covered a lot of ground since we first considered Seurat's *Grande Jatte*. By stepping away from the canvas, we observed places for three motives—self-interest, interpersonal relationships, and moral principles. Emphasizing deontology, we discussed how justice considerations are translated into moral actions, paying special attention to cognitive processing. Finally, we applied this model to the applied issues raised by the contributors to this book. Along the way, we passed Buddhism, Joan of Arc, and the students' rights movement of the 1960s. We illustrated our key points with examples from South African real estate sales, medical history, and the American fast food industry. Justice, as we have seen, is a pervasive element of human social life. It pervades much of what we do and feel.

We care about justice for a variety of reasons. In the long run, it is likely to yield beneficial outcomes and is indicative of full standing in social collectives. While there is no denying the importance of these considerations, our review of the justice literature further suggests that deontological concerns—a sense of ourselves as principled actors—are also an important part of organizational justice. Consequently, some people, some times, are moved to behave morally because they view it as the right thing to do.

NOTES

1. Batson (1991, 1995) reviews this model in the context of prosocial behavior. This is related, though not identical with, just behavior (Batson, 1996). Regardless, the two literatures have influenced one another, and the mood enhancement model is very similar for both justice and altruism. For instance, when articulating his position, Greenberg (2001) cites the work of Batson. The principal difference between Batson's viewpoint and that of Greenberg is that the former seems relatively more skeptical of the mood enhancement model than the latter. Based on the findings of several studies, Batson argues that the mood enhancement effect does not provide a complete account of prosocial human behavior (e.g., Batson, Batson, Griffitt, Barrientos, Brandt, Sprengelmeyer, & Bayly, 1989; Batson, Dyck, Brandt, Batson, McMaster, & Griffitt, 1988; Dovidio, Allen, & Schroeder, 1990; Dovidio, Piliavin, Gaertner, Schroeder, & Clark, 1991).

2. Fortunately, the female students did substantially better. McNeel reports that their insights helped enlighten many of their male peers.

3. In their research, Bebeau and her colleagues prefer to use the term "ethical sensitivity" rather than "moral sensitivity." The two concepts are quite similar, and the use of one rather than the other will not change the conclusions drawn here. Given this, we elected to use the term "moral sensitivity" throughout.

4. The AMA's early efforts had a dark side. They tended to oppose legitimate competitors, such as homeopathy (Fruend & McGuire, 1991). Likewise, they also worked to discourage the entry of women and African Americans into the medical profession (Starr, 1982).

REFERENCES

Academy of Management. (2001). *Standards of Professional Conduct for Academic/Management Consultants.* http://csep.iit.edu/coe/amdmc-a.htm.

Ajzen, I. (1988). *Attitudes, personality, and behavior.* Chicago: Dorsey Press.

Ambrose, M.L., Harland, L.K., & Kulik, C.T. (1991). Influence of social comparisons on perceptions of organizational fairness. *Journal of Applied Psychology, 76,* 239-246.

American Educational Research Association, American Psychological Association, and National Council of Measurement in Education. (1999). *Standards for educational and psychological tests.* Washington, DC: American Educational Research Association.

American Psychological Association. (December, 1992). Ethical principles of psychologists and code of conduct. *American Psychologist.*

Anderson, L., Rupp, D.E., Thornton, G.C. III (2001). *Selecting people for the 21st century: Issues for the high tech industry and the impact of technology on today's organizations.* Manuscript in preparation.

Avolio, B.J. (1999). *Full leadership development: Building the vital forces in organizations.* Thousand Oaks, CA: Sage.

Barnhart, C.L. (1958). (Ed.). *Thorndike—Barnhart comprehensive desk dictionary* (Vol. I). Garden City, NY: Doubleday & Company.

Batson, C.D. (1991). *The altruism question: Toward a social psychological answer.* Hillsdale, NJ: Erlbaum.

Batson, C.D. (1995). Prosocial motivation: Why do we help others? In A. Tesser (Ed.), *Advanced social psychology* (pp. 332-381). New York: McGraw-Hill.

Batson, C.D. (1996). Empathy, altruism, and justice: Another perspective on partiality. In L. Montada & M. J. Lerner (Eds.), *Current societal issues about justice* (pp. 49-66). New York: Plenum.

Batson, C.D., Batson, J.G., Griffitt, C.A., Barrientos, S., Brandt, J.R., Sprengelmeyer, P., & Bayly, M.J. (1989). Negative-state relief and the empathy-altruism hypothesis. *Journal of Personality and Social Psychology, 61*, 413-426.

Batson, C.D., Dyck, J.L., Brandt, J.R., Batson, J.G., Powell, A.L., McMaster, M.R., & Griffitt, C. (1988). Five studies testing two new egoistic alternatives to the empathy-altruism hypothesis. *Journal of Personality and Social Psychology, 55*, 52-77.

Bazerman, M.H. (1998). *Judgment in managerial decision making.* New York: John Wiley & Sons.

Bazerman, M.H., & Neale, M.A. (1992). *Negotiating rationally.* New York: The Free Press.

Bazerman, M.H., Schroth, H.A., Shah, P.P., Diekmann, K.A., & Tenbrunsel, A.E. (1994). The inconsistent role of comparison others and procedural justice in reactions to hypothetical job descriptions: Implications for job acceptance decisions. *Organizational Behavior and Human Decision Processes, 60*, 326-352.

Bebeau, M.J. (1994). Influencing the moral dimensions of dental practice. In J.R. Rest & D. Narvaez (Eds.), *Moral development in the professions* (pp. 121-146). Hillsdale, NJ: Erlbaum.

Bebeau, M., & Brabeck, M. (1989). Ethical sensitivity and moral reasoning among men and women in the professions. In M. Brabeck (Ed.), *Who cares?* (pp. 144-163). New York: Praeger.

Bebeau, M., Rest, J.R., & Yamoor, C.M. (1985). Measuring dental students' ethical sensitivity. *Journal of Dental Education, 49*(4), 225-235.

Bebeau, M.J., & Waithe, M.E. (1988). Undergraduate preparation in philosophy, humanities, and social sciences as predictors of the ability to identify and reason about ethical issues in dentistry. *Journal of Dental Education, 52*(1), 49.

Bem, D.J. (1970). *Beliefs, attitudes, and human affairs.* Monterey, CA: Brooks/Cole.

Bennett, W.J. (1994). *The index of leading cultural indicators: Facts and figures on the state of American society.* New York: Simon & Schuster.

Berliner, H.S. (1975). A larger perspective on the Flexner Report. *International Journal of Health Services*, 573-592.

Berliner, H.S. (1976). "Starr wars." *International Journal of Health Services, 13*, 671-675.

Bethell, T. (1998). *The noblest triumph: Property and prosperity through the ages.* New York: St. Martin's Griffin.

Bettmann, O.L. (1974). *The good old days—They were terrible!* New York: Random House.

Bies, R.J. (1987). The predicament of injustice: The management of moral outrage. In L.L. Cummings & B.M. Staw (Eds.), *Research in organizational behavior* (Vol. 9, pp. 289-319). Greenwich, CT: JAI Press.

Bies, R.J. (1993). Privacy and procedural justice in organizations. *Social Justice Research, 6*, 69-86.

Bies, R.J. (2001). Interactional (in)justice: The sacred and the profane. In J. Greenberg & R. Cropanzano (Eds.), *Advances in organizational justice* (pp. 89-118). Stanford, CA: Stanford University Press.

Blasi, A. (1980). Bridging moral cognition and moral action: A critical review of the literature. *Psychological Bulletin, 88,* 1-45.

Blau, P.M. (1986). *Exchange and power in social life.* New Brunswick, NJ: Transaction, Inc.

Bobocel, D.R., McCline, R.L., & Folger, R. (1997). Letting them down gently: Conceptual advances in explaining controversial organizational policies. In C.L. Cooper & D.M. Rousseau (Eds.), *Trends in organizational behavior* (Vol. 4, pp. 73-88). New York: John Wiley & Sons.

Bolger, N., DeLongis, A., Kessler, R.C., & Schilling, E.A. (1989). Effects of daily stress on negative mood. *Journal of Personality and Social Psychology, 57,* 808-818.

Brady, F.N. (1985). A Janus-headed model of ethical theory: Looking two ways at business/society issues. *Academy of Management Review, 10,* 568-576.

Brady, F.N. (1990). *Ethical managing: Rules and results.* New York: Macmillan.

Bredemeier, B.J.L., & Shields, D.L.L. (1994). Applied ethics and moral reasoning in sports. In J.R. Rest & D. Narvaez (Eds.), *Moral development in the professions* (pp. 173-187). Hillsdale, NJ: Erlbaum.

Brockner, J., Tyler, T.R., & Cooper-Schneider, R. (1992). The influence of prior commitment to an institution on reactions to perceived unfairness: The higher they are, the harder they fall. *Administrative Science Quarterly, 37,* 241-261.

Conlon, D.E. (1993). Some tests of the self-interest and group-value models of procedural justice: Evidence from an organizational appeal procedure. *Academy of Management Journal, 36,* 1109-1124.

Corey, S.M. (1937). Professed attitudes and actual behavior. *Journal of Educational Psychology, 28,* 271-280.

Cronbach, L.J., & Meehl, A.J. (1955). Construct validity in psychological tests. *Psychological Bulletin, 52,* 281-302.

Cropanzano, R., & Byrne, Z.S. (2001). When it's time to stop writing polices: An inquiry into procedural justice. *Human Resource Management Review, 11,* 31-54.

Cropanzano, R., Byrne, Z.S., Bobocel, D.R., & Rupp, D.R. (2001a). Moral virtues, fairness heuristics, social entities, and other denizens of organizational justice. *Journal of Vocational Behavior, 58,* 164-2001.

Cropanzano, R., Byrne, Z.S., Bobocel, D.R., & Rupp, D.R. (2001b). Self-enhancement biases, laboratory experiments, George Wilhelm Fredrich Hegal, and the increasingly crowded world of organizational justice. *Journal of Vocational Behavior, 58,* 260-272.

Cropanzano, R., Chrobot–Mason, D., Rupp, D.E., & Prehar, C.A. (in press). Accountability for corporate injustice. *Human Resource Management Review.*

Cropanzano, R., & Grandey, A.A. (1998). If politics is a game, then what are the rules?: Three suggestions for ethical managers. In M. Schminke (Ed.), *Managerial ethics: Morally managing of people and processes* (pp. 133-152). Mahwah, NJ: Erlbaum.

Cropanzano, R., James, K., & Citera, M. A. (1993). A goal hierarchy model of personality, motivation, and leadership. In L.L. Cummings & B. M. Staw (Eds.), *Research in organizational behavior* (Vol. 15, pp. 267-322). Greenwich, CT: JAI Press.

Cropanzano, R., Prehar, C., & Chen, P.Y. (in press). Using social exchange theory to distinguish procedural and interactional justice. *Group and Organization Management.*

Cropanzano, R., Rupp, D.E., Mohler, C.J., & Schminke, M. (2001). Three roads to organizational justice. In J. Ferris (Ed.), *Research in personnel and human resource management* (Vol. 20, pp. 1-113). Greenwich, CT: JAI Press.

Damon, W.(1977). *The social world of the child.* San Francisco, CA: Jossey-Bass.

Dawes, R.M. (1991). Social dilemmas, economic self-interest, and evolutionary theory. In D.R. Brown & J.E.K. Smith (Eds.), *Recent research in psychology: Frontiers of mathematical psychology: Essays in honor of Clyde Coombs.* New York: Springer-Verlag.

Dawes, R.M. (1994). *House of cards: Psychology and psychotherapy built on myth.* New York: The Free Press.

Dawes, R.M., van de Kragt, A.J.C. & Orbell, J.M. (1990). Cooperation for the benefit of us—Not me or my conscience. In J. Mansbridge (Ed.), *Beyond self-interest.* Chicago: University of Chicago Press.

Deckop, J.R., Mangel, R., & Cirka, C.C. (1999). Getting more than you pay for: Organizational citizenship behavior and pay-for-performance plans. *Academy of Management Journal, 42,* 420-428.

Dovidio, J.F., Allen, J.L., & Schroeder, D.A. (1990). The specificity of empathy-induced helping: Evidence for altruistic motivation. *Journal of Personality and Social Psychology, 59,* 249-260.

Dovidio, J.F., Piliavin, J.A., Gaertner, S.L., Schroeder, D.A., & Clark, R.D., III. (1991). The arousal:cost-reward model and the process of intervention: A review of the evidence. In M.S. Clark (Eds.), *Prosocial behavior* (pp. 86-116). Newbury Park, CA: Sage.

Ermann, M.D., & Lundman, R.J. (Eds). (1987). *Corporate and governmental deviance: Problems of organizational behavior in contemporary society* (3rd Ed.). New York: Oxford University Press.

Etzioni, A. (1988). *The moral dimension: Toward a new economics.* New York: The Free Press.

Flexner, A. (1910). *Medical education in the United States and Canada.* Bulletin, number 4. New York: Carnegie Foundation for the Advancement of Teaching.

Folger, R. (1994). Workplace justice and employee worth. *Social Justice Research, 7,* 225-241.

Folger, R. (1998). Fairness as a moral virtue. In M. Schminke (Ed.), *Managerial ethics: Moral management of people and processes* (pp. 13-34). Mahwah, NJ: Erlbaum.

Folger, R. (2001). Fairness as deonance. In S. Gilliland, D. Steiner, & D. Skarlicki (Eds.), *Theoretical and cultural perspectives on organizational justice* (pp. 3-33). Greenwich, CT: Information Age Publishers.

Folger, R., & Cropanzano, R. (1998). *Organizational justice and human resource management.* Thousand Oaks, CA: Sage.

Folger, R., & Skarlicki, D.P. (2001). Fairness as a dependent variable: Why tough times can lead to bad management. In R. Cropanzano (Ed.), *Justice in the workplace (Vol. 2): From theory to practice* (pp. 97-118). Mahwah, NJ: Erlbaum.

Folkman, S., Lazarus, R.S., Gruen, R.J., & DeLongis, A. (1986). Appraisal, coping, health status, and psychological symptoms. *Journal of Personality and Social Psychology, 50,* 571-579.

Frese, M., & Sabini, J. (1985). (Eds). *Goal directed behavior: The concept of action in psychology.* Hillsdale, NJ: Erlbaum.

Freund, P.E.S., & McGuire, M.B. (1991). *Health, illness, and the social body: A critical sociology.* Englewood Cliffs, NJ: Prentice Hall.

Fukuyama, F. (1995). *Trust: The social virtues and the creation of prosperity.* New York: The Free Press.

Gergen, K. J. (1969). *The psychology of behavioral exchange.* Reading, MA: Addison-Wesley.

Gordon, M. (2000). *Joan of Arc.* New York: Penguin Books.

Grandey, A.A., & Cropanzano, R. (1999). The conservation of resource model applied to work-family conflict and strain. *Journal of Vocational Behavior, 54,* 350-370.

Greenberg, J. (1990). Looking fair vs. being fair: Managing impressions of organizational justice. In B. M. Staw & L. L. Cummings (Eds.), *Research in Organizational Behavior* (Vol. 12, pp. 111-157). Greenwich, CT: JAI.

Greenberg, J. (2001). Setting the justice agenda: Seven unanswered questions about what, why, and how. *Journal of Vocational Behavior, 58,* 210-219

Grzywacz, J.G., & Marks, M.F. (2000). Reconceptualizing the work-family interface: An ecological perspective on the correlates of positive and negative spillover between and family. *Journal of Occupational Health Psychology, 5,* 111-126.

Halberstam, J. (1993). *Everyday ethics: Inspired solutions to real-life dilemmas.* New York: Penguin Books.

Hatfield, E., Walster, G.W., & Piliavin, J.A. (1978). Equity theory and helping relationships. In L. Wispe (Ed.), *Altruism, sympathy, and helping: Psychological and sociological principles* (pp. 115-139). New York: Academic Press.

Herbert, R.L. (1991). *Georges Seurat: 1859-1891.* New York: The Metropolitan Museum of Art.

Holbrook, R.L., Jr., & Kulik, C.T. (1996, April). *Strength of membership influences on reactions to bank loan procedures.* Paper presented at the annual meeting of the Society for Industrial and Organizational Psychology, San Diego, CA.

Holley, D.M. (1999). *Self-interest and beyond.* St. Paul. MN: Paragon House.

Hosmer, L.T. (1996). *The ethics of management* (3rd Ed.). Chicago: Irwin.

James, K. (1993). The social context of organizational justice: Cultural, intergroup, and structural effects on justice behaviors and perceptions. In R. Cropanzano (Ed.). *Justice in the workplace: Approaching fairness in human resource management* (pp. 21-50). Hillsdale, NJ: Erlbaum.

James, K., Lovato, C., & Khoo, G. (1994). Social identity correlates of minority workers' health. *Academy of Management Journal, 37,* 383-396.

Jones, T.M. (1991). Ethical decision making by individuals and organizations: An issue-contingent model. *Academy of Management Review, 16,* 366-395.

Kahneman, D., Knetsch, J.L., & Thaler, R.H. (1986). Fairness and the assumptions of economics. *Journal of Business, 59,* 285- 300.

Kohn, A. (1990). *The brighter side of human nature.* New York: Basic Books.

Kollock, P. (1998). Social dilemmas: The anatomy of cooperation. *Annual Review of Sociology, 24,* 183-214.

Konovsky, M.A. (2000). Understanding procedural justice and it's impact on business organizations. *Journal of Management, 26,* 489-511.

Konovsky, M.A., & Pugh, S.D. (1994). Citizenship behavior and social exchange. *Academy of Management Journal, 37,* 656-669.

Kors, A.C., & Silvergate, H.A. (1998). *The shadow university: The betrayal of liberty on America's campuses.* New York: The Free Press.

Krehbiel, P.J., & Cropanzano, R. (2000). Procedural justice, outcome favorability, and emotion. *Social Justice Research, 13,* 337-358.

Lees, C.D., & Cordery, J.L. (2000). Job analysis and job design. In N. Chmiel (Ed.), *Introduction to work and organizational psychology: A European perspective* (pp. 45-68). Malden, MA: Blackwell Publishers.

Lerner, M.J. (1980). *Belief in a just world: A fundamental delusion.* New York: Plenum Press.

Lerner, M.J., & Miller, D.T. (1978). Just world research and the attribution process: Looking back and looking ahead. *Psychological Bulletin, 85,* 1030-1051.

Lind, E.A. (1995). Justice and authority in organizations. In R. Cropanzano & M.K. Kacmar (Eds.), *Organizational politics, justice, and support: Managing the social climate of the workplace* (pp. 83-96). Westport, CT: Quorum.

Lind, E.A. (2001). Thinking critically about justice judgments. *Journal of Vocational Behavior, 58,* 220-226.

Lind, E.A., & Tyler, T.R. (1988). *The social psychology of procedural justice.* New York: Plenum.

Mansbridge, J.J. (1990). (Ed.). *Beyond self-interest.* Chicago: University of Chicago Press.

Masterson, S.S., Lewis, K., Goldman, B.M., & Taylor, M.S. (2000). Integrating justice and social exchange: The differing effects of fair procedures and treatment on work relationships. *Academy of Management Journal, 43,* 738-748.

May, W.E. (1983). *The physician's covenant: Images of the healer in medical ethics.* Philadelphia: Westminster Press.

McCabe, D.L., & Treviño, L.K. (1996). What we know about cheating in college. *Change, January/February,* 29-33.

McFarlin, D.B., & Sweeney, P.D. (2001). Cross-cultural applications of organizational justice. In R. Cropanzano (Ed.), *Justice in the workplace (Vol. 2): From theory to practice* (pp. 67-118). Mahwah, NJ: Erlbaum.

McNeel, S.P. (1994). College teaching and student moral development. In J. R. Rest & D. Narvaez (Eds.), *Moral development in the professions: Psychology and applied ethics* (pp. 27-49). Hillsdale, NJ: Erlbaum.

Meara, N.M. (2001). Just and virtuous leaders and organizations. *Journal of Vocational Behavior, 58,* 227-234.

Miller, D.T. (1999). The norm of self-interest. *American Psychologist, 54,* 1053-1060.

Miller, D.T., & Ratner, R.K. (1996). The power of the myth of self-interest. In L. Montada & M. J. Lerner (Eds.), *Current societal issues about justice* (pp. 25-48). New York: Plenum.

Miller, D.T., & Ratner, R.K. (1998). The disparity between the actual and assumed power of self-interest. *Journal of Personality and Social Psychology, 74,* 53-62.

Montada, L. (1998). Justice: Just a rational choice? *Social Justice Review, 12,* 81-101.

Myers, D.G., & Diener, E. (1995). Who is happy? *Psychological Science, 6,* 10-19.

Ordóñez, L.D., Benson, L., III., & Beach, L.R. (1999). Testing the compatibility test: How instructions, accountability, and anticipated regret affect prechoice screening of options. *Organizational Behavior and Human Decision Processes, 78,* 63-80.

Ordóñez, L. D., Connolly, T., & Coughlan, R. (2000). Multiple reference points in satisfaction and fairness assessments. *Journal of Behavioral Decision Making, 13,* 329-344.

Paloutzian, R.F., & Kirkpatrick, L.A. (1995). Religious influences on personal and societal well-being. [Special issue]. *Journal of Social Issues, 51*(2), 1-11.

Plous, C. (1993). *The psychology of judgment and decision making.* New York: McGraw-Hill.

Ployhart, R.E., & Ryan, A.M. (1997). Toward an explanation of applicant reactions: An examination of organizational justice and attributional frameworks. *Organizational Behavior and Human Decision Processes, 72,* 308-335.

Ployhart, R.E., & Ryan, A.M. (1998). Applicants' reactions to the fairness of selection procedures: The effects of positive rule violations and time of measurement. *Journal of Applied Psychology, 83,* 3-16.

Ployhart, R.E., Ryan, A.M., & Bennett, M. (1999). Explanation for selection decisions: Applicants' reactions to informational and sensitivity features of explanations. *Journal of Applied Psychology, 84,* 87-106.

Rest, J.R. (1979). *Development in judging moral issues.* Minneapolis, MN: University of Minnesota Press.

Rest, J.R. (1984). The major components of morality. In W.M. Kurtines & J.L. Gewirtz (Eds.), *Morality, moral behavior, and moral development* (pp. 24-38). New York: John Wiley & Sons.

Rest, J.R. (1994). Background: Theory and research. In J. R. Rest & D. Narvaez (Eds.), *Moral development in the professions: Psychology and applied ethics* (pp. 1-26). Hillsdale, NJ: Erlbaum.

Roch, S.G., Lane, J.A.S., Samuelson, C.D., Allison, S.T., & Dent. J.L. (2000). Cognitive load and the equality heuristic: A two-stage model of resource overconsumption in small groups. *Organizational Behavior and Human Decision Processes, 83,* 185-212.

Rokeach, M. (1973). *The nature of human values.* New York: The Free Press.

Rupp, D.E., & Cropanzano, R. (in press). Multifoci justice and work relationships: The mediating effects of social exchange. *Organization Behavior and Human Decision Processes.*

Russell, J. (1965). *Seurat.* New York: Frederick A. Praeger.

Samuelson, C.D., & Allison, S.T. (1994). Cognitive factors affecting the use of social decision heuristics in resource-sharing tasks. *Organizational Behavior and Human Decision Processes, 58,* 1-27.

Sanchez, J.I. (1994). From documentation to innovation: Reshaping job analysis to meet emerging business needs. *Human Resource Management Review, 4,* 51-74.

Schminke, M. (1998). The magic punchbowl: A nonrational model of ethical management. In M. Schminke (Ed.), *Managerial ethics: Moral management of people and processes* (pp. 197-214). Mahwah, NJ: Erlbaum.

Schminke, M., Ambrose, M.L., & Noel, T.W. (1997). The effect of ethical frameworks on perceptions of organizational justice. *Academy of Management Journal, 40,* 1190-1207.

Schwab, D.P. (1980). Construct validity in organizational behavior. In B. Staw & L.L. Cummings (Eds.), *Research in organizational behavior* (Vol. 2, pp. 3-43). Greenwich, CT: JAI Press.

Sears, D.O., & Funk, C.L. (1991). The role of self-interest in social and political attitudes. In M.P. Zanna (Ed.), *Advances in experimental social psychology* (Vol. 2, pp. 2-91). New York: Academic Press.
Self, D.J., & Baldwin, D.C., Jr. (1994). Moral reasoning in medicine. In J.R. Rest & D. Narvaez (Eds.). *Moral development in the professions* (pp.147-162). Hillsdale, NJ: Erlbaum.
Schlosser, E. (2001). *Fast food nation: The dark side of the all-American meal.* Boston, MA: Houghton Mifflin.
Schoemaker, P.J.H. (1982). The expected utility models: Its variants, purposes, evidence and limitations. *Journal of Economic Literature, 20,* 529-563.
Schor, J.B. (1991). *The overworked American: The unexpected decline of leisure.* New York: Basic Books.
Sherman, S.J., & Fazio, R.H. (1983). Parallels between attitudes and traits as predictors of behavior. *Journal of Personality, 51,* 308-345.
Sheppard, B.H., Blumenfeld-Jones, K., Minton, W.J., & Hyder, E. (1994). Informal conflict intervention: Advice and dissent. *Employee Responsibilities and Rights Journal, 7,* 53-72.
Singer, P. (1979). *Practical ethics.* Cambridge, UK: Cambridge University Press.
Sitkin, S.B., & Bies, R.J. (1993). The legalistic organization: Definitions, dimensions, and dilemmas. *Organization Science, 4,* 345-351.
Sitkin, S.B., & Roth, N.L. (1993). Explaining the limited effectiveness of legalistic "remedies" for trust/distrust. *Organization Science, 4,* 367-292.
Skarlicki, D.P., & Latham, G.P. (1996). Increasing citizenship behavior within a labor union: A test of organizational justice theory. *Journal of Applied Psychology, 81,* 161-169.
Skarlicki, D.P., & Latham, G.P. (1997). Leadership training in organizational justice to increase citizenship behavior within a labor union. *Personnel Psychology, 50,* 617-633.
Skitka, L.J. (in press). Do the means always justify the ends, or do the ends sometimes justify the means? A value protection model of justice. *Personality and Social Psychology Bulletin.*
Skitka, L.J., & Houston, D.A. (in press). When due process is of no consequence: Moral mandates and presumed defendant guilt or innocent. *Social Justice Research.*
Skitka, L.J., & Mullen, E. (2001). When procedural fairness fails to account for perception of justice done: Moral mandates and the Elián González. *Unpublished Manuscript.*
Smith, P. (1997). *Seurat and the avant-garde.* New Haven, CT: Yale University Press.
Society for Industrial and Organizational Psychology. (1987). *Principles for the validation and use of personnel selection procedures* (3rd ed). College Park, MD: Author.
Society of Human Resource Management (August 6, 1999). *Code of Ethics.* http://cseo.uut.edu/codes/coe/Human_Resource_Management.html.
Sowell, T. (1995). *The vision of the anointed: Self-congratulation as a basis for social policy.* New York: Basic Books.
Sowell, T. (1996). *Migrations and cultures: A world view.* New York: Basic Books.
Sowell, T. (1999). *The quest for cosmic justice.* New York: The Free Press.
Sprinthall, N.A. (1994). Counseling and social role taking: Promoting moral development and ego development. In J. R. Rest & D. Narvaez (Eds.), *Moral develop-*

ment in the professions: Psychology and applied ethics (pp. 85-99). Hillsdale, NJ: Erlbaum.
Starr, P. (1982). *The social transformation of American medicine.* New York: Basic.
Sullivan, J.J. (1989). Self theories and employee motivation. *Journal of Management, 15,* 345-363.
Tangney, J.P. (1995). Shame and guilt in interpersonal relationships. In J.P. Tangney, & K.W. Fischer (Eds.), *Self-conscious emotions: Shame, guilt, embarrassment, and pride* (pp. 114-139). New York: John Wiley & Sons.
Taylor, M.S., Tracy, K.B., Renard, M.K., Harrison, J.K., Carroll, S.J. (1995). Due process in performance appraisal: A quasi-experiment in procedural justice. *Administrative Science Quarterly, 40,* 495-523.
Thoma, S. (1994). Moral judgments and moral action. In J.R. Rest & D. Narvaez (Eds.), *Moral development in the professions: Psychology and applied ethics* (pp. 199-211). Hillsdale, NJ: Erlbaum.
Tomaka, J., & Blascovich, J. (1994). Effects of justice beliefs on cognitive appraisal and subjective, physiological, and behavioral responses to potential stress. *Journal of Personality and Social Psychology, 67,* 732-740.
Treviño, L.K. (1986). Ethical decision making in organizations: A person-situation interactionist model. *Academy of Management Review, 11,* 601-617.
Treviño L.K., & Bies, R. J. (1997). Through the looking glass: A normative manifesto for organizational behavior. In C. L. Cooper & S. E. Jackson (Eds.), *Creating tomorrow's organizations* (pp. 439-452). New York: John Wiley & Sons.
Turillo, C. J., Folger, R., Lavelle, J.J., Umphress, E., & Gee, J. (in press). Is virtue its own reward? Self-sacrificial decisions for the sake of fairness. *Organizational Behavior and Human Decision Processes.*
Tyler, T.R. (1991). Using procedures to justify outcomes: Testing the viability of a procedural justice strategy for managing conflict and allocating resources in work settings. *Basic and Applied Social Psychology, 12,* 259-279.
Tyler, T.R. (1994). Psychological models of the justice motive: Antecedents of distributive and procedural justice. *Journal of Personality and Social Psychology, 67,* 850-863.
Tyler, T.R. (1997). The psychology of legitimacy: A relational perspective on voluntary deference to authorities. *Personality and Social Psychology Review, 1,* 323-345.
Tyler, T.R., & Blader, S.L. (2000). *Cooperation in groups; Procedural justice, social identity, and behavioral engagement.* Philadelphia: Psychology Press.
Tyler, T.R., & Dawes, R.M. (1993). Fairness in groups: Comparing the self-interest and the social identity perspectives. In B.A. Mellers & J. Baron (Eds.), *Psychological perspectives on justice: Theory and applications* (pp. 87-108). Cambridge, MA: Cambridge University Press.
Tyler, T.R., & Degoey, P. (1995). Collective restraint in social dilemmas: Procedural justice and social identification effects on support for authorities. *Journal of Personality and Social Psychology, 69,* 482-497.
Tyler, T.R., Degoey, P., & Smith H. (1996). Understanding why the justice of group procedures maters: A test of the psychological dynamics of the group-value model. *Journal of Personality and Social Psychology, 70,* 913-930.
Tyler, T.R., & Lind, E.A. (1992). A relational model of authority in groups. In M.P. Zanna (Ed.), *Advances in experimental social psychology* (Vol. 25, pp. 115-191). San Diego, CA: Academic Press.

Tyler, T.R., & Smith, H.J. (1998). Social justice and social movements. In D. Gilbert, S.T. Fiske, & G. Lindzey (Eds.), *Handbook of social psychology* (Vol. 4, pp. 595-629). Boston, MA: McGraw – Hill.

Van den Bos, K. (2001). Fundamental research by means of laboratory experiments is essential for a better understanding of organizational justice. *Journal of Vocational Behavior, 58,* 254-259.

Vallacher, R.R., & Wegner, D.M. (1985). *A theory of action identification.* Hillsdale, NJ: Erlbaum.

Velasquez, M.G. (1992). *Business ethics: Concepts and cases* (3rd Ed.). Englewood Cliffs, NJ: Prentice Hall.

Wade-Benzoni, K.A., Tenbrunsel, A.E., & Bazerman, M.H. (1996). Egocentric interpretations of fairness in asymmetric, environmental social dilemmas: Explaining harvesting behavior and the role of communication. *Organizational Behavior and Human Decision Processes, 67,* 111-126.

Walster, E., Walster, G. W., & Berscheid, E. (1978). *Equity: Theory and research.* New York: Allyn & Bacon.

Wanous, J. P., Keon, T. L., & Latack, J. C. (1983). Expectancy theory and occupational/organizational choices: A review and a test. *Organizational Behavior and Human Performance, 32,* 66-86.

Weiss, H.M., & Cropanzano, R. (1996). An affective events approach to job satisfaction. In B.M. Staw & L.L. Cummings (Eds.), *Research in organizational behavior* (Vol. 18, pp. 1-74). Greenwich, CT: JAI Press.

Weiss, H.M., Suckow, K., & Cropanzano, R. (1999). Effects of justice conditions on discrete emotions. *Journal of Applied Psychology, 84,* 786-794.

INFORMATION ON CONTRIBUTING AUTHORS

Robert J. Bies is a Professor of Management in the McDonough School of Business, Georgetown University, Washington, D.C. He received his Ph.D. in Business Administration (Organizational Behavior) from Stanford University. Professor Bies's research interests include organizational justice, revenge in the workplace, trust and distrust dynamics, and the delivery of bad news. His research has been published in *Academy of Management Journal, Academy of Management Review, Journal of Applied Psychology, Journal of Management, Research in Organizational Behavior, Research on Negotiation in Organizations, Organization Science,* and *Organizational Behavior and Human Decision Processes.* Professor Bies is on the editorial boards of *Journal of Applied Psychology, Journal of Management,* and *The International Journal of Conflict Management.*

Russell Cropanzano is a Professor of Organizational Behavior in the Department of Management and Policy of the University of Arizona. Dr. Cropanzano is a member of the Academy of Management, the American Psychological Society, and the Society for Organizational Behavior. He is a fellow in the Society for Industrial/Organizational Psychology. Currently, Dr. Cropanzano serves on the editorial boards for the *Journal of Applied Psychology, Journal of Management, Journal of Personality and Social Psychology,* and *Organizational Behavior and Human Decision Processes.* He has published over 70 scholarly articles and chapters. In addition, Dr. Cropanzano is a co-author of the book, *Organizational Justice and Human Resources Management,* which won the 1998 Book Award from the International Association of Conflict Management. Dr. Cropanzano is also active internationally, having given talks in Australia, France, New Zealand, and the United Kingdom.

John H. Ellard is Associate Professor of Psychology at the University of Calgary. He did his Ph.D. work at the University of Waterloo. Prior to assuming his position at Calgary, he held a Post-Doctoral fellowship at the Institute for Social Research, University of Michigan. His research exploring aspects of the justice motive has appeared in leading journals such as the *Journal of Personality and Social Psychology, Journal of Experimental Social Psychology, Personality and Social Psychology Bulletin, Journal of Applied Psychology,* and *Social Justice Research.*

Stephen W. Gilliland is a Professor of Management and Policy and Vice Dean of the Eller College of Business and Public Administration at the University of Arizona. He received his Ph.D. from Michigan State University and was previously on the faculty at Louisiana State University. Stephen's research interests include organizational justice, individual decision making, and the application of these areas to human resource policies and procedures. He has published numerous articles on these issues in the *Academy of Management Review, Journal of Applied Psychology, Personnel Psychology, Organizational Behavior and Human Decision Processes,* and *Journal of Management.* He is currently on the editorial boards of the *Journal of Applied Psychology* and *Personnel Psychology* and previously served on the board of the *Academy of Management Journal.* Stephen was the 1997 recipient of the Ernest J. McCormick Award for Early Career Contributions from the Society for Industrial and Organizational Psychology.

Barry Goldman is an Assistant Professor of Management and Policy at the Eller College of Business and Public Adminstration at the University of Arizona. He received his Ph.D. in Management and a J.D. from the University of Maryland. Previously, he was in the private practice of law. His research interests include organizational justice and understanding the antecedents to employee legal-claiming against one's employing organization. Broadly speaking, he has a strong interest in understanding the reaction of management and employees to legal issues. He has published articles in the *Academy of Management Journal, Personnel Psychology,* and the *Journal of Applied Psychology.*

Robert L. Holbrook, Jr. is an Assistant Professor of Management Systems in the College of Business at Ohio University. He received his Ph.D. from the University of Illinois at Urbana-Champaign in 1997. His research interests include organizational justice, demographic diversity, and corporate social responsibility. His work has been published in the *Journal of Organizational Behavior, Human Resource Management Review,* and *Social Justice Research.*

Audrey Korsgaard is an Associate Professor of Management at the Moore School of Business at the University of South Carolina. She received a Ph.D. from New York University. Audrey's research interests include organizational justice, interpersonal trust, and work values. She has published articles on these topics in the *Academy of Management Journal, Academy of Management Review, Journal of Applied Psychology, Organizational Behavior and Human Decision Processes,* and *Journal of Management.* She is currently on the editorial boards of the *Journal of Management* and *Entrepreneurship Theory & Practice.*

Carol T. Kulik is a Professor of Management at the University of Melbourne in Australia. She received her Ph.D. in 1987 from the University of Illinois at Urbana-Champaign. Her research interests include demographic diversity, organizational fairness, and cognitive processes in organizations. She serves on the editorial boards of the *Journal of Organizational Behavior,* the *Journal of Management, Administrative Science Quarterly,* and the *Academy of Management Journal.* Her work has been published in the *Academy of Management Review, Journal of Applied Psychology, Journal of Management, Journal of Organizational Behavior,* and *Administrative Science Quarterly.*

Gerold Mikula is Professor of Social Psychology in the Department of Psychology at the University of Graz, Austria, where he also got his Ph.D. His research interests cover the experience of injustice, division of family labor, justice and social conflict, social interdependence, personal relationships, and interpersonal attraction. He has published articles in the *Personality and Social Psychology Bulletin, European Journal of Social Psychology, European Review of Social Psychology, International Journal of Psychology, Journal of Applied Social Psychology* and *Social Justice Research.* He is currently an associate editor of *Social Justice Research,* and previously served as co-editor of the *Zeitschrift fuer Sozialpsychologie.* In addition he has served, and still serves partially, on the editorial boards of *European Journal of Social Psychology, European Review of Social Psychology, Social Psychology Quarterly, Journal of Personal and Social Relationships,* and *Zeitschrift fuer Sozialpsychologie.* Gerold is past-president of the European Association of Experimental Social Psychology (1987-1990) and the Austrian Society of Psychology (1997-1999).

Deborah E. Rupp is an Assistant Professor in the Department of Psychology and the Institute for Labor and Industrial Relations at the University of Illinois, Urbana-Champaign. She has co-authored several articles and book chapters in the area of organizational justice. She is currently conducting research on multi-foci justice as well as the deontological model of organizational justice. Her research has appeared in *Organizational Behavior and Human Decision Processing, Journal of Vocational Behavior, Human Resource Management Review,* and the *Comprehensive Handbook of Psychological Assessment.* Other areas within which she has conducted research include the assessment center method and workplace age bias. She has also been working with Sun Microsystems' Educational Consulting Services developing assessment centers to certify international consultants.

Harry J. Sapienza is a Professor of Management and the Curtis L. Carlson Chair in Entrepreneurial Studies at the University of Minnesota. He received his Ph. D. from the University of Maryland and was previously on the faculty at the University of South Carolina. Harry's research interests include interorganizational relationships, strategic decision making, and organizational justice. His work focuses on these issues in the context of high-potential new ventures. He has published numerous articles on these topics in the *Academy of Management Journal*, the *Strategic Management Journal*, the *Journal of Business Venturing*, *Entrepreneurship Theory & Practice* and several other journals. He is currently on the editorial boards of the *Journal of Business Venturing*, *Entrepreneurship Theory & Practice*, *Venture Capital* and *Enterprise and Innovation Management*.

Daniel P. Skarlicki is an Associate Professor in the Faculty of Commerce at the University of British Columbia, Vancouver, Canada. He received his Ph.D. from the University of Toronto and previously taught at the University of Calgary and at Tulane University in New Orleans. Dr. Skarlicki teaches in executive programs in Asia, Mexico, United States, and South America. He has won numerous teaching and international research awards. His research has appeared in several top scholarly journals, including the *Academy of Management Journal, Administrative Science Quarterly, Journal of Applied Psychology, Personnel Psychology*, and *Applied Psychology, An International Review*. In 1993, he received the Robert S. Wherry best paper award at the Society for Industrial and Organizational Psychology and he is also the recipient of the Ascendant Scholar Award of the Western Academy of Management for 2000. He serves on the editorial board of the *Journal of Organizational Behavior* is editor of a special issue on organizational justice in *Human Resource Management Review* and *International Journal of Conflict Management*.

Dirk D. Steiner is Professor of Psychology at the Université de Nice-Sophia Antipolis in Nice, France where he directs the Applied Social Psychology Team of the Laboratoire de Psychologie Expérimentale et Quantitative. He is also the director of doctoral studies in Psychology there. He earned his Ph.D. in Industrial/Organizational Psychology at the Pennsylvania State University and began his academic career at Louisiana State University before moving to France. He has published research in both English and French on topics such as job satisfaction, organizational justice in personnel selection, and performance appraisal in journals such as *Journal of Applied Psychology, International Journal of Selection and Assessment, Journal of Occupational and Organizational Psychology*, and *Human Relations*. Currently, he is conducting research on the cognitive processing of organizational justice information and on the role of organizational justice in applicant and employee evaluation practices. He is an associate editor of the journal, *Revue Internationale de Psychologie Sociale/International Review of Social Psychol-*

ogy and a member of the editorial board of *Cahiers Internationaux de Psychologie Sociale.*

Dianna Stone is a Professor of Management and Psychology at the University of Central Florida. She received her Ph.D. from Purdue University. Her research interests include organizational justice, reactions to personnel selection techniques, information privacy, human resources technology, and diversity in organizations including issues of race, disability and culture. Results of her research have been published in the *Journal of Applied Psychology, Personnel Psychology,* the *Academy of Management Review, Organizational Behavior and Human Decision Processes,* and the *Journal of Management.*

Eugene F. Stone-Romero received his Ph.D. from the University of California-Irvine and is now Professor of Psychology at the University of Central Florida where he directs the Ph.D. program in Industrial and Organizational Psychology. He is a Fellow of the Society for Industrial and Organizational Psychology, the American Psychological Association, and the American Psychological Society. The results of his work on numerous issues, including negative affectivity, cross-cultural issues, job design, reactions to feedback, work-related values, job satisfaction, moderator variable detection strategies, performance ratings, privacy in organizations, job involvement, and work quality have been published in such outlets as the *Journal of Applied Psychology, Organizational Behavior and Human Performance, Personnel Psychology, Journal of Vocational Behavior, Academy of Management Journal, Journal of Management, Educational and Psychological Measurement, Journal of Educational Psychology, Journal of Applied Social Psychology, International Review of Industrial and Organizational Psychology,* and *Research in Personnel and Human Resources Management.*

Sherry Thatcher is an Assistant Professor in the Management Information Systems Department at the University of Arizona. Her research interests include the social effects of computer communication technologies on interpersonal communication, individual perceptions, and organizational productivity; behavioral and organizational aspects of virtual work; and global information technology. Her research has been published in *Research on Managing Groups and Teams, International Journal of Conflict Management,* and *Performance Improvement Quarterly.*

Thomas M. Tripp is an Associate Professor of Management & Systems at Washington State University, teaching at its Vancouver, Washington campus. He received his Ph.D. in Organizational Behavior from Northwestern University in 1991. His research focuses on workplace revenge and on how to measure negotiator effectiveness. His research has been published in *Journal of Applied Psychology, Organizational Behavior and Human Decision Pro-*

cesses, *Journal of Behavioral Decision Making, Group Decisions and Negotiations,* and *Journal of Applied Social Psychology.*

Riel Vermunt is associate professor in social and organizational psychology at Leiden University, the Netherlands. Riel's research interest include distributive justice, procedural justice, organizational justice, the self and their applications on economic games, stress reduction, self-esteem threat and boosting of self-esteem. He has published articles on these issues in *Journal of Applied Psychology, Journal of Applied Social Psychology, Journal of Personality and Social Psychology,* and *Journal of Experimental Social Psychology.* He has also published in Dutch. He is one of the founders of the International Society of Social Justice Research, founded the journal *Behavior and Organization,* and is currently Director of Education of the Social Psychology Graduate School "Kurt Lewin Institute" in the Netherlands. Riel is also a visiting professor until 2005 at the University of Skövde, Sweden.

HD
6971.3
.E45
2002